Women and
Twentieth-Century Protestantism

Women and Twentieth-Century Protestantism

EDITED BY
Margaret Lamberts Bendroth
and Virginia Lieson Brereton

University of Illinois Press
URBANA AND CHICAGO

⊗ This book is printed on acid-free paper.

Library of Congress Cataloging-in-Publication Data
Women and twentieth-century Protestantism / edited by
Margaret Lamberts Bendroth and Virginia Lieson Brereton.
p.   cm.
Includes bibliographical references and index.
ISBN 0-252-02691-8 (alk. paper)
ISBN 0-252-06998-6 (pbk. : alk. paper)
1. Protestant women—History—20th century.
I. Bendroth, Margaret Lamberts, 1954– .
II. Brereton, Virginia Lieson.
BX4817.W65   2002
280'.4'082—dc21   2001001933

Contents

Acknowledgments

This book is the final product of a three-year project, Women and Twentieth-Century Protestantism, funded by the Pew Charitable Trusts. It is also a fully collaborative project. Early on, the editors benefited from the guidance and support of the project steering committee: Ann Braude, Catherine Brekus, Delores Carpenter, Carolyn De Swarte Gifford, Judith Weisenfeld, and Barbara Welter. Larry Eskridge and Jennifer House Farmer at the Institute for the Study of American Evangelicals oversaw the logistics of publicity, mailing lists, and conference organizing, always in a winsome and efficient manner. Over the three years of our work together, Patricia Appelbaum moved from able office assistant to an equally able collaborator; we owe her deep thanks for her patience and hard work on behalf of this project. We are also grateful to colleagues and friends who read and critiqued manuscripts, participated in our public conference, or offered timely encouragement: Steve Warner, Edith Blumhofer, Elisabeth Lasch-Quinn, Yvonne Chireau, Richard Fox, David Watt, Jodie Davie, Peter D'Agostino, Mark Noll, Joel Carpenter, and Michael Hamilton. Andover Newton Theological School provided the institutional base for this project, for which we are also grateful. Lorrie Menninga provided much-needed expert editorial assistance in the final stages. Finally, but certainly not least of all, we thank Jack Brereton and Norman Bendroth for a range of contributions to this project. Their critical reading of manuscripts, advice on office equipment, rides to and from airports, and frequently well-timed humorous suggestions made the three years of our work together pass with amazing speed.

Introduction

MARGARET LAMBERTS BENDROTH
AND VIRGINIA LIESON BRERETON

Like scores of books about women in the modern world, this one tells stories of struggle and achievement. It documents a movement for equality that
has been, on the whole, amazingly successful in American society and in
Protestant churches. Although the transformation is hardly universal or complete, vast numbers of women now enjoy a range of personal choices nearly
unthinkable at the turn of the century.

Historical writing about women and religion has tended to focus on this
narrative of achievement, viewing the twentieth century as a scorecard of
wins and losses with success usually measured in terms of access to church
governing bodies and ordination rights. Obviously, these are important
events. But the experiences of women in white, middle-class, mainline
churches, whose stories tend to dominate such accounts, are hardly predic-
tive of the rest. Continuing resistance to women's ordination, especially within many conservative denominations, indicates that the full picture is really
a mixed patchwork of contradictory beliefs and social attitudes. A deeper look
also suggests that ordination, for many Protestant women, is only one of
many possible means toward religious empowerment.

This book of essays attempts to launch a new and wider investigation into
the story of women and religion in the twentieth century. The authors, participants in a joint project entitled "Women and Twentieth Century Protestantism," examine some familiar narratives but from a variety of racial and
ethnic viewpoints; they ask skeptical questions about the nature of women's
"progress" in American church life and come up with some surprising answers. They bring to light an alternative set of historical texts that give voice
to a broad range of Protestant women and with analytical nuance probe the

meaning and impact of feminism. These essays offer no single story line and make no pretense of exhaustiveness. But taken as a whole, they suggest some important interpretive themes to guide future exploration of women's religious experience.

The essays are grouped into five sections. The first provides four different accounts of women's changing leadership roles and the impact of feminism on Protestant institutions. The second takes up another important strand, the changing configuration of women, religion, and domesticity in the post-Victorian era. The third presents examples of women constructing their own religious experiences, often through narratives, and the fourth investigates the impact of professionalization on women's religious work. The last section encompasses broader cultural questions surrounding women's religious identity in the twentieth century.

From these separate discussions, several major interpretive issues emerge, the first dealing with the core question of Protestant identity. Although many of the authors reference the formal divisions between more liberal "mainline" and more conservative "evangelical" groups—differences rooted in historic theological and denominational conflicts—these terms are not necessarily as central to their analysis as one might expect. More critically, many of the essays deal in one way or another with a fundamental question: What is a Protestant? That query is less important if we are dealing with the histories of Protestant institutions and organizations. But when we look at individuals and groups not securely anchored in church institutions, we are in less familiar territory. Problems of definition are particularly knotty with regard to women, who have ample reason to detach religiosity from its often restrictive institutional moorings. That is even more true of women writers and artists who may use a Protestant vocabulary of faith but one that does not dovetail with the received teaching of the Sunday school or pulpit. Understanding Protestant identity in the twentieth century is, of course, a long-term process, especially as denominational and doctrinal loyalties have attenuated in recent decades. These essays do not pretend to solve such questions, especially in regard to women artists, but they do raise them in new and provocative ways.

Secularization is another important theme of this volume. Few scholars now assume that religion will and must fade from modern life; even the most conservative forms of belief have demonstrated remarkable staying power—indeed, the more liberal forms as well. Yet it is also clear that religion has receded from many areas of American public life—from public schools, courtrooms, academia, government, and commerce—and even some areas of private life. Scholars have considered this departure from a variety of angles, but our study suggests that the modern experience of religious displacement has had a gendered dimension as well.

Secularization has occurred in combination with two waves of feminism, one peaking between 1890 and 1920 and the second, which is still evolving, beginning in the early 1970s. Feminism has proved to be one of the most complex issues of the twentieth century. As in the case of other grand concepts, its definition has changed according to particular historical context. Before the Nineteenth Amendment gave women the vote in 1920, self-professed feminism tended to revolve around questions of political and legal rights, suffrage in particular. During the same era, though, many other women sought access to public life by emphasizing their differences from men, arguing that as women they both could and needed to make the world a more righteous (and often Christian) place. The second wave of feminism has, if anything, been even more diffuse, incorporating concern for political, legal, and economic rights as well as for female consciousness-raising in addition to discussion about changing modes of work, marriage, child-raising, education, and female activism. No one group of women has owned the ascription of "feminist," although in recent decades it has proved politic to eschew that label even while acting and thinking in "feminist" ways.

The interaction of feminism and Protestantism has been similarly complicated. Many women's historians have assumed that *feminism* and *religion* were mutually exclusive terms, although some have claimed a heroic role for religion in conferring a gospel freedom upon women. More and more, however, scholars have come to recognize a complex and often fraught relationship between the two, and readers will find evidences of those complexities everywhere in these essays.

The changing place of religion over the past century and more has profoundly affected women's lives. At the beginning of the twentieth century, churches were their primary bridge into the larger social world. Protestant women busied themselves in large, influential movements for social reform, including child welfare, temperance, and urban relief work; women from vastly different social backgrounds forged partnerships in nationally based home and foreign missionary societies. Women were the backbone of the social gospel movement of the turn of the century, which involved Protestants in burning social causes of the day. The unmistakable fact of that dominance ultimately inspired (somewhat paradoxical) worries about churches becoming overly "feminized" and therefore doomed to ineffectiveness. The term *feminized* itself confusingly suggests a style of Protestant piety and also refers to the sheer numbers of women in the pews and in organizational roles.

By the 1920s, Protestants could no longer assume an identity of interests between women and religion. The society forged by World War I, with its bustling mass economy and new sexual mores, offered more secular bridges to the world beyond the home. Church work was no longer "women's business." As if to symbolize this development, many formerly independent women's missionary organizations were merged into denominational missionary bodies in the 1910s and 1920s, often against the better judgment of the women. They were in a difficult position: As champions of cooperation and organizational efficiency, they had difficulty spurning the overtures of male church leaders, yet they rightly suspected their influence would wane in the new organizations.

The relationship of women to the forces of "modernity"—that nexus of industrial, urban, commercial, and bureaucratic forms that came to define twentieth-century life—is extremely complex. Women have not, of course, enjoyed equal access to the secularizing intellectual, political, and economic world. Still, they have participated enthusiastically where they could, especially in the professionalization of religious work. But other women resisted the domination of experts and became healers instead of doctors, Bible school teachers instead of college professors. These contrasts suggest the importance of gender in the construction of modern religious understanding and the close relationship between women's changing social role and the shifting status of religion in the twentieth-century world.

Until recently, women have also not enjoyed equal access to the theological discussions that have arisen in response to modernity. Until the 1970s they did not attend theological seminaries in large numbers other than to enroll in the practical fields of missions and religious education. Thus, for example, they were not prominent in the rise of neo-orthodoxy, associated in the United States with Reinhold and H. Richard Niebuhr and designed to counter liberal Protestantism's optimism about the possibilities for the attainment of peace and justice.

Perhaps because of their exclusion from the theological realm, women tended to retain hope in the benefits of social activism—particularly in regard to racial cooperation and the welfare of women and children—more consistently and more intensely than many of their male counterparts. Often not having as much stake in Protestant hierarchies, they were inclined to address social and political ills with more boldness than their brothers. And they tended to be ecumenists and cooperators. Less influenced by theological distinctions, they had a penchant for shunning doctrinal controversies (including the modernist-fundamentalist one of the 1920s) and operating across denominational, ethnic, and racial boundaries typified by their enthusiastic participation in the preeminent Protestant ecumenical organization, the National Council of Churches. American Protestant women, then, have tended to be pragmatists. The ascription seems to apply across the spectrum of those whose stories are told in these essays—black, white, Latina, Asian, conservative, and liberal Protestant women.

Like many collaborative ventures, this book opens more questions than it resolves. It is only one part of a much larger historical project of documenting and interpreting the religious experiences of twentieth-century people. Many gaps remain, of course, and we do not pretend to speak the final word. We hope, in fact, that this book will be among the first of many more to come.

PART 1

New Dimensions of the Separate Sphere: Women and Religious Institutions

FEMINISM HAS HAD a powerful and enduring impact on twentieth-century Protestant church leadership and institutional structures. The essays in this section document the scope and persistence of egalitarian ideals in a variety of settings. As Susan Hartmann demonstrates, the National Council of Churches—an ecumenical organization representing mostly mainline Protestant groups—helped incubate second-wave feminist ideals well before the secular movement rose to public prominence. The Latina Pentecostals in Gastón Espinosa's study establish the powerful reach of women's rising aspirations for leadership across the span of twentieth-century North American culture.

The impact of egalitarian feminism within Protestant denominations is not always easy to trace, however. In the late-nineteenth century, Protestant women did not directly challenge male hegemony but rather built power in separate institutions. Women's missionary and social reform organizations provided unique opportunities to exercise public leadership and to manage vast sums of money raised from their female constituents in the pews. But women involved in missionary concerns were not, on the whole, cultural radicals. Although, strictly speaking, the power of women's missionary organizations challenged conventional notions of femininity, the leaders of these groups did not wish to jeopardize their independence by challenging the male monopoly over the pulpit.

During the 1920s, however, women's missionary organizations lost their separate status as they underwent forced mergers with their "parent" societies. The choice between maintaining separate power and pushing for more equal access to denominational leadership was not an easy one. Women's groups that resisted "equality" sometimes fared better than those that chose incorporation into larger denominational institutions. The Woman's Missionary Union of the Southern Baptist Convention was one of the few that stayed independent, managing to survive through strong, largely volunteer leadership, continuing denominational loyalty, and a religious ideology of service. These Southern Baptist women would not have called themselves feminists in any sense of the word, and they certainly did not see missionary work as a vehicle of women's rights. Yet as Paul Harvey demonstrates, the

Woman's Missionary Union was a genuinely powerful institution. During the denomination's lean years, the Southern Baptist missionary program owed its survival to the financial stability of its women's auxiliary.

Opposition to feminism among Protestant groups is similarly complex. Women who reject identification with the secular movement may still refer to themselves as "liberated" and evidence their sense of feminine power by rigorous pursuit of spiritual leadership. Espinosa's account of Latina Pentecostals demonstrates the complex challenge that egalitarian feminism poses to women in conservative religious institutions. His essay stands in ironic juxtaposition to Hartmann's examination of the religious roots of second-wave feminism, normally perceived as an entirely secular movement.

The rise of modern feminist ideals is central to the plot line of twentieth-century women's history. It is also an important aspect of women's religious history—yet not in any simple or obvious way. As the essays in this section suggest, the uneven progress of egalitarian feminist ideals within Protestant churches is conditioned by a variety of social factors, including race, ethnicity, and regional identity. Since the early twentieth century women's aspirations have taken a variety of different forms in Protestant churches. Feminism is only one of many narratives that have shaped that story.

1. Saints but Not Subordinates: The Woman's Missionary Union of the Southern Baptist Convention

PAUL HARVEY

BEGINNING IN 1979 and culminating in the early 1990s, fundamentalists assumed control of the nation's largest Protestant denomination, the Southern Baptist Convention (SBC). Led by a lawyer and a seminary professor from Texas and closely affiliated with a burgeoning nationwide network of conservative activists, Southern Baptist insurgents purged "moderates" from convention posts and took over the boards of trustees of major southern Baptist seminaries. They also sought to gain greater institutional authority over one Southern Baptist institution that they did not control directly—the Woman's Missionary Union (WMU) of the Southern Baptist Convention. Although something of a modus vivendi between the denomination and the WMU has been worked out, lingering tensions have raised the specter of a gender gap in Southern Baptist life.

The tension in the 1980s was unusual given the history of the WMU working as the engine that fueled the denomination's missions programs. The very existence of the WMU owes much to the conservative and patriarchal legacy of the SBC and to the fact that WMU members of the past have been content to remain in an auxiliary (that is to say, an institutionally subordinate) status. WMU leaders historically have preached an ethic of being saints and subordinates; in more recent and politically charged times they have used the language of sainthood—self-sacrifice for missions—to resist being made subordinates.

Leaders of the WMU would not—do not—give themselves the inflammatory label "feminist." Yet neither do members of the WMU fit the southern evangelical stereotype of a submissive woman. Southern Baptist women have not adopted the agenda of the religious right. Rather, they have focused on the missionary goals and aims articulated by their founding mothers. By doing so, they have successfully resisted attempts to subsume the WMU into larger, male-dominated denominational structures.

Just as the Southern Baptist Convention is the nation's largest Protestant denomination, the Woman's Missionary Union remains the largest Protestant woman's missionary society in America. The gigantic Southern Baptist home and foreign missionary enterprise, in fact, has depended heavily on the ceaseless fund-raising work of Southern Baptist women past and present. Organizers of the WMU in the nineteenth century created a society that has worked so successfully as an "auxiliary" that Southern Baptist men, until recently at least, have known better than to disturb it. WMU leaders have focused their organizational acumen on creating a financial system that put to shame the haphazard ways in which men managed denominational funds. Among mainstream Protestant groups, the WMU is notable for having preserved its sex-segregated independence long after most women's mission groups—such as the American Baptist Woman's Missionary Society of northern Baptists or the Woman's Foreign Mission Society of the Methodist Episcopal Church, South, in the early twentieth century—were incorporated into larger denominational structures. In fact, historically it has been the very conservatism of Southern Baptist men that has allowed Southern Baptist women to maintain control over the workings of their organization.

The story of the WMU complicates the dominant narrative of women and twentieth-century American Protestantism. Evangelical in theology, implicitly feminist in some of their actions, yet also accepting of the self-sacrificial rhetoric of their foremothers, WMU members draw from the mixed heritage of southern evangelical women. They are neither fundamentalist nor feminist, although elements of both have found their way into the WMU's history. They remain an "auxiliary" to the Southern Baptist Convention yet are in subterranean conflict with the current denomination's stridently fundamentalist leadership. Their tradition required that women who were saints would also be subordinates; they have, however, subtly transformed this tradition and showed that, for contemporary Southern Baptist women, to be a saint one cannot be a subordinate.

Women and Religion in the Nineteenth-Century North and South

In the nineteenth century, as historians have told the story of gender and evangelicalism in the United States, Protestant women inspired by the perfectionist doctrines of the Second Great Awakening swelled the ranks of the early abolitionist movement and energized the first wave of feminism. Women filled an increasing number of pews, led husbands and children to the altar in the Second Great Awakening, and resonated to the loving familial metaphors that suffused the sermons and hymns of the era.[1] Protestant women in the South exist only in the margins of this story. They could not be involved in abolitionism, and few would publicly identify themselves as proponents of women's rights. Yet even in the South a trend toward "feminization"—in the exercise of church discipline, in theological movements away from Calvinism, and in the adoption of the psychology of moral influence—penetrated religious life as the nineteenth century progressed.[2]

Protestant women in the early twentieth century, as this narrative line continues, allied themselves with progressive social reformers. Women assumed increasingly active roles in organizations of benevolence, converting missionary societies into agencies that combined evangelism with social reform. Southern churchwomen embraced social gospel reform with an enthusiasm rare among their male counterparts. Behind the scenes, black women often instigated and prodded in their own tentative gestures at interracial cooperation.[3] At the same time, women in southern Holiness, Primitive Baptist, and other sectarian groups, although rarely social-gospelers and not ordinarily involved in missionary societies, ignored the strictures imposed on women in the pulpit or on the religious stump. They crisscrossed the heartland on twentieth-century itinerant treks and chronicled their heroism in memoirs for the faithful.[4]

Later in the twentieth century—to complete this version of the story—men assumed control of bureaucracies of benevolence formerly managed by women. Although women, as always, made up a majority of those in the pews, their influence was not commensurate with their physical presence in the churches. Rather than being allied with progressive social reform, women's religious activism seemed instead to be concentrated on the political right. Accompanying this has been a secularization of progressive social activism— or so many historians have assumed.[5]

In the dominant narrative of Protestant women in the United States from the mid-nineteenth century to the present, women move from the progressive Protestant mainstream to the antiprogressive Protestant right wing. This essay will test the dominant story line using subjects largely ignored in the larger story line: women in the Southern Baptist Convention.[6]

Led by established men in the community but attended mostly by farmers of modest means, nineteenth-century white Southern Baptist churches exemplified the conservative ideal of the divinely ordained gender and racial hierarchy. Women sometimes exercised voting rights in matters of discipline and fellowship but more rarely in the election of church officers and pastors. Protestant men ritually praised the moral influence of the true evangelical woman. In reality, however, as women well knew, informal influence never equaled formal power. The slow growth of temperance societies in the South and heated controversies raised by figures such as Frances Willard (condemned by southern ministers for advocating female preaching) suggested the limitations of moral suasion. The well-publicized leadership of abolitionist women in the early feminist movement personified white Southern Baptist fears of the blurring of carefully delimited racial and gender boundaries. A Mississippi Baptist association noted how "owing to the fact that the question of Woman's Rights in other fields has been pushed to such an offensive extent in more northern latitudes, our people have been bitterly opposed to our women being brought forward in any cause."[7] Moreover, the localism treasured by the thousands of small, scattered Baptist congregations throughout the region created difficulties for Southern Baptist women who could not participate in denominational institutional structures such as associations and convention meetings to commune with Baptist sisters in other regions. The preponderance of rural churches and the tenuous urban civic life of the nineteenth-century South simply made it difficult for members of organizations to gather at all, particularly for women who could not travel alone without scandal. Denominational hierarchies also blocked women who organized for female laity rights and mission work. That was true even after the Civil War, when white southern churches struggled to rebound from economic devastation.[8]

In the late nineteenth century, however, as bourgeois values and benevolent societies gained a foothold in plain-folk southern denominations, regionally based women's religious societies slowly emerged. Beginning at first in individual churches and extending through statewide networks, such societies in the 1880s and 1890s coalesced into regionwide organizations. Among Methodists, the Woman's Home Missionary Society of the Methodist Episcopal Church, South, formed in the 1880s, soon engaged women throughout the region in varied progressive causes. Beginning their work with visions of guiding the "unenlightened" of the region, they gradually formed implicit alliances with black women in various denominations (especially among women in the Colored Methodist Episcopal and African Methodist Episcopal Zion traditions). In the twentieth century, white Southern Methodist women, many of them trained at Scarritt College in Nashville, formed a significant part of the tiny cadre of the progressive white South.[9]

Organization of the Woman's Missionary Union

In the late nineteenth century, Southern Baptist churchwomen increasingly chafed at quietist prescriptions for female piety even while continuing to work within the language of the "refined southern woman." "The gospel is the Magna Charta of human liberty. It will eventually sweep away all despotism," a Texas woman proclaimed in 1881. In the 1870s and 1880s, Southern Baptist women formed state mission societies that disseminated information supplied by denominational boards. Denominationalists worried that "if we do not accord to women places where their powers can be employed along with ours, they will do as our Northern sisters did, leave us and open up fields for themselves." Missionary society organizers assured skeptics that Southern Baptist women would not form a separate board that pursued its own fields of work. That would be "out of harmony with the clinging tendril nature of the refined Southern woman," they explained. Rather, as was true for many other southern denominational groups, white and black, they formed a woman's auxiliary designed to enlist support for larger denominational causes.[10]

This careful rhetoric toward independent women's organizations has been a constituent feature of the WMU since its inception. Meeting in Richmond, Virginia, in 1888, a group of actively pious, well-bred, white Southern Baptist women organized the Woman's Missionary Union, Auxiliary to the Southern Baptist Convention. They disclaimed "all intention of independent action," seeking instead to stimulate "the missionary spirit and the grace of giving, among the women and children of the churches." Annie Armstrong, a native of Baltimore who headed the WMU from its founding until 1906, dismissed as "absurd" the charge that her organization would push for "women's rights." Still, the WMU gradually has become an advocate for a twentieth-century southern evangelical womanhood, one resembling neither the nineteenth-century "true woman," twentieth-century feminist activism, or contemporary fundamentalism. The WMU has also grown into a huge professional religio-philanthropic organization that now stands ideologically in conflict to the SBC in a way that would shock Armstrong.[11]

After organizing in 1888, the WMU's members soon proved their mettle as fund-raisers for Southern Baptist mission causes. In 1890 there were about five hundred small, individual societies in Baptist churches throughout the region, few of which collected funds for denominational work. Only 12 percent of southern Baptist churches supported mission organizations of any kind. By 1910 the WMU had raised approximately 30 percent of the money expended by the home and foreign mission boards, a number that would

grow significantly over the next three decades. Their work in enlisting individual churches in missions projects, WMU advocates pointed out, simply encouraged women's work for women, not "speaking from the rostrums,
Women's Rights, dynamite, [or] Nihilism." Denominational leaders happily announced that "these noble Christian women are gladly cooperating with
our Boards, and . . . manifest no disposition to . . . usurp authority."[12]

The earliest icon for the WMU was Charlotte Diggs Moon, whose life story
provided a dramatic backdrop and most effective symbol for mammoth
annual money-raising festivals. After a privileged upbringing in Virginia and
a seriously considered offer of marriage, "Lottie" Moon gave her life over to
mission work in the interior of China from the 1870s to 1915. While person-
ifying an ideal of female selflessness, she lived a far more complex reality than
portrayed in the various hagiographic accounts of her life. She began her
mission efforts with typical Victorian evangelical conceptions of the degradation of the heathen and the place of Anglo-Saxon America in world evangelism. By the end of her career, however, she had adopted native dress; giv-
en hungry Chinese her own food, thus hastening her own death; and pleaded
with those sending literature from home to employ a less tendentious term
than *Chinese heathen.* She struggled to transform southern evangelical expressive styles into a form comprehensible to Chinese women.

Moon fiercely defended southern evangelical norms, although her life
modeled something very different. In 1901 she wrote home in support of the
WMU's plans to develop a training school for female missionaries at Southern Baptist Theological Seminary in Louisville, Kentucky. Southern women
trained in the North, she reasoned, absorbed dangerous views of their extended roles. Northern missionaries believed that, as Moon put it, "they not
only may but *must* do things that grate on the sensibilities of people with
Southern feelings and ideals. . . . I am Southern to the core and while I ad-
mire and love many Northern people, I don't want Northern ideals of womanhood introduced into our Southern Baptist missions." She strategically
aimed her reasoning at those opposing any kind of theological education for
women. Her efforts were successful, and women began entering what became
the William Owen Carver School of Social Work in the Louisville seminary.
Although Moon was herself not directly involved in the actual organization
of the WMU, she perfectly represented the role of the WMU in her own careful negotiating of opportunities in the perceived roles of southern evangelical women.[13]

Along with Moon, Annie Armstrong was midwife at the birth of the new
white southern Baptist woman. After a childhood of some privilege in the
Upper South, she rejected marriage and spent her adult years in feats of or-

ganizing and fund-raising. The creation of the WMU itself, opposed as it was by some denominational stalwarts, was no mean accomplishment, nor was her work as corresponding secretary of the WMU. In 1901 she organized the first full-scale survey of SBC churches and missions work, sending out more than 5,600 mailings. Using her own money for support, Armstrong traveled tirelessly for nearly two decades and while in Baltimore spent long days in the Woman's Mission Room organizing WMU drives. Armstrong sent so many care packages to missionaries in the newly developing Southwest that she came under fire for neglecting foreign missionaries. The annual offering collected each Easter in Southern Baptist churches is called the Annie Armstrong offering in recognition of her primary interest in and devotion to home missions. Fund-raising strategies adopted by the WMU and later by the SBC, such as the weekly envelope system, facilitated long-range denominational planning based on plausible budgets.[14]

Tirelessly active and zealously evangelical, Armstrong pioneered roles for younger white southern evangelical women. As she impatiently put it, "I have heard so much about the 'woman's sphere,' and her going beyond proper bounds, that I think I am beginning to feel on this point as the children do when they are told 'children should be seen and not heard.'" Women's work was, she said, "much of it hidden work, as are the springs which feed the watercourses of mighty rivers." To those who scoffed at what "sentiment" might accomplish, she answered, "It is woman's sentiment which has in the last forty years changed the codes of many states, and revolutionized the thoughts of the nation, on the subject of temperance. The creation of sentiment is as womanly as powerful."

At the same time, Armstrong rarely challenged the conventions of women in southern religious life. She expressed both the nineteenth-century vision of heroic voluntarism in benevolence and the newer model of professionalized philanthropy. Yet in her heart she remained closer to the earlier ideal of heroic voluntarism in benevolence, as suggested in her incessant rhetoric of self-sacrifice, her refusal to take any pay for her seventy-hour weeks of work, and her resistance to regularizing the leadership structure of the WMU itself. Armstrong knew how to negotiate delicate gender questions so as to ease fears of violating biblical injunctions. She never appeared in a pulpit if she could be construed as acting in a ministerial role. She preferred to "help in a work without appearing publicly" and avoid "being a target for criticism." The growth of her organization, she felt, had not cost activists "one iota of womanliness, but gain in all that goes to make up a rounded Christian character." The success of the WMU proved "competency and business sense in managing new lines of missionary effort, bringing them to successful result," she triumphantly concluded. Yet this "business sense" itself depended on the comfortable background of Annie and her sister Alice, daughters of a successful family in Baltimore and friends to Richard Edmonds, a ceaseless propagandist for the New South and influential entrepreneur.[15]

Armstrong's language and practice of self-sacrifice worked well as a pragmatic plan to make women's religious activism acceptable to the traditionalist constituency that filled the pews of Southern Baptist churches. Armstrong herself began a practice common among future WMU leaders of forming alliances with influential men in the SBC, who would then make the public case for the WMU's work. As Armstrong wrote to James M. Frost, secretary of the Sunday School Board of the SBC, "We can go a certain distance and there have to stop and unless we have the support of our brethren the work does not assume the proportions it should. If I had to appear before the public as the one who was responsible for some measures which I have suggested and the Boards have carried out . . . I could not have borne it." Armstrong was, by all accounts, a forceful personality who behind the scenes generally directed men in what to do; she was not one to take orders or countenance resistance to her ideas.[16]

In the early twentieth century, as the WMU moved into a new era of acceptance and power, Armstrong lost control over her child. When the WMU engineered plans to form a training school for women at the Southern Baptist Theological Seminary in Louisville, Armstrong opposed it adamantly and even at times slanderously, accusing its supporters of political "wire-pulling" and of wanting to create a matrimonial bureau for men studying at the seminary. She also fought against increasing the power of the president of the WMU and making the job of corresponding secretary (the executive post in the organization) into a salaried professional position. When she lost both fights in 1906 she resigned. Incredibly, even though she lived into the 1930s, she never again attended a WMU meeting and distanced herself from the further development of the organization. Armstrong chose a different course from her Methodist counterpart Belle Bennett, who very publicly campaigned for women's rights within the Methodist Episcopal Church, South.

Armstrong's legacy, however, served future generations of WMU members, and the SBC itself, very well. Recognizing her organizational achievements, the SBC later praised her: "Possessed of a power to grasp and master details that amounts to genius; given a vision of the possibilities of organization and development among our people that few have ever had; having a love for souls amounting to a passion; loving God fervently and willing to make her life an unbroken day of sacrificial service to him, she has been to us and our work what few others could have been."[17]

The Professionalization of Self-Sacrifice:
The WMU, Missions, and Social Activism in the
Mid-Twentieth Century

The growth of the SBC into a twentieth-century benevolent machine owes much to the organization and fund-raising techniques devised by WMU leaders. Armstrong tried to mold the WMU in her own image—to energize a self-sacrificing group of volunteers who would devote themselves to raising money for Southern Baptist missions. The status of the founding mothers as reasonably comfortable urban white women made possible such a vision. Much to Armstrong's consternation, however, the organization gradually followed the imperatives of professional philanthropy, including the employment of a full-time staff.

Armstrong's spiritual daughter, Kathleen Mallory, maintained the tradition of single-minded heroism in the cause of missions support. Mallory lived in a single-room apartment in Birmingham during her thirty-six-year tenure as WMU director, never accepting more than $3,000 in pay, even during the years after World War II. She recognized that by keeping the WMU clear of denominational infighting, support for missionary causes would grow. Asked to back a proposal to admit women as messengers to SBC meetings, Mallory responded to a male colleague, "The unwieldy personnel of the Convention is well known to you and we do not believe that our women would ever feel free to take part in discussions on the floor." In this case it was men who pressed for an expansion of women's roles in the SBC. "Women would do their best work on committees where the woman's view is often badly needed," Texas Baptist James B. Gambrell wrote to Mallory. To him, it was "incongruous, that the men of our churches should control all the work, when so large a part of it is done by the women." Opening the SBC to women was, he concluded, as "inevitable" as woman suffrage.[18]

The independent auxiliary status of the WMU made even more sense as the twentieth century progressed. During the 1920s, Southern Baptist missions overexpanded in response to an exuberant postwar fund-raising drive that soon produced far less in receipts than had been pledged. To worsen matters, Southern Baptist mission boards witnessed a financial scandal. As boards struggled to find a way out of debt, the depression nearly wiped missions out of existence. In fact, the plight of the Southern Baptist missions compelled Kathleen Mallory to seek legal counsel to ensure that WMU assets would not be seized to pay off debts of the Foreign Mission Board. For many of the interwar years the WMU provided nearly the only money that paid missionaries and not creditors. In 1928, despite numbering only 13.3 percent of membership in SBC-affiliated churches, the WMU contributed 59 percent of the budget of the Foreign Mission Board of the Convention; by 1931 it was nearly 70 percent.

The WMU's fund-raising capabilities and business acumen extended to future generations. It not only developed new techniques for systematic fund-raising but also, until the 1950s, controlled the disbursement of its funds. The WMU espoused tithing as a regular part of the churchgoers' duties long before the SBC formed its own Stewardship Commission to systematize fund-raising. In the 1930s, in fact, while Southern Baptists as a whole rated last in per capita mission giving for major denominations at $1.87 per churchgoer, WMU members contributed $4.49 per member.

After World War II, as the South modernized and the SBC cultivated a national constituency, the WMU tapped into new reserves of churchgoers' dollars and collected tens of millions annually toward the support of Southern Baptist mission enterprises. Ironically, the growth of the SBC missionary force (to more than 1,200 in the early 1950s and more than 7,500 in the 1980s) necessitated that the WMU relinquish control of the disbursement of funds to (male) denominational professionals. The WMU itself lacked the staff to oversee the distribution of its funds and handle the complexities of specific situations of missionaries. Since the 1980s the WMU has organized annual mission offerings in excess of $60 million, allowing the SBC to be one mainstream Protestant denomination with a growing missionary force and total number of members. The annual Lottie Moon offering of the WMU, amounting to more than $66 million in 1986, was the single largest source of support for the missionaries supported by Southern Baptists. The offering commemorates a woman whose life dramatically contradicted the norms of women's roles preached by the southern patriarchy. That contradiction is smoothed over, however, by presenting Moon as exemplifying rather than subverting southern evangelical womanhood.[19]

The WMU and the Social Gospel in the Twentieth Century

The WMU far outpaced the SBC not only in inspiring giving to denominational causes but also in formulating social responses to the gospel in a region suspicious of the social gospel. While denominational leaders argued over the precise degree of emphasis on evangelism versus social action, women found no conflict, potential or actual, between the two. WMU leaders adopted "community uplift" as a principal rather than a peripheral theme (the opposite of men in the SBC, who relegated ideas of religious progressivism to token "social service commissions" whose job it was to meet year-ly to pass resolutions). In the early twentieth century the WMU created its own Personal Service Committee, signaling in part a shift from the nine-teenth-century individualistic ethos to a Progressive Era stress on social ac-tion. The WMU passed its first temperance resolution in 1891, several years before the SBC endorsed Prohibition. In many towns and cities, WMU mem-bers to a woman also joined the Woman's Christian Temperance Union.

In the twentieth century, WMU Personal Service extended into new areas, including settlement-house work, child labor law advocacy, and other sta-ples of the progressive movement. Most WMU leaders did not publicly sup-port or oppose woman suffrage. WMU president Fannie E. S. Heck, certain-ly a politically active woman, asserted that the WMU could as well achieve its purposes without suffrage as with it and that alienating potential support-ers by joining the suffrage campaign might hinder the growth of the orga-nization. Heck, however, served as vice president of the Southern Sociolog-ical Congress and placed social action onto the WMU agenda. Her opposition to making suffrage an issue for the WMU appears to have been tactical rather than philosophical. Heck engaged in a whirlwind of charitable, reformist, and missionary society activities in North Carolina and participated in ecumen-ical conferences for missionary leaders from various denominations. At her urging, the WMU began publishing a journal known originally as *Our Mis-sion Field,* which continues publication under the title *Royal Service.*

During Heck's years at the helm, and into the 1920s and the depression era, the WMU closely followed trends in progressive thought and action. At the beginning of anti-child labor campaigns, Baptist women in North Carolina appealed for fewer work hours so children's lives "be not completely stunt-ed and crushed mentally, morally, and physically." They also expressed ap-proval of national efforts (such as *Muller v. Oregon*) to limit women's work hours. While full of the same condescension of middle-class progressives generally toward the poor, they also supported educational programs, child labor restrictions, and racial uplift. Suggesting measures to meet the needs of "the unlovely people about us"—factory children, cotton mill workers, mountain women, and African Americans—South Carolinians advocated active measures from Baptists to alleviate the "poverty, ignorance, disease, and crime" afflicting poor southern women. Expressing a typically postmil-lennialist southern progressive vision, North Carolina Baptist women en-dorsed "child labor and temperance legislation, welfare work, prison reforms, social service centers, every activity of this kind" as a way to "make the world ready for His coming." Prominent Baptist women served on public boards and commissions that investigated child labor abuses, pushed for Prohibition legislation, condemned convict leasing and other abuses in the penal system, and fostered tentative efforts at interracial cooperation.[20]

By including the traditional staples of Protestant moral fervor along with more contemporary social ills, the WMU articulated a southern religious social consciousness that outpaced male denominational leaders. Southern Baptist women's religious progressivism peaked in the World War I years. The national WMU set as its agenda support for "those forces in our country which make for righteousness: patriotism working toward universal and permanent peace, prohibition, Sabbath observance, the sacredness of the home, the effort toward a more general re-establishment of the family altar, and the crusade against poverty, disease, illiteracy, vice, and crime." The WMU also began settlement centers in 1913 and was directing some thirty-two by 1925. The Woman's Missionary Union Training School in Louisville soon focused its efforts on training graduates to work in settlement houses that ministered to immigrant, working-class, and black populations in cities. The largest Southern Baptist settlement was in Louisville, where the Good Will Center at 512 East Madison Street employed women educated at the training school that Annie Armstrong had fought to block.[21]

Later in the twentieth century, WMU members heard frequent social gospel addresses long after the social gospel itself had fallen into disfavor. Women such as Ethlene Boone Cox spoke publicly for WMU causes—in Cox's case to a crowd of forty-seven thousand in a stadium in Atlanta. During the 1930s and 1940s, WMU president Olive Martin deliberately inserted "heretics" (her somewhat light-hearted term) into public-speaking engagements at Southern Baptist women's meetings, including early feminist theologians such as Georgia Harkness. She also invited several black women to the podium to speak, challenging southern social customs with another sort of heresy. Women such as Cox and Martin tapped into the developing tradition of a moderate white southern appeal to the religious conscience of the region, which civil rights leaders later exploited with great effectiveness. Christian women, WMU leaders believed, should treat all people with Christian charity and kindness. That view inherently clashed with southern norms of racial subjugation.[22]

The WMU also tentatively engaged in projects involving interracial cooperation. The organization's leaders spoke of these as work "among" black women, expressing the condescending conception of their mission. Still, it was a decided improvement over the determination of denominational men to "manage the Negro." The WMU drew from the legacy of feminine caring for the less fortunate (including African Americans); over time, members took from that tradition a willingness to engage in some limited interracial dialogue and gradually learned that kindness alone was no panacea for the race problem in the South. Indeed, some learned that the race problem was a white problem at base. Again, it was the theology of southern evangelical womanhood—which allowed for woman's "gentle touch" in social conflicts—that afforded them more leeway than men in dealing with racial issues. The theological racism of the Southern Baptist tradition, emanating from prominent pastors and denominational agencies, was not the same barrier to members of the WMU as it was to progressive-minded men, for WMU had developed a quiet counter-tradition of biracial cooperation.

Southern evangelical women cultivated interracial contacts with little of the public fanfare of male efforts toward the same end. In this area as in so many others, Annie Armstrong, child of the Upper South, set an early example. She aided Nannie Burroughs in forming the Woman's Convention, Auxiliary to the National Baptist Convention and worked with Richard Boyd, founder and manager of the National Baptist Publishing Board, and Burroughs to provide Sunday school literature to black Baptist churches. For some years, the SBC contributed toward the salary for missionaries among black women and funds for Sunday school literature. "You have no idea of how . . . thankful I am that God is allowing us this opportunity to help to elevate the colored woman as well as to assist the work in Africa," Armstrong wrote a denominational colleague. "It will prove to the colored people that we are anxious to help them." The "life long acquaintance" of southern whites with their black servants, she imagined, would furnish "the most favorable of opportunities" for the uplift of black women. Northern women entertained unrealistic expectations about missionary work, she alleged. "There may be more romance in it to those at a distance," but there were "larger possibilities in it for us." Armstrong arranged for the Home Mission Board of the SBC to employ black women as field workers in the Woman's Convention of the National Baptist Convention, and she appeared together with one of these women, Lillie Easterly Barker, at a board meeting in Atlanta. Despite Armstrong's penchant for paternalistic language, which normally riled Nannie Burroughs, the two women maintained a good working relationship. If Burroughs had drawn the line at paternalistic rhetoric, it would have been virtually impossible to work with any white agencies at all. She later expressed appreciation for Armstrong by calling her "the trail blazer in Christian cooperation between white and Negro Baptist women of the south. . . . No woman in America has ever done more to encourage Negro Baptist women in their work."[23]

Such effort in biracial cooperation, with its implications of controversy, grew slowly among the rank and file, but over time it took root. Few Southern Baptist women participated in early interracial efforts such as the Commission on Interracial Cooperation headed by the Methodist Will Alexander and championed by the Atlanta Baptist minister M. Ashby Jones. The Training School at Southern Baptist Theological Seminary, as one progressive southern woman later reminisced of her years there in the 1930s, mostly taught the "same old Sunday school stuff," dissatisfying those who wanted to move beyond Progressive Era pieties about "uplifting" the Negro. In the 1930s and 1940s, Burroughs and other black women worked successfully with Una Roberts Lawrence, chair of the Personal Service Committee of the WMU. An advocate of interracial work, appointee to the Committee on Farm Security in the New Deal, and an admirer of Eleanor Roosevelt, Lawrence insisted that work for (or even with) African Americans become part of the "Personal Service Standard" for WMU organizations. In 1929, when she took office, 255 missionary societies reported some effort in that direction. By 1936 that number was 2,437. Impressive as the increase was, it nevertheless represented only 7 percent of all missions organizations. Lawrence renewed the WMU's contacts with Nannie Burroughs, contributing funds for the distribution of mission literature. In 1947 Burroughs was featured on the cover of *Royal Service,* which only a year before had pronounced the demands of blacks "frightening, difficult, dangerous, revolutionary and unreasonable."[24] The WMU integrated the Training School in Louisville in 1952 and in 1957–58 endorsed *Brown v. the Board of Education of Topeka, Kansas.* Locally, WMU workers affiliated themselves with groups such as Church Women United. They usually did so unofficially rather than risk the reputation of the WMU by involving it in even slightly controversial causes.

In many local communities, white Baptist and Methodist women provided unsung but important support for the work of civil rights organizations, whether it involved driving domestic workers during the Montgomery bus boycott or more direct political actions such as the efforts of Church Women United to thwart the plans of Gov. Orval Faubus during and after the 1957 Little Rock school crisis. During the course of the 1960s, the WMU gradually nudged Southern Baptists into an acceptance of desegregation, couching it in terms of opportunities for mission work with blacks. Moderate Southern Baptists such as Foy Valentine, a long-time chair of the Social Service Commission of the SBC and an advocate of racial reform in the South, depended on the work of WMU leaders to ease the way for acceptance of the achievements of the civil rights movement.[25]

White Southern Baptist women of the twentieth century, then, tread gingerly into new roles. They were neither as publicly involved as their Methodist sisters nor as removed from worldly affairs as Holiness and Pentecostal women. They kept southern garb firmly in place in the process while raising and distributing remarkable sums of money, running complex organizations, and poking holes in the region's racial and gender mythologies. And they did so in a denomination that maintained its regional identity and remained conservative and cautious in even slightly breaching regional mores.

Power Struggles: Women and Fundamentalism in the Contemporary Southern Baptist Convention

The advantages of auxiliary status have become even clearer in recent years. It has allowed those women who have remained within the SBC to resist attempts to incorporate their organization within the larger confines of the denomination itself—in other words, to put it under male rule. Independent auxiliary status has also allowed WMU members to support moderate social reform. In some ways, a gender gap in SBC politics has developed that mirrors the one often noted in national politics. The WMU has maintained its traditional missions and social emphasis while the SBC enlists in the agenda of the religious right, issuing public condemnations of everything from flag burning to Ellen DeGeneres and endorsing "wifely submission" to husbands.[26]

What explains the ability of the WMU to maintain its organizational independence? Its perseverance is remarkable given the larger pattern in other denominations of women's mission societies being subsumed into larger groups headed by male executives. Early in the twentieth century, for example, the Southern Methodists combined various missionary agencies into the Missionary Council and later into the Board of Missions, which has various departments of service. Perhaps conservative religious groups, because of their literal interpretations of biblical restrictions on women's ordination, are most amenable to single-sex benevolent societies. That is certainly true of groups in the Pentecostal traditions, many of which have had a tradition of female exhorters and evangelists but over time have grown increasingly conservative on questions of men and women's roles. Most of them encouraged separate women's mission groups at the same time that such groups were integrated out of existence in mainstream Protestant denominations.[27]

Such an argument provides little reason for cheer. If organizational independence does not open opportunities beyond those available to a previous generation, then the model of empowerment drawn from nineteenth-century women's culture cannot be applied to twentieth-century groups. Annie Armstrong lived a life available to few southern women who followed conventional models. The same is not as true for Armstrong's contemporary successors. While Annie Armstrong was a confidant and ally of denomina-

tional leaders, in more recent years WMU leaders and SBC denominationalists have eyed each other with some suspicion.

In the 1980s, as the power struggle within the SBC raged, conservatives
suspected WMU leaders of encouraging women in ministerial vocations that
the Bible assigned to men. In 1984 SBC delegates passed a resolution encouraging "the service of women in all aspects of church life and work other than
pastoral functions and leadership roles entailing ordination." They noted that
"concerns of Christian doctrine and practice" should not be determined by
"modern cultural, sociological, and ecclesiastical trends or by emotional factors"—including the contemporary women's rights movement. The resolution implicitly accused some WMU leaders and female seminarians of advancing a political agenda favorable to women's rights, including ministerial
ordination. Contentious issues over women's roles in SBC-affiliated churches
and in seminaries have continued to smolder. In the 1990s, for example, Albert Mohler, Jr., the young president of Southern Baptist Theological Seminary in Louisville, ousted a well-known female biblical scholar from his
institution, a battle chronicled in the documentary *Battle for the Minds.* Seminarians supportive of women's rights to ministerial ordination began publishing a newsletter, *Folio,* that drew the ire of denominational officials. WMU
leaders dissociated themselves from the newsletter and proclaimed their
neutrality on issues of women's ordination, using the traditional Baptist language about the issue being a decision of the local church and not of any
larger entity.[28]

The institutional power of the WMU remains undeniable, but the current
crop of denominational officials has sought ways to bring the WMU more
closely under the denominational wing or to circumvent traditional WMU
roles in favor of newly sanctioned groups directly under the denominational imprimatur. As part of a denominational "restructuring," SBC leaders
began to sponsor and fund women's mission groups that challenged the historic dominance of the WMU in channeling support for Southern Baptist
missions. Early in 1998, while acknowledging that leaders of alternative
groups had given "verbal affirmation of [the] WMU and assurance that they
did not intend to run us out of business," the WMU Executive Board also
expressed concern that "since both missions offering promotion and missions education for the local church have been reassigned to the mission
boards, we have waited with some tension for clarification of our place in
these two areas formerly considered the responsibility of the WMU." The
board wondered how to diminish "confusion among women in the local
church" whose limited time and resources would be called upon to support
what appear to be multiple organizations pursuing the same task. Although

the board said, "We have cooperated so long that we hardly know how not to do so," it also added, "We will have to learn to operate in a more ambiguous atmosphere than we have known in the recent past."[29]

The incredible successes of the WMU in Southern Baptist life, moreover, have not translated into effective leverage in moving women into new levels of religious leadership unavailable to previous generations. Given the present SBC male leadership's hostility to women in the ministry, the stained-glass ceiling will grow even more impenetrable. Denominational officials have rejected any notion of women in ordained ministerial roles, citing scriptural authority that "women should not usurp authority over men in the church."[30] Although nearly one in four denominational employees are women, most are concentrated at the lower echelons of the denominational hierarchy. Only about 10 percent of professional church staff personnel are women, and fewer than 1 percent of female ministers nationwide are Southern Baptist. At present, the outlook for ordained women in Southern Baptist churches appears bleak; many are moving on to American Baptist churches or to other denominations where jobs are more plentiful and less controversial. The WMU's successes have barely nudged upward the mobility of women in the nation's largest Protestant denomination. In this sense, members of the WMU have been saints and subordinates.

Or perhaps that is too pessimistic a conclusion. Armstrong's vision of the self-sacrificial women supporting and enlarging the denomination's mission program while also abjuring any public roles of authority cannot be sustained indefinitely. Since the fundamentalist resurgence in the SBC in 1979, the WMU has supported women in a variety of church-related occupations in a denomination inclined to excommunicate churches that ordain women. Carolyn Weatherford, a recent director of the WMU, cagily argued that a group called Women in Ministry, formed to encourage Southern Baptist women in ministerial roles, was not forcing women's ordination down Southern Baptist throats. Speaking to the controversial informal alliance of the WMU and an ad hoc informal fellowship known as Southern Baptist Women in Ministry (SBWIM), Weatherford maintained that the term *women in ministry* really meant "women in church-related vocations," whether or not the women involved were ordained. At the same time, Weatherford acknowledged the price of the intractability of gender discrimination in church work: "Some women have been seriously disappointed when they accepted God's call to special service, [and] then were unable to find places of service." She termed this a "serious dilemma. If WMU is to be honest with girls about listening to God's call, we must be informed and concerned about the problems they encounter." Women not ordained but serving as effectual ministers, she insisted, were tilling the ground for future generations of theologically trained women. For that reason among others, the SBC's leadership has continued to eye uneasily the auxiliary power at its side. As Alma Hunt explains her view of WMU work, "Don't think we're not progressive. We're just not militant."[31]

The mothers of the WMU founded their group as an auxiliary precisely because it allowed the organization to fit well within the confines of southern evangelical culture. That same culture, however, allowed them to retain control of their own missionary agency and to pursue and develop the tentative social emphasis on religion that characterized their earlier years. Since male authority in the SBC has grown increasingly conservative, however, the WMU has charted a different course from that of the denomination, even though there are plenty of conservative and fundamentalist women in the WMU itself. For many Southern Baptist women, a twentieth-century women's religious culture that is neither fundamentalist nor feminist has provided their route for testing new models of southern evangelical womanhood.

Notes

1. For a variety of views on women and religion in antebellum America, see Mary Ryan, *Cradle of the Middle Class: The Family in Oneida County, New York, 1790–1865* (New York: Cambridge University Press, 1981); Ann Douglas, *The Feminization of American Culture* (New York: Knopf, 1977); Colleen McDannell, *The Christian Home in Victorian America, 1840–1900* (Bloomington: Indiana University Press, 1986); and Sandra S. Sizer, *Gospel Hymns and Social Religion: The Rhetoric of Nineteenth-Century Revivalism* (Philadelphia: Temple University Press, 1978).

2. Jean Friedman's *The Enclosed Garden: Women and Community in the Evangelical South, 1830–1900* (Chapel Hill: University of North Carolina Press, 1985) began more recent discussions of southern women and religion. Other studies of contrasting interpretation include those by Stephanie McCurry, *Masters of Small Worlds: Yeoman Households, Gender Relations, and the Political Culture of the Antebellum South Carolina Low Country* (New York: Oxford University Press, 1995), who argues for the strengthening of male patriarchal rule through evangelical institutions, and Christine Leigh Heyrman, *Southern Cross: The Beginnings of the Bible Belt* (New York: Knopf, 1997), who paints a complex and emotionally compelling portrait of southern women's attraction to evangelicalism.

3. Glenda Gilmore, *Gender and Jim Crow: Women and the Politics of White Supremacy in North Carolina, 1896–1920* (Chapel Hill: University of North Carolina Press, 1996); Ralph Luker, *The Social Gospel in Black and White: American Racial Reform, 1885–1912* (Chapel Hill: University of North Carolina Press, 1991); John Patrick McDowell, *The Social Gospel in the South: The Woman's Home Mission Movement in the Methodist Episcopal Church, South, 1886–1939* (Baton Rouge: Louisiana State University Press, 1982); Patricia Martin, "Hidden Work: Baptist Women in Texas, 1880–1920," Ph.D. diss., Rice University, 1982;

Jacqueline Rouse, *Lugenia Burns Hope: Black Southern Reformer* (Athens: University of Georgia Press, 1989).

4. For an autobiographical account and close study of a Holiness woman who served as the unofficial founder of the Church of the Nazarene, see Mary Lee Cagle, *Life and Work of Mary Lee Cagle: An Autobiography* (Kansas City: Nazarene Publishing House, 1928), and Robert Stanley Ingersol, "Burden of Dissent: Mary Lee Cagle and the Southern Holiness Movement," Ph.D. diss., Duke University, 1989. For analyses of women claiming authority in backcountry primitivist traditions, see Beverly Patterson, *The Sound of the Dove: Singing in Appalachian Primitive Baptist Churches* (Urbana: University of Illinois Press, 1995), and Elaine Lawless, *Handmaidens of the Lord: Pentecostal Women Preachers and Traditional Religion* (Philadelphia: University of Pennsylvania Press, 1988).

5. This is the implication of the documents and essays collected in Rosemary Radford Ruether and Rosemary Skinner Keller, eds., *Women and Religion in America*, 4 vols. (Minneapolis: Fortress Press, 1981–86). For a critique of this view, see Elizabeth Fox-Genovese, "Two Steps Forward, One Step Back: New Questions and Old Models in the Religious History of American Women," *Journal of the American Academy of Religion* 53 (1985): 465–71.

6. For a full recounting of the history of the denomination, see Robert Baker, *The Southern Baptist Convention and Its People, 1607–1972* (Nashville: Broadman Press, 1974). For a more analytical examination of the denomination from the Civil War to the 1920s, see Paul Harvey, *Redeeming the South: Religious Cultures and Racial Identities among Southern Baptists, 1865–1925* (Chapel Hill: University of North Carolina Press, 1997). For a full and well-researched history of the WMU written by an insider but with a professional historian's competence, see Catherine Lee Allen, *A Century to Celebrate: History of the Woman's Missionary Union* (Birmingham: Woman's Missionary Union, 1987). This essay draws heavily on Allen's extensive archival research.

7. Leslie K. Dunlap, "Family Descent: Race, Politics, and Sexual Morality in the Woman's Christian Temperance Union," Ph.D. diss., Northwestern University, 1998; *Christian Index*, June 7, 1888; Fair River Baptist Association (Miss.), *Minutes*, 1884, 17. For women and the war, see George Rable, *Civil Wars: Women and the Crisis of Confederate Nationalism* (Urbana: University of Illinois Press, 1989), and Drew Faust, *Mothers of Invention: Women of the Slaveholding South in the American Civil War* (Chapel Hill: University of North Carolina Press, 1996).

8. Friedman, *The Enclosed Garden*, chapter 1; Harvey, *Redeeming the South*, 25–27.

9. McDowell, *The Social Gospel in the South;* Mrs. R. W. MacDonell, *Belle Harris Bennett: Her Life Work* (1928, repr. New York: Garland, 1987); Mary E. Frederickson, "'Each One Is Dependent on the Other': Southern Churchwomen, Racial Reform, and the Process of Transformation, 1880–1940," in *Visible Women: New Essays on American Activism*, ed. Nancy Hewitt and Suzanne Lebsock (Urbana: University of Illinois Press, 1993), 296–324; Gilmore, *Gender and Jim Crow*.

10. "Mrs. Jenny Beauchamp," *Baptist Record*, May 19, 1881 (first quotation); Southern Baptist Convention (hereafter SBC) *Annual*, 1882, 38 (second quotation); *Baptist Record*, Aug. 9, 1888 (third quotation).

11. Constitution of the WMU, 1888, (first quotation), Southern Baptist Historical Library and Archives, Nashville, Tenn. (hereafter SBHLA); "Cleia," *Christian Index*, June 5, 1884.

12. Allen, *A Century to Celebrate*, 117, 337, 354; Tennessee Baptist State Convention *Minutes*, 1895, 34 (first quotation); SBC *Annual*, 1915, 30–31 (second quotation).

13. Charlotte Diggs Moon to James M. Frost, n.d., James M. Frost Papers, box 23, folder 6, SBHLA; Moon to R. J. Willingham, Nov. 7, 1901 (quotation), Edgar Young Mullins letter files, Boyce Library, Southern Baptist Theological Seminary, Louisville, Ky. For an analysis of the symbology of Moon and her central role in contemporary fund-raising efforts, see Irwin Hyatt, *Our Ordered Lives Confess: Three Nineteenth-Century Missionaries in East Shantung* (Cambridge: Harvard University Press, 1976), and Paul Harvey, "The Politicization of White and Black Southern Baptist Missionaries, 1880–1930," *American Baptist Quarterly* 13 (Sept. 1994): 204–20. For more on the training school, see T. Laine Scales, *All That Fits a Woman: Training Southern Baptist Women for Charity and Mission, 1907–1926* (Macon: Mercer University Press, 2000).

14. For a full recounting of Armstrong's life, see Bobbie Sorrill, *Annie Armstrong: Dreamer in Action* (Nashville: Broadman Press, 1985).

15. The quotations in this and the preceding paragraph are from Annie Armstrong to T. P. Bell, July 8, 1893, James M. Frost Papers, box 1, folder 1A, SBHLA (first quotation); Woman's Missionary Union (hereafter WMU) *Report*, 1894, 10 (second quotation); WMU *Report*, 1896, 9 (third quotation).

16. Annie Armstrong to J. M. Frost, Oct. 6, 1906, James M. Frost Papers, box 15, folder 10a, SBHLA (first quotation); Allen, *A Century to Celebrate*, 354 (second quotation).

17. Allen, *A Century to Celebrate*, 354.

18. *Baptist Standard*, July 13, 1916, 10 (first quotation); Catherine Allen, *Laborers Together with God: Twenty-two Great Women in Baptist Life* (Birmingham: The Union, 1987), 172 (second quotation).

19. For facts and figures on the financial successes of the WMU and the key importance of WMU-inspired offerings in keeping alive Southern Baptist missions in the 1920s and 1930s, see Allen, *A Century to Celebrate*, 150–55.

20. Woman's Missionary Union, Auxiliary to the Baptist State Convention of North Carolina, *Report*, 1919, 22, 93 (first quotation); Woman's Missionary Union, Auxiliary to the Baptist State Convention of South Carolina, *Minutes*, 1912, 39–40 (second quotation); see also Gregory Vickers, "Models of Womanhood and the Early Woman's Missionary Union," *Baptist History and Heritage* 24 (Jan. 1989): 41–53; Gregory Vickers, "Southern Baptist Women and Social Concern, 1910–1929," *Baptist History and Heritage* 23 (Oct. 1980): 3–12; and Martin, "Hidden Work."

21. SBC *Annual*, 1917, 90 (quotation); Allen, *A Century to Celebrate*, 211.

22. Allen, *A Century to Celebrate*, 220–21.

23. Annie Armstrong to James M. Frost, Jan. 26, 1897, James M. Frost Papers, box 3, SBHLA (first quotation); WMU *Report*, 1895, 14 (second quotation); WMU *Report*, 1897, 15–20 (third quotation); National Baptist Convention *Journal*, 1902, 58–60 (fourth quotation); Allen, *A Century to Celebrate*, 244–48.

24. Allen, *A Century to Celebrate*, 248.

25. Ibid., 215–20, 248; interview with Thelma Lewis in Southern Oral History Program interviews, Southern Historical Collection, Wilson Library, University of North Carolina at Chapel Hill. For more on Lawrence, see the excellent collection of the Una Roberts Lawrence Papers, SBHLA, which contains voluminous material on race relations. See also

Foy Valentine, *A Historical Study of Southern Baptists and Race Relations, 1917–1947* (New York: Arno Press, 1980), a reprint of his remarkably prescient dissertation completed in the 1940s.

26. See Nancy Ammerman, *Baptist Battles: Conflict and Change in the Southern Baptist Convention* (New Brunswick: Rutgers University Press, 1985), and Ellen Rosenberg, *The Southern Baptists: A Subculture in Transition* (Knoxville: University of Tennessee Press, 1989), for more on women and the fundamentalist resurgence in the SBC.

27. For a broader analysis of the complicated relationship between fundamentalism and gender conceptions, see Betty DeBerg, *Ungodly Women: Gender and the First Wave of American Fundamentalism* (Minneapolis: Fortress Press, 1990), and Margaret Lamberts Bendroth, *Fundamentalism and Gender, 1875 to the Present* (New Haven: Yale University Press, 1993).

28. Resolution on Ordination and the Role of Women in Ministry, SBC *Annual*, 1984, 65; Carolyn Weatherford, speech to Montana Southern Baptist Fellowship, Oct. 1, 1984, copy in Weatherford Collection, WMU Archives, record group 6A5A4, box 17, WMU History Research Collection, Birmingham, Ala.

29. Executive Board Minutes, General Session, 1998, 3–6, WMU Archives, WMU History Research Collection.

30. Statement by SBC president Charles Stanley on women's ordination, reprinted in *Folio*, n.d., copy provided by WMU Archives.

31. Carolyn Weatherford, form letter composed in response to inquiries about the WMU and Women in Ministry, July 17, 1984, WMU Archives, record group 6A5A4, box 17, WMU History Research Collection (first quotation); Anne Thomas Neil and Virginia Garrett Neely, eds., *The New Has Come: Emerging Roles among Southern Baptist Women* (Washington: Southern Baptist Alliance, 1989); David T. Morgan, *The New Crusades, the New Holy Land: Conflict in the Southern Baptist Convention, 1969–1991* (Tuscaloosa: University of Alabama Press, 1996); Allen, *A Century to Celebrate,* 338 (second quotation).

2. "Your Daughters Shall Prophesy": A History of Women in Ministry in the Latino Pentecostal Movement in the United States

GASTÓN ESPINOSA

"SHE BENT OVER and touched my shoulder. As I brushed the sand out of my eyes to wake up, she began talking fast in some language I had never heard before. . . . Then the other language stopped, and she said: 'Son, I have had the most glorious experience! I have just been baptized in the Holy Ghost and have been given the gift of tongues!'" Thus Adolfo Valdez described his mother's spirit baptism at the Azusa Street Revival in 1906. "These are blessed times, son," Susie Villa Valdez went on to declare. "The Holy Ghost is here on earth—like at Pentecost. Thank God we are alive to see fulfillment of the promises of the Bible!"[1]

Villa Valdez's Pentecostal message took the devout Catholic family by storm. The very next week she took her husband and son to the Azusa Street Revival in Los Angeles, where they, too, were converted. Not able to confine her newfound enthusiasm to the walls of the Azusa Street Mission, she began preaching throughout southern California. Her prophetic ministry helped give birth to the Latino Pentecostal movement in the Americas.[2]

The stories of women such as Villa Valdez and more than 1,200 Latina clergy in the United States and Puerto Rico have been virtually ignored by scholars of American religious history.[3] Even more painful and ironic is the total absence of Latina clergy in the recent flurry of historical and sociological studies on women in the ministry.[4] The reasons for this gap in the literature are cultural barriers and the myth that all Latinas/os are Spanish-speaking Roman Catholic immigrants. Other studies have shattered this myth. The majority of the thirty-five million Latinos in the United States are bilingual and citizens. Furthermore, only 65 percent of all Latinos are Catholic; 25 percent (between eight and nine million) are Protestant.[5]

The little that has been written on Latinas in religion has focused almost exclusively on the contemporary struggles of Catholic and mainline Protestant women from a decidedly feminist and/or liberationist perspective.[6] Although this scholarship has filled an important gap in the literature, the stories of millions of non-feminist Latina Catholics, Pentecostals, Baptists, Methodists, Mormons, Jehovah's Witnesses, and others have gone largely untold.[7] Aside from the work of María Pérez y González and Virginia Sánchez-Korrol, almost nothing has been written from a critical scholarly perspective on the history of the Latina Evangelical and Pentecostal clergy in the United States.[8] That is unfortunate because Latino Pentecostalism represents one of the most dynamic and diverse movements in the Latino community.[9]

Contrary to the Barfoot and Sheppard thesis, there was no great reversal in the accumulation of power or right to ordination for Latinas in the early twentieth century such as there was in Anglo-American Pentecostalism.[10] Instead, the history of clergywomen in Latino Pentecostalism has been long but checkered. Latinas have faced an uphill struggle against gender discrimination and the right to full ordination. Pentecostal women have practiced a kind of paradoxical domesticity whereby they are exhorted to be end-times prophetesses in the public sphere and devoted mothers and good wives in the private sphere. Despite the seemingly paradoxical lives they live, Pentecostal women are, by their own accounts, "liberated."

There are more than 150 Latino Pentecostal denominations and five to seven million Latino Pentecostal Christians in the United States, Mexico, and Puerto Rico.[11] Each has its own unique traditions and customs. Despite the great diversity within the movement, the two main varieties of Latino Pentecostalism are Trinitarian and Oneness. Oneness Pentecostals reject the traditional doctrine of the Trinity and insist that a person must be baptized in Jesus' name only for salvation (Acts 2:38). In general, the Trinitarian Latino Pentecostal movement has adopted a more prophetic attitude (openness to women preachers and leadership over men) toward women in the ministry, whereas the Oneness movement has adopted a more priestly attitude (generally restricting the role of women to lay leadership over women and youths only).[12] Positions on women in the ministry have been shaped by degree of institutional acculturation and cultural orientation to U.S. values and gender roles. This study is based on original primary and secondary research in Spanish and English sources, a dozen interviews, and unpublished oral history research. Most of the names of informants have been changed to protect their anonymity.[13]

Mexican Women at the Azusa Street Revival, 1906–9

The Latino Pentecostal movement was born at the fabled Azusa Street Revival in 1906. The revival served as a sacred center and springboard from which the Latino Pentecostal movement spread rapidly throughout the United States, Mexico, and Puerto Rico. Although the first Latinos at Azusa Street left few written records of their experiences, fragmentary evidence indicates that men and women contributed to the revival.

The second edition of *Apostolic Faith* newspaper noted that "there are a good many Spanish speaking people in Los Angeles. The Lord has been giving the language, and now a Spanish preacher, who, *with his wife,* are preaching the Gospel in open air meetings." That couple was Abundio and Rosa López, who began attending the Azusa Street Mission on May 29, 1906, shortly after it opened in April. In one of the few written testimonies by Mexicans at the revival, the Lópezes stated, "We testify to the power of the Holy Spirit in forgiveness, sanctification, and the baptism with the Holy Ghost and fire. . . . We want to be used for the salvation and healing of both soul and body."[14]

The Lópezes organized the first Pentecostal ministry in Los Angeles in the historic Mexican Plaza District. They also served as lay ministers at the Azusa Street Revival and conducted evangelistic work in San Diego. Abundio López's three-year ministry at the Azusa Street Mission was rewarded by William J. Seymour, who ordained him to the ministry in 1909. Although Rosa López's clerical status is less clear, she was one of the first Spanish-speaking Pentecostal evangelists in North America.[15]

The Azusa Street Revival attracted not only Mexican immigrant women such as Rosa López but also Mexican Americans such as Susie Villa Valdez. After her conversion in 1906, the seamstress-turned-evangelist took the Pentecostal message to prostitutes, alcoholics, and immigrants living in the slums of Los Angeles and in the migrant farm labor camps of Riverside and San Bernardino. Adolfo Valdez stated of his mother, "I remember her hard but rewarding spiritual-social work with prostitutes and skid-row alcoholics done in the Lord's name. . . . My mother visited the slums, playing her guitar and singing sacred songs in the poorly lit streets for anyone who would listen. . . . She heard the troubles of many lonely and depressed people and usually introduced them to Christ. Around midnight she would walk . . . home, often arriving as late as 2 A.M."[16] Villa Valdez combined evangelism, social work, and musical talent to reach out to the poor and marginalized in California for the rest of her life.

Although no concrete evidence proves that Rosa López and Susie Villa Valdez were ordained to the ministry, evidence does indicate that they actively engaged in evangelistic preaching, social work, and pastoral ministry to men and women. Given the historic *machismo* in Mexican culture and society, it is not surprising that Latinas do not figure more prominently in the early literature. The tension between the prophetic and priestly at Azusa Street and in early Pentecostalism began to crystallize along theological and denominational lines after Latinos left the mission. That split is evident when comparing the role of women in the ministry in the two largest Latino Pentecostal denominations in the United States: the Apostolic Assembly of the Faith in Christ Jesus, Inc., and the Hispanic Districts of the General Council of the Assemblies of God.

Women in the Ministry in the Oneness Pentecostal Movement: The Apostolic Assembly of the Faith in Christ Jesus, Inc.

The Oneness Pentecostal movement strictly prohibits the ordination and licensure of women to the ministry. In fact, women are prohibited from exercising any kind of spiritual authority over men in the church. That is remarkable given the fact that both Anglo-American and black Oneness Pentecostal denominations have ordained women to the ministry since they were founded.

The Oneness Pentecostal movement erupted onto the stage of history in 1913 at the Worldwide Pentecostal Camp Meeting at Arroyo Seco near Los Angeles. At the camp meeting, R. E. McAlister reported that God revealed to him that the Apostles baptized in the name of Jesus Christ (Acts 2:38), not in the trinitarian formula (Matthew 28:19). That controversial teaching led to one of the first major theological schisms in the Pentecostal movement. A number of Anglos, blacks, and Mexicans at Arroyo Seco embraced the Oneness message. One former Azusa Street participant named Juan Martínez Navarro joined the Oneness movement and shortly thereafter, around 1912 or 1913, persuaded Francisco Llorente to accept the Oneness message.[17]

The preaching of Navarro and Llorente led to the conversion and/or baptism of Marcial de la Cruz and Antonio Castañeda Nava. In 1916 Llorente, de la Cruz, and Nava became loosely affiliated with the Pentecostal Assemblies of the World (PAW) because it was one of the few legally incorporated Oneness denominations in the United States. The linguistic barriers that separated Anglo and black Oneness Pentecostals from their Mexican counterparts allowed Mexicans to develop independently of the larger Oneness movement. In 1928 Francisco Llorente died. A year later Nava assumed leadership of the movement, and in 1930 he severed its loose affiliation with PAW. He incorporated the movement as the Apostolic Assembly of the Faith in Christ Jesus, Inc.[18] In 1999 the Apostolic Assembly claimed seventy-five thousand members and seven hundred churches throughout the United States and Latin America.[19]

Although the exact reasons why Nava and the Mexican contingent split off from PAW are uncertain, it may have had something to do with growing differences in doctrine and comportment standards. Although the Apostolic Assembly is theologically similar to other Oneness denominations, it does differ in its strict prohibition of women in the ministry. Furthermore, Latino Oneness Pentecostals insist that women must wear a headcovering when they pray and refrain from cutting their hair and wearing cosmetics and jewelry; skirts and dresses must be worn instead of pants. Although women are encouraged to exercise their spiritual gifts, men are considered the heads of their households.[20]

Apostolic Women in the Ministry

The current ban on women in the ministry in the Apostolic Assembly is complicated by the fact that Latinas served as deaconesses, evangelists, and planters of churches in the early Oneness movement. It is well known in Apostolic Assembly lore that Romanita Carbajal de Valenzuela was the first person reportedly to take the Oneness message to Mexico. Little is known about her life, except that she fled to Los Angeles from Villa Aldama, Chihuahua, Mexico, in the wake of the Mexican Revolution. There, she was converted to Pentecostalism around 1912 and, Apostolic historian Nellie Rangel asserts, attended the Azusa Street Revival. In November 1914 Valenzuela returned to Villa Aldama and converted twelve members of her family to Pentecostalism. Her work led to the formation of the first Oneness church in Mexico. Shortly thereafter she converted a Methodist pastor named Ruben Ortega to the Apostolic doctrine and placed him in charge of the congregation. After instructing Ortega in Pentecostal theology, she returned to Los Angeles, where she helped her husband (or relative) Genaro Valenzuela pastor the Spanish Apostolic Faith Mission on North Hill Street. After 1914, however, Carbajal de Valenzuela faded into anonymity.[21]

Romanita Carbajal de Valenzuela was not the only woman to minister in ways now prohibited by the Apostolic Assembly. Rangel notes that in 1928 Nicolasa de García, Delores (Lolita) de Gonzáles, and María Apolinar Zapata all served as deaconesses, an office that Apostolic women are now prohibited from holding.[22] The fact that Francisco Llorente allowed women to minister as deaconesses in 1928 may indicate that it was under Nava's presidency, not Llorente's, that the Assembly began to tighten its restrictions on women in the ministry. Llorente's openness was probably shaped by his direct personal contact with the black and Anglo Oneness movements and his marriage to Juanita Peach, an Anglo-American Methodist, in 1927. His decision to marry an Anglo-American Methodist woman who may have not been as committed to Latin American cultural and comportment norms may in part explain why the union led to controversy within the Apostolic Assembly.

After Llorente's sudden death in 1928, Nava assumed control of the Apostolic Assembly in 1929 and appears to have tightened the restriction on women in the ministry. A year later, he also decided to sever the Apostolic Assembly's ties with PAW, a denomination that ordained women to the ministry. These factors, combined with Nava's Mexican cultural orientation, no doubt influenced his opposition to women in the ministry.[23]

Nava, a recent immigrant from Durango, Mexico, had neither attended the Azusa Street Revival (where he would have seen women in important prophetic roles) nor received any kind of systematic training in Oneness doctrine from PAW. It is not surprising that he did not support the ordination of women. His theological and cultural reference points in Mexico were the Roman Catholic Church, with its historic opposition to women in church office. The decisive factor was likely what Nava believed was the Assembly's commitment to the Bible, which, in his mind prohibited women from the ordained ministry. The transition from a decentralized movement under Llorente to a centralized one under Antonio Nava after 1929 may have helped contribute to the present ban on women in the ministry (ordained or diaconal). That ban was not called into question in a major way until the 1990s.

At present, the greatest challenge to the ban on women in the ministry comes from young, acculturated, second- , third- , and fourth-generation college and graduate students who have been influenced by the feminist and Chicano movements and by denominations that ordain women. Unlike their parents or grandparents, their primary cultural reference points are in the United States rather than Latin America.

Felipe Agredano-Lozano argues that some Apostolics "vigorously" disagree with the Assembly's views on women in the ministry. As one disgruntled Apostolic stated, "I don't know who's this going to get hurt. . . . Somebody in the Assembly forgot that Deborah was a judge. Somebody in the Assembly forgot that Miriam helped Moses along with Aaron. Somebody in the Assembly forgot that Mary Magdalene also preached with Paul, followed him and ministered to him. . . . All these women did all these things and yet, we still live under patriarchal establishment and patriarchal rules and bylaws."[24] An Apostolic at a United Pentecostal Church Bible College stated that once he had actually heard a woman preach, "it was hard not to believe it [women preachers]. It's only because we have been taught to believe in that way." The growing ambivalence was summed by one Apostolic who stated, "I still haven't made up my mind yet, but I think a woman can make a difference in the ministry. I'm ready to see couples minister together."[25]

The ban on women in the ministry has had another consequence. As Egla Montero has stated, "Some women have . . . left the Apostolic Assembly and taken their gifts to the Assemblies of God because they feel that there is no room for them in the Apostolic Assembly. . . . They have been called by God to preach, so they have taken their ministry to the Assemblies of God or the United Pentecostal Church." She warns, however, that "their ministries are not as powerful as they thought they would be."[26]

Despite the categorical restriction banning women from the ordained and teaching ministry, Apostolic women do evangelize and teach men, whether on the mission field, in high school and college-age Sunday school classes, in marriage seminars, or when men attend their Sunday school lessons and national women's conventions. Montero admits that teaching men is a challenge, because they "don't like to be taught by women," but she also notes, "There have been times when exceptions have been made."[27] Montero sees no reason why the denomination cannot allow gifted women to teach men under special circumstances.

It would be wrong, however, to imply that Montero and most Apostolic women support the idea of women in the pastoral ministry. In fact, she and the vast majority of Apostolic women firmly reject that idea on the grounds that Jesus did not have women apostles and that Paul forbade women from exercising spiritual authority over men.[28]

"Tamales Have Built Our Churches": The Ladies' Auxiliaries

Despite the prohibition on women in the ministry, it would be wrong to conclude that they do not exercise power and influence in the Assembly. This culturally imperialistic and reductionist view of historical agency ignores the realities of millions of non-feminist, working-class, minority, and immigrant women who have pursued other creative strategies of empowerment and

influence. Rather than take the monolithic and ahistorical view that wom-
en's voices are either radically subversive or co-opted through the creation
of a false dual consciousness, we do better to recognize that many women
often, like men, live paradoxical and contradictory lives. In fact, Pentecostal
and Evangelical women are constantly affirming and subverting the established order. Like the U.S.-Mexican border itself, Latinas consciously criss-
cross the borders of "patriarchy" and "matriarchy" all the time. For that reason, scholars need to look for new models of historical agency that take into
account the realities of non-feminist women. Feminist scholars, for example, have often overlooked or even criticized denominational women's organizations as places of empowerment.[29] The Ladies Auxilary in the Apostolic Assembly is one example of a paradoxical space where women find
historical agency and power and yet still work within the power structure of
the organization.

Although the Ladies' Auxiliary traces its roots to the 1930s, the first national
organization did not occur until 1950. The auxiliary grew from 150 adult
women in 1950 to more than twelve thousand in 1996. The organization encourages ethnic and spiritual unity, spiritual and moral growth, confrater-
nity, family, and divine community. The auxiliary is also the main fund-raising organization in the Assembly.[30]

The growing power and influence of Apostolic women is evident in their
fund-raising projects. The most important, the annual Blue Flower Project
(Flor Azul), began in 1972–73 to benefit the foreign missions department. In
1996 auxiliary president Georgina Mazón reported that the project had raised
$420,000. For that reason and many others, Apostolic Assembly president
Baldemar Rodríguez described the auxiliary's contributions to the denomination as "indispensable."[31] Summarizing the growing clout of Apostolic
women, Patty Galaviz proudly observes, "Tamales have built our churches."[32]
Indeed, tamales have built more than just churches. The auxiliaries' fund-
raising projects have also given women a voice, which, one woman prophet-
ically stated, will one day lead to women on the national board.

There have been attempts to check the growing power of the Ladies' Auxiliary, however. At one of the group's national retreats in the mid–1990s,
Apostolic men took over the teaching positions—a role historically controlled
by women. One Apostolic claimed this was done because "women were
'usurping' too much authority." The decision prompted one Apostolic pastor's wife to state angrily, "The Assembly took a few steps too many, back-
wards."[33] A few women responded by talking about protesting the Assembly's decision. One confided that she had been asked to lead a protest against
the decision but declined because she believed most women would not back

her up once the conflict began. She noted, however, that if a protest movement was done at the right time, place, and by the right person, the "rest will follow." General Secretary Bishop Daniel Sánchez described the takeover as an isolated incident and insisted that women run their own national conferences without inference from men. Whatever the case may have been, evidence indicates that the growing economic clout and number of strong, articulate women in the Assembly is prompting at least a few of the men to reassert their spiritual and institutional authority.[34]

Whether Apostolic women will fully reclaim the prophetic voices of women such as Romanita Carbajal de Valenzuela in the near future is uncertain. What is clear is that year by year the Assembly becomes more and more dependent on Ladies' Auxiliaries' fund-raising efforts to keep its missions and church planting projects afloat. As one Apostolic put it, "If women were to unite under an economic front, boycott the kitchen, and stop making tamales, the World Missions Program and the construction projects of many temples [churches] would immediately come to a complete stop."[35] If the national leadership does not anticipate these changes and find a way to appease, accommodate, or co-opt women, it may find itself in conflict with Carbajal de Valenzuela's successors.

The Latino Trinitarian Pentecostal Movement: The Hispanic Districts of the Assemblies of God

The role of women in the ministry in the nine Hispanic Districts of the Assemblies of God is both similar to and different from that of the Apostolic Assembly. It is similar in that both denominations affirm a kind of paradoxical domesticity, whereby Pentecostal clergywomen are admonished to be end-times prophetesses in the public sphere and devoted mothers and good wives in the private sphere of the home. Pentecostals see no contradiction in asking women to exercise their spiritual gifts under the direction of men.

The major difference between Oneness and Trinitarian Pentecostalism is that although both admonish women to exercise their spiritual gifts, only the Trinitarian Pentecostal movement allows them to exercise a prophetic ministry to other men in the ordained ministry. This position is justified by a passage in Joel 2, which states that in the last days of the world God would pour God's spirit on all flesh and that their sons and daughters shall prophesy.

The Latino Trinitarian Pentecostal movement, which makes up approximately 80 to 90 percent of all Latino Pentecostals in the United States and Puerto Rico, has a lengthy but inconsistent history of credentialing women to the ministry. On that issue, the Hispanic Districts of the Assemblies of God are influenced by the larger Anglo-American Assemblies of God, which has ordained women since it was founded in Hot Springs, Arkansas, in 1914. The founder of the Hispanic Districts, Henry C. Ball, adopted a prophetic view of women in the ministry when he began his ministry to Mexicans in south Texas in 1915.[36] By 1997 the ministry Ball founded had grown to an estimated 1,740 Latino AG churches and more than 290,000 adherents, making it the largest Latino Pentecostal denomination in the United States.

The Hispanic District's doctrinal beliefs are virtually identical to those of the larger General Council of the Assemblies of God. They teach that a person must be born again (John 3) to go to heaven and that speaking in tongues is the initial physical evidence of the baptism with the Holy Spirit (I Cor. 12, 14). In contrast to the Apostolic Assembly, they are Trinitarian in theology and ordain women to the ministry. They believe that Jesus Christ will return any day to set up his thousand-year millennial kingdom on earth. Although they place a heavy emphasis on holy living, they do not have a strict dress code and do not require women to wear head covering. Women are allowed to cut their hair and wear modest jewelry and cosmetics, in sharp contrast to virtually all Latino Oneness Pentecostal denominations.

Latina Assemblies of God Women in the Ministry

The first Assemblies of God evangelists to be effective in ministering among Latinos in the United States were Anglo American.[37] The most important woman was Alice E. Luce. A former British Episcopalian missionary to India, Luce converted to Pentecostalism there and later felt "called" to evangelize Mexico. After H. C. Ball ordained her in 1915, she and Sunshine Marshall (Ball) conducted evangelistic work in Monterrey, Mexico. The bloody Mexican Revolution (1910–17) thwarted their plans, however, and four months later they returned to Texas, where they assisted Ball's evangelistic work along the border.[38]

In 1918 Luce left Texas to pioneer Assemblies of God work in Los Angeles. Like Abundio and Rosa López twelve years earlier, she rented a hall in the Mexican Plaza District and began conducting evangelistic services. Her work was difficult. In 1920 she lamented, "The 'new issue' [Apostolic] error is the greatest difficulty here—they are trying to steal away our flock all the time."[39] The burgeoning Apostolic movement was a real threat to Luce's fifty-member congregation. Despite the difficulties she faced as an Anglo woman ministering in Mexican Los Angeles, she conducted open-air services and prayers for the sick. Luce had a tremendous impact on the formation of the Latino Pentecostal movement. Not only did Luce establish the precedent of women in prophetic ministry, but she and other evangelists such as Aimee Semple McPherson and Kathryn Kuhlman also inspired Latinas such as Nellie Bazán, Francisca Blaisdell, Concepción Morgan Howard, and countless others to go into the ministry.

Dionisia Feliciano was the first Latina to be recorded as ordained by the Assemblies of God. She and her husband Solomon were ordained in San Jose, California, in July 1916. Feliciano pioneered Assemblies of God work in California, Puerto Rico, and the Dominican Republic from 1913 to the 1940s. During her stay in Puerto Rico she inspired many women to go into the ministry.[40]

Manuelita (Nellie) Treviño Bazán (1895–1995) was one of the first Mexican American women ordained to the Pentecostal ministry in the United States. H. C. Ball ordained her and her husband, Demetrio, in 1920, and they ministered in Texas, New Mexico, and Colorado. She preached from the pulpit at least thirty times a year, conducted door-to-door evangelistic work, composed poetry, raised ten children, and wrote articles for *La Luz Apostólica* (the Assemblies' Spanish-language periodical) in addition to an autobiography. She also personally planted three churches in Texas, Colorado, and New Mexico during her seventy-five years in the ministry.[41]

Although Nellie Bazán was allowed to exercise her prophetic ministry on a regular basis in the Assemblies of God, she was also expected to submit to her husband's spiritual authority at home. As at the Azusa Street Revival, women's roles in the Hispanic Districts were paradoxical—women were exhorted to exercise their prophetic gifts yet also submit to their husbands' authority. Early Latino Pentecostals did not believe that the point of having prophetic gifts was to erase gender distinctions but rather to empower women for Christian service in the cataclysmic end-time drama that lay ahead.

While Nellie Bazán ministered in Texas, Colorado, and New Mexico, Francisca D. Blaisdell (ca. 1885–1941) conducted evangelistic work in Arizona and northern Mexico. In 1916 she began preaching Pentecostalism, and around 1922 she organized the first Assemblies of God women's organization in North America. A year later, she was ordained to the ministry by Juan Lugo and H. C. Ball. Blaisdell pastored her own churches in Douglas, Arizona; Agua Prieta, Sonora, Mexico (1932–33, 1938–39); and El Paso, Texas (1933–35).[42]

Like Blaisdell, Concepción (Chonita) Morgan Howard (1898–1983) was a Mexican immigrant. Unlike Nellie Bazán, her father was an Anglo and her mother was a Mexican. Howard was converted to Pentecostalism in 1913 in the small mining town of San Jose de las Playitas, Sonora, Mexico. Not long after her conversion and baptism around 1913, she felt called to the ministry. As a result, she traveled the dusty evangelistic trail on horseback in northern Mexico and Arizona, preaching the Pentecostal message. She eventually traveled to California, where she came under the influence of George and Carrie Judd Montgomery, two former Azusa Street participants. With their encouragement she began evangelistic work in California around 1915. Four years later, in 1919, she met and married a young Anglo Pentecostal preacher, Lloyd Howard, who was pastoring a small group of Mexicans in the border town of Pirtleville, Arizona. She co-pastored with her husband. In 1928 the Assemblies of God recognized Chonita Morgan Howard's evangelistic talent and ordained her to the ministry.[43]

In addition to Howard's pastoral and evangelistic work, she served as the second president of the Women's Missionary Council (Concilio Misionero Femenil) from 1941 to 1962. From 1966 to 1968 she pastored Betel Asamblea de Dios in Douglas, Arizona. From 1915 to 1968, Howard conducted pioneer evangelistic work in California, Arizona, New Mexico, and northern Mexico. Her fifty-five year pioneer ministry touched the lives of thousands of Latinas and helped establish AG work on both sides of the border. Despite the fact that most Latinas were ordained or credentialed as evangelists, some, such as Howard, did pastor their own churches.[44]

The ministry of Latinas in the United States helped set the precedent for women in the ministry in Mexico. The first Mexican women credentialed to the ministry in the Assemblies of God, all in the 1920s, were Srita Cruz Arenas, Catarina García, Juana Medellín, and Raquel Ruesga.[45]

Despite the fact that Latinas have been ordained since 1916, Virginia Aguilar, Gloria Garza, Alex and Anita Bazán, and everyone else I interviewed agreed that it was uncommon before 1950 for a single woman to pastor her own church or even be ordained to the pastoral ministry. More often than not, women were licensed rather than ordained and served as auxiliaries.[46] Latinas who married Anglo pastors had a much better chance of being fully ordained than women married to Latino men. Although the number of Latinas ordained from 1916 to the 1970s was low, there has been a sharp increase since the early 1980s. The liberalizing tendency of a younger generation has shaped this trend.

Aimee García Cortese's life and ministry in the Hispanic District of the Assemblies of God provides an excellent window into the struggle that women have faced in the ministry. Born to Puerto Rican parents in New York City in 1929, Cortese was raised in a small, Spanish-speaking, Pentecostal storefront church in the early 1940s and 1950s. Reacting against the legalism she saw in Pentecostalism, she became briefly involved with a Lutheran and then a Methodist church before returning to the Assemblies of God in the late 1950s.[47]

After graduating from the Assemblies of God–sponsored Instituto Biblico Hispano in New York City and from Central Bible College in Springfield, Missouri, she sought ordination from the Spanish Eastern District in New York in 1957. The request was denied for no reason other than her gender. Angry at such overt sexism, Cortese protested the decision to J. Roswell Flower, superintendent of the Assemblies of God. In July 1958, she wrote, "I am appealing to the Executive Presbytery of the Assemblies of God, because of the rejection of my application for ordination with the Spanish Eastern District [Council of the Assemblies of God]. The rejection was a complete violation of the constitution of the Assemblies of God, Article VI, section 4, part B. I met all the requirements of our Credential Committee and had the full backing and blessing of every Official of my District, but because of pure prejudice against the ministry of women, I was rejected."[48] After a long-drawn-out struggle, she was finally ordained by the Spanish Eastern District in 1962, but only after Anglo-American leaders in Springfield pressured it to do so.

Cortese's experience captures the dilemma that Latinas have faced in the Hispanic Districts. Although on the one hand they are encouraged to exercise their spiritual and prophetic gifts, on the other they are quietly discouraged from seeking full ordination or pastoring their own churches. It appears, however, that Cortese's cultural orientation toward Anglo America and Anglo leaders enabled her to scale some of the barriers of sexism. Only after Anglo leaders in Springfield intervened and put pressure on the Spanish Eastern District did it finally ordain her in 1962.

Cortese's active ministry has touched the lives of thousands. Reflecting the gender bias still prevalent in the Hispanic Districts, after she was ordained she still found it difficult to find a job as a pastor. That prompted her to organize her own church, Crossroads Tabernacle, in 1982 in the South Bronx. As she observes, "If you want to get a church you have to start your own." She reportedly holds no grudges against the Spanish Eastern District, however, perhaps because her ministry in the South Bronx has met with phenomenal success. It has grown from thirty-seven people in 1982 to 1,500 in 1997, making it one of the largest predominantly Latino churches in New York state. The gender discrimination she faced in the Hispanic Districts is slowly abating, Cortese observes.[49] A growing number of women such as Aimee García Cortese, Julie Ramírez, and Julia Hernández are pastors of Pentecostal churches of more than five hundred members across the United States.[50]

Despite guarded openness to prophetic women's voices in the Assemblies of God, many Latinas who wanted complete autonomy and freedom before 1960 have ministered outside the AG. In 1939 the Rev. Leoncia Rosado Rosseau ("Mama Leo") helped found what during the early 1940s became the Damascus Christian Church denomination in New York City, and in 1957 she pioneered one of the first church-sponsored drug-rehabilitation programs in the United States through the Damascus Youth Crusade.[51] During the 1940s, the Rev. Juana García Peraza left AG work in Puerto Rico to found her own denomination, Mita Congregation.[52] Still other Latinas, such as the Rev. Aurora Chávez, worked with Spanish-speaking Pentecostal denominations in the Southwest, for example, the Concilio Peña de Horeb, which granted greater freedom to women in ministry. Chávez, like Aimee Semple McPherson, wore a cape and conducted evangelistic tent-healing crusades in Los Angeles and throughout the Southwest during the 1950s.[53] Latina Pentecostal women looked to Anglo-American Pentecostal women pastors and evangelists as role models and means by which to justify their own ministries. Although some decided to leave the Assemblies of God to pioneer their own ministries, most, such as Cortese, have chosen to remain.

Latina Women in the Ministry in the 1990s

Congruent with Blumhofer's findings in Anglo-American Pentecostalism, although the Hispanic Districts have officially ordained women for most of the twentieth century they discreetly kept women out of leading pastoral and administrative positions until the 1980s.[54] Those who did pastor churches often worked in small ones or in missions where men were unwilling to go. Although Latinas have never served as leaders of the nine Hispanic Districts, Aimee García Cortese was the first woman invited to speak prime-time at an annual Assemblies of God general convention.[55] Furthermore, the Rev. Carmen H. Pérez was the first woman to be nominated for the executive presbyter position in the Assemblies of God. These moves can be interpreted as genuine gestures of gender and racial inclusivity. They can also be interpreted, however, as tokenism and a safe way of including women who would not be a real threat to male leadership because they could never garner the nationwide support needed to be elected or make any serious structural changes.

Despite the difficulties that women such as Cortese have faced, the Hispanic Districts have turned a new leaf—at least in the number of women they are credentialing. By 1997 the Spanish Eastern District, which once gave Cortese such problems, had the highest percentage and largest number of credentialed and ordained women among the Hispanic Districts. The total number of Latina clergy (ordained, licensed, and certified) in the Assemblies of God increased from 624 in 1990 to 741 in 1997. The number of Latinas fully ordained in the Assemblies of God almost doubled, going from eight women in 1990 to 141 in 1997. In 1998 the percentage of clergywomen in the Hispanic Districts (25.1 percent) was significantly higher than the average for Anglo-American Districts (15.8 percent) nationwide.[56] The Assemblies of God now claims more Latina clergy than any other denomination, including the United Methodist Church—which in 1998 had ninety to a hundred.[57]

In short, although the number and percentage of Anglo-American clergy-women in the Assemblies of God in general have declined, the Hispanic Districts have experienced a sharp increase in number since the early 1980s. Much of the growth is due to progressive-minded national leaders such as Jesse Miranda, who have pushed for credentialing more women to the ministry.

Women and Theological Education: The Role of Bible Institutes

A major reason that Latinas have been able to exercise a prophetic voice in the Hispanic Districts is education. Women have been allowed to receive formal ministerial and theological training in the Latino Pentecostal movement since at least 1926, something Apostolic Assembly women have been (and still are) unable to receive in the United States. The percentage of women who attend Bible school has been historically quite high. It is significant that a woman founded the second Spanish-speaking Pentecostal Bible Institute in the United States. In 1926 Alice Luce founded Berean Bible Institute—later called the Latin American Bible Institute (LABI)—in San Diego. The first graduating class at Berean Bible Institute in 1928 consisted of three women: D. Adeline Sugg, Ursula Riggio, and María Grajeda. Women have always made up a significant portion of the graduating classes of Latin District Bible schools.[58] Theological training has been pivotal in opening doors to ministry, theologizing, and writing for periodicals such as *La Luz Apostólica* and *The Word*.[59]

Saving Souls and Sick Bodies: The Women's Missionary Council

The majority of Mexican women who graduated from the Bible institutes in California, Texas, New York, and Puerto Rico did not go into the ordained ministry. Many chose to become actively involved in the national women's organization. The Women's Missionary Council (WMC) grew from one woman in 1922 to more than 44,600 Latinas in 1995, making it one of the largest Latina organizations in the United States.[60] The purpose of the council was to encourage and propagate evangelistic and social work in the U.S.-Mexico borderlands. Ball's description of the WMC in 1931 still hold true:

> We have what is known as the Women's Missionary Councils in most of our assemblies, and this organization has been the means of banding the sisters together to work and pray for the salvation of souls as well as for the relief of the poor, and sick visitation. Thousands of tracts and Gospels have been distributed by the sisters, many sick ones healed and revival prayed down upon

quite a number of our assemblies . . . the women meet every morning to pray, and in most of the other places they hold weekly meetings for Bible study and prayer.[61]

The WMC has had less of an impact on the Hispanic Districts than has the Ladies' Auxiliary, because the WMC does not have a unified, national organization. Each of the nine Hispanic Districts elect their own presidents and organize their own projects.

"We've Got a Voice, but We Also Know Our Place": Feminism, *Chicanismo,* and the Construction of Latina Identity

When confronted with sexism in the Hispanic Districts, the Rev. Gloria Garza, like all of the women I interviewed, did not turn to the feminist movement for help or support. Furthermore, like every other Apostolic or Assemblies of God woman I interviewed, Garza stated that Pentecostal women did not support the feminist movement because they said it was too radical, pushy, tied to the gay movement, and a luxury that their working-class schedules could not afford. As one young, strong-willed Apostolic woman stated, "When ladies think of the feminist movement they think of the gay community . . . [and] the stereo-type I don't need a man. I tell my husband [a bishop in the Apostolic Assembly] that a woman's place is in the house *and* the Senate."[62] In a slightly sarcastic tone, she concluded, "We've got a voice, but we also know our place." Ironically, although many Latinas had no interest in the feminist movement, their own confident personalities resonate with many contemporary feminists.

In line with their attempt to distance themselves from the feminist movement, Latina Pentecostals react negatively to the patronizing and condescending view that they are in need of liberation.[63] "We have always been liberated," Montero stated sharply. "First of all we have been liberated from sin. People feel that because we talk about subjection and being subject to our husbands and to the ministry, they feel we are stepped on and are doormats, but it's totally the opposite."[64]

Although the vast majority of married women whom I interviewed were opposed or indifferent to the largely white feminist movement, they had mixed feelings about the Chicano movement.[65] Gloria Garza believes it to be good but states that most people in the Hispanic Districts were indifferent and uninterested in getting involved because of the movement's perceived cultural nationalism, antireligious spirit, and political activism. Nevertheless,

Egla Montero observes, "In a left-handed way it [the Chicano movement] had a positive impact. It helped a lot of us to really see our roots and place in society." Although she recognizes some good in the movement, she explains, "I don't care for the word 'Chicano,' because to me it's just a slang word. I don't care to be called a 'Chicana.'"[66] Echoing that sentiment, Assemblies of God pastor Anita Soto states, "'Chicano' is a nickname from the world. I don't believe too much in that. We are for the whole world, not just for 'Chicanos.'"[67]

Despite distancing themselves from the Chicano movement, Latina clergy recognized the important work of Latino activists such as former Hispanic District evangelist Reies López Tijerina and the Catholic farm labor leader César Chávez. Egla Montero, who lived in Delano, California, recalls picking cotton and potatoes with Chávez and regards him up as a role model, a man who "was amongst us" and believed in a cause.[68]

While many Latina Pentecostal women distanced themselves from the feminist movement and to a lesser degree the Chicano movement, they openly embraced Anglo Pentecostal and evangelical values. Apostolic and Hispanic District women, for example, listen to Pentecostal preachers such as Oral Roberts, Kathryn Kuhlman, T. D. Jakes, John Hagee, and Benny Hinn on the radio and television. Montero testifies, in fact, that she was healed at an Oral Roberts healing crusade in Bakersfield.[69]

After denominational literature and books, the most important evangelical influence on gender roles was James Dobson, whose books, magazines, and *Focus on the Family* radio program resonated with Latin American gender roles and notion of family. Dobson's Focus on the Family ministry has also shaped Latina Pentecostal gender roles in the home. Latina Pentecostal ministers see no inherent contradiction in being a "godly mother" and wife and a dynamic evangelist or pastor. Pentecostal clergywomen do not believe the two are mutually exclusive.[70]

Although many women warmly supported Dobson's ministry, they did not support another evangelical, Pat Robertson. Rose Nodal, for example, states that she used to watch Robertson on television until he became involved in politics.[71] None of the women whom I interviewed seemed interested in mixing politics and religion. Perhaps that is why they were reluctant to embrace the Chicano and feminist movements or evangelical politics.

Conclusion

This investigation into the diverse and complex history of women in the Latino Pentecostal movement has only scratched the surface of a hitherto untold story. Contrary to the scholarly literature about the decline of women in the ministry in the Anglo-American Pentecostal movement, the Hispanic Districts are experiencing unprecedented growth. That surge, however, has not developed without a struggle, as Aimee García Cortese's story illustrates.

It would be inaccurate, though, to equate these struggles with Latina feminism. In fact, strong and articulate clergywomen such as Leoncia Rosado Rosseau, Gloria Garza, Aimee García Cortese, and many others reject secular feminism because of what they perceive as its rejection of the traditional Latin American and biblical gender roles and notion of family. From a feminist perspective, Latina Pentecostals might seem to live paradoxical lives. Yet they believe they have real power to transform lives and communities. For them, the message of repentance, forgiveness, and a born-again, Spirit-filled relationship with Jesus constitute true liberation. Far from being "doormats" suffering from a false consciousness, Pentecostal women believe they have found real freedom despite the problems they face. If we take seriously how most Latina Pentecostal women perceive themselves, then they are by their own account "liberated" and "empowered." There are clear limitations to their "freedom in Christ," but the stories of Latina clergy such as Susie Villa Valdez, Romanita Carbajal de Valenzuela, Aimee García Cortese, and many others challenge conventional interpretations of women and religion, historical agency, and what it means to be a truly liberated woman.

Notes

I wish to thank the Pew Charitable Trusts, Virginia Brereton, Margaret Bendroth, and the steering committee of the Women and Twentieth Century Protestantism project for their generous support in the research and writing of this essay.

1. A. C. Valdez and James F. Scheer, *Fire on Azusa Street* (Costa Mesa, Calif.: Gift Publications, 1980), 3–4.

2. Valdez and Scheer, *Fire on Azusa Street*, 3–6, 23–26, 117.

3. The exact number of Latina clergy in the United States and Puerto Rico is impossible to establish because most denominations do not keep records by ethnicity and because credentialing classifications differ from denomination to denomination. Despite that fact, the 1,200 figure is a rough estimate based on reports given to me by denominational representatives. In 1998 there were 841 Pentecostal, ninety-five United Methodist, thirty American Baptist, twelve Foursquare, and twelve Latin American Council of Christian Churches clergywomen in the United States and Puerto Rico. That number also includes an estimated two hundred clergywomen in small Pentecostal denominations and in countless independent churches.

4. Barbara Brown Zikmund, Adair T. Lummis, and Patricia Mei Yin Chang, *Clergywomen: An Uphill Calling* (Louisville: Westminster John Knox Press, 1998); Mark Chaves,

Ordaining Women: Culture and Conflict in Religious Organizations (Cambridge: Harvard University Press, 1997); Paula D. Nesbitt, *The Feminization of the Clergy in America: Occupational and Organizational Perspectives* (New York: Oxford University Press, 1997); Frederick W. Schmidt, Jr., *A Still Small Voice: Women, Ordination, and the Church* (Syracuse: Syracuse University Press, 1996); Edward C. Lehman, *Women Clergy: Breaking Through Gender Barriers* (New Brunswick: Transaction Books, 1985).

5. In 1993, 65.8 percent of all Hispanics claimed Roman Catholic allegiances. Barry A. Kosmin and Seymour P. Lachman, *One Nation under God: Religion in Contemporary American Society* (New York: Harmony Books, 1993), 137–42. Kosmin and Lachman also found that 52 percent of Puerto Ricans, 53.8 percent of Latin Americans, and 59 percent of high school students of Mexican origin claimed Roman Catholic allegiances.

6. Ada María Isasi-Díaz and Yolanda Tarango, *Hispanic Women: Prophetic Voice in the Church* (Minneapolis: Fortress Press, 1992); Ada María Isasi-Díaz, *En la Lucha, In the Struggle: A Hispanic Women's Liberation Theology* (Minneapolis: Augsburg-Fortress Press, 1993); Jeanette Rodríguez, *Our Lady of Guadalupe: Faith and Empowerment among Mexican-American Women* (Austin: University of Texas Press, 1994); Ada María Isasi-Díaz, "The Cultural Identity of the Latina Woman: The Cross-Disciplinary Perspective of Mujerista Theology," in *Old Masks, New Faces: Religion and Latino Identities* (New York: Bildner Center for Western Hemisphere Studies, 1995), 93–116; Adair Lummis and Allison Stokes, "Catholic Feminist Spirituality and Social Justice Actions," *Journal for the Scientific Study of Religion* 6 (1994): 103–38.

7. In 1998 an estimated five hundred thousand Latino Jehovah's Witnesses and Mormons were attending more than 2,350 Spanish-language congregations throughout the United States and Puerto Rico. That estimate is probably too low because it does not include second- through fifth-generation Latinos attending Anglo congregations. Gastón Espinosa, "From One to Many: A Short History of Mexican American Religious Pluralism in the Borderlands," in *Chicano Religions: Essays in the Mexican American Religious Experience,* ed. Gastón Espinosa and Mario T. García (Berkeley: University of California Press, in press).

8. María Elizabeth Pérez y González, *Latinas in Ministry: A Pioneering Study on Women Ministers, Educators, and Students of Theology* (New York: New York City Mission Society, 1994); Virginia Sánchez-Korrol, "In Search of Unconventional Women: Histories of Puerto Rican Women in Religious Vocations before Mid-Century," in *Barrios and Borderlands: Cultures of Latinos and Latinas in the United States* (New York: Routledge, 1994), 141–51. For information on Latina mainline Protestantism, see Milagros Peña and Lisa M. Frehill, "Latina Religious Practice: Analyzing Cultural Dimensions in Measures of Religiosity," *Journal for the Scientific Study of Religion* 37 (1998): 620–35; Loida Martel Otero, "Women Doing Theology: Una Perspectiva Evangélica," *Apuntes* 67 (Fall 1994): 67–85; Minerva N. Garza, "The Influence of Methodism on Hispanic Women through Women's Societies," *Methodist History* (Jan. 1996): 78–89; Minerva Garza Carcaño, "Una Perspectiva Bíblico-teológica Sobre la Mujer en el Ministerio Ordenado," in *Voces: Voices from the Hispanic Church,* ed. Justo L. González (Nashville: Abingdon Press, 1992), 24–31, 112–21; and Jill Martínez, "Worship and the Search for Community in the Presbyterian Church (U.S.A.): The Hispanic Experience," *Church and Society* (March–April 1986): 42–46.

9. Andrew Greeley estimates that more than sixty thousand U.S. Latinos leave the Roman Catholic Church every year for Evangelical and Pentecostal Christianity—more than one million "defected" (his word) between 1973 and 1988. Greeley describes this mass defection as "an ecclesiastical failure of unprecedented proportion." I argue that this mass defection actually began in the early twentieth century and not the 1960s and 1970s as often asserted. Andrew Greeley, "Defection among Hispanics," *America* (July 1988): 61–62; Gastón Espinosa, "*El Azteca:* Francisco Olazábal and Latino Pentecostal Charisma, Power, and Faith Healing in the Borderlands," *Journal of the American Academy of Religion* 67 (Sept. 1999): 597–616.

10. Charles H. Barfoot and Gerald T. Sheppard, "Prophetic vs. Priestly Religion: The Changing Role of Women Clergy in Pentecostal Churches," *Review of Religious Research* 22 (1980): 2–17. The dichotomy between the prophetic and priestly should not be overdrawn. Within most Pentecostal traditions there are elements of both. Furthermore, even in those denominations that allow women a prophetic voice, Edith Blumhofer has correctly noted that this voice is often muzzled or marginalized. Nonetheless, although I do not agree with all that Barfoot and Sheppard suggest, their terminology and notions of the prophetic and priestly are helpful in comparing and contrasting women's roles in the Latino Pentecostal movement.

11. David B. Barrett, ed., *World Christian Encyclopedia: A Comparative Study of Churches and Religions in the Modern World, A.D. 1900–2000* (New York: Oxford University Press, 1972), 486–91; Patrick Johnstone, *Operation World* (Grand Rapids: Zondervan Publishing House, 1993), 379–80, 459.

12. The main Trinitarian Pentecostal denominations in the United States are the Hispanic Districts of the Assemblies of God; the Pentecostal Church of God, M.I.; Victory Outreach International; Church of God, Cleveland, Tennessee; Church of God of Prophecy; International Foursquare Gospel; Universal Church of the Kingdom of God; and Latin American Council of Christian Churches. The main Oneness Pentecostal denominations in the United States are the Apostolic Assembly of the Faith in Christ Jesus, Inc.; the Apostolic Church of the Faith in Christ Jesus of Mexico; the Light of the World Church; and the United Pentecostal Church.

13. I draw upon a number of oral interviews conducted by Felipe Agredano-Lozano, an Apostolic and Harvard Divinity School graduate. Felipe Emmanuel Agredano-Lozano, "The Apostolic Assembly at the Crossroads: The Politics of Gender," unpublished paper presented at the Society for Pentecostal Studies, Wheaton, Ill., 1994.

14. Abundio López and Rosa López, "Spanish Receive Pentecost," *Apostolic Faith* 1 (Oct. 1906): 4, emphasis added.

15. Gastón Espinosa, "Borderland Religion: Los Angeles and the Origins of the Latino Pentecostal Movement in the U.S., Mexico, and Puerto Rico, 1900–1945," Ph.D. diss., University of California, Santa Barbara, 1999, esp. chapter 3.

16. Valdez and Scheer, *Fire on Azusa Street*, 3–4, 23–25, 45.

17. Benjamin Cantú and José Ortega, *Historia de la Asamblea Apostólica de la Fe en Cristo Jesús, 1916–1966* (Mentone, Calif.: Sal's Printing Service, 1966), 6–7.

18. Cantú and Ortega, *Historia de la Asamblea Apostólica*, 5–10, 26.

19. According to Apostolic Assembly president Baldemar Rodríguez, there are fifty-five thousand Apostolic adherents in the United States. There are an additional 345 churches,

635 ordained and licensed ministers, and fifteen to twenty thousand Apostolics in fifteen countries (primarily Latin America) around the world. Baldemar Rodríguez, "Denominational Statistical Information Form for the Apostolic Assembly of Faith in Christ Jesus, Inc.," Jan. 1996, 1–2 (copy in my possession).

20. Article 71 of the Apostolic Assembly Constitution states: "During worship services men should keep their heads uncovered and women should keep their heads covered (I Corinthians 11:4–7; Psalms 100:4). . . . The woman should not cut or pleat her hair." Apostolic Assembly, *Apostolic Assembly Constitution* (Rancho Cucamonga, Calif.: Apostolic Assembly of the Faith in Christ Jesus, 1996), 76. The Apostolic Assembly Sunday school workbook instructs: "Contrary to the humanistic philosophy of man, God has established an order of authority for the family. . . . The chain of command is as follows: Christ, father, mother, then children. Whenever this order is distorted, confusion usually arises in the family bringing forth chaos and the possible disintegration thereof. . . . The Father has the God-given responsibility to lead his family in all areas of life. Under God, he is to lead them in an ordered home life. He leads them in honest endeavors by setting a true example backed up by his actions at home, and insisting that this be a rule of family life. This leadership must be executed with great care." Sam Valverde, ed., *Apostolic Expositor* (Second Quarter 1996): 27–28, 55.

21. Rangel assumes that because Valenzuela was in Los Angeles, she must have attended the Azusa Street Revival. She offers no evidence for that, however. Whether or not Valenzuela attended the Azusa Street Mission, there is little reason to doubt that she was not influenced by the strong female Pentecostal voices she encountered in Los Angeles. Nellie Rangel, *Historia de la Confederación Nacional de Sociedades Femeniles "Dorcas"* (Rancho Cucamonga, Calif.: Apostolic Assembly of the Faith in Christ Jesus, 1986), 23.

22. Rangel, *Historia de la Confederación Nacional,* 162; Cantú and Ortega, *Historia de la Asamblea Apostólica,* 23.

23. Cantú and Ortega, *Historia de la Asamblea Apostólica,* 21–26.

24. Agredano-Lozano, "The Apostolic Assembly at the Crossroads," 2, 4.

25. Ibid., 12–13. Ramírez has noted that many acculturated Apostolics find United Pentecostal Church (UPC) services attractive. Daniel Ramírez, "A Pentecostal Perspective," *Nuestro* (Jan.–Feb. 1984): 40.

26. Egla Montero is one of the most famous and important leaders in the Apostlic Assembly. Tape-recorded telephone interview with Egla Montero, Texas, Jan. 1997, Latino/a Pentecostal Oral History Project.

27. Interview with Egla Montero.

28. Ibid.

29. Mary Daly wrote, "The so-called 'sisterhoods' of patriarchy were and are in fact mini-brotherhoods, serving male interests and ideals. The ladies' auxiliaries . . . have all served the purposes of sexist society. In contrast to these, the new sisterhood is the bonding of women for liberation from sex role socialization." Mary Daly, "The Women's Movement: An Exodus Community," *Religious Education* 67 (Sept.–Oct. 1972): 327–33.

30. Rangel, *Historia de la Confederación Nacional,* 229–31; telephone interview with Georgina Mazón, Los Angeles, Jan. 1997; Ladies Auxiliary, *Confederación Nacional de Sociedades Femeniles Dorcas Reglamentos* (Rancho Cucamonga, Calif.: Asamblea Apostólica de la Fe en Cristo Jesús, 1994), 19–20 (by-laws).

31. Telephone interview with Baldemar Rodríguez, Santa Barbara, Calif., Jan. 1996.

32. Patty Galaviz is a leader of the Ladies Auxiliary in southern California. In addition to raising a family, she works full time in a management position for a national corporation. Tape-recorded telephone interview with Patty Galaviz, Ventura, Calif., Feb. 1997.

33. Agredano-Lozano, "The Apostolic Assembly at the Crossroads," 14–15.

34. Although this may not be the official position of the Apostolic Assembly, it represents the sentiments of some within the Assembly. Telephone interview with Daniel Sánchez, Rancho Cucamonga, Calif., spring 1997; Agredano-Lozano, "The Apostolic Assembly at the Crossroads," 10–15.

35. Agredano-Lozano, "The Apostolic Assembly at the Crossroads," 11.

36. This has not always been the case. Evidence indicates that some men wanted women's roles restricted in the Assemblies of God. See, for example, "A Timely Word," *The Pentecostal Evangel* 15 (Sept. 1923): 9; and Minutes of the Fifteenth Annual Session of the Arkansas-Louisiana District Council of the Assemblies of God, 1927, 12, Assemblies of God Archives, Springfield, Mo.; see also Espinosa, "Borderland Religion," chapter 4; and Victor De León, *The Silent Pentecostals* (Taylor, S.C.: Faith Publishing, 1979), 14–19.

37. Sherri L. Doty, *A/G Language Report of 1997* (Springfield, Mo.: Assemblies of God, 1998).

38. Gary B. McGee, "Pioneers of Pentecost: Alice E. Luce and Henry C. Ball," *A/G Heritage* 5 (Summer 1985): 4–6, 12–15; De León, *The Silent Pentecostals*, 19–23.

39. Alice E. Luce, Missionary File (1920), 1, Assemblies of God Archives, Springfield, Mo.

40. According to Dionisia Felicano's Assemblies of God ordination certificate, she was ordained an evangelist and missionary on July 28, 1916. David Ramos Torres, *Historia de la Iglesia de Dios Pentecostal, M.I.* (Río Piedras, P.R.: Editorial Pentecostal, 1992), 46.

41. Alex Bazán is the son of Nellie Bazán. He, too, is an ordained minister in the Assemblies of God. Tape-recorded interview with Alex Bazán and Anita Bazán, Escondido, Calif., Nov. 1996, Latino/a Pentecostal Oral History Project; Nellie T. Bazán, "Historia: Cincuenta Años de Cristiana y de Ministerio Cristiano," *La Luz Apostólica* 52 (Dec. 1967): 7–8; Nellie Bazán with Elizabeth B. and Don Martínez, Jr., *Enviados de Dios: Demetrio and Nellie Bazán* (Miami: Editorial Vida, 1987).

42. De León, *The Silent Pentecostals*, 144–45.

43. C. Morgan Howard, "Historia de los Primeros Cincuenta Años de las Asambleas de Dios," *La Luz Apostólica* 52 (Sept. 1967): 7; De León, *The Silent Pentecostals*, 146–48.

44. Howard, "Historia de los Primeros," 7; De León, *The Silent Pentecostals*, 146–47. Bazán, Blaisdell, and Howard were not the only women to pastor churches. Although the exact numbers of Latinas who did so are uncertain, Natividad Nevarez, María Inostroza, and Elvira Perales all pastored their own churches as well. Nevarez was ordained a "pastor" in 1937, where she served as co-pastor of the famous Aposento Alto Church in Los Angeles. María Inostroza was also ordained during the 1930s and pastored churches during the 1940s and 1950s. Ministerial files for Natividad Nevarez and María Inostroza (in my possession); Elvira Perales, "Una Mujer Pionera," *La Luz Apostólica* 51 (June 1967): 6.

45. Minutes of the District Council of the Assemblies of God of Texas and New Mexico, June 1928, 34–36, Assemblies of God Archives, Springfield, Mo.; Luisa Jeter de Walker, *Siembra y Cosecha: Reseña Histórica de las Asambleas de Dios de México y Centroamérica* (Deerfield, Fla.: Editorial Vida, 1990), 1:19–20.

46. Aguilar was credentialed in 1936. Tape-recorded telephone interviews with Virginia Aguilar, Texas, June 1996; Gloria Garza, Kingsville, Tex., Jan. 1997; Rose Nodal, Santa Maria, Calif., Jan. 1997; and Alex Bazán and Anita Bazán. All interviews conducted as part of the Latino/a Pentecostal Oral History Project.

47. Interview with Aimee García Cortese, New York City, March 1998, Latino/a Pentecostal Oral History Project (Cortese has also provided a copy of her vita); Korrol, "In Search of Unconventional Women," 149–51.

48. Interview with Aimee García Cortese; Aimee García Cortese to J. Roswell Flower, July 11, 1958, in author's possession.

49. Aimee García to J. Roswell Flower, July 11, 1958.

50. Ibid.

51. Mama Leo was converted to Pentecostalism in Puerto Rico and migrated to New York City in the 1930s, where she came under the influence of Francisco Olazábal. After Olazábal's death, she and her husband founded the Damascus Christian Church. Korrol, "In Search of Unconventional Women," 146–47; Espinosa, "Borderland Religion," chapter 6; Espinosa, *"El Azteca."*

52. Ramos Torres, *Historia de la Iglesia de Dios Pentecostal,* 126–31; Carmín Cruz, *La Obra de Mita* (Puerto Rico: s.n., 1990); Donald T. Moore, "La Iglesia de Mita y Sus Doctrinas," *Siguiendo la Sana Doctrina* (Sept.–Oct. 1988): 96–104; Mita Congregación, "Centenario del Natalicio de la Persona de Mita," *El Nueva Dia,* July 6, 1997, 2–8

53. Aurora Chávez, *Gran Campaña de Salvación y Sanidad Divina* (Aug. 1957), flier with picture (in my possession).

54. During the 1980s, Latinas began to be elected as presbyters to Hispanic Districts. Edith Blumhofer, "The Role of Women in the Assemblies of God," *A/G Heritage* 7 (Winter 1987–88): 13–17; Edith L. Blumhofer, *Restoring the Faith: The Assemblies of God, Pentecostalism, and American Culture* (Urbana: University of Illinios Press, 1993), 174–75.

55. Aimee Cortese, "Together . . . in Christ," *The Pentecostal Evangel,* Oct. 14, 1979, 4–6; Robert Edwards, "Woman up for AG Post as Doors Begin to Open," *News-Leader* (Springfield, Mo.), Aug. 8, 1993, 1A, 6A.

56. I include all credentialed women. More than half of the 741 Latina clergy in the United States were granted their credentials after 1990. Sherri L. Doty, *Ministers Status/Gender Summary* (Springfield, Mo.: Assemblies of God, 1998): 1–2.

57. The information on the United Methodist Church is from an interview with M. Lynn Scott, director of clergywomen concerns, United Methodist Church, July 1998.

58. For example, from 1939 to 1960, 230 of the 556 graduates from the Hispanic American Bible Institute of the Assemblies of God in New York City were women. An incomplete survey indicates that women made up a majority of the graduating classes at their Bible schools in New York City (1940, 1943, and 1948), Texas (1952 and 1958), and California (1926, 1958, and 1959). Instituto Biblico Hispano del Este Asamblea de Dios, *El Vencedor 1986: Edición Cincuenteria, 1936–1986* (New York: Instituto Biblico Hispano del Este Asamblea de Dios, 1986), 155–58; see also *The Pentecostal Evangel,* June 15, 1935, Dec. 28, 1952, June 30, 1954, May 1, 1955, July 20, 1958, and May 8, 1960.

59. During the 1960s and 1970s, for example, Nellie Bazán, Mary Ruth Prado, and Linda Ruíz wrote regular articles for *La Luz Apostólica* and *The Word.*

60. In 1995 the total number of Latina adult and young women involved in denomi-

nationally sponsored women organizations and girls clubs ("missionettes") was 67,465 (414,377 for all AG women and girls). Of that number, 44,609 (242,294 for all AG women) were adult women. Women's Ministries Department, Women's Ministries and Missionettes, *1995 Annual Church Ministries Report* (Springfield, Mo.: Assemblies of God, 1997).

61. H. C. Ball, "Healed for Service among Mexicans," *Latter Rain Evangel* (Jan. 1931): 11.

62. Interviews with Gloria Garza and Patty Galaviz. This sentiment was shared by AG women such as one key clergywoman who stated that the feminist movement had no impact on the Hispanic Districts because the "movement was tied with homosexuality." Gloria Garza, a graduate of LABI in Texas, has completed two years of college. She has been in the ministry since 1955 and has been a leader in the Women's Missionary Council (WMC) for more than thirty-five years. She served as president of the WMC for the Gulf Latin District of the Assemblies of God from 1979 to 1998 and has been a major catalyst in the call for women in the ministry. Interview with Gloria Garza.

63. This sentiment is also common in Anglo Pentecostalism. Elaine J. Lawless, *Handmaidens of the Lord: Pentecostal Women Preachers and Traditional Religion* (Philadelphia: University of Pennsylvania Press, 1988), xix, 69.

64. Interview with Egla Montero.

65. The Chicano movement (1965–75), which was political as well as social, emphasized civil rights against the social and racial indignities that Mexican Americans faced in the United States. The movement called upon Chicanos/as to become involved politically and fight for social justice. It was that aspect of the movement that turned off most, but clearly not all, Mexican American Pentecostals. *Chicanismo* is an attitude and social stance that demands political action, social justice, and pride in *la raza* (Latino people).

66. Interview with Egla Montero.

67. The Rev. Anita Soto is the senior pastor Calvary Temple (Templo Calvario) in the historic barrio of Santa Barbara. She has been in the ministry in California for more than twenty years. Her Latin American immigrant congregation of eighty to a hundred meets in an industrial garage in the industrial section of the city. Interview with Anita Soto, Santa Barbara, June 1996.

68. Interviews with Egla Montero and Gloria Garza.

69. Interview with Egla Montero.

70. Ninety percent of the Latina Pentecostal clergy in the United States and Puerto Rico in the 1990s supported Dobson's Focus on the Family ministry. Gastón Espinosa, "En la Lucha: The Changing Roles of Latina Pentecostal Women in Ministry," presented at the American Academy of Religion, San Francisco, Nov. 1998. For additional evidence, see Vidal Enriquez, "Dia de la Madre," *La Luz Apostólica* 55 (May 1971): 1; Josue Sánchez, "La Familia: El Padre: La Cabeza del Hogar," *The Word* (Jan.–Feb. 1983): 4–6; and Josue Sánchez, "La Familia: Le Herencia de los Hijos," *The Word* (Jan.–Feb. 1983): 10–12, 24.

71. The Rev. Rose Nodal is a Puerto Rican who grew up in New York City, where she converted to Pentecostalism and then attended the AG Bible school from 1947 to 1950. She has been in the ministry since 1949 and is the senior pastor for a 160- to 200-member church in Santa Maria, Calif. Interview with Rose Nodal, June 1996. Although 90 percent of Latina clergy said they voted, only 30 percent supported Pat Robertson and the Christian Coalition. Espinosa, "En la Lucha."

3. Expanding Feminism's Field and Focus: Activism in the National Council of Churches in the 1960s and 1970s

SUSAN M. HARTMANN

> What if I am a woman? Did [God] not raise up Deborah to be a
> mother, and a judge in Israel: Did not queen Esther save the lives of
> the Jews?

SINCE THE EARLY DECADES of the nineteenth century, religion has inspired women's challenges to the status quo, as it did for Maria Stewart. An African American and the first American-born woman to defend women's rights in public, Stewart upheld her claim with Scripture. A few years later, in 1837, abolitionist and feminist Sarah Grimké insisted that "no where does God say that he made any distinction between [men and women] as moral and intelligent beings."[1] Yet the scriptural justification and inspiration that energized women's challenges to sex role limitations rested uneasily within thoroughly patriarchal institutions. Some feminists such as Elizabeth Cady Stanton simply withdrew from traditional religion, which she identified as "the chief obstacle in the way of women's elevation." Frances Willard acknowledged the impulse to forsake a church that denied "women's equality within the house of God," but she remained. "I love my mother-church so well," she declared, "that I would fain give her a little time in which to deal justly by the great household of her loving, loyal and devoted daughters."[2] As was true for Willard, strong bonds tied many twentieth-century feminists to their traditional religious institutions. Women affiliated with the National Council of Churches of Christ in the U.S.A. (NCCC) saw the church as their church, too, based on women's ample presence and contributions, and they determined to make liberal Protestantism embrace their feminist claims.

Such women are virtually invisible in scholarship about second-wave fem-

inism in the United States, which has focused overwhelmingly on the secular women's movement expressed in organizations such as the National
Organization for Women (NOW) and manifested in women's liberation
groups throughout the country. Arising from this research is a portrayal of
feminism as a white, middle-class movement that emerged around 1966.
Turning our attention to religious women, however, revises that understanding in nearly every respect. We find, first, that religion played a pivotal role
in inspiring and sustaining feminist activism. Second, liberal Protestant
women articulated feminist ideas in the early 1960s, anticipating the secular
feminism that emerged later. Third, African American women played leading roles in the feminism that developed in the NCCC. Finally, the agenda
of this spiritually inspired feminism embraced the concerns of poor wom-
en, women of color, and lesbians as well as those of white, economically comfortable, heterosexual women.

Although the National Council of Churches was as male-dominated as
most institutions in the 1960s, the organization's predominantly liberal orientation—in which social reform was as central to Christianity as personal
salvation—both inspired feminist action and provided an environment that
feminists could exploit. Founded in 1908 by social gospel progressives, in the
1960s the NCCC was the largest ecumenical organization in the United States,
representing more than thirty million Christians in thirty-three Orthodox
and Protestant denominations. As movements for racial and economic justice arose in the 1960s, the white, liberal denominations and the NCCC re-
aligned their agendas to address the needs of oppressed groups and emphasized concepts of liberation, inclusiveness, and the oneness of all humans in
Christ.[3] Feminists then expanded that agenda and rhetoric to include wom-
en. In fact, the theological bases for their assertion of women's equality gave
religious feminists especially high levels of confidence and commitment to
their cause. To them, sexism was a sin, and feminism became part of spreading Christ's mission in the world.

Church Women United and the Seeds of Interracial Feminism

Feminist pressures arose early in Church Women United (CWU), a group
of denominational women's organizations founded in 1941. Having become
a general department in the National Council of Churches in 1950, it operated, according to a historian of the NCCC, as "a bit of a burr under the saddle
to the overwhelmingly male leadership" of the organization. As Virginia
Brereton has demonstrated, CWU leaders operated both as insiders in their

ability to influence the NCCC and as outsiders in their distance from real power and authority.[4]

From its inception, CWU leaders chafed at the disparity between women's vast contributions to church work and their near absence in decision-making positions. During the 1950s and 1960s CWU prompted investigations of denominational policies and practices regarding ordination of women and their participation in policy-making. Long before the resurgence of feminism, CWU expressed dissatisfaction at women's exclusion from church administration and decision making, calling in 1954, for example, for ecumenical councils to "provide for a more adequate participation of the Council of Church Women in policy building."[5]

CWU also acted on issues concerning women in the secular world, working for federal equal pay legislation and promoting positive approaches to women's employment in the 1950s.[6] In 1965 CWU created the Committee on the Changing Role of Women, which boldly evaluated the interpretation of Scripture and the churches' teaching about women. In a forceful statement calling for "a radical challenge to the Church," it rebuked male religious leaders for interpreting Scripture "in such a way as to minimize the personhood of women." Several years before consciousness-raising swept through the secular women's movement, the report articulated the need to "help women to validate their interior feelings" and gain confidence in themselves. It anticipated that "forces of both men and women will rise against us if we really move" but insisted that churches had to respond to women's changing roles. The report's ideas and rhetoric borrowed much from the black freedom struggle and at the same time demonstrated the feminist stirrings present within organized religion at an early date.[7]

CWU leaders increasingly felt "hamstrung by a group of uniform regulations to which every department must conform" and resentful of the gap between CWU's substantial financial contributions and women's actual influence in the larger organization. Claire Randall, associate executive director of CWU, stated bluntly, "[T]his has been the role of women in the church—to be used. We are used to dispense the ideas men have decided upon, to feed the money to support the projects that men have decided on and are running."[8]

The NCCC's response to the "Black Manifesto," a demand by black activists in the summer of 1969 that the churches marshall their resources behind economic development projects to alleviate black poverty, did not help matters. CWU leaders expressed dismay at the "missing dimensions" of the churches' responses, that is, a "lack of concern for women disadvantaged by poverty" and a "lack of women in the decision-making bodies to which the church is promising large funds." They called together black women leaders and representatives of women's denominational organizations to discuss economic justice for women. The resulting statement demanded a role for women "from varied segments of our society in the decision making processes" and sought "major funds . . . for innovative projects which encourage the economic development of women." CWU created its own Commission on Economic Justice for Women, chaired by Coretta Scott King.[9]

The extent to which women in CWU attacked racism and involved African American women in leadership positions distinguished religious feminism from the mainstream liberal women's movement. CWU had taken an early and consistent stance against discrimination. In 1945 national board members stayed in private homes rather than patronize hotels that refused to serve African Americans. In 1948 the organization attacked school segregation as "contrary to our Christian principles and inimical to the democratic pattern." In 1960, before the full flowering of the black freedom struggle, CWU began a three-year project, Assignment Race, sending interracial pairs of women to train local churchwomen in antiracist action. African American women held important paid and volunteer positions in CWU, and in 1971 the organization chose Clare Collins Harvey, the granddaughter of a slave, as its president.[10]

Church Women United challenged mainstream feminism's tendency to identify needs and interests of white, middle-class women as those of all women. Launching a project called the Commission on Woman in Today's World in 1969, CWU staff contested the notion of a universal Woman by inquiring pointedly, "Who are the disadvantaged and deprived women? In what ways and why?"[11] The awareness that race and class shaped gender both reflected the involvement of African American women in creating CWU's agenda and facilitated further interracial feminist efforts.

When CWU became independent of the NCCC in 1970, its headquarters remained in the building that housed the council and several denominations, its members continued to participate broadly in NCCC programs, and its antiracist tradition influenced the feminism developing in both CWU and the NCCC. As the council responded to women's demands and took up feminist issues, African American women sometimes headed and often occupied places near the center of projects. Those projects, in turn, maintained a strong focus on the needs and interests of women of color.

Feminist Networks and Leaders in the NCCC

In 1969, shortly before CWU declared its independence, it gave birth to a women's caucus at the NCCC's general assembly meeting in Detroit. Seeking to "place the question of women's liberation in the main stream of the church's concern," CWU leaders invited all the women attending the meeting to a briefing. That briefing turned into a full-fledged caucus as individuals worked through the night to draw up a statement alerting "the churches that the era of tokenism was over."[12]

Peggy Billings, an executive in the United Methodist Church, read the women's statement as more than a hundred women rose to demonstrate that she spoke for all of them. Focusing on "women's liberation in the life of the Church," Billings cited statistics showing that women were poorly represented in decision-making bodies. She read, "Women are rising . . . black and white, red and brown, to demand change" in an institution dominated by "white-skinned male clergy over forty." Billings asserted that the caucus was here to stay: "You will be sick of this theme, but we will not stop raising it." Afterwards, two of the caucus leaders rejoiced: "For the first time in history men made no effort to laugh us off and made no funny remarks all week."[13]

The caucus raised the theme of women's liberation throughout the 1970s and beyond. By the 1974 NCCC meeting, it attracted three-fourths of the women delegates, including more than token numbers of black women. African American women continued to be highly visible in the caucus, which beginning in 1977 was led by the Rev. Joan M. Martin, a black on the NCCC's professional staff.[14] The caucus functioned in a number of ways that enabled feminists to influence the NCCC. It increased contact between delegates and staff women who implemented NCCC programs. It pushed by-law changes that required minimum percentages of women delegates to the governing board, and it pressed for more women on the professional staff at NCCC headquarters. By 1979 women's representation on the governing board had increased from 6 to 24 percent, and their presence on the NCCC's professional staff had grown from 10 to 35 percent in 1984.[15]

Enabling women to draw "upon our strength and support for mutual empowerment," the caucus taught them how to participate effectively in board meetings. Because delegates frequently approved resolutions with little or no discussion, the caucus devised ways to draw greater attention to their issues. For example, upon introduction of a resolution supporting the creation of a memorial to black leader Mary McLeod Bethune, all of the women rose to second the motion and several spoke about her life. That event demonstrated not just the caucus's attention to strategy and tactics but also the cooperation between black and white women that characterized much caucus activity.[16]

Feminist activism in the NCCC paralleled developments in the denominations, several of which, including the United Methodist Church, the United Church of Christ, and the (northern) United Presbyterian Church, established task forces on women during the early 1970s.[17] Frequently, women's feminist efforts overlapped among their denominational governing body, their denominational women's organization, Church Women United, and the National Council of Churches. Cynthia Wedel served in leadership roles in CWU and Episcopal Church Women before joining the NCCC as a division head in the 1960s. The Rev. Davida F. Crabtree and Valerie E. Russell served on the United Church of Christ's task force on women and were active in the NCCC women's caucus. NCCC caucus members Peggy Billings and Theressa Hoover held executive positions in the Women's Division of the United Methodist Church. Thelma Stevens promoted feminist goals through the women's caucus, CWU, and the Women's Division of the United Methodist Church. The sense of community and feminist reinforcement that women received in multiple arenas perhaps balanced the difficulties of sustaining active membership in several bodies.

The birth of the women's caucus coincided with the election of the first woman president of the National Council of Churches. An important symbolic achievement, Cynthia Wedel's presidency gave feminists a tremendous lift. Although she characterized herself as not especially militant, she had accumulated considerable feminist experience through her work in CWU and as a member of the President's Commission on the Status of Women and its successor. Clearly influenced by the "young and sometimes rather militant women . . . pressing for opportunities," Wedel recognized in 1969 that organized religion must respond. Shortly after her election, she placed equal opportunity for women and new structures in which "we would no longer be relegated to the 'women's work'" on the NCCC's agenda.[18]

Even more important to NCCC feminists was the election of Claire Randall in 1974 as general secretary. When Randall, who had held administrative posts in the Presbyterian Church U.S. and the CWU, assumed the highest staff position in the NCCC, the *New York Times* characterized the event as "a break with two thousand years of tradition." Although the presidency of the council changed every three years, the general secretary served five-year terms, and Randall won reelection in 1979. Moreover, the general secretary ran the organization on a day-to-day basis, wielding significant influence as she oversaw implementation of policies set by the governing board.[19]

As associate executive director of Church Women United, Randall had played a key role in creation of the women's caucus. She chaired the NCCC's task force on abortion in 1972 and 1973 and publicly approved the Supreme Court decision in *Roe v. Wade,* even though the council itself would not. Although there were limitations on what Randall could deliver for women, her position as the highest staff executive considerably amplified the force of feminism in the NCCC. She continued her wholehearted support of the women's caucus, which she frequently hosted at governing board meetings. She vigorously challenged the use of masculine language and imagery, refusing to let it pass when it crept into board meetings. She acted on feminist proposals from staff women when such action did not require governing board approval. And she implemented feminist resolutions approved by the board in the strongest fashion possible. When Randall's position occasioned invitations to participate in secular feminist activities, she responded enthusiastically, speaking, for example, at Equal Rights Amendment (ERA) ratification rallies and serving on the National Commission on the Observance of International Women's Year and on the President's Advisory Committee for Women.[20]

Feminists and the NCCC Structure

Feminists persuaded the NCCC governing board to support various projects of the secular women's movement. The board gave its blessing to the observance of International Women's Year and the National Women's Conference held in Houston in 1977. It called upon the federal government to fund safe and wholesome day-care facilities for all children of working parents. And it leapt to the aid of the federal government's increasingly beleaguered affirmative action policy, urging churches to pursue educational efforts and legal strategies, including the filing of amicus curiae briefs.[21]

The NCCC governing board passed three resolutions backing ratification of the ERA, which Randall implemented energetically with efforts that included personal lobbying of officials. The decentralized structure of the council, however, enabled specific divisions to go even further in support for the ERA without having to obtain governing board approval. In 1976, largely upon the initiative of CWU, more than twenty representatives of Catholic, Jewish, and Protestant organizations formed the Religious Committee for the ERA (RCERA) to demonstrate widespread religious support for the amendment. Claire Randall was one of five speakers at its founding press conference. The council as a whole did not join the coalition, but its Division of Church and Society (DCS) did. The DCS not only housed RCERA but also donated funds and staff time, developed resource materials, and helped train church activists. Although ERA ratification failed, NCCC efforts were nonetheless significant in aligning the moral authority of organized religion with feminist aspirations.[22]

In contrast to feminists' ability to marshall NCCC support for the ERA, they could not obtain endorsement of women's right to abortion, even after the

Supreme Court legalized abortion in 1973 and after an NCCC committee and task force studied the issue. That failure reflected ecumenical concerns. The council was seriously exploring the possibility of Roman Catholic membership, and the eight Eastern Orthodox churches that were already members had become increasingly disenchanted with the council's liberal direction. One Orthodox delegate warned that a policy statement affirming abortion "would seriously jeopardize our continued relationship with the NCCC."[23]

In 1977, after Congress had begun to restrict federal funding for abortions, two caucus members found a way to unlock the council's silence. Peggy Billings suggested an NCCC resolution opposing the denial of federal Medicaid funds for abortion, and Chris Cowap, a staff member in the Division of Education and Ministry (DEM), found a previous policy statement on which to base such a stand, a 1963 council assertion of the rights of all persons to receive government benefits without discrimination. On this foundation, caucus members obtained a governing board resolution disclaiming any policy on the merits of abortion but supporting the principle that a right guaranteed to all must not be denied to some because of economic status. Moreover, the resolution urged governments to guarantee equal access to legal abortions by ensuring adequate funding. Armed with that resolution, in 1980 Randall authorized NCCC filing of an amicus curiae brief with the Supreme Court challenging the denial of Medicaid reimbursements for abortions. The inclusive position of NCCC feminists on reproductive freedom embraced abortion rights for poor women as well as action against sterilization abuse.[24]

The divisional autonomy that enabled strong activism relating to the ERA and abortion also facilitated a number of other initiatives. Each NCCC division had a unit committee composed of representatives from denominations. Instead of going to the governing board, divisions could initiate activities by securing the consent of their unit committees and obtaining funds from denominations.[25] Thus, the Division of Church and Society established the Justice for Women Program, and the Division of Education and Ministry created the Commission on Women in Ministry and the Task Force on Sexism in the Bible. With leadership by African American women, these bodies undertook projects that particularly emphasized the needs of disadvantaged women.

In the DCS, whose work focused on secular issues, two feminists held positions in which they could draw attention to women's concerns. Chris Cowap, an Episcopalian and former staff employee of CWU, was staff associate for economic justice in the division; Peggy Billings represented the United Methodist Church on the division's unit committee. In 1975 Billings and Cowap raised concerns about harassment of the women's movement by the FBI and other law-enforcement agencies, which were interrogating members of radical feminist and lesbian communities as part of a nationwide search for radical fugitives, including Katharine Ann Power and Susan Saxe. Several women went to jail for refusing to answer FBI or grand-jury questions. Billings, Cowap, and others believed that officials' actions frequently violated civil rights and amounted to intimidation of the women's movement. Concerned also about the spread of intimidation to women's centers supported by religious bodies, they, along with women representing Church Women United and denominational organizations, formed the Committee of Concern.[26]

Billings and Cowap persuaded the DCS unit committee to endorse and house the Committee of Concern, which then persuaded the NCCC to file an amicus curiae brief on behalf of two women who refused to testify before a New Haven grand jury. Although the judge refused the plea and sentenced the women to eighteen months in jail, NCCC intervention signaled religious support for the women's liberation movement, attracted publicity to the case, and warned the government that FBI and grand-jury actions would receive close scrutiny. The Committee of Concern also sponsored public briefings, contacted legislators, and wrote to seven hundred women's organizations, offering them information and support. These efforts joined women across denominational lines and linked the largest ecumenical organization with the radical branch of secular feminism.[27]

In 1975 the DCS named justice for women among its top four priorities, and in 1977 it raised sufficient funds to inaugurate the Justice for Women (JFW) Program, with Joan M. Martin as its staff associate. In her training at Princeton Theological Seminary Martin had experienced "otherness" both as a black and as a woman and had decided that, for women of color, "the luxurious choice of which oppression to fight is not an option." Dedicating her work to "doing what I dare call Black feminist theology," Martin promoted racial diversity among representatives to the JFW program. Her leadership helped NCCC feminism embrace the particular concerns of women of color and reflect the ways in which race shaped gender. For example, while acknowledging that domestic violence and rape crossed class and racial lines, Martin explained black women's unique vulnerability as victims of violence. Police often ignored or responded slowly to calls coming from black communities, she maintained, and "the woman is likely to be insulted if the police do show."[28]

With members from denominations, ecumenical organizations, and secular women's groups, JFW's working group addressed a broad assortment of issues, including domestic violence, sterilization abuse, affirmative action, relationships between sexism and racism, and the incarceration of women. JFW promoted links between the NCCC and secular organizations through its representation on the National Affirmative Action Task Force, for example, and at the first National Hispanic Women's Conference.[29]

JFW served feminist needs in a variety of ways. It provided physical and emotional space so women could find others who had mutual concerns and engage in joint action, benefits especially important to those who felt isolated in their denominations. Although JFW had to raise its own budget, NCCC sponsorship lent credibility to program activities. The program's stationery named the Division of Church and Society, but at the top in even larger letters was imprinted "National Council of the Churches of Christ." In reporting activities of divisions, the press frequently attributed such action to the NCCC rather than to the particular sub-unit. The council's imprimatur gave women's units the appearance of having greater support than they could have mustered had their actions required authorization from the governing board.

JFW, which focused on women's issues in the secular world, was not the only sub-unit where feminism flourished under NCCC shelter. The Commission on Women in Ministry (COWIM) attacked sex discrimination in the churches and advanced women's opportunities as ministers, professionals, and support staff in the denominations. With more than one hundred members, COWIM operated in the Division of Education and Ministry, which was headed by Emily V. Gibbes. The first African American woman named as an associate general secretary of the NCCC, Gibbes had served as executive secretary for United Presbyterian Women and as president of Church Women United in Pennsylvania. In response to suggestions from Claire Randall and others for a center to encourage women's employment in the churches, she launched COWIM in September 1974.[30]

Usually attracting about fifty persons from ecumenical organizations and denominations—including Roman Catholics—COWIM's semiannual meetings incorporated consciousness-raising sessions and structures that encouraged broad participation. The paucity of ordained women and the difficulties they experienced as ministers claimed a large part of COWIM's attention. Its very first activity announced militant intentions by sponsoring the "Service in Celebration of Women in Ministry," where three women newly ordained in violation of their Episcopal Church's hierarchy celebrated the Eucharist. Although the service neither had nor needed the sanction of the NCCC governing board, it appeared to suggest council support of the Episcopal women, and some bishops expressed displeasure at NCCC "involvement" in what they considered the internal affairs of their church.[31]

From COWIM's inception it concerned itself with inclusiveness. At its first meeting, members noted the scarcity of minority women and strategized to remedy that underrepresentation. Setting a goal of 50 percent minority representation, the commission pressed denominations to appoint women of color and sought out such women to join as individuals. Every meeting addressed strategies for recruiting minority women, and although the commission fell short of its goal, non-whites usually composed about 30 percent of attendance. COWIM ensured minority participation in leadership by expanding its steering committee to include three women appointed by its Task Force on Ethnic Women in Ministry. More broadly, it organized a conference of minority women in ministry—the first of its kind. Some two hundred women—African American, Latina, Asian American, and Native American—gathered in Washington, D.C., in 1978 to explore the particular concerns of minority women serving as ministers and church employees.[32]

Feminists in COWIM tackled racial oppression with much greater intensity and commitment than did most of their secular sisters, in part reflecting the leadership of Emily Gibbes and the persistence of Joan Martin and other women of color. COWIM also continued a tradition of interracial cooperation among religous women that stretched from the abolitionist movement to the antiracist work of Church Women United.[33] NCCC women, like men, had been sensitized to racism in the 1960s when liberal churches allied themselves with the civil rights movement. White women also learned from black women, who challenged them to investigate their privilege and examine their complicity in racial and economic injustice. Tutored by black women who could not separate their identities into race and gender (and who anticipated the academic theory about the interconnectedness of race, class, and gender that emerged in the 1980s), white women in the NCCC came to see their part in the struggle against racism as inseparable from their feminism. They proved willing to combat their prejudice by engaging in the consciousness-raising sessions that became a regular part of COWIM meetings. One participant characterized the confrontation with racial oppression as a "chaotic and creative process of giving birth to a feminist model of ministry in our midst," one that grew out of an examination of "the relationship between *all* forms and experiences of oppression."[34]

In this spirit COWIM also took on discrimination against homosexuals, creating the Task Force on Gay Women in Ministry to investigate issues facing lesbians in the church and society. As they had with racism, COWIM members confronted their feelings about sexuality through consciousness-raising and role-playing sessions. The commission sought to change attitudes by publishing for member denominations a resource packet on gay issues and ministry. It also facilitated a support network for lesbians by co-sponsoring a conference, "Journey to Freedom, Lesbian-Feminist-Christian," in March 1979. In addition, COWIM protested instances of discrimination by churches and public agencies. For example, it wrote to several Methodist seminaries that expelled or refused to admit gay students and protested a church's firing of a woman who came out as a lesbian.[35]

While its ardent commitment to justice for racial and ethnic minorities, lesbians, and gay men formed COWIM's most distinguishing feature, the commission worked in multifarious ways to support and empower all women in ministry. It published a resource guide and co-sponsored an annual national conference for women seminarians. For already ordained women, it held Women in Ministry weeks, gathering together women from across the country and from diverse denominations and ministerial responsibilities. It also reached beyond NCCC's constituency and wrote to support Sister Teresa Kane, who had confronted Pope John Paul II on women's ordination during his visit to Washington, D.C., in 1979.[36]

The Challenge to Male-Exclusive Language

More visible and consequently more controversial than COWIM was a second feminist enterprise undertaken by the DEM, the elimination of sexism from religious language. The NCCC women's caucus and feminists in member denominations had protested the use of male-exclusive language in worship and discussion. Evangelical feminist Virginia Mollenkott spoke for many devout women alienated by the traditional language of worship that made them feel "linguistically and structurally excluded. . . . If God is always manlike, and never womanlike," she protested, "then men are God-like and women are not." By 1974 several churches, including the United Church of Christ, the United Presbyterian Church, and the Lutheran Church of America, had examined language in religious materials and published guides to more inclusive speech. Attention soon turned to the NCCC and its DEM, which held copyright to the Revised Standard Version of the Bible and under whose charge a body of distinguished scholars, the RSV Bible Committee (RSVBC), issued new editions of the Scripture.[37]

Professional, practical, and spiritual considerations posed huge obstacles to the feminist project of eliminating male language from the Bible. As scholars, RSVBC members were deeply invested in the Scripture as they and men like them had translated it. Feminist claims against that "ownership" challenged both their professional standards and their masculine authority. Furthermore, biblical revision affected the division's million-dollar budget, which depended in part on royalties from the RSV Bible. Finally, male theologians worried about the effects of transforming language on the many Christians—men and women—who actually did encounter God as a "he" and held sacred the Scripture that they had made part of their lives.[38]

In 1974 Emily Gibbes appointed the Task Force on Sexism in the Bible, which was composed of women who had solid credentials as biblical scholars. Phyllis Trible, for example, specialized in the Old Testament as an associate professor at Andover Newton Theological Seminary. A prolific writer, Elisabeth Schussler Fiorenza was associate professor of theology at the University of Notre Dame. Letty M. Russell had served as pastor of a Presbyterian Church in East Harlem and currently taught theology at Yale's Divinity School. Gibbes herself represented the NCCC staff. Task force members saw their work as striving to reconcile their heart-felt Christianity with their feminist aspiration to be fully equal under God. Describing herself as "a feminist who loves the Bible," Phyllis Trible later portrayed their task as that of "redeem[ing] the past (an ancient document) and the present (its continuing use) from the confines of patriarchy."[39]

In 1976 the task force published a study guide for church members, *The Liberating Word: A Guide to Nonsexist Intepretation of the Bible,* with chapters written by four of its members, all professors of theology. They explained the power of language and the imperative "to liberate the interpretation of God's Word from male bias." They demonstrated how biblical texts reflected the patriarchal environment of their construction and provided examples of alternate, feminist readings. Acknowledging that altering language describing God was "difficult and dangerous," they suggested avoiding the use of patriarchal terms such as *Master* and *Father* to refer to God and speaking of Jesus as male only when referring to his earthly life as a man. Designed for religious leaders, seminarians, and lay study groups in the parishes, the 120-page paperback attracted attention in major media such as *Time* and the *Washington Post* as well as in church magazines.[40]

The Task Force on Sexism enjoyed less success with the RSVBC. Members expressed interest in working with the revision committee and submitted names of competent female scholars, yet when four vacancies arose in the thirty-five-member RSVBC, the committee added just two women along with two men.[41] After lengthy discussion in June 1976, the committee agreed to eliminate male expressions that did not appear in the original Greek or Hebrew, but it refused to consider changing language that identified God as male. Bruce M. Metzger, professor of theology at Princeton University and chair of the RSVBC, declared himself "unwilling to monkey around with God language . . . and cease calling God Father." Changing passages that "reflect

the historical situation of ancient patriarchal and masculine-oriented society" would result in "betrayal of what translation is supposed to be." These
male theologians devoted primary allegiance to the context out of which
Scripture arose, whereas feminists placed more importance on the community into which it was conveyed.[42]

Subsequent discussions left feminists disheartened and convinced that
RSVBC members "were not hearing the questions or issues being raised." In
response, the Commission on Women in Ministry sponsored a public forum
where both feminists and traditionalists could be heard. Convened at NCCC
headquarters in December 1977, the forum attracted some one hundred people as well as articles in the *New York Times* and *Christian Science Monitor*.
In 1978 the DEM's unit committee mandated further dialogue between feminists and the RSVBC by authorizing yet another body, the Task Force on
Issues of Biblical Translation, which had representation from both the RSVBC
and the original task force.[43]

The final recommendations of the Task Force on Issues of Biblical Translation revealed both the influence of feminists in the NCCC and the limits
of their power. Representing the views of five women and eight men, the task
force report defined a fundamental dilemma: The RSVB "must not lend aid
and comfort to sexist attitudes and interpretations," but it must provide readers "access to the language and conceptuality of the ages in which the biblical texts took shape." Resolution of the quandary essentially acknowledged
the RSVBC's independence and its tenacious hold on tradition. The report
did praise the committee's "good beginning" in avoiding sexist translations
and encouraged "more substantial revisions," providing a whole series of
recommendations that resembled those in *The Liberating Word*. It also recommended appointment of scholars "with feminist perspectives" as regular members of the RSVBC. But the task force's most important recommendation indicated that feminist concerns would have to be met through other
means.[44]

The task force proposed development of a new lectionary, a series of primary Bible passages that are read aloud at services throughout the church
year, which could provide the opportunity to try new language and give people a chance to get used to it. The proposal clearly represented a momentous
step for the DEM, whose unit committee struggled for months before authorizing the lectionary project while thousands of letters poured into the
NCCC denouncing it as an effort to "de-sex" the Bible. "You sound and act
like Communists," blasted one, while a disgusted women asserted that "people in this country . . . have gone crazy over this women's liberation idea."
Some letters resulted from a direct-mail campaign conducted by groups in

the religious right, such as the Religious Roundtable, which castigated "Bible butchers" for "tampering with the word of God." Careful to explain what the project intended to do and why, the DEM, backed by the NCCC leadership, took the heat and carried through the project. The first volume of the *Inclusive Language Lectionary* was published in 1983.[45]

Reference to God as "Father and Mother," substituting "Human One" for "Son of man," and a host of other changes proved too much for leaders of some NCCC denominations. The nine Eastern Orthodox churches urged the governing board to dissociate itself from the lectionary, and the president of the Lutheran Church in America advised his parishes not to use it. Bruce Metzger, chair of the RSVBC, deemed the new language referring to the Deity "altogether unacceptable." Reminding critics that the new lectionary was "experimental and voluntary" and not meant to replace the Bible, the NCCC held its ground, completing it with new volumes in 1984 and 1985. Although most ministers turned their backs on the lectionary, worshipers in a substantial minority of churches became accustomed to hearing the Scripture in women-affirming language. The Presbyterian Church U.S.A. took no official position, but it began immediately to educate its 3.2 million members about the lectionary, and its spokesperson called it a step toward "breaking down some of the walls of separation felt by women and others who feel excluded by male language and imagery."[46]

Moreover, NCCC sponsorship of projects related to inclusive language, beginning with the Task Force on Sexism in the Bible in 1975, had an impact ranging beyond the lectionary. For example, the Lutheran Church in America, which had advised its ministers not to use the NCCC lectionary, published its own in 1987. Advertised as more conservative than the NCCC's, it nonetheless excised masculine pronouns for God and eliminated many of the male references to Jesus. And NCCC feminists did influence the 1989 edition of the RSV Bible. The still overwhelmingly male editors clung to the masculine references to God, but they eliminated many of the masculine pronouns referring to humans. Above all, religious women's distress with sexist language reached an audience different from that of secular feminists, broadening considerably public consciousness about the power of gendered words.[47]

Looking back at feminism among Protestant women in the 1960s and 1970s, Theressa Hoover recalled, "These intelligent, angry younger women articulated our frustrations also. . . . Their determination to revise patriarchal culture and politics energized us."[48] Yet in acknowledging the spark generated by secular feminists, Hoover told only half the story. The ideas and actions of CWU and other churchwomen's organizations helped lay a foundation for the resurgence of feminism in the 1960s. Moreover, religious feminists enjoyed access to women and men beyond the reach of the secular women's movement, and their theologically based arguments broadened the ideological foundation of feminism. They enlarged the field and focus of feminism in the 1970s and aligned the largest ecumenical organization behind important goals of the women's movement.

Religious feminists struggled to practice an interracial feminism sooner and with more intensity than most of their secular counterparts. Fortified by a theological foundation emphasizing inclusiveness, the tradition of antiracist effort in CWU, and participation in the liberal churches' engagement with the struggle for black freedom, NCCC women constructed a feminism that attacked the interlocking forms of oppression experienced by women of color, lesbians, and poor women. Above all, African American women's considerable presence and leadership ensured that inclusivity and antiracism formed an integral core of the feminism that emerged in the NCCC.

The actions of women in the NCCC extended beyond its boundaries, encouraging women's presence in religious leadership and a wording of Scripture that included and valued women. Moreover, the NCCC endowed moral authority on such demands of the secular women's movement as the ERA, reproductive freedom, and nonsexist language. All of this activity under the council's umbrella served as a counterweight when antifeminists marshalled religious arguments, and it prevented the right from monopolizing the church's voice on feminist issues.

Notes

1. "Mrs. Stewart's Farewell Address to Her Friends in the City of Boston. Delivered September 21, 1833," reprinted in *Black Women in Nineteenth-Century American Life: Their Words, Their Thoughts, Their Feelings,* ed. Bert James Loewenberg and Ruth Bogin (University Park: Pennsylvania State University Press, 1976), 198–200; Sarah Grimké, "Province of Women: The Pastoral Letter," *The Liberator,* Oct. 6, 1837.

2. Stanton quoted in Elisabeth Griffith, *In Her Own Right: The Life of Elizabeth Cady Stanton* (New York: Oxford University Press, 1984), 210; Frances E. Willard, *Glimpses of Fifty Years: The Autobiography of an American Woman* (Chicago: Woman's Temperance Publication Association, 1889), 465.

3. Henry J. Pratt, *The Liberalization of American Protestantism: A Case Study in Complex Organizations* (Detroit: Wayne State University Press, 1972), 13–16, 120, 160–64; James F. Findlay, Jr., *Church People in the Struggle: The National Council of Churches and the Black Freedom Movement, 1950–1970* (New York: Oxford University Press, 1993), 6, 173, 178; A. James Reichley, *Religion in American Public Life* (Washington, D.C.: Brookings Institution, 1985), 245, 247, 251–53, 257–67.

4. The organization began as the United Council of Church Women and used the name

United Church Women until 1966, when it became Church Women United, the name I use throughout this essay. Findlay, *Church People in the Struggle,* 49; Virginia Brereton, "United and Slighted: Women as Subordinated Insiders," in *Between the Times: The Travail of the Protestant Establishment in America, 1900–1960,* ed. William R. Hutchison (New York: Cambridge University Press, 1989), 147–48, 163–64.

5. The following are in the NCC Records at the Presbyterian Historical Society, Philadelphia, Pa.: Mary Ely Lyman, "Goals, and Some Steps to Take," Sept. 29, 1953 (RG 3, box 13); "Questions for Research and Survey: Some Questions from a Meeting of the Secretarial Conference," Dec. 16, 1960 (RG 14, box 9); "General Policy and Strategy Committee Concerning a Letter to Heads of Member Communions about a Study of Men and Women in the Churches," June 6, 1962 (RG 4, box 28); "Cooperation of Men and Women," 1962 (RG 14, box 9). The quotation is in "Suggested Criteria for Organizational Participation of Councils of Church Women in State and Local Councils of Churches," Aug. 2, 1954 (RG 4, box 9).

6. Cynthia Wedel, *Employed Women and the Church: Study and Discussion Guide for Church Groups* (New York: National Council of Churches of Christ in the U.S.A., 1959); Board of Managers, United Church Women, "Christian Social Relations Resolution on Equal Pay," May 2, 1962, RG 4, box 28, NCCC Records, Presbyterian Historical Society.

7. The following are in RG 10, box 1, NCC Records of the Presbyterian Historical Society: UCW, Committee on the Role of Women, "Reports and Recommendations," April 29, 1965; Minutes, Committee on Laity and Cooperation of Men and Women, May 13, 1965; Mrs. Theodore O. Wedel to Dr. Harvey Cox, Oct. 1, 1965; and Report of Consultation, Committee on the Changing Role of Women, Oct. 13, 1965 (all quotations).

8. Brereton, "United and Slighted," 162–63; Margaret Shannon to Dr. [R. H. Edwin] Espy, Aug. 29, 1968, RG 10, box 1, NCCC Records, Presbyterian Historical Society; "The Status of Women in the Church," May 9, 1969, 16–17, Papers of Pauli Murray, box 139, folder 2536, Schlesinger Library, Radcliffe College (hereafter Murray Papers).

9. Margaret Shannon to Pauli Murray, Aug. 15, 1969, and Murray, "Some Queries," both in box 119, folder 2136, Murray Papers; Church Women United press release, Sept. 26, 1969, and Margaret Shannon to Dr. R. H. Edwin Espy et al., Oct. 3, 1969, both in RG 5, box 17, NCCC Records, Presbyterian Historical Society.

10. Findlay, *Church People in the Struggle,* 49–50; Brereton, "United and Slighted," 154. Brereton points out (156) that UCW women "prided themselves on taking . . . unorthodox social, political, and economic stances." Margaret Shannon, *Just Because: The Story of the National Movement of Church Women United in the U.S.A., 1941 through 1975* (Corte Madera, Calif.: Omega Books, 1977), 116–37 (emphasis added); United Church Women, Executive Committee Minutes, Oct. 1952, 11, box 62, folder 1, and Carrie E. Meares, "Three-Year Project: Assignment: Race 1961–1964," Confidential Reports I and II, box 62, folder 6, both in Records of Church Women United, General Commission on Archives and History, United Methodist Church, Drew University; Ruth Weber, "The New President," *The Church Woman* 37 (June–July 1971): 18–24.

11. Commission on Woman in Today's World (agenda), Nov. 7, 1969, box 119, folder 2135, Murray Papers.

12. The following are in box 119, folder 2135, Murray Papers: Claire Randall to Pauli Murray, Nov. 19, 1969; Commission on Woman in Today's World (agenda), Nov. 7, 1969;

and Thelma Stevens and Claire Randall to Members of the Commission on Woman in Today's World and Denominational Liaison Members, Dec. 16, 1969.

13. Stevens and Randall to Members of the Commission.

14. Notes on Women's Meetings at the NCCC Governing Board, Oct. 11–12, 1974, and Joan M. Martin to Members of PPEC, Nov. 18, 1977, both in Justice for Women Files (hereafter JFW Files), Division of Church and Society (hereafter DCS), NCCC National Office (hereafter NCCC-NO), New York, N.Y.

15. Mary Gene Boteler to Women of the NCCC Governing Board, Feb. 5, 1982, Joan Milton to Joan Martin, May 4, Oct. 23, 1979, Jorge Lara-Brand to Lacy Camp, Nov. 16, 1978, and "A Decade of Women's Issues in the NCCCUSA: Next Steps," Nov. 1979, all in JFW Files, DCS, NCCC-NO; interview with Chris Cowap, New York City, Oct. 15, 1984.

16. Joan M. Martin to NCCC Governing Board, Oct. 27, 1980, Files of the Division of Overseas Ministries, NCCC-NO; interview with Chris Cowap.

17. The following are in RG 5, box 20, NCC Records of the Presbyterian Historical Society: Study Commission on the Participation of Women in the United Methodist Church, "The Status and Role of Women in Program and Policy Making Channels of the United Methodist Church," June 1, 1972; Report from the Task Force on Women in Church and Society to the Executive Council and to the Ninth General Synod of the United Church of Christ, March 8, 1973; and United Presbyterian Church in the U.S.A., "Report of the Interim Task Force on Women—1973"; see also Lois A. Boyd and R. Douglas Breckenridge, *Presbyterian Women in America: Two Centuries of a Quest for Status* (Westport: Greenwood Press, 1983), 225–26 and 51–57 (2d ed., 1996).

18. The following are in the NCC Records of the Presbyterian Historical Society: Minutes, National Council of Churches General Nominating Committee, Jan. 24, April 2, 1969 (RG 3, box 7), and NCCC press releases, Dec. 2, 4, 1969 (RG 2, box 5); see also "Cynthia Wedel: Woman with a Mission for the Seventies," *The Church Woman* 36 (March 1970): 3; Cynthia C. Wedel, "Agenda for the Future," *The Church Woman* 36 (March 1970): 20; and "The Status of Women in the Church," 24.

19. Pratt, *The Liberalization of American Protestantism,* 106–8, 120. The *New York Times* is quoted in "Claire Randall Elected Top Administrator of NCCC," *The Church Woman* 40 (Jan. 1974): 32.

20. "Claire Randall," Oct. 1973, RG 5, box 18, NCCC Records, Presbyterian Historical Society; "Claire Randall: NCCC's New General Secretary-Elect," *Tempo* 3 (Oct. 1973): 1, 4, 7; Claire Randall, "Women in the World of Now," *Church Women* 36 (March 1970): 17; Minutes of the NCCC General Board, June 11–12, 1971, 9, RG 3, box 4, NCCC-NO; Elizabeth Hambrick-Stowe, "A Conference on Women and Theology," *The Church Woman* 39 (Feb. 1973), 30–32; *NCCC Chronicles* 77 (Fall 1977): 2, and 78 (Fall 1978): 2; National Council of Churches of Christ in the U.S.A., *Report for the Triennium, 1976–1978* (New York: National Council of Churches of Christ in the U.S.A., 1979), 71.

21. Minutes of the NCCC Governing Board, Oct. 11–13, 1974, Nov. 10, May 5, 1977, May 12, 1978, NCCC-NO.

22. Minutes of the NCCC Governing Board, March 6, 1975, May 6, 1977, May 9, 1980, NCCC-NO; memo from Joan Martin to Arleon Kelley, June 16, 1980, and Annual Program Report, JFW Program Area, 1979, 1980, both in JFW Files, DCS, NCCC-NO; press realeases, Religious Committee for the ERA, Feb. 6, Sept. 21, 1977, boxes 120, 121, Records

of ERAmerica, Library of Congress, Washington, D.C.; "ERA Means 'Equal Rights Amendment,'" *The Church Woman* 42 (Oct. 1976): 29.

23. Kay Leslie, "The Abortion Issue and the Churches," *Tempo* (July–Aug. 1972): 3–4; *The Religious Newsweekly,* Feb. 17, 1970, 2. The following are in the NCC Records of the Presbyterian Historical Society: Muriel S. Webb to Members of the General Board (RG3, box 4); Minutes of the NCCC General Board, Feb. 11–14, 1972 (RG 5, box 15); "Proposed Policy Statement on Abortion" as presented to the Governing Board, Dec. 8, 1972 (RG 5, box 15); Claire Randall to NCCC Task Force on Abortion, Dec. 14, 1972, March 12, 1973 (RG 5, box 15); General Planning and Program Committee, NCCC, *Program Budget Directions for 1971* (RG 3, box 12); *Capsule,* March 3, 1970, 5, Feb. 1, 1972, 1 (RG 15, box 1); Ed Luidens and Ann Patrick Ware to Christian Unity Section Staff Team, Feb. 20, 1973 (RG 5, box 14); Minutes of the NCCC General Board, Dec. 2, 1972, 12–13, NCCC-NO. Quotation from NCCC press release, March 1, 1973 (RG 15, box 4).

24. Interview with Chris Cowap; Minutes, NCCC Governing Board, Nov. 11, 1977, Claire Randall to Cong. Daniel J. Flood, Nov. 16, 1977, and Minutes of DCS Unit Committee, March 17–18, 1980, 9–21, all in JFW Files, DCS, NCCC-NO; Thomas M. Shapiro, *Population Control Politics: Women, Sterilization and Reproductive Choice* (Philadelphia: Temple University Press, 1985), 137, 197–99.

25. Opponents of the NCCC's liberal stance have criticized the sub-units' lack of accountability to the general board. See K. L. Billingsley, *From Mainline to Sideline: The Social Witness of the National Council of Churches* (Washington, D.C.: Ethics and Public Policy Center, 1990).

26. Peggy Billings et al. to Sisters, April 16, 1975, and Peggy Billings, "Memorandum of Concern. Re: Harassment of Women's Movement," April 14, 1975, both in Commission on Women in Ministry Files, NCCC-NO (hereafter COWIM Files); "Groups Hit 'Antiwomen' FBI Tactics," *Boston Globe,* May 4, 1975.

27. Minutes, Unit Committee, DCS, May 8, 1975, 4, DCS Files, NCCC-NO; "Church Women, Feminists Fight FBI Harassment," *Minneapolis Tribune,* June 9, 1975; Susan Savell to Sisters and Brothers, July 10, 1975, COWIM Files; Richard Harris, "Annals of Law," *The New Yorker,* April 19, 1976, 42–97.

28. Minutes, Executive Committee, DCS, Dec. 15, 1976, 2, and JFW Program Area, Annual Program Reports to DCS Program Planning and Evaluating Council, July 1979, July 1980, both in JFW Files, NCCC-NO; Sara Maitland, *A Map of the New Country: Women and Christianity* (Boston: Routledge and Kegan Paul, 1983), 92–93; Joan Martin, "Speaking Out from a Black Perspective," *The Church Woman* 44 (Nov. 1978): 11–13.

29. JFW Program Area, Annual Program Reports to DCS Program Planning and Evaluating Council, July 1979, July 1980, JFW Files, NCCC-NO.

30. NCCC press release, June 9, 1972, RG 15, box 4, NCCC Records, Presbyterian Historical Society; "Emily Gibbes Receives Award at New York University," *The Church Woman* 44 (March 1978): 36, 53. The following are in the COWIM Files: Burnice Fjellman, "COWIM: How It All Began," July 1978; Burnice Fjellman to Friend, Oct. 29, 1973; and NCCC, Professional Church Leadership, COWIM, Proceedings, Sept. 30–Oct. 1, 1974.

31. Organization for COWIM, March 17, 1975, COWIM Files; Fjellman, "COWIM: How It All Began"; Summary of Proceedings, COWIM meeting, Sept. 30–Oct. 2, 1974, 7, 10, COWIM Files; untitled announcement of Service in Celebration of Women in Ministry,

Oct. 27, 1974, COWIM Files; Minutes of the NCCC Governing Board, March 4–6, 1975, NCCC-NO.

32. Minutes, Unit Committee, Division of Education and Ministry (hereafter DEM), Oct. 10–11, 1974, 3, DEM Records, NCCC-NO; Organization for COWIM, March 17, 1975, COWIM Files; Summary of Proceedings, COWIM meeting, Feb. 5–7, 1975, 3–4, and Oct. 6–8, 1975, 3–4, 5, 10, COWIM Files; "Event Will Assess Job Outlook for Minority Women in Ministry," *NCCC Chronicles* 78 (Spring 1978): 7; "Unique Event Gathers Minority Churchwomen," *NCCC Chronicles* 78 (Summer 1978): 7.

33. On inter-racial work among religious women, see, for example, Evelyn Brooks Higginbotham, *Righteous Discontent: The Women's Movement in the Black Baptist Church, 1880–1920* (Cambridge: Harvard University Press, 1993), 88–119; Jacquelyn Dowd Hall, *Revolt against Chivalry: Jessie Daniel Ames and the Women's Campaign against Lynching,* rev. ed. (New York: Columbia University Press, 1993), 66, 163; Susan Lynn, *Progressive Women in Conservative Times: Racial Justice, Peace, and Feminism, 1945 to the 1960s* (New Brunswick: Rutgers University Press, 1992), 65; and Shannon, *Just Because,* 116–37.

34. Report on COWIM meetings, Oct. 6–8, 1975, Oct. 3–4, 18–20, 1976, 2, and Susan Savell to Sisters and Brothers, March 15, 1975, both in COWIM Files.

35. The following are in the COWIM Files: summary of COWIM meetings, Feb. 5–7, 1975, 2, Oct. 6–8, 1975, 4, 7, Feb. 16–18, 1976, 3, 5, Oct. 18–20, 1976, 1, 3, Oct. 25–27, 1978, 5–7, March 21–23, 1979; Patricia E. Farris to Mai Gray, Sept. 11, 1979; Linda Brebner to Sisters, Sept. 19, 1979; and summary of COWIM meeting, Oct. 25–27, 1978, 5–7.

36. The following are in the COWIM Files: summary of COWIM meetings, Oct. 18–20, 1976, 1–2, Oct. 25–27, 1978, 3; Burnice Fjellman to William Holladay, Oct. 24, 1977; and *COWIM Communicator,* Dec. 17, 1979, 1.

37. *The Church Woman* 49 (Winter 1983–84): 34; Letty M. Russell, ed., *The Liberating Word: A Guide to Nonsexist Interpretation of the Bible* (Philadelphia: Westminster Press, 1976), 89, 120.

38. Statement of Members of the Task Force on Biblical Translation, June 12, 1980, 6, 7–8, 10, DEM Records, NCCC-NO.

39. Russell, *The Liberating Word,* 107–8; Task Force on Sexism in the Bible, June 3–4, 1975, DEM Records, NCCC-NO; Phyllis Trible, "The Pilgrim Bible," in *We Belong Together: Churches in Solidarity with Women,* ed. Sarah Cunningham (New York: Friendship Press, 1992), 15–16. For other examples of the passion that Christian women felt about sexism in the Bible, see Maitland, *A Map of the New Country,* chapter 6; and Nelle Morton, *The Journey Is Home* (Boston: Beacon Press, 1985).

40. Russell, *The Liberating Word,* 15, 89–93; Minutes of the Unit Committee, DEM, Dec. 8–9, 1976, 10–11, and Report, Task Force on Sexism in the Bible, June 1–2, 1977, both in the DEM Records, NCCC-NO.

41. *NCCC Chronicles* 1 (Summer 1975): 7; Task Force on Sexism in the Bible, June 3–4, 1975, DEM Records, NCCC-NO.

42. Report of the RSV Bible Committee to the meeting of the DEM Unit Committee, Dec. 8–9, 1976, and Minutes, Unit Committee, Dec. 8–9, 1976, both in the DEM Records, NCCC-NO.

43. The following are in the DEM Records, NCCC-NO: Minutes, Unit Committee, DEM, June 1–2, 1977, 14–16; COWIM Steering Committee, meeting notes, June 3, 1977, 8;

Report of the Task Force on Issues of Biblical Translation, May 9, 1979, 1–3, 6–8; and Minutes, Unit Committee, DEM, Nov. 16, 1979, 3–7. In the late 1970s the RSVB committee had just one female member.

44. The following are in the DEM Records, NCCC-NO: Report of the Task Force on Issues of Biblical Translation, May 9, 1980, 8–10; Statement of Members of the Task Force on Biblical Translation, June 12, 1980; Minutes of Unit Committee, DEM, June 12, 1980, 14–19; and Minutes of the Unit Committee, DEM, Nov. 25, 1980, 8–20.

45. *NCCC Chronicles* 80 (Fall 1980): 1, 7; *New York Times,* Oct. 16, 1983, 27. The following are in the DEM Records, NCCC-NO: D. E. & M. Lectionary Project, n.d. [ca. early 1981]; Questions and Answers on Inclusive Biblical Language, n.d.; and Inclusive Language Lectionary Committee, n.d.

46. *New York Times,* Nov. 12, 1983, 24; *United Press International,* Dec. 2, 1983, July 13, 1984; *Time,* Oct. 24, 1983, 57; *New York Times,* Nov. 12, 1983, 24; Allen Kratz, "Inclusive Language Lectionary," *Nor'easter* (Dec. 1983): 15.

47. *The Record,* April 25, 1987, C14; *Los Angeles Times,* May 27, 1989.

48. Theressa Hoover, *With Unveiled Face: Centennial Reflections on Women and Men in the Community of the Church* (New York: Women's Division, General Board of Global Ministries, The United Methodist Church, 1983), 34.

PART 2

Religion, Modernity, and the Protestant Domestic Strategy

THE STORY OF women and religion is inextricably bound up with the history of the family. Domestic piety was at the center of late-nineteenth and early twentieth-century Protestant culture, reflecting the depth of its assurance in the moral and spiritual superiority of women. As guardians of the home, middle-class women even managed to forge a strong social presence, arguing for greater political and economic power in the name of "home protection." Despite the obvious limitations of this strategy, it proved surprisingly durable, adapting to a variety of cultural settings. Rumi Yasutake's essay on the Japanese Woman's Christian Temperance Union illustrates the way in which "home protection" served different purposes in American, Japanese, and Japanese-American society.

But by the turn of the century, the intrinsic ties between morality and domesticity had begun to fray. A new marital ideal, which emphasized emotional and sexual companionship, gradually replaced the older Victorian model with its strict gender categories and respect for duty and authority. Parents also had to contend with an emerging youth culture, oriented toward commercialism and the rapidly growing secular marketplace of pleasure and entertainment. The home ceded ground to other social institutions as well: hospitals and doctors cared for the sick, public schools educated children, and merchandisers furnished ready-made clothing and food.

Protestant churches adapted to the new family model with some difficulty, for they had long relied on a domestic strategy to teach religion to children and to press for moral reforms. But, as Christopher Coble's essay on the Christian Endeavor movement demonstrates, new institutions stepped in to fill the void. Christian Endeavor in effect took over the religious role of Protestant mothers, training young people in the traditional faith while also introducing them to the new ways of the twentieth century, in particular the new more relaxed forms of social interaction between the sexes and the "emancipation of youth" from the supervisory gaze of parents.

Auxiliary parachurch organizations took on greater importance in Protestant institutional culture as the century progressed. As Colleen McDannell's description of Focus on the Family suggests, they have also grown in sophistication, harnessing the modern communications revolution in the service of "family values," and, McDannell argues, easily accommodating styles of language and interaction that feminist scholars have identified as "women's ways of knowing."

The three essays in this section sketch the outlines of a broad transformation in the religious role of women as it has been mediated through the family. In many ways, the Protestant domestic strategy looks remarkably intact— some of the home protection rhetoric from the Woman's Christian Temperance Union has certainly survived in Focus on the Family. But in other ways, it is clearly obsolete. The moral and social power of the family and Protestant motherhood have been parcelled out to other institutions, both religious and secular. The reasons behind these changes, and the historical shape of their unfolding, are still open for investigation.

4. The Role of Young People's Societies in the Training of Christian Womanhood (and Manhood), 1880–1910

CHRISTOPHER COBLE

ACCORDING TO 1906 U.S. census statistics, a dramatic increase in church membership took place during the last decades of the nineteenth century. Yet in spite of a generally optimistic outlook on church growth, Protestant church leaders noted with concern the indifference among young people toward church attendance.[1] Children, they lamented, filled Sunday school classrooms but disappeared around age thirteen or fourteen.[2] Thomas Chalmers, a well-known pastor from Brooklyn, voiced that worry: "The Sunday-school was a quite vigorous operation, but there was no link which joined it to the church. There came a time in the life of every youth when he considered himself too big for Sunday-school and not yet old enough to acquiesce in the somber regime of a full-fledged Christian. There was a wide desert through which the waters of Christianity and church life had to run, and there was considerable leakage away into the sands of sin and indifference."[3]

Young people, it seemed, fell into a gap between the Sunday school and the church; they were too old for the childish activities of the Sunday school but not ready to enter the adult world of the congregation. Francis Clark, a Congregational pastor in Portland, Maine, noted with alarm that "while the parents may be at the church to save the respectability of the family, the children are anywhere and everywhere else. They are out riding or walking, or are sleeping at home, or reading a flash newspaper or exciting novel."[4] The concern about the absence of children and young people was compounded by the admission that many pastors were unsure what to do with the young even when they did attend. The emerging conventional wisdom of the period recognized that young people were in a deeply impressionable and critical period of life. If the church did not capture them at this time, they might be lost forever. Religious leaders faced a pressing question: How could the churches attract, nurture, train, and finally incorporate young people into membership?

One answer was young people's societies. The two largest, the Young People's Society of Christian Endeavor and the Epworth League of the Methodist Episcopal Church, counted more than 4.9 million members in 1899, equivalent to 25 percent of the total membership in Protestant churches. Founded in 1881 by Francis Clark, by 1899 Christian Endeavor claimed more than 3.3 million members in 55,813 local societies representing thirty denominations and seventy-five countries. The societies became the primary vehicle for the religious formation of young people and in the process challenged older forms of piety, working to reform and enliven the "somber regime of a full-fledged Christian."[5]

Many of these reforms focused specifically on gender expectations. Societies strove to open opportunities for women, capture their considerable energies, and expand their opportunities for leadership in the churches. By encouraging and channeling the piety of the young women, they hoped likewise to inspire the young men to emulation.

Closing the Gap: Young People's Societies' Strategy for Religious Formation and Training

While they bemoaned the gap between the Sunday school and church membership, Protestant leaders at the end of the nineteenth century also examined the shortcomings of existing strategies for recruiting, training, and incorporating new members. Such strategies came out of the revival tradition and assumed the necessity of an individual experience of conversion. Depicted most vividly in the techniques of Charles Finney, old-style revivalism centered in a religious and psychological crisis in which potential converts recognized their state of sinfulness and depravity, realized their dependence on God's grace, and made a life-changing decision to follow Christ. Conversion was marked by a movement from hopelessness to joy and resulted in an utterly transformed life. In this scheme at its strictest, the conversion experience was also a prerequisite for church membership.

The conversion strategy had direct consequences for child-rearing practices.[6] Godly parents were to teach children about their sinful nature and prepare them for a conversion experience in early adulthood.[7] Children, in essence, were in a holding pattern outside the church until they achieved that pivotal, transformative experience. The revival tradition targeted young people; not surprisingly, most conversions in the early part of the nineteenth century occurred in the teenage years, much earlier than the average age in the previous century.[8] This pattern persisted into the turn of the century, when Edwin Starbuck, in a seminal study of religious conversion, found that almost all conversions occurred between the ages of thirteen and twenty-five and almost never outside that range.[9] In the most desirable scenario, children experienced a religious conversion in their later Sunday school years and entered church membership in due course. In such cases, conversion represented a rite of passage from childhood to adulthood.[10] The interval between the time a child completed Sunday school and joined a church was understood as a period of waiting for the work of the Spirit, during which pastors and parents constantly reminded young people of their precarious state before God.

By mid-century, this revival strategy had come under increasing criticism, and a second strategy of Christian growth became dominant in many Protestant churches.[11] Reversing the emphasis on the innate depravity of children, critics of the revival strategy instead stressed the innocence and beauty of this period of life.[12] Childhood was to be celebrated and prolonged, and child-rearing was to be accomplished within a protected environment where children could develop moral character and practice the virtues and skills necessary for the adult world.

Articulated most clearly in Horace Bushnell's definitive work *Christian Nurture,* this strategy of Christian growth emphasized the necessity of raising children within an environment of love. Bushnell's well-known charge that "a child is to grow up a Christian and never know himself otherwise" was the centerpiece of this understanding.[13] Instead of keeping a child outside the church in preparation for a conversion experience, Christian growth focused on maintaining an environment in which the child would grow up practicing virtues necessary for developing Christian character.[14] The responsibility for religious formation was placed on parents, specifically the mother, and the primary location was the home. According to Bushnell, parents created an environment in which children, surrounded by Christian virtues, need never undergo a traumatic religious experience. The goal was to create a seamless path from birth in the home to adulthood in the church.

This strategy of Christian growth meshed easily with the domestic ideology of separate spheres and its sharp separation between the private sphere of the home and the public sphere of business and politics.[15] The home, presided over by women, was a refuge from the fierce world of commerce, a moral environment for the formation of character, and a base for work in the world. Not surprisingly, the home thus defined easily became the primary location for religious formation—the church, in many ways, secondary. Domestic ideology, together with the strategy of Christian nurture, emphasized the need for parents to maintain stronger, more enduring religious and economic oversight over their children. This control became both feasible and necessary as, within the emerging industrial society, the size of families decreased, particularly in the new middle-class, and families sought to delay the age of children's entry into the work force so that they could be prepared for better-paying, more prestigious careers.[16]

By the last decades of the nineteenth century, the domestic model and its allied strategy of Christian growth had come under increasing criticism. A growing number of religious leaders worried about an increasing "indifference" to church attendance among young people and traced that apathy to the pressures placed on families and churches by the advancing industrial and urban revolution. Although warnings against religious declension have been constant in American religious life over the centuries, those who sounded the alarm in the late nineteenth century correctly assumed that the vast social and economic changes of their time were having far-reaching impacts on the family, congregational life, and the religious nurture of the young.

At the end of the century, middle-class families found themselves in an ironic situation: They were smaller and more intimate but had less control over the economic fortunes and the religious formation of their members. One pressure on families resulted from a shift in the market economy from entrepreneurial capitalism, which involved small businesses and partnerships, to a consumer, corporate culture that rested on large, bureaucratic corporations.[17] The displacement of small businesses and shops changed styles of work as middle-class workers became white-collar clerks and career tracks were made routine. When entry-level jobs became increasingly standardized, families lost much influence over the career trajectories of their children. At the same time, an increasing number of clubs, department stores, and entertainment opportunities—many aimed at women and young people— competed for their leisure hours.[18] Pastors complained that parents had lost control of the religious training of children. As Francis Clark warned, "We in this generation are just beginning to feel the evil effects of this loose family government and home training in regard to church-going. The generation immediately preceding ours slackened the reins, and the empty pews in many churches show that the young colts have run away."[19]

A second pressure on the traditional domestic strategy was ideological and arose from the gathering strength of the woman suffrage and prohibition movements in the late nineteenth century. As Susan B. Anthony, Elizabeth Cady Stanton, and other radical leaders pushed publicly for the recognition of women's rights, the Woman's Christian Temperance Union (WCTU) organized women into a powerful political force for prohibition and other social goals. Frances Willard, the leader of the WCTU, particularly encouraged other women to speak publicly for religious and political causes and in so doing push the limits of traditional gender restrictions.

Another pressure on families and their efforts at religious nurture arose from a growing confidence in scientific methods and a corresponding "rise of experts" who cast doubt on the "natural" child-raising abilities of wives and mothers.[20] In 1890 Thaddeaus Wakeman, a social critic, acknowledged the power of science when he answered the question "What is the American creed?" in these words: "The answer is, that which he knows to be true,— and that, in one word is *Science.* The majority of the American people are already *practically secularists*—people of this world. . . . Our people are unconsciously welcoming the incoming sway of the Science of Man; and this is proved by their absence from the Churches."[21]

The new positivist scientific method systematically addressed all areas of life and was articulated by "experts" who presided over bodies of knowledge in their fields, ranging from medicine and social work to business management, homemaking, and child-rearing. Frances Willard celebrated the resulting rise of "scientific motherhood": "Children will be born of set purpose and will cut their teeth according to a plan. The empirical maxims and old wives' fables of the nursery will give way to the hard-earned results of scientific investigation. The best work of the mother will be intelligently done, on the basis of heredity, pre-natal influence, and devout obedience to the laws of health."[22] No longer revered for their innate abilities and natural instincts, women— particularly mothers—now needed to learn the craft of "domestic science."[23]

The experts challenged and complicated the old domestic ideology. In effect, in arguing that outside specialists needed to intervene in the home and assist parents in the education and formation of children, they questioned the home's centrality. "Facts" and expertise now superseded its former God-given authority. G. Stanley Hall as well as other pioneers in the field of "child-study" identified specific developmental stages and tasks for children and in the process worked to standardize the process of maturation. Compulsory education laws ensured that all children would attend school and receive a common educational experience—again, standardizing the process of socialization into the American way of life and removing it from the home.[24] By the end of the century, parents theoretically retained major responsibility for raising their children, but in fact they now shared this task with experts and government agencies.

Protestant leaders, recognizing the growing weakness of families, increasingly pointed to the failure of the home-based strategy of Christian growth to incorporate young people into churches. A key element of the criticism was that the Christian growth strategy never encouraged—or forced—young people to decide to follow a Christian life.[25] Ironically, that criticism echoed the earlier revivalist invocations of crisis in the lives of young people, but this time the expectation was endorsed and shaped by experts. The pioneering psychological studies of Edwin Starbuck and G. Stanley Hall defined adolescence as a distinctive period in human development, a time of crisis and a search for significant commitments. As Starbuck's classic study of religious conversion concluded, "There is a normal period between the innocence of childhood and the fixed habits of maturity, while the person is yet impressionable and has already the capacity for spiritual insight when conversions most frequently occur."[26] "The whole future of life," Hall wrote, "depends on how the new powers now given suddenly and in profusion are husbanded and directed."[27] Young people, according to the experts, were in a critical period of life, a period marked by hope and danger.

Yet churches were failing to take advantage of this period in the lives of youths to capture their imaginations, elicit a commitment to the Christian life, or direct their energies toward the work of the church. Rufus Miller, addressing the International Convention of Christian Endeavor in 1893, summed up the attitude of many church leaders: "The church must meet the changed conditions of modern life and the new phases of our aggressive civilization. The family is no longer the sole channel through which the church can reach the world."[28] Leaders argued that the churches needed a new strategy to close the gap between childhood and adulthood. A great deal was at stake. If they could succeed in harnessing the "new powers" of youth, then young people would become the leading edge of the revitalization and renewal of Protestant churches.

Within this changed social and cultural context, Christian Endeavor, along with other young people's societies based on the Endeavor model, developed several common methods. First, they introduced a model of religious formation that used the strongest aspects both of the revival and Christian nurture strategies.[29] The societies established a segregated, insulated space for the religious nurture of young people. Young people also learned specific skills, from leading prayer meetings to organizing community-service activities.[30] But Christian Endeavor also re-introduced elements of the revival tradition. Each person who joined a society had to take the Christian Endeavor pledge. In signing that pledge, members promised to participate in all meetings, engage in daily devotions, support the local church, and judge all their actions by the standard of their commitment to Christ.[31] Signing the pledge was intended as a resolution to religious crisis, compelling a clear commitment to follow a Christian life. Thus, the societies did everything they could to capture and direct the energies of young people during a pivotal period in their lives.

Young people's societies also served as a "stepping-stone" between the home, the realm of childhood, and the adult world of the church. Ideally, youths would move from the child-centered lessons of the Sunday school to the youth-centered activities of the societies, and finally into the adult-oriented work of the church. Paralleling trends in secular education, the three-step process was intended to standardize the religious experience of young people and establish a common path into church membership.

Christian Endeavor societies also provided a strategy for reinvigorating the somewhat passive forms of traditional piety. Endeavor leaders believed that young people were a "latent force" within many local congregations, largely untapped because church life was so often "cold and dry." If youths could cultivate a piety that would direct their energies toward good works, they would be the leaven for revitalizing the adult church.[32] Following that logic, Endeavor societies gave young people specific tasks to perform and emphasized participation, activism, and transdenominational cooperation.

The rapid expansion of young peoples' societies at the turn of the century indicated that their strategy for attracting and holding youth in the churches was succeeding. The growth in numbers suggests that, to a large extent, societies did manage to attract and form three generations of Protestant youths. But there was a cost for mothers—their displacement as primary religious nurturers for sons and daughters. The home was no longer the primary location for the formation and training of the young; that site had shifted to an age-specific society within a local church.[33] While mothers still carried the major responsibility for the religious formation of younger children, they shared this task with the church once adolescence was reached.[34] What made that significant was the conviction that youth—and not childhood—was the most critical period for nurture and training. Thus, mothers no longer controlled the key moments of religious formation but yielded responsibility for that task to "experts," specifically pastors, adult lay leaders, and even other young people.[35]

The Role of Young People's Societies in Reforming Gender Roles and Expectations

Developing Women's Leadership

A fundamental principle of Christian Endeavor was that, contrary to earlier nineteenth-century practices, young women and men should pray, work, and play together.[36] Addressing the delegates of the 1887 Christian Endeavor convention, Annie Hill articulated the logic of this principle:

There have been for many years Christian organizations for young men only, prayer-meetings for young ladies only, reform societies for men, and similar organizations for women; but the difficulty with all has been that they are distinctively for the one or the other. There has not been sufficient recognition of the necessity of a common ground of labor within and as a part of the church. . . . It is in accordance with the Creator's own laws that [men and women] should work together. This has been recognized and used as a fundamental principle in the Societies of Christian Endeavor. We believe that in Jesus Christ there is neither male nor female; that . . . all work together, so, in the life that concerns our best selves, we should work hand in hand.[37]

Hill's words reflected the underlying theological commitment of Christian Endeavor: Women and men are created equal, and the truest expression of the Christian faith demands the full participation of both.

Hill also indicated Endeavor's indebtedness to the ideology of female reform leaders such as Frances Willard, who often appeared at Christian Endeavor conventions and wrote a weekly column for the movement's publication.[38] Francis Clark, in reflecting on the success of the movement, remarked, "One of the glories of the Christian Endeavor movement is . . . that it brings together young men and women in an equality of service . . . and that the society is not complete, and cannot as a rule do its best work, if composed of only one sex."[39] Thus, Christian Endeavor societies were based on a theological commitment to gender mutuality already fundamental to the larger world of reform movements like the Woman's Christian Temperance Union.

This basic commitment to equality also dictated the everyday work of Endeavor societies, as recorded in carefully kept notebooks from local societies. Both young women and men took the same pledge and made the promise to participate in the society's meetings. Endeavor rules required both sexes to speak at weekly prayer meetings and to alternate leadership. Young men and women took turns chairing committees, organizing meetings, and leading the work of the society, and they shared all duties, privileges, and responsibilities. The only exception was that young women were discouraged from holding the office of president, but local notebooks demonstrate that this injunction was often ignored.

The influence of these practices was striking. Speaking in 1893 before the World's Congress Auxiliary at the Columbian Exposition, Alice Scudder described the impact for women within churches: "No organization intrusted to the church has done more for the development of woman than has the Christian Endeavor Society." Scudder explained:

Christian Endeavor has removed the conventionalities of the past, and woman may rise to the religious privileges of her brother. No longer must she sit in silence and hear, "Thus far shalt thou go and no farther"; no longer need she find her highest church attainment in arranging tableaux and passing ice-cream, but rather she is expected to exert her positive influences. The church expects her to use her talents. . . . Thanks be to Christian Endeavor, which counts woman more than a cipher in the religious gatherings of the church, and which has removed forever the thought of her as one of the "lowest of all God's creatures."[40]

Women were expected—and required—to develop and use their skills in all areas of church life, including speaking publicly and leading prayer meetings. The ultimate goal of pushing women into church leadership roles was clear. Elbert Russell, a leading Quaker scholar and Endeavor supporter, noted, "The time is coming, through [Christian Endeavor's] influence, when the churches can no longer exclude from the ministry of Christ those who have shown in Endeavor meetings such pre-eminent fitness for service. The young men who have grown up, performing service side-by-side [with] . . . their Endeavor sisters, will not find it in their hearts to deny them a share in the larger work of the church."[41] With the societies emphasizing mutuality and equality, the full ordination of women seemed only a short distance away.

Although reports about Christian Endeavor justly celebrated the advancement of women within churches, the actual results were more mixed, in part because critics from outside Endeavor exercised a subtle—sometimes not so subtle—influence on the society's practice. External criticism came, not surprisingly, from traditionalists who charged that requiring young women to lead public prayer meetings was both inappropriate and unchristian. Citing St. Paul's admonition in his letter to the Corinthians that women remain silent in worship, critics argued that Endeavor practices were unscriptural and pushed for women to remain under the authority of men within the church.

The admonitions took their toll. Although, theoretically, women enjoyed full equality with men, they were often limited by an early form of the "glass ceiling" in the national leadership of the Endeavor movement. Women were allowed, and in fact encouraged, to hold all offices in local societies, yet trustees and senior leaders at the national level were almost entirely men, as were most platform speakers at conventions. The notable exception was that women received national leadership responsibilities for Endeavor's work with junior societies composed of pre-teenaged children, a division of labor that reinforced traditional domestic patterns. This pattern remained unchanged until the national restructuring of the movement in the 1910s. Under the new model that resulted, field secretaries helped organize and lead the work of Endeavor at the regional level. Both young men and women filled these positions equally, thus providing an avenue for advancing women's leadership within the national movement.[42]

The more damaging resistance arose not from external critics but from the young women themselves. Some of them, at least initially, were reluctant to speak publicly or take positions of leadership in mixed-sex prayer meetings.[43] In a few societies, women were willing to speak but refused to chair prayer meetings. In response, Endeavor leaders stressed over and over the importance of full participation by every member at prayer meetings and in the work of the society; participation, they urged, was a key to spiritual growth both for the speaker and the listener. Endeavor even developed literature designed to encourage all members, particularly women, to speak publicly in meetings. As Endeavor leader Emily Wheeler summed up the argument, "If the love of Christ is within you, if you are full of Christ's spirit and are praying for those around you, you cannot be silent. . . . If you really know Christ, you will long to let others know how grand and beautiful a thing it is to have Christ as an intimate friend."[44]

Endeavor literature even presented a stepped strategy for building confidence and encouraging participation. A member would move from the simple recitation of a scripture or hymn verse, to reading a short written prayer, to finally speaking extemporaneously about faith in Christ. Minutes from meetings of local societies diligently charted attendance and participation. Although rarely claiming complete participation, these minutes noted that most Endeavor members, including women, fulfilled their obligations and spoke at the weekly prayer meetings. Yet the resistance revealed the difficulty women experienced in moving beyond deeply ingrained gender habits.

The results of Endeavor's efforts to open opportunities for women in Christian leadership within the church were, of course, less than revolutionary. The societies introduced young women, as well as men, to new possibilities for leadership. Through Christian Endeavor, many women were able to break new ground and participate more fully in the work of local churches. Some undoubtedly surprised themselves with their boldness and their unexpected abilities. They spoke publicly, led mixed-sex prayer meetings, and organized and executed mission projects beside their Christian brothers. Young women clearly made significant gains, but these stopped short of complete equality. The power of the domestic ideology, it appears, still set the limits on such opportunities. All the same, gender arrangements had started to undergo major alterations in an important—and formative—area of American Protestant life.

Christian Marriage

Christian marriage was inevitably a major concern—actually, an obsession—within the Christian Endeavor movement. Endeavor leaders had good reasons for their preoccupation. Some estimates suggested that at least one-third of members married a person whom they had met at a society prayer meeting or event.[45] Reflecting that reality, Christian Endeavor was dubbed "Courting Endeavor" and accused of maintaining a "flirtation society" where young people were motivated by lust rather than religious growth. Endeavor leaders bristled at this suggestion but still took pains to point out that youth societies—where young women and men worshipped, met under the supervision of a pastor, and grew in "affection through Christian work"—were excellent places to meet a future spouse.[46] The societies were one of the few places where respectable young Christians of both sexes were allowed to mix freely and work closely together on mutual projects. From a parent's perspective, the groups were protected, supervised spaces where sons and daughters could meet and interact with other eligible young people. Thus, the expectation that Endeavor would and should steer young people toward matrimony encouraged leaders to address the topic of Christian marriage at every opportunity.

The Endeavor ideal of Christian marriage reflected the movement's fundamental theological commitment to gender equality. Christian marriage was a covenant between two "equally consecrated" individuals and rested upon a mutual commitment to Jesus Christ.[47] Accordingly, the ideal marriage consisted of an equal relationship between a man and woman pursuing a common life in Christ. When in 1903 the *Christian Endeavor World* asked readers whether they thought a wife should promise to obey in a marriage ceremony, the response was an emphatic "Never!" "The ideal married life," one member wrote, "is never inspired by a sense of inequality, but rather of perfect equality and equal rights, by harmony and a life-journey sweetened by loving helpfulness." Other members asserted, "Man and woman are created equal," and "the husband and wife will serve each other, spurred by love, the gift of God, sole ruler in their hearts and home."[48]

The stress on equality in marriage had direct implications for the selection of an ideal spouse. Endeavor publications warned young women against marrying a man in order to reform him; a man who had bad habits at marriage would likely only keep them.[49] They also urged young women to resist marrying anyone who was not a committed Christian. This dramatic lesson was played out in *Chrissy's Endeavor,* a novel about a local Endeavor society and promoted widely by the movement's leaders. In the story, the heroine, Chrissy, goes against her parents' wishes and turns down a proposal from the most sought-after bachelor in town because he does not share her commitment to Christ. Instead, she marries a plain but deeply religious man, and they share a wonderful life together.[50] The Endeavor message was clear: The primary criterion for a spouse is a person who shares a commitment to Jesus.

Endeavor leaders pushed women, whether married or single, not to be satisfied with a life confined within older domestic constraints but to use their talents in all areas. "Let it take a great deal to satisfy you," they challenged young women. "Do not count yourself to have reached the sum total of human bliss, and to have achieved the *sole raison* for feminine existence as soon as you have secured a husband and a home of your very own. . . . Do not be satisfied if your brother, or father, or husband leaves you outside many of his interests. Have a hand and a heart for everything."[51] Endeavor literature positively portrayed young women who resisted love and family demands in order to pursue a life of Christian service.[52] These messages to young women came through strongly within the local societies, which reinforced their verbal messages by providing the space for women to practice a wide variety of leadership skills.

In the end, although Endeavor training challenged many traditional expectations it never completely replaced older domestic ideals. The stress on equality worked to modify the sharp distinction between female and male spheres, but the belief that women and men had different innate qualities persisted. The uneasy mix between traditional domestic expectations and new opportunities for women was most visible in descriptions of the ideal spouse. Young men were urged to seek out women who were capable, sweet-tempered, good housekeepers, in complete sympathy with a husband's goals, and able to create a loving atmosphere at home. Young women were advised to find a man who was a good provider, possessed good habits, had a gentle and affectionate nature, exhibited bravery and truthfulness, and was a comforter and helpmate.[53] On the surface, this description of ideal spousal qualities did not reveal much change from the mid-nineteenth century. Yet beneath the conventional prescription was the expectation of a marriage based on a partnership and mutual work. The ideal Endeavor relationship was both equal and complementary.

Endeavor leaders made explicit challenges to young Christian women. "You have a contribution to make," Francis Clark declared, "a peculiar and unique contribution, simply because you are a woman. God has given you these qualities, not simply that you may make yourself attractive, that you may win a husband or a home or some position in the business or professional work which women can fill; but He has given them to you that you may use them for Him."[54] True women possessed special characteristics of "refinement, spiritual grace, and delicacy of thought." But they also needed to use these gifts in unconventional ways and not allow traditional domestic constraints to limit them. Thus, the true Christian woman was gentle and patient as well as independent, self-sufficient, and courageous.

Along with a new womanhood, Christian Endeavor also presented an alternative ideal of Christian manhood. The new ideal still emphasized the traditional male virtues of strength, bravery, and chivalry. It also encouraged young men to cultivate qualities previously considered part of the feminine sphere, including gentleness and a deep sensitivity to others. More significantly, Endeavor literature identified piety as a manly characteristic; men—not women—were believed to have the potential for the deepest faith. That sentiment was articulated clearly and forcefully by the heroine of *Chrissy's Endeavor:* "I have often thought that young men, of all others, ought to be Christians, because Jesus Christ was a young man, you know, and they would be in intimate fellowship with him in a sense that none others could."[55] The ability to establish that type of relationship with Jesus set men apart and signaled that they were—or could become—more pious than women.

Christian Endeavor taught women and men to form marriages based on mutuality and centered on a common life in Christ. Traditional roles were to be abandoned when they did not serve that purpose. At the same time, Endeavor teachings maintained the distinctive qualities of women and men, and the descriptions of an ideal spouse continued to follow traditional patterns. The truth was that the distinctions were blurring, with the result that the roles of Christian womanhood and manhood were shifting markedly—not as fast as some leaders wished but shifting nonetheless.

A Piety for the Twentieth Century

Many threads may be woven together to describe the piety that was taught to Endeavor young people and carried into the churches in the twentieth century. Most fundamentally, this piety required a life-defining commitment to follow Jesus Christ. The act of signing the Christian Endeavor pledge established a filter through which all future activities would be judged. The importance of this personal decision was articulated most sharply in the leading question of Charles Sheldon's popular novel *In His Steps:* "What would Jesus do?"[56]

The common pledge to Jesus Christ defined the style of piety in several ways. First, it established a basis for equality between young women and men. Both signed the pledge and were expected to fulfill the responsibilities inherent in their commitment to Christ. Second, the pledge challenged traditional gender restrictions. When such restrictions blocked the full expression of the pledge (or promise to follow Christ), then they were to be abandoned. The piety of the Christian Endeavor movement thus offered a critique of traditional gender expectations and a guide to evaluating alternatives. Third, the style of piety stressed activism. Whether participating in a prayer meeting, organizing a church social, or carrying out a service project in the local community, Christian faith was to be expressed continuously both in word and deed. Countering the passive tone of the mid-nineteenth-century prayer meeting, Christian Endeavor's mark of true faith lay not in gesture or language primarily but in an eagerness to engage in acts of service. Finally, Protestant faith within the scope of the Endeavor movement took on a particularly ecumenical character. Although young people's societies respected denominational differences, the common commitment cut across doctrinal disagreements and helped define the basis for cooperative mission among Protestant churches.

Although the long-term influence of Christian Endeavor and other similar young people's societies is hard to gauge, its immediate impact on Protestant churches is easy enough to detect. The number of Endeavor societies continued to multiply throughout the first decades of the twentieth century. A wide range of prominent Protestant and American leaders, including Fred Smith and John Dewey, would report the significance of their early training in Christian Endeavor. In the early part of the twentieth century, young people's societies such as Christian Endeavor were a pervasive feature of Protestant churches, and a majority of young Protestants passed through their ranks.

Yet despite these measurements of success, significant challenges arose from several directions. In one, a countermovement of single-sex young people's societies emerged in the 1890s as a corrective to the progressive teachings of Endeavor concerning gender. Based on a conviction that Endeavor taught young men a feminine style of piety, male religious societies such as the Boys' Brigade and other societies within the broader "muscular Christianity" movement introduced a style of piety that emphasized the manly character of Christianity, attempted to create a place within churches specifically for young men, and, in the process, reinforced the essentialist characteristics of women and men.[57] A second challenge focused on an unintended consequence of Endeavor's success, the fact that many young people who were brought back into the church through Christian Endeavor were slow to move out of the societies and into positions of leadership within churches. As a result, the average age of Endeavor members crept upward, for the movement's organizational structure provided no clear exit or "graduation" points. It was never entirely clear when a young person was ready to move from the youth-centered society to the adult-oriented church.

From another direction, a group of religious educators and psychologists pushed for more age-segregated and developmentally specific groupings of children and youths. They argued that Christian Endeavor's broad mix of young people was too loose, and they deplored what they saw as a single-minded emphasis on pledge-signing.[58] For its part, Endeavor responded to this critique by organizing its societies along more specific age groupings. Yet in the process the impact of the pledge was blunted, and many societies lost their hard, activist edge.

In its heyday, however, Christian Endeavor played a key role in training Protestant young people. The societies provided a vehicle for introducing progressive ideals that challenged traditional gender roles and opened opportunities for women (and new ways for young men to define themselves) within Protestant churches. Yet the legacy of the movement is ambiguous. Although the societies pushed both young women and men to reach beyond traditional expectations, they did not expand the campaign to include wholesale change in Protestant churches. For that reason, Christian Endeavor and the various points of resistance to its progressive program reflect the complexities of women's experience within twentieth-century Protestantism—an experience that has consistently defied a simple narrative of progress.

Notes

1. According to U.S. census data, the number of Christian church members grew from 38,061 in 1850 to 161,151 in 1890, reflecting a 424 percent increase. Using information from denominational yearbooks and almanacs, the historian Daniel Dorchester found that the number of communicants in evangelical Protestant churches rose from 3,529,988 in 1850 to 10,065,963 in 1886, a 285 percent increase in membership. Despite the growth in churches and church members, many prominent pastors, such as Russell Conwell, noted many empty pews and an increasing indifference toward church attendance. For more statistical information see U.S. Bureau of the Census, *Religious Bodies: 1906* (Washington, D.C.: Government Printing Office, 1906), 23, and Daniel Dorchester, *Christianity in the United States: From the First Settlement Down to the Present Time* (New York: Hunt and Eaton, 1890), 733. See also Henry K. Carroll, *The Religious Forces of the United States: Enumerated, Classified, and Described on the Basis of the Government Census of 1890; with an Introduction on the Condition and Character of American Christianity* (New York: Christian Literature, 1893), xvii, xxxvi–xxxvii, xlvi–xlvii, lvi.

2. For a discussion of the vitality of nineteenth-century Sunday schools, see Anne Boylan, *Sunday School: The Formation of an American Institution, 1790–1880* (New Haven: Yale University Press, 1988).

3. Thomas Chalmers, *The Juvenile Revival; or, The Philosophy of the Christian Endeavor Movement* (St. Louis: Christian Publishing, 1893), 35.

4. Francis Clark, *The Children and the Church and the Young People's Society of Christian Endeavor as a Means of Bringing Them Together* (Boston: Congregational Sunday School and Publishing Society, 1882), 95–96.

5. A partial listing of young peoples' societies organized in the late nineteenth century include the Young Peoples' Society of Christian Endeavor (1881); Brotherhood of Saint Andrew (1886); Daughters of the King (1886); Brotherhood of Andrew and Philip (1888); Epworth League (1888); Baptist Young Peoples' Union (1891); International Order of King's Daughters and Sons (1891); Young Peoples' Christian Union of the United Brethren (1891); and Luther League (1895). For a fuller discussion of the formation of these groups, see Leonard Woolsey Bacon and Charles Addison Northrop, *Young People's Societies* (New York: Lentilhon, 1900), and Frank Erb, *The Development of the Young People's Movement* (Chicago: University of Chicago Press, 1917).

6. Philip Greven, *The Protestant Temperament: Patterns of Child-rearing, Religious Experience, and the Self in Early America* (Chicago: University of Chicago Press, 1977).

7. In the early nineteenth century, the focus of Sunday schools shifted from a mission to the poor to the preparation of children of church members for conversion. See Anne Boylan, *Sunday School.*

8. Joseph Kett, *Rites of Passage: Adolescence in America 1790 to Present* (New York: Basic Books, 1977), 64.

9. Edwin Starbuck, *The Psychology of Religion: An Empirical Study of the Growth of Religious Consciousness* (London: Walter Scott, 1900), 28ff.

10. Kett, *Rites of Passage,* 80ff.

11. For example, Stout and Brekus note the shift at mid-century from a strategy of revival to Christian nurture at Center Church, New Haven. Harry Stout and Catherine Brekus, "A New England Congregation: Center Church, New Haven, 1638–1989," in *American Congregations,* vol. 1: *Portraits of Twelve Religious Communities,* ed. James P. Wind and James W. Lewis (Chicago: University of Chicago Press, 1994), 28, 56.

12. The works of John Locke and Jean-Jacques Rousseau were influential in the shift in the conception of childhood. Hugh Cunningham, *Children and Childhood in Western Society since 1500* (New York: Longman, 1995), 61–70.

13. Horace Bushnell, *Christian Nurture* (1861, repr. Cleveland: Pilgrim Press, 1994), 10.

14. Bushnell, *Christian Nurture,* 100.

15. Kathryn Kish Sklar, *Catharine Beecher: A Study of American Domesticity* (New York: Norton, 1973); Colleen McDannell, *The Christian Home in Victorian America, 1840–1900* (Bloomington: Indiana University Press, 1986).

16. Stephanie Coontz, *The Social Origins of Private Life: A History of American Families, 1600–1900* (New York: Verso Press, 1988).

17. T. J. Jackson Lears, *No Place for Grace: Antimodernism and the Transformation of American Culture, 1880–1920* (Chicago: University of Chicago Press, 1981), 9.

18. Sheila Rothman, *Woman's Proper Place: A History of Changing Ideals and Practices, 1870 to Present* (New York: Basic Books, 1978), 18.

19. Clark, *The Children and the Church,* 96.

20. Barbara Ehrenreich and Deirdre English, *For Her Own Good: 150 Years of Experts' Advice to Women* (Garden City: Doubleday Anchor Books, 1979).

21. Paul F. Boller, Jr., *American Thought in Transition: The Impact of Evolutionary Naturalism* (Chicago: Rand-McNally, 1969), 120, cited in Ehrenreich and English, *For Her Own Good,* 71.

22. Frances Willard, "Address of Frances Willard, President of the National Council of the United States, at Its First Triennial Meeting, Albaugh's Opera House, Washington, D.C., February 22–25, 1891," in *Votes for Women: Selections of the National American Woman Suffrage Association Collection 1848–1921*, Rare Books Division, Library of Congress.

23. Ehrenreich and English (*For Her Own Good,* 209) describe this argument as the rise of "educated motherhood."

24. Joel H. Spring, *The American School 1642–1993* (New York: McGraw-Hill, 1994), 188.

25. Francis Clark, *Training the Church of the Future* (New York: Funk and Wagnalls, 1902); Charles McKinley, *Educational Evangelism: The Religious Discipline of Youth* (Boston: Pilgrim Press, 1905).

26. Starbuck, *The Psychology of Religion,* 35–36.

27. G. Stanley Hall, *Adolescence* (New York: D. Appleton, 1904), xv.

28. Rufus Miller, *Report of the International Convention of Christian Endeavor, Montreal, Canada, 1893* (Boston: United Society of Christian Endeavor, 1893), 60.

29. Clark, *Training the Church of the Future.*

30. Christian Endeavor societies organized their work through a committee structure. Every member in a Christian Endeavor society was required to serve on a committee. The responsibilities for committees included planning the prayer meeting, recruiting and screening new members, organizing missionary programs and projects, leading social activities, and supporting the work of the pastor. Committees were kept small, and membership rotated every six months in order to give each member a wide variety of experiences.

31. The fullest version of the Christian Endeavor pledge stated: "Trusting in the Lord Jesus Christ for strength, I promise Him that I will strive to do whatever He would like to have me do; that I will make it a rule of my life to pray and read the Bible every day, and to support my own church in every way, especially by attending all her regular Sunday and mid-week services, unless prevented by some reason which I can conscientiously give to my Saviour; and that just so far as I know how, through my whole life, I will endeavor to lead a Christian life. As an active member, I promise to be true to all my duties, to be present at and to take some part, aside from singing, in every Christian Endeavor prayer meeting, unless hindered by some reason which I can conscientiously give to my Lord and Master. If obliged to be absent from the monthly consecration meeting of the Society I will, if possible, send at least a verse of Scripture to be read in response to my name at the roll-call." Francis Clark, *The Christian Endeavor Manual* (Boston: United Society of Christian Endeavor, 1903), 58–59.

32. S. W. Adriance, *The Beginnings of the Society of Christian Endeavor* (Boston: United Society of Christian Endeavor, 1889).

33. Clark, *The Christian Endeavor Manual.*

34. In Christian Endeavor literature, parents are sometimes portrayed as antagonistic to the participation of their children in the society. Endeavor members were urged to inform parents respectfully of the importance of Endeavor work and maintain membership within the society.

35. Christian Endeavor literature suggested that mothers appreciated help in sharing the responsibility for Christian nurture. Mrs. Russell Brown, *A Mother's View of Christian Endeavor* (Indianapolis: Christian Woman's Board of Missions, n.d.).

36. For an introduction to single-sex societies, see Gail Bederman, "'The Women Have Had Charge of the Church Long Enough': The Men and Religion Forward Movement of 1911–12 and the Masculinization of Middle-Class Protestantism," *American Quarterly* 41 (Sept. 1989): 432–65.

37. Annie Hill, "Equal Duties: Ought the Young Men and Women to Share Equally in the Duties and Privileges of Our Society," *The Golden Rule,* Aug. 4, 1887, 8–9.

38. For example, Frances Willard appeared on the platform and spoke at every international convention of the Christian Endeavor movement during the 1890s. In this period, attendance at Endeavor conventions ranged between thirty thousand and fifty-six thousand registered delegates.

39. The statement makes an implicit criticism of single-sex societies. Francis Clark, "Young Men in Christian Endeavor: A Place which They Alone Can Fill," *Christian Endeavor World,* Feb. 12, 1914, 384.

40. Alice Scudder, "Woman's Work in the Society of Christian Endeavor," *Christian Endeavor World,* June 15, 1893, 749.

41. Elbert Russell, *Primitive Quakerism and Christian Endeavor* (Richmond: Indiana Yearly Meeting, 1897), 15–16.

42. As one example, the papers of Elizabeth Wishard in the Indiana State Library, Indianapolis, describe her work as a field secretary.

43. Harriet Clark, "Beginnings," in *Fifty Years of Christian Endeavor: A Jubilee Record and Forecast, 1881–1931,* ed. W. Knight Chaplin and M. Jenie Street (London: British Christian Endeavour Union, 1931).

44. Emily Wheeler, "St. Paul's Advice to Sisters," *The Golden Rule,* Sept. 5, 1889, 789–90. For another example of the literature, see *Help for the Timid* (Boston: United Society of Christian Endeavor, n.d.).

45. Francis Clark, "To Married Endeavor Members," *Christian Endeavor World,* Nov. 2, 1893.

46. "Where to Choose a Wife" (editorial), *The Golden Rule,* Oct. 6, 1887.

47. Clark, "To Married Endeavor Members," 88.

48. "Should the Wife Promise to Obey in the Marriage Ceremony?" *Christian Endeavor World,* Dec. 3, 1903, 202.

49. "Reform still Needed" (editorial cartoon), *Christian Endeavor World,* Nov. 2, 1893, 83.

50. "Pansy" [Isabella Macdonald Alden], *Chrissy's Endeavor* (Boston: Lothrop, 1889).

51. "Our Women's Column," *The Golden Rule,* Oct. 28, 1886, 13.

52. Two examples are Jessie Brown, *The Iron-clad Pledge: A Story of Christian Endeavor* (Cincinnati: Standard Publishing, 1890), and Grace Livingston Hill, *Crimson Roses* (New York: Grosset and Dunlap, 1928).

53. J. R. Miller, "Choosing a Wife" and "Choosing a Husband," *Christian Endeavor World,* Jan. 6, 7, 1898, 294–95.

54. Francis Clark, "Young Women in Christian Endeavor: Their Unique Place in Society," *Christian Endeavor World,* March 12, 1914, 465.

55. "Pansy," *Chrissy's Endeavor,* 144. It is significant that this insight was made by a young woman.

56. Charles Sheldon, *In His Steps; "What Would Jesus Do"?* (New York: H. M. Caldwell, 1896).

57. Bederman, "'The Women Have Had Charge of the Church Long Enough'"; Clifford Putney, "Muscular Christianity: The Strenuous Mood of American Protestantism," Ph.D. diss., Brandeis University, 1994.

58. Hall, *Adolescence*; George A. Coe, *The Spiritual Life: Studies in the Science of Religion* (New York: Eaton and Mains, and Cincinnati: Jennings and Pye, 1900).

5. Transnational Women's Activism: The Woman's Christian Temperance Union in Japan and the United States

RUMI YASUTAKE

In 1886 MARY C. LEAVITT, the first "round-the-world missionary" of the World Woman's Christian Temperance Union (World WCTU), ended her organizing tour to Japan regretfully, "for a great work could be done in this country, whose people [were] so eager for all good things, moral and religious; welcoming with especial favor everything that [would] improve the nation, and raise it to a higher rank among the nations of the earth."[1]

WCTU activism was rooted in American Protestant churchwomen's evangelism and the development of a Victorian ideology of womanhood. In predominantly Protestant nineteenth-century America, middle-class women gained moral authority by claiming that they were innately more pious and pure than men. Emboldened by their moral authority, they participated in evangelical, benevolent, and reform activities outside their homes and expanded their domestic roles as mothers and guardians of the home into the public sphere. The numerous churchwomen's societies that had emerged at the local level in the early nineteenth century developed into national organizations after the Civil War. Two that were typical were denominational Protestant missionary societies and the interdenominational WCTU. Like the male-led Protestant mission boards, they crossed boundaries of race, class, and nation as an expression of messianic and millennialist impulses.[2]

From the beginning, the WCTU had international aspirations and drew founding members from denominational missionary societies. During the late 1870s it began Anglo-American and transatlantic cooperation with British and Canadian women, and Frances Willard's organizing tour to the West Coast resulted in the formation of the World WCTU in 1883.[3] Willard, who had nurtured her international vision in Methodist churches, argued, "The mission of the White Ribbon women is to organize the motherhood of the world for the peace and purity, the protection and exaltation of its homes. . . . We must be no longer hedged about by the artificial boundaries of states and nations; we must utter as women what good and great men long ago declared as their watchword: The whole world is my parish and to do good my religion."[4] One year after the inception of the World WCTU, Leavitt left San Francisco to start her westward voyage, returning to New York seven years later.

The worldwide expansion of WCTU activism depended greatly upon the preexisting international network of Anglo-American Protestant foreign missionary women. They and World WCTU workers both believed that those who followed the Protestant faith were morally superior and that the Protestant culture was more desirable than others in advancing women's status. Thus, they worked for evangelization and social reform of their host countries. One important difference between the two groups was that World WCTU members were more willing to use secular language than Protestant missionary women, and they engaged in a greater diversity of activities to make the world more "home like" (a more woman-friendly environment). The temperance cause was important to middle-class WCTU members because they believed it would keep homes safe from irresponsible breadwinners as well as wife-beaters and child-abusers. At the same time, when scientific knowledge was undermining the authority of religion in late-nineteenth-century America, temperance was an increasingly important universal cause. Willard underscored the temperance cause, recognizing its potential in creating female mass movements in the United States and worldwide. Advocating her famous "do-everything" policy, Willard argued that "everything [was] not in the Temperance Reform, but the Temperance Reform should be in everything." By emphasizing temperance, the WCTU was able to push its activism in every direction beyond the female sphere.[5]

Another important difference between the women's missionary and temperance groups was that, unlike Protestant missionary societies, which were subordinate to male-controlled general boards, the WCTU was exclusively for women and governed by women. While Protestant foreign missionary women limited their purview to "woman's work for woman" to avoid competition with male missionaries, World WCTU members approached both men and women to achieve their goals. Despite their differences, however, members of the World WCTU and Protestant missionary women cooperated closely in foreign fields. In non-Western nations, the most enthusiastic supporters for Leavitt's efforts were Anglo-American Protestant missionary women and English-speaking native men.[6]

By the time Leavitt left Japan in 1886, she had organized several local unions among Japanese men and women. By 1894, following Leavitt's footsteps, at least six World WCTU workers had visited and toured Japan in a short period.[7] Unlike other countries in which women's unions were often led by Anglo-American missionary women, Japanese local unions were usually headed by Japanese men or women.[8] Responding to a call of World WCTU missionary Mary West, the local Japanese women's societies coalesced into Japan's first women's national organization, the Japan Woman's Christian Temperance Union (Nihon Fujin Kyofu Kai), in 1893.[9] In 1895, Anglo-American Protestant missionary women working in Japan formed a separate national organization for resident Western women.

From 1896 to 1913 five additional WCTU missionaries arrived in Japan. They were called "resident missionaries" or "resident correspondents" and stayed in Japan for a longer period, striving to transmit WCTU methods and strategies to Japanese women.[10] Furthermore, when a substantial number of Japanese emigrated overseas at the turn of the century, the Japan WCTU extended its influence to those immigrant communities. In 1905 the Japan WCTU's overseas branch unions were founded among Japanese immigrant women on the West Coast of the United States. Those branch unions, in turn, were linked with local California unions through American Protestant missionary women working among Japanese.

Founding the Japan WCTU

When Mary Leavitt visited Japan in 1886, the nation was still in a craze for "civilization and enlightenment." Japan's initially unwilling encounter with the expansionist West served as a catalyst for the Meiji Restoration, replacing Tokugawa feudal order with an imperial rule in 1868. In the 1870s and 1880s, in a nationalistic fervor to build a modern, centralized state capable of withstanding Western powers, Japan eagerly adopted Western systems and ideas. Popular rights activists who had studied Western political liberal thought demanded a constitution and a people's assembly. Because, in the Japanese view, Protestantism and political liberal thought from the West were inseparable, Japanese Christians and popular rights activists were not two distinct groups but were closely connected during the 1870s and 1880s.[11]

Although Leavitt interacted most closely with English-speaking Japanese men, her organizing tour galvanized Japanese churchwomen in this receptive atmosphere. Forming local WCTU unions, Japanese graduates of, and teachers at, female mission schools, spoke, wrote, and petitioned the government for women's causes. These middle-class Japanese women welcomed

Protestant sexual moral values and the ideal of companionate marriage in order to break the feudalistic role of women as a "borrowed womb" with which to secure a male heir for her husband's household and an "obedient daughter-in-law" who served her in-laws. Moreover, by developing strong ties with radical popular rights theorist Emori Ueki, who extended the discussion of "natural rights" to women, WCTU activism in the late 1880s became highly political. Japanese women in the circle of the Tokyo WCTU took the leadership in memorializing the Meiji government and campaigning for sexual equality and women's economic and political rights.[12]

As it turned out, however, the promulgation of the Meiji Constitution in 1889 and the opening of the Imperial Diet in 1890 reversed the liberal political tide of early Meiji Japan. After establishing the new constitutional monarchy, Japan reinforced its oligarchic politics and state power rather than expanding popular rights. In addition, to ensure loyalty to the new nation, which was hurrying its industrialization and military buildup, the despotic Meiji government reemphasized the myth that defined the emperor as "the lineal descendant of the Sun Goddess" and required the absolute loyalty of his subjects. As the 1890s unfolded, the liberal political current was submerged under a strong backlash against the rapid Westernization and modernization of the preceding era, including both the spread of Christianity and women's activism in its attack. The public responded with heightened xenophobic and nativistic sentiments. Christians who believed in "the one and only God" were suspected of being potential traitors to imperial Japan, and Japanese women who left their homes to publicize their demands were viewed as threats to the virtues of Japanese womanhood.

Thus, by the mid–1890s Japanese Christian women's activism was deeply in trouble. The membership of the Japan WCTU quickly declined amid the mounting conservatism. Under the relatively weak presidency of Kajiko Yajima, who was employed full time by a Presbyterian female mission school in Tokyo, the Japan WCTU lacked the means to protect its activities from public criticism or integrate local churchwomen's societies under its umbrella. Only sixteen women representing two local unions attended the third annual convention of the Japan WCTU in April 1896.[13]

It was at this point that the first World WCTU resident missionary in Japan, Clara Parrish, arrived and stepped in to rescue the waning fortunes of the Japan WCTU. Arriving in Japan in October 1896, Parrish reported on the troubled condition of the fledgling organization: "The printed directory of the native women gives the names of the officers of ten local unions, but a correspondence with them reveals the fact that nearly all are greatly discouraged. What wonder! Mrs. Yajima is busy with her school work, and can not go to give the needed instruction and inspiration, and there has been no one else. Under similar conditions, enthusiasm would wane anywhere."[14]

To consolidate the group's organizational basis, Parrish resorted to the WCTU network of Anglo-American Protestant missionary women who had in 1895 established the "Auxiliary in Japan" of the World WCTU, a separate national organization for female foreign residents in Japan. Although the auxiliary also suffered from the conservative and nativistic tide of the 1890s, it was able to take advantage of denominational bonds that connected missionaries in different cities and the interdenominational network that linked missionaries residing in the same city. Thus the auxiliary successfully created a nationwide interdenominational WCTU network among Protestant missionary workers in Japan.[15]

Parrish, a former national organizer for the WCTU's Young Women's Union in America, also recognized the importance of the coming generation of educated women. She used female mission schools, which were under the management of auxiliary members, as frequent sites for lectures and appearances during her extensive organizing tours. She skillfully involved Japanese students of mission schools and quadrupled the paid membership of the Japan WCTU to exceed a thousand. As a result, at the fourth World WCTU annual convention held in Toronto in 1897, the Japan WCTU was awarded a banner for having the largest increase in its percentage of membership. At the same time, Parrish called upon auxiliary members to identify themselves more closely with Japanese unions and to "strengthen the hands of their sisters." Her efforts led to the unification of the auxiliary and the Japan WCTU, "two entirely separate circles." In 1898 the "Auxiliary in Japan" of the World WCTU became the "Foreign Auxiliary [of the Japan WCTU] in Japan." As a result, it began to pay a portion of its members' yearly fees to the Japan WCTU and to send representatives to annual conventions of the Japan WCTU.[16]

To revive WCTU activism in Japan, Parrish also promoted WCTU philosophy and methods as advocated by Frances Willard, both to the WCTU of Japan and the Foreign Auxiliary. For example, in the manual written for World WCTU officers, Willard instructed that "agitate, educate and organize . . . [were] the deathless watchwords of success" and provided pragmatic and detailed methods of how to organize and manage WCTU unions and activities.[17] Parrish initiated efforts to translate this manual and other WCTU leaflets and tracts into the Japanese language. She also encouraged Protestant missionary women to use WCTU materials and work for WCTU causes during their regular gospel activities.[18] In keeping with the do-everything policy, Parrish also pressured the Japan WCTU to take on broader lines of work at its 1897 convention. As a result, fifteen departments were created, including "Work among Soldiers" and "Scientific Temperance Instruction in the Public Schools."[19]

In the rising tide of anti-foreign and anti-Christian sentiments of the 1890s, Foreign Auxiliary members, whose female mission schools were losing students, recognized the efficacy of the do-everything policy. At the beginning of Parrish's residency, Protestant missionary women were "not in sympathy with WCTU methods," believing them too secular. But they soon realized that the WCTU's temperance work could not only be combined with their evangelical efforts but actually was a distinct help to their work. One missionary commented that it was "easier to get the people to attend a temperance meeting" than a "regular gospel service."[20]

Parrish's endeavor to transfer WCTU methods at the critical moment were generally welcomed by the Japan WCTU and the Foreign Auxiliary and were assimilated into WCTU activism in Japan. Some of her efforts, however, met strong resistance and required accommodation. For example, when Parrish realized that any mention of the word *Christian* had been dropped from the Japanese name of the Japan WCTU, she insisted on reinserting that word. Both the Japan WCTU and the Foreign Auxiliary objected, arguing that "the union could not and would not thrive if it was known to be a Christian organization" in Japan. Although Parrish believed that the Japan WCTU had been successfully persuaded to change its name to include "Christian," the women of the Japan WCTU did not use the new name in public until 1905.[21]

Along this same line, Japanese WCTU members never agreed with World WCTU missionaries about the merits of emphasizing the temperance cause. In Japan, drinking sake was an important ritual deeply rooted in national culture and history; advocating temperance challenged tradition and thus caused female social activism to receive public reproach. Furthermore, interpreting Parrish's effort for do-everything as an attempt to advocate non-drinking for its own sake above any other causes, Japan WCTU members confronted Parrish and declared that it was impossible to promote not drinking until Japanese women "heightened their virtue" and obtained independence.[22] Despite pressure from World WCTU missionary women, the Japan WCTU never required each individual to make a total-abstinence pledge in order to become a member.[23]

Thus, in part because of Japanese reservations about WCTU strategies, Parrish worked more closely with Japanese male Christians who were the main supporters of the World WCTU's efforts for temperance. Arriving in Meiji Japan, which had just started its nation-building efforts, World WCTU workers who preceded Clara Parrish had introduced the temperance cause as an important factor to promote industrialization and modernization of Japan. By tactfully using scientific and empirical language, the World WCTU emphasized patriotic goals and stressed the importance of total abstinence in developing and advancing the nation of Japan.[24] Although distrust of Christianity ran deep among the Japanese, the temperance cause as advocated by World WCTU missionaries was welcomed by progressive Japanese men— Christians, non-Christians, and anti-Christians alike—all of whom agreed that temperance "would bring good health, increased production, a higher education, and a purer morality" throughout the nation.[25]

Working closely with Japanese Christians, Parrish formed the National Temperance Alliance of Japan (Nihon Kinshu Domei Kai) in 1898, which united twenty Japanese male temperance societies throughout the nation together with one foreign male society. Unlike the Japanese women's organization, the alliance's member societies required every individual to make an abstinence pledge and strove to promote non-drinking and non-smoking in Japan. The alliance was open to "a national or foreign, Christian or non-Christian temperance society," and it "cordially invited" five selected women of the Japan WCTU to become "associate members of the Board of Control."[26]

Collaborating with male temperance workers, Protestant missionary women, and Japanese WCTU members, Clara Parrish triumphantly transformed two Japan WCTU national conventions during her residency in Japan into the largest temperance meetings ever held in the country.[27] Ironically, however, Parrish's emphasis on the temperance cause, and her particular understanding of womanhood and Japanese exigencies, exerted a conservative influence on Japanese women's WCTU activism. She emphasized the domestic role of women in social reform in order to ensure the support of Japanese men, who were not eager to lose their customary power, and to help the WCTU dodge public criticism against women's involvement in social causes.

At the two Japan WCTU conventions held during Parrish's residency, the group's officers presided, and Japanese and foreign WCTU women presented reports and participated in business discussions, but the most gala occasions were reserved for male speakers who emphasized women's assistant roles in social reform. Parrish excitedly reported the attendance of "the real nobility of the country," including "Hon. Mr. [Keigo] Kiyoura," a member of the former Matsukata Cabinet at the 1898 convention. Kiyoura, in Parrish's words, argued "with great eclat" that "everything depended upon the home" and that "woman was the centre of the home influence." What Kiyoura meant, however, was to deny women's right to political participation by asserting that they should execute their duties at home and that their organizations should use their influence rather than political methods to "purify societies."[28]

Nonetheless, thanks to Parrish's efforts the Japan WCTU consolidated its organizational basis, securing cooperative relationships with the Foreign Auxiliary and the National Temperance Alliance and pushing Japanese women into positions of leadership. Clara Parrish summed up her satisfaction at the fifth World WCTU convention in 1900:

> We saw the National W.C.T.U. Convention of Japan grow from a purely local meeting of half a dozen women, with no delegated powers, and therefore could not be called a convention at all, to a meeting of four or five hundred members, some of them coming a distance of fully five hundred miles. We saw these bodies organized as conventions are in the West, with secretaries, press reporters, committees on credentials, courtesies, publications, telegrams, and even a stenographer. We saw our banners and mottoes displayed; our flags intertwined. We saw native women preside, with the grace and dignity of queens, during the whole of a three days' session, and we saw them introduce to immense audiences at night some of the most distinguished "honorables" of the land.[29]

Accommodating to Japanese Nationalism and the Emperor System

Although World WCTU resident missionaries emphasized the temperance cause, WCTU activism in Japan could not carve a niche in late Meiji Japan without accommodating to the emperor system and the heightened nationalism stirred by the Sino-Japanese War (1894–95) and the Russo-Japanese War (1904–5). During the Sino-Japanese War, Japanese WCTU members followed the example of non-Christian women supporting the war. The Japan WCTU published a booklet for the bereaved of soldiers, which praised the "glorious" death of soldiers for the nation and preached the Gospel to the bereaved, promising they would regain strength and peace by believing in God.[30]

Ten years later, during the Russo-Japanese War, the WCTU's "work among soldiers" was promoted by Kara Smart, a World WCTU resident missionary who worked in Japan between 1902 and 1906. In both peace and war, Soldiers' Department workers in the United States held temperance and gospel meetings, provided "temptation-free" socials, established soldiers' homes and libraries, and brought delicacies and provisions to the sick and wounded, always carrying pledge cards on their rounds. In the United States, the department's Workers expressed their motherly concern for "the boys" in service, who were away from home and in the midst of temptations, and their ultimate goal was prohibition among soldiers. In 1901 their efforts led Congress to pass the anti-canteen section of the Army Reorganization Bill, which banned the sale or distribution of any intoxicating liquors upon any premises used for military purposes by the United States.[31]

In 1904 Smart and the superintendent of the Japan WCTU's Work among Soldiers Department, Fukiko Shimizu, called both foreign and Japanese local WCTU members to participate in their efforts and raise funds for temperance and evangelistic work among Japanese soldiers. Responding to the call, some WCTU workers visited hospitals with gospel and temperance literature. Others met soldiers on station platforms and "busied themselves in sewing on missing buttons, mending rips, and in many other ways making as comfortable and pleasant as possible the [troops'] brief sojourn." Still others visited battleships to welcome foreign and Japanese crews.[32]

Transferred to Japanese members, however, the WCTU's work among soldiers was transformed into Japanese women's activism to prove their loyalty to the emperor and the nation. Notwithstanding the frequent accusation that Japanese Christians were potential traitors of imperial Japan, the majority of them were as patriotic and loyal to the emperor as non-Christians and anti-Christians. For them, being pious Christians did not conflict with being good subjects to the "lineal descendant of the Sun Goddess." Japanese Christians of the time had been brought up worshipping nature and the spirits of their ancestors at home and then converted to Christianity at school or church. Not fully comprehending Protestant theology and church dogmas, they could easily combine the Christian emphasis to be selfless for God's cause with a patriotic and familial devotion to emperor, nation, and family.

The most successful among the WCTU methods of work for soldiers were the "comfort-bag" campaigns, in which bags containing such amenities as candies and letters of gratitude, in addition to temperance and purity leaflets, pledge cards, and Bibles, were sent to the front and to hospitals. In 1904 Japan WCTU members sewed and filled six hundred bags and sent them to the navy as a trial effort. Soon the troops responded with letters and postcards of gratitude, and the Japanese government requested the Japan WCTU to procure more bags to be sent to the army as well as the navy. The comfort-bag campaign soon became a nationalistic phenomenon to show support for the war. People from all walks of life, including members of the imperial household and the aristocracy, joined the efforts. Spurred by this favorable response to their activism, members of the Japan WCTU joyfully carried out the comfort-bag campaign. They sold machine-made bags, supplied sewing directions, collected a huge number of filled bags, and inspected each one to remove items such as cigarettes and antiwar and antigovernment literature. The government provided free transportation for the bags and instructed WCTU members to "send no less than ten thousand bags at one time and as many as ten thousand lots." Japan WCTU president Kajiko Yajima, whom the government made individually responsible for every bag, bore "the burden joyously and fearlessly" and announced that the Japan WCTU "would not only reach that high mark, but would go beyond it."[33]

Japan's expansion over neighboring nations at the turn of the century coincided with U.S. desire to check the increasing influence of Russian powers in China. Thus American WCTU and Protestant missionary women acceded to the Japan WCTU's jingoistic efforts. Although the Foreign Auxiliary formed the Department of Peace and Arbitration in 1904 to "counteract the tendency for militarism in the world," its members allowed the Japan WCTU to use female mission schools as centers for the comfort-bag campaigns.[34]

World WCTU missionaries even endeavored to take advantage of Japanese national pride to promote temperance. During the Spanish-American War, Clara Parrish recognized the "fact" that "of the young men who had volunteered in the United States, ninety percent of those who used cigarettes were rejected as unfit to serve their country, while only ten percent of nonusers failed to pass their medical examinations." An officer of the National Temperance Alliance of Japan introduced a bill to the Imperial Diet prohibiting minors from smoking. The bill became a law in 1900 to ensure the health of future soldiers.[35] After the Russo-Japanese War, Kara Smart commented, "The war, instead of hindering our work, as we once [had] feared it would, magnified a thousand fold our opportunities and opened avenues for our entrance we [had] thought could not be reached perhaps for years." With the comfort-bag campaign a massive success, Smart asked for and received World WCTU funds to supply temperance and purity leaflets for inclusion in the bags.[36]

Enthusiastically supporting Japan's imperialistic wars, the Japan WCTU became a respected member of imperial Japan and at last could publicly carry the word *Christian* in its Japanese name.[37] Thus, by accommodating Japanese jingoism, WCTU movements in Japan gained some room for their own cause. If the American WCTU protected and promoted its social activism "for God" and for the cause of temperance in predominantly Protestant, nineteenth-century America, WCTU activism in late-Meiji Japan became acceptable and respectable by dedicating its efforts to the emperor and the nation.[38]

From Japan to California

Even while it was creating a niche for churchwomen's activism in Japan, the Japan WCTU expanded its influence to Japanese immigrant communities on the West Coast of the United States. After the Meiji Restoration in 1868, young samurais who had lost their means of living crossed the Pacific to improve their career opportunities by mastering Western knowledge and technology. In San Francisco, the pioneer Japanese immigrants were self-supporting students who created communities during the 1870s. Learning English and American practices at church-sponsored activities, they increasingly came under the strong influence of American church people and their moral values. The first Issei organization formed in California was the Gospel Society (Fukuinkai), an interdenominational organization of Japanese students who associated themselves with Methodist, Presbyterian, and Congregational churches in San Francisco. Assisted by American church people in San Francisco, the society rented rooms in the Methodist Episcopal Chinese Mission House to hold regular meetings, provide accommodations to Japanese immigrants in need, give English classes, and help Japanese students find jobs as "school boys" or "school girls" who lived with American families and did housework while attending school.[39]

Japanese immigrant communities, composed mainly of self-supporting students, grew rapidly and diversified in the 1890s. To replace Chinese workers, whose entry had been denied by the Chinese Exclusion Act of 1882, Japanese laborers began to arrive in California in the late 1880s. As a result, gender-imbalanced Japanese immigrant communities and their brothels and gambling dens became increasingly visible. To prevent anti-Asian sentiments from focusing on the Japanese, Issei elites struggled to avoid having the stigma of immorality be attached to their communities. They campaigned to eradicate prostitution and gambling in the communities and petitioned the Japanese government to stop the emigration of indigent Japanese. In 1891 the Japanese Ministry of Foreign Affairs began efforts to control the migration of Japanese prostitutes. By 1918 the measures agreed upon by the Japanese and U.S. governments ceased immigration of working-class Japanese to the U.S. mainland.[40]

Sharing the belief with Issei elite men that the immoral stereotype of Chinese women was an important cause for the American public's hostility against Chinese, the Japan WCTU also played a role in the effort to ban Japanese prostitutes. In the late 1880s in San Francisco, Issei women activists, some of whom were present or former Japan WCTU members, met every steamer from Japan and attempted to dissuade newly arriving women from engaging in the "shameful business." In 1890 an immigrant who had kept her membership in the Tokyo WCTU wrote to sister members in Japan, urging them to petition the government to stop the migration of Japanese prostitutes. Internalizing Protestant American middle-class moral values, urban middle-class Japanese WCTU members felt the "greatest grief" in having their country's reputation sullied by "vile" women. The Japan WCTU supported the Foreign Ministry's attempts to pass a bill that would punish both procurers and prostitutes who went abroad to engage in the "shameful business."[41]

Those efforts to preserve the reputation of Japan and its subjects brought about the formation of Japan WCTU branches on the West Coast. In 1905 two Japan WCTU officers visited the United States. One, Chiyoko Kozaki, who later became a president of the Japan WCTU, toured the West Coast with her husband, a minister well known both in Japan and Issei communities in the United States. Although she received the hospitality of prominent Issei families, she also encountered numerous shops in the Japanese parts of towns where suspected prostitutes conducted their business. Although Kozaki reported that she felt "so pitiful" for such women, who, she explained, were generally lured by "villains," she considered their visibility to be responsible for rising anti-Japanese sentiments in early-twentieth-century California.[42] Kozaki wrote:

> The reason why Japanese are excluded by white people is that many of those arriving in this land are not educated Japanese who know manners but country people who even have never seen Tokyo. They are indifferent to socialization or courtesy and do not care about maintaining their dignity. Their behaviors are often disgraceful to white people, and thus Japanese tend to be criticized. So I hope people who are sensible to these matters will come in large number. I think it is most meaningful that branch unions of the Japan WCTU are formed as many as five or six in such lands on the [Pacific] Coast in order to show the dignity of Japanese people to the overseas.[43]

Kozaki encouraged the migration of well-educated Japanese to the United States and, to demonstrate their respectability, called for the organization of Japan WCTU branches on the West Coast. She, along with another Japan WCTU officer who visited the Pacific Coast in the same year, endeavored to form Japan WCTU branch unions among Issei churchwomen, many of whom had graduated from female mission schools in Japan and some of whom had been active in the Japan WCTU. As a result, in 1905 Japan WCTU branch unions were formed in Seattle, Portland, Oakland, Los Angeles, and Riverside.[44]

The Issei unions soon became affiliated with the California WCTU, which had begun work among Asians in the 1880s by focusing first upon Chinese immigrants through its Department of Work among Foreigners. The California WCTU's work among the Chinese set the pattern for their later efforts among the Japanese. WCTU members who closely interacted with Chinese were sympathetic to their clients, whom they viewed as much soberer than

Irish and German immigrants. They also dissented from nativist prejudice against the Chinese. Witnessing the public's anti-Chinese hostility, a California WCTU officer wrote that she felt "a burning shame" about how Chinese had been treated in a "professedly Christian land."[45] In 1895 the California WCTU established the Oriental Work Department to concentrate on efforts among Asian immigrants. Mrs. L. P. Williams, an active member of the Woman's Home Missionary Society (WHMS) of the Methodist Episcopal Church, became its superintendent.[46] During the 1890s, native-born Chinese sons started to reach voting age, and in 1898 the Supreme Court ruled in *Wong Kim Ark v. the United States* that Chinese who had been born in America could not be stripped of their citizenship despite the anti-Asian attitudes of the public.[47]

Because evangelical efforts among adult Asians had not been as fruitful as Williams had hoped, such developments encouraged her to focus on the coming generation. Especially because public schools in California increasingly excluded Asian children, she saw a special mission for American churchwomen in "Americanizing" Asian children by conducting Sunday schools and providing teachers and materials for their separate, ethnic schools.[48] As Williams wrote:

> Fifteen years ago there was hardly to be seen a Chinese or Japanese child in America. Today there are two thousand of the former in San Francisco—little urchins in yellow blouses, born under the Stars and Stripes laugh at Congressional Legislation and close-barred gates, as the Supreme Court of the United States has recently declared that all boys born in the United States are citizens and voters, when of age. Shall these have a pagan or Christian citizenship? The former might imperil our institutions. India, China, and Japan must have their schools, but is it no less important that we in America push our educational work among these people on our own shores?[49]

As the number of Japanese immigrants in California increased during the late 1890s, Williams began to distribute WCTU tracts and leaflets that had been translated into the Chinese language.[50] When Kara Smart returned from Japan and moved to California, she strengthened the link between the Issei unions and the California WCTU. In 1907 an independent department was established to carry out the organization's work with the Japanese, and Smart was its first superintendent. She was succeeded by the Rev. Mary Bowen in 1909 and by Clara E. Johnson in 1913. These superintendents of the Japanese Department reported on the activities of Issei unions and conducted their own work among the Japanese, using missionary and church networks. Smart, who had spent four years in Tokyo, obtained Japanese-language materials from the Japan WCTU and forged connections with Protestant ministers working among the Japanese, such as H. B. Johnson, superintendent of the M.E. Japanese Mission, and H. H. Guy, the Pacific Coast superintendent of Japanese Work under the Christian Church Mission. Mary Bowen, a former missionary of the WHMS of the Methodist Episcopal Church and the founder of the Independent Japanese Mission in Sacramento, emphasized evangelical and rescue efforts. Clara Johnson created a Little Temperance League among Japanese children in Berkeley. Relying upon the influence of her husband, the Rev. H. B. Johnson, and a Japanese pastor under his supervision, she distributed WCTU materials among Issei church members. She also encouraged California churchwomen to participate in "Americanizing" the Japanese and their children by conducting Sunday schools, evening classes, and Bible studies.[51]

While the California WCTU aimed to exercise moral influence on Japanese immigrants, especially on their native-born children, Japanese WCTU members in both Japan and northern California had a different focus. They cultivated community interests and were most concerned about the reputation of the Japanese. Thus, Issei unions were much more closely connected to other Issei community organizations than to the California WCTU. Issei members of the WCTU worked together with Issei Christian churches and the Japanese Association in America, which was formed under the auspices of the Japanese government to protect the interests of Japanese immigrants.

Among the unions formed in California, only the Oakland chapter sustained its WCTU activism for a substantial period—until 1941.[52] It published a bimonthly newsletter, *Japanese Women's Herald in America* (Zaibei Fujin Shinpo) from around 1907 to 1941. Probably one of the earliest, and one of the few, publications by and for Issei women, the newsletter had readers even outside California and a circulation of eight hundred in 1913.[53] Although I could find only a few issues, the small number of articles on Issei WCTU activism carried in the newsletter, the Japan WCTU journal, and Issei community newspapers indicate that Issei WCTU activism in California was for mutual support and improvement. As in the case of black churchwomen activists studied by Evelyn B. Higginbotham, Issei WCTU women both embraced and contested the dominant values and norms of American churchwomen and their societies.[54] When the earthquake hit San Francisco in 1906, Oakland Issei WCTU members endeavored to provide shelter for Issei refugees escaping from the city. The following year, as it became apparent that Japanese prostitutes who had escaped from San Francisco were resuming business in Oakland, the Issei Oakland WCTU members who emulated American middle-class Protestant moral values like Japanese WCTU members in Japan collaborated with American and Issei church people, the Japanese Association in America, Issei youth organizations, and local authorities to eliminate houses of "ill fame" and drive away Japanese women in the "shameful business."[55]

Yet Issei WCTU women emphasized maintaining "respectable" Japanese middle-class women's lives by advocating intellectual and cultural self-improvement. One Issei WCTU member insisted that to "bring back and heighten *kyoyo* (culture/education)" was indispensable among Issei women who were immersed in daily chores in the new land.[56] Another member, whose article was reprinted in an Issei newspaper in Sacramento in 1912, argued that it was especially necessary for Issei women in America to read books and increase their knowledge for the improvement of the "Yamato Minzoku (Japanese race)."[57] Some Issei WCTU members joined in organizing Issei YWCAs in California and in providing classes in Japanese flower arranging and cooking in order to reproduce Japanese middle-class family life in America. Because they experienced American prejudice against Asians, Issei churchwomen made extra efforts to maintain pride in their cultural heritage while emulating dominant American values and customs. They also endeavored to preserve the reputations of the Japanese and their communities.[58]

Conclusion

The transnational activism of the World WCTU spread from the United States to Japan and back to the Issei communities on the West Coast of the United States and involved American and Japanese women and men of various expectations. The politics of women's moral authority was effectively used to expand women's influence outside their homes in the United States. The WCTU and Anglo-American Protestant women, spurred by evangelism and confidence in their cultural superiority, crossed the boundaries of race, class, and nation to help "uplift" Japanese women to the American standard. Internalizing this cultural hierarchy, Japanese women's efforts to improve the status of women became intertwined with their nationalistic pride and goals to achieve equal status with Western powers and civilization. As a result, as WCTU activism was practiced by the Japanese, Willard's universal vision of creating a woman-friendly, temperate environment for the protection of the home became nationalistic.

Ian Tyrrell, who emphasized "collaboration and solicitation" by non-American and non-Western women in his study of World WCTU activism in the former British Empire, argued that the leaders of the World WCTU movement in America were "as much the victims of misleading assessments of power and potential at the periphery as they were instigators of their own illusions."[59] In the transnational expansion of WCTU activism to Japan and Issei communities in California, Japanese women and men interpreted and accommodated American Protestant middle-class gender ideology and their methods of activism to the anti-Christian and jingoistic sociohistorical conditions of Meiji Japan and the Japanese immigrant communities of anti-Asian California. It was an uneasy collaboration among American and Japanese churchpeople who held different views and had different interests and resources that enabled the transnational expansion of the WCTU from the United States to Japan and then back to Japanese immigrant communities in California.

Notes

A number of individuals commented on this essay at different stages, including Ellen C. DuBois, Sharon L. Sievers, Rebecca Mead, Anastasia Christman, Susan Englander, Virginia L. Brereton, Margaret L. Bendroth, Carolyn De Swarte Gifford, James Opp, Maureen Fitzgerald, Mark Chaves, David Watt, Fred. G. Notehelfer, Mariko Tamanoi, and Valerie Matsumoto. I would like to thank all of them.

1. Mary C. Leavitt, "Our Round-the-World Missionary," *Union Signal,* Dec. 30, 1886.

2. For the politics of Protestant missionary and WCTU members, see Barbara L. Epstein, *The Politics of Domesticity: Women, Evangelism, and Temperance in Nineteenth-Century America* (Middletown: Wesleyan University Press, 1981), 67–151; Ruth Bordin, *Women and Temperance: The Quest for Power and Liberty, 1873–1900* (New York: Rutgers University Press, 1990); Peggy Pascoe, *Relations of Rescue: The Search for Female Moral Authority in the American West, 1874–1939* (New York: Oxford University Press, 1990); and Suzanne M. Marilley, "Frances Willard and the Feminism of Fear," *Feminist Studies* 19 (Spring 1993): 123–46. Concerning the internationalization of their evangelical female activism, see, for example, R. Pierce Beaver, *All Loves Excelling: American Protestant Women in World Mission* (Grand Rapids: Eerdmans, 1968); Jane Hunter, *The Gospel of Gentility: American Women in Turn-of-the-Century China* (New Haven: Yale University Press, 1984); Patricia R. Hill, *The World Their Household; The American Woman's Foreign Mission Movement and Cultural Transformation, 1870–1920* (Ann Arbor: University of Michigan Press, 1985); and Ian Tyrrell, *Woman's World/Woman's Empire: The Woman's Christian Temperance Union in International Perspective, 1880–1930* (Chapel Hill: University of North Carolina Press, 1992).

3. Tyrrell, *Woman's World/Woman's Empire,* 11–34.

4. Frances E. Willard, *Do Everything: A Handbook for the World's White-Ribboner,* reprinted in *The Ideal of "The New Woman" According to the Woman's Christian Temperance Union,* ed. Carolyn De Swarte Gifford and Donald W. Dayton (New York: Garland Publishing, 1988), 11.

5. Williard, *Do Everything,* 4–6.

6. See, for example, Mary C. Leavitt, "Reconnoitering in the Sandwich Islands," *Union Signal,* Dec. 25, 1884, 4, and Mary C. Leavitt, "Our Round-the-World Missionary," *Union Signal,* April 26, 1888, 4.

7. They were Pandita Ramabai and Emma B. Ryder (1888), Jessie A. Ackerman (1890, 1901), Mary A. West (1892), and Elizabeth W. Andrew and Kate C. Bushnell (1894).

8. During her tour in Asia, Leavitt reported that native women took leadership in their unions in Japan and Ceylon, while Anglo-American women did so in other countries. Mary C. Leavitt, "Our Round-the-World Missionary," *Union Signal*, Oct. 4, 1888.

9. The Japan Woman's Christian Temperance Union, *The Centennial History of the Japan Woman's Christian Temperance Union* (Nihon Kirisutokyo Fujin Kyofu Kai Hyaku-nenshi) (Tokyo: Domesu Shuppan, 1986), 35–40, 93–94.

10. The WCTU's resident missionaries were Clara Parrish (who worked in Japan from 1896 to 1898), Eliza Spencer-Large (1898–1910), Kara G. Smart (1902–6), Flora E. Strout (1908–10), and Ruth F. Davis (1909–13). Except for Spencer-Large, a former Canadian Methodist foreign missionary who lived in Japan, the women were American.

11. Akio Dohi, *The History of Protestant Religion in Japan* (Nihon Purotesutanto Kiri-sutokyoshi) (Tokyo: Shinkyo Shuppan, 1980), 90–103.

12. *The Centennial History of the Japan Woman's Christian Temperance Union*, 35–87. For an overview of Japanese WCTU activism in the 1880s and 1890s, see Sharon L. Sievers, *Flowers in Salt: The Beginning of Feminist Consciousness in Modern Japan* (Stanford: Stanford University Press, 1983), 87–113.

13. "The Japan WCTU Annual Convention Report" (Nihon Fujin Kyofu Kai Nenkai Kiji), *Fujin Shinpo*, April 28, 1896, 31–32.

14. Clara Parrish, "Impressions of Japan," *Union Signal*, Jan. 28, 1897.

15. Mary F. Denton, "World's W.C.T.U.," *Japan Evangelist* 3 (Feb. 1896): 173–76.

16. Clara Parrish, "World's W.C.T.U.," *Japan Evangelist* 5 (Jan. 1898): 23–27; Carolyn E. Davidson, "World's W.C.T.U.," *Japan Evangelist* 5 (Oct. 1898): 320; "Report of Our Seventh Round-the-World Missionary, Miss Clara Parrish, at the World's Convention," *Union Signal*, July 12, 1900, 4.

17. Willard, *Do Everything*, 35.

18. Clara Parrish, "World's W.C.T.U.," *Japan Evangelist* 5 (Jan. 1898): 24, and 5 (Aug. 1898): 237. The Japanese-language version of Frances Willard's *Do Everything* manual is in *Bankoku Kirisutokyo Fujin Kyofu Kai Annai* (The Guide of the World WCTU), trans. Takeshi Ukai (Tokyo: Kyobunkan, 1898).

19. Other Japan WCTU departments were entitled "Evangelistic," "Loyal Temperance Legion" (children's work), "Mothers' Meetings," "Narcotics," "Social Purity," "Sabbath Observance," "Sunday School Work," "Work among Young Women in Schools and Colleges," "Press Work," "Literature," Heredity," "Unfermented Wine at the Sacrament," and "Legislation and Petitions." Clara Parrish, "The World's W.C.T.U.," *Japan Evangelist* 4 (May 1897): 253–54; *The Centennial History of the Japan Woman's Christian Temperance Union*, 136.

20. Clara Parrish, "World's W.C.T.U.," *Japan Evangelist* 4 (April 1897): 220, and 5 (Jan. 1898): 25; Carolyn E. Davidson, "World's W.C.T.U.," *Japan Evangelist* 6 (Sept. 1899): 270.

21. "A Letter from Miss Parrish," *Union Signal*, Aug. 26, 1897; Clara Parrish, "World's W.C.T.U.," *Japan Evangelist* 4 (May 1897): 254; *The Centennial History of the Japan Woman's Christian Union*, 214; "The W.C.T.U. of the World," *Union Signal*, March 17, 1904.

22. Taneko Yamaji, "To Our Readers" (Yomu Hito ni Tsugu), *Fujin Shinpo*, May 11, 1898, 157.

23. According to Japan WCTU officer Kikue Takahashi, the WCTU in Japan does not require a pledge of total abstinence from members even now. Interview with Kikue Takahashi, Tokyo, July 29, 1994.

24. For example, Mary West, a World WCTU missionary who visited Japan in 1892, emphasized the merit of abstinence in Japan's industrial development while she promoted women's activism. Because she died while on a lecture tour of Japan, many of her lectures were published in commemorative form. Her lectures included "Citizenship"; "Harm from Liquor and Tobacco" (Sake to Tabako no Gai); "The Evil Effect of Drinking on Japanese Industry" (Nihon no Kogyo ni Oyobosu Insyu no Heigai); "The Relationship between Temperance and Industry" (Kinshu to Kogyo no Kankei); "The Relationship between Women and Temperance Work" (Fujin to Kyofu Jigyo Tono Kankei); and "The World WCTU Movement" (Bankoku Fujin Kyofukai no Undo).

25. "W.C.T.U. in Japan," Union Signal, May 26, 1887.

26. "More Advanced Steps in the Line of Temperance Reform," Japan Evangelist 4 (Sept. 1897): 359–60; "How Beautiful It Is to Be with God—Frances E. Willard," Japanese Evangelist 6 (Feb. 1899): 53–55; "The Bylaws of the National Temperance Alliance of Japan" (Nihon Kinshu Domei Kai Kisoku), The Light of Our Land (Kuni no Hikari), Oct. 29, 1898, 13.

27. Clara Parrish, "World's W.C.T.U.," Japan Evangelist 4 (May 1897): 251–54, and 5 (May 1898): 151–56.

28. "The Convention," Japan Evangelist 5 (May 1898): 151–56; Keigo Kiyoura, "On the Development of the WCTU" (Fujin Kyofu Kai no Hattatsu ni Tsuite), Fujin Shinpo, Aug. 20, 1898, 264–70.

29. "Report of Our Seventh Round-the-World Missionary, Miss Clara Parrish, at the World's Convention," Union Signal, July 12, 1900, 4.

30. Nihon Fujin Kyofukai, The Booklet Given to the Bereaved of Soldiers (Gunjin no Izoku ni Okuru Sho) (Tokyo: Shueisha, 1894).

31. Carolyn E. Davidson, "W.C.T.U. Department," Japan Evangelist 3 (March 1901): 81–82; "W.C.T.U. Department," Japan Evangelist 11 (April 1904): 131–33.

32. "W.C.T.U. Department," Japan Evangelist 11 (March 1904): 90 and 11 (April 1904): 133; Fukiko Shimizu, "About the Soldiers' Department" (Gunjinka ni Tsuite), Fujin Shinpo, Feb. 25, 1904, 3–7; "The WCTU Welcomes the Crews of Battleships Nisshin and Kasuga" (Kyofukai no Nisshin Kasuga Kokaiin Kangei), Fujin Shinpo, Feb. 25, 1904, 9–10.

33. Kara Smart, "Work for Soldiers in Japan," Union Signal, Dec. 29, 1904; "W.C.T.U. Department," Japan Evangelist 11 (Dec. 1904): 388–91.

34. "W.C.T.U. Department," Japan Evangelist 11 (Aug. 1904): 268–69, and 12 (Aug. 1905): 280.

35. Clara Parrish, "World's W.C.T.U.," Japan Evangelist 5 (Aug. 1898): 238–39; Carolyn E. Davidson, "World's W.C.T.U.," Japan Evangelist 7 (April 1900): 118–23.

36. Kara Smart, "An Appeal from Miss Smart," Union Signal, April 13, 1905.

37. The Centennial History of the Japan Woman's Christian Temperance Union, 241.

38. The YMCA movement in late-Meiji Japan underwent a similar transformation. See Jon Thares Davidann, A World of Crisis and Progress: The American YMCA in Japan, 1890–1930 (Bethlehem: Lehigh University Press, 1998).

39. Yuji Ichioka, The Issei: The World of the First Generation of Japanese Immigrants, 1885–1924 (New York: Free Press, 1988), 16–19; Ryo Yoshida, "Japanese in California and Chris-

tianity" (Kariforunia no Nihonjin to Kirisutokyo), in *Japanese Christian Movements in North America* (Hokubei Nihonjin Kirisutokyo Undoshi), ed. Doshisha University Institute for the Study of Humanities and Social Sciences (Tokyo: PMC Shuppan, 1991), 166–72.

40. Ichioka, *The Issei*, 51–56.

41. "Letter from Sister Masue Kawaguchi" (Kawaguchi Masue Shi no Shojo), *Tokyo Fujin Kyofu Zasshi*, Aug. 16, 1890. A part of the letter is translated and cited by Sievers in *Flowers in Salt* (96). See also "Bill to Protect Japanese Women Overseas" (Graikoku ni Okeru Nihon Fujo Hogo Hoan), *Tokyo Fujin Kyofu Zasshi*, March 21, 1891, 8–10; Toyoju Sasaki, "Work of Women and Civilization" (Fujin Bunnmei no Hataraki), *Jogaku Zasshi*, May 21, 1887, 86–88; "Japanese Women Engaging in Degrading Business in America" (Zaiber Nihon Joshi no Sengyosha), *Tokyo Fujin Kyofu Zasshi*, March 21, 1891, 8–10; and *Draft of a Petition on the Establishment of a Law to Control Overseas Prostitutes* (Zaigai Baiinfu Torishimariho Seitei ni Kansuru Kenpakusho Soan) (Tokyo: Shueisha, 1892).

42. Chiyoko Kozaki, "Account of Travels in the United States" (Beikoku Junkaiki), *Fujin Shinpo*, May 25, 1906, 16–21.

43. Chiyoko Kozaki, "Journal of Travels in the United States" (Beikoku Junkai Nikki), *Fujin Shinpo*, Dec. 25, 1905, 14–15.

44. "The First Overseas Branch Union" (Saisho no Gaikoku Shibu), *Fujin Shinpo*, Sept. 25, 1905, 7; "Oakland WCTU" (Okurando Fujin Kyofu Kai), *Fujin Shinpo*, Dec. 25, 1905, 367; "U.S. Riverside WCTU" (Beikoku Ribasaido Fujin Kyofu Kai), *Fujin Shinpo*, Jan. 25, 1906, 27–28; "Portland WCTU" (Potorando Fujin Kyofu Kai), *Fujin Shinpo*, April 25, 1906, 26; "Los Angeles WCTU" (Rosanzerusu Fujin Koyfu Kai), *Fujin Shinpo*, Feb. 25, 1906, 74.

45. *Minutes of the Woman's National Christian Temperance Union* (1880): 63–64, (1881): lxii, and (1886): lxxxviii–lxxxix.

46. Dorcas J. Spencer, *A History of the Woman's Christian Temperance Union of Northern and Central California* (Oakland: West Coast Printing, 1913[?]), 123.

47. Sucheng Chan, *Asian Americans: An Interpretive History* (Boston: Twayne Publishers, 1991), 92.

48. *Minutes of the Annual Convention of the WCTU of California* (1896): 60–61, (1898): 66–67, and (1904): 67.

49. *Minutes of the Annual Convention of the WCTU of California* (1898): 66.

50. *Minutes of the Annual Convention of the WCTU of California* (1897): 51, and (1898): 66. Japanese intellectuals of the time could read Chinese well.

51. *Minutes of the Annual Convention of the WCTU of California* (1908): 46–47, (1915): 81–82, (1916): 74, (1921): 82, and (1925): 125.

52. After its inception, the Japan WCTU's newsletter, *Fujin Shinpo*, carried reports from each union for a short while. The Los Angeles union was active, but their reports ended in 1908. Both Japanese and American WCTU records reported that Issei unions in Los Angeles and Riverside affiliated themselves with the WCTU of Southern California in 1906. The Southern California WCTU's Annual Report of 1924, however, the earliest report to which I had an access, did not list these two unions. Annual reports of the WCTU of Southern California show that one Japanese union was formed under the Los Angeles City Federation in 1930 and another under the Los Angeles County Young People's Branch/Youth Temperance Council in 1934.

53. Ochimi Kubushiro, *Dedicated to Eliminating Prostitution* (Haisho Hitosuji) (Tokyo: Chuo Koronsha, 1973); *Minutes of the Annual Convention of the WCTU of California* (1913), 77, (1917), 82, and (1925), 125.

54. Evelyn B. Higgenbotham, *Righteous Discontent: The Women's Movement in the Black Baptist Church, 1880–1920* (Cambridge: Harvard University Press, 1993).

55. "Correspondence from Oakland" (Okurand Tsushin), *Fujin Shinpo,* Oct. 25, 1907, 22–23, and June 25, 1908, 180–81.

56. Kubushiro, *Dedicated to Eliminating Prostitution,* 78–79.

57. Naok Kawata, "Japanese Women in America and Learning" (Zaibei Fujin to Shuyo), *Sacramento News* (Ofu Nippo), Feb. 7, 1912.

58. For more accounts of Protestantism in Japanese American communities, see Ryo Yoshida, "A Socio-Historical Study of Racial/Ethnic Identity in the Inculturated Religious Expression of Japanese Christianity in San Francisco, 1877–1924," Ph.D. diss., Graduate Theological Union, Berkeley, 1989, and Brian Hayashi, *"For the Sake of Our Japanese Brethren": Assimilation, Nationalism, and Protestantism among the Japanese of Los Angeles, 1895–1942* (Stanford: Stanford University Press, 1995).

59. Tyrrell, *Woman's World/Woman's Empire,* 6.

6. Beyond Dr. Dobson: Women, Girls, and Focus on the Family

COLLEEN MCDANNELL

SHORTLY AFTER the conviction of Renee Polreis for beating her two-year-old adopted son to death with wooden spoons, a background article appeared in the Sunday edition of the *Denver Post*. "Some parenting experts who espouse fundamentalist Christian beliefs," began staff writer Carol Kreck, "have long advocated the use of a 'neutral object' in the spanking of children instead of the hand. Looking to the Bible for guidance, they say it's better to use a paddle or a wooden spoon or a belt for spanking." In the third sentence, Kreck quotes the nationally known source for such ideas: "'The hand,' writes Christian psychologist James Dobson, 'should be seen as a[n] object of love—to hug, pat and caress.'" In an attempt to explain why a forty-three-year-old businesswoman would bludgeon to death a child she had known less than six months, the reporter associated domestic violence with what she called "fundamentalist Christian beliefs."[1]

The association of child abuse with religion is not unique to the Polreis case. The FBI justified, at least in part, the bombing of the Branch Davidian compound because agents suspected that David Koresh abused the community's children. Pedophilia cases involving Catholic priests and altar boys have become a staple of popular publishing. In 1990 Rutgers University historian Philip Greven presented a frightening history of physical punishment by religious parents. As did *Denver Post* reporter Carol Kreck, Greven includes James Dobson in the "long line of corporal-punishment advocates obsessed with the wills of children."[2] A 1995 study of divergent models of child-rearing also cited Dobson's views. According to sociologists John P. Bartkowski and Christopher G. Ellison, conservative Protestant parenting specialists "strongly" endorse corporal punishment because of their acceptance of biblical literalism and their belief that human nature is sinful.[3]

Since the nineteenth century, American women, children, and religion have frequently shared the same place in societal structure and national mythology. Concerns over the condition of one typically spill over to the other. I am convinced that the current "culture wars" over who should control children is an extension of the "gender wars" of the past generation over who should control women. During these periods, both liberal and conservative Americans have envisioned an Armageddon where the chaotic forces of evil threaten the stability of "the family." In the 1970s, either feminism or fundamentalism was variously destroying womanhood. In the 1980s and 1990s, childhood was either being perverted by secular humanists or bludgeoned to death by the religious right.

In a rare moment of agreement, both conservatives and liberals alike place James Dobson near the center of the "war" over the family. His name appears in newspapers and scholarly articles, and an estimated five million people listen to his daily radio program.[4] Dobson's organizational headquarters in Colorado Springs, Colorado, receives ten thousand letters daily, most of which are requests for print, audio, and video materials produced by his nonprofit organization, Focus on the Family. Of that daily mail, approximately one thousand letters will be of a significant personal nature, and a staff member will send a written reply. Working with an annual budget of $110 million, 1,300 men and women attempt to accomplish Dobson's goal of "turning hearts toward home" so that "people will be able to discover the founder of homes and the creator of families—Jesus Christ."[5]

It is difficult for me to imagine why in one month forty thousand people would visit the corporate headquarters of a man whose conception of the family purportedly is a variation of "men rule, women submit, and children obey."[6] Yet that quotation from political scientist Michael Liensch supposedly summarizes conservative Christian thinking on the family. Liensch accompanies a host of scholars and journalists who conclude that fundamentalists are preoccupied with exercising control over the bodies of women and children. To overstate James Dobson's concern for discipline or to see Focus on the Family as merely a mouthpiece for right-wing politics is to miss its influence. This essay attempts to explain why, on their way to Pikes Peak and the Air Force Academy, people stop to tour an office building.

Contemporary scholarly and journalistic focus on the Christian religious right has led us to believe that conservative Protestantism is primarily a male-dominated religious force that seeks to reform public institutions through political action. Although I do not doubt that this is the agenda of many, the focus on men, politics, and the public sphere has blinded us from seeing other aspects of conservative Christianity.[7] Focus on the Family's strength is not in its ability to motivate its audience to send thousands of letters to political leaders—which it can and does do. Dobson's organization is successful precisely because its message makes sense to the majority of conservative churchgoers—women and children. Christian women and children who are trying to integrate "the World" with "the Spirit" find constructive information and community support in Focus on the Family's publications and broadcasts.

Focus on the Family is not an organization that seeks to create a Christian America out of a nation of unbelievers. Although Dobson can pen "culture war" rhetoric with the best of conservative ideologues, he and his organization spend their energy supporting the lives of those who already believe. Most of Focus on the Family's budget goes to funding its family ministries, while only 3.8 percent pays for public policy research and outreach. Around 70 percent of its radio broadcasts deal with marriage or the family, with 5 percent commenting on politics or current events.[8]

Although Focus on the Family materials boast that the broadcasts reach five million listeners a day, what it does not mention is that James Dobson's thirty-minute program is aired only on Christian radio stations. Many non-Christians have read *Focus on the Family,* a magazine mailed to 2.1 million people who pay nothing for the subscription. A more telling figure, however, is that there are 447,000 paid subscribers to *Brio, Breakaway, Club House,* and *Club House, Jr.,* magazines that clearly address the lives of Christian children and teenagers. *Brio,* a publication for Christian teenaged girls, is mailed to 170,000 households, whereas the more political *Citizen* is sent to only eighty-six thousand. This essay moves beyond the crusading spirit of James Dobson and describes Focus on the Family as a major parachurch organization that speaks to conservative Christians and is listened to by large numbers of women and children.

Let me begin by placing Focus on the Family in the larger context of popular American Protestantism. During the nineteenth century, domestic Christianity—both worship in the family and worship of the family—was an integral part of mainstream Protestantism. By the early twentieth century, however, the assumption that an idolized home was the foundation of patriotism and piety had diminished in liberal and moderate Protestant thought. Modern social theories of the 1920s and 1930s that altered the views of liberal Protestants did not have the same effect on conservatives. Fundamentalist Protestants articulated their domestic ideology with the same vigor and commitment as they did their views on evolution and biblical criticism. Their continued support of Victorian separate spheres ideology was seen by the dominant culture as another example of their antimodern stance and only contributed to their exclusion from the power centers of politics, business, education, and entertainment.[9]

Following World War II, social mobility and economic prosperity enabled some conservative Protestants in the South and Midwest to enter the middle class. By the 1960s, a segment of the youth culture in the West was experimenting with "getting high on Jesus." Consequently, by the early 1970s a change was taking place in American Protestantism that had a profound impact on what it meant to be a "Christian." Some believers were saying that Christianity was not merely a set of beliefs and rituals but that God demanded the total commitment of the whole person. A relationship with Christ required that faith be integrated into every aspect of living; Sunday church-going was not enough. This holistic attitude of the Jesus movement combined with postwar economic expansion to create a Christian culture outside of clerical control. Believers began to write, publish, distribute, and buy Christian books. They did the same for Christian music, household decorations, clothing, and jewelry. Christian "academies" and eventually home schooling became popular as believers found ways to blend religion into their everyday lives. Teaching, retailing, clerical work, and administration—all would become acceptable Christian ministries. No longer would the triad of pastor, church, and seminary dominate Protestantism.[10]

Consequently, in 1970 when Tyndale House, a Christian publishing company, offered James Dobson an advance contract to write what would become *Dare to Discipline,* they knew that a book by a child development specialist had a good chance of selling. The same year that *Dare to Discipline* was published, Hal Lindsey's best-selling *The Late Great Planet Earth* appeared, and a year later *The Living Bible,* a paraphrase of the Scriptures in a breezy, modern style. In the first few months of its publication, *The Late Great Planet Earth* sold more than 130,000 copies, and *The Living Bible* held the number-one best-seller position well into 1973. In that year, Marabel Morgan published *Total Woman,* a Christian reflection on marriage relations that by 1975 was selling between ten and twenty thousand copies per week.[11] These unusually high book sales helped launch the Christian retailing industry by feeding the hunger for books geared to lay Christians. James Dobson would be one of several writers whose career would profit by the expansion of the Christian retailing industry. He appeared on the Christian landscape at the right time and with the right credentials.

Conservative Christianity survived the initial frenzy of the Jesus movement, the money and sex scandals of several televangelists, and the election of another Democratic president. If a young mother had bought *Dare to*

Discipline when it first appeared in 1970, she could now be passing her dog-eared copy on to her daughter with the hope that it might help *her* raise *her* rambunctious daughter. Or, grandmothers might buy the revised *The New Dare to Discipline* (1992) in book or audiocassette form. I refer to grandmothers, mothers, and daughters because it is women who outnumber men in conservative Protestant congregations, just as they do in liberal Protestant groups. This continues a trend starting in the mid-eighteenth century of women's numerical dominance in American Protestantism. Indeed, historian Ann Braude concludes that the history of American religion is the history of women.[12] For example in 1936, the year James Dobson was born, for every one hundred women in his denomination of the Church of the Nazarene there were only fifty-seven men.[13] As the essays in this volume demonstrate, Protestant women have reached into every aspect of church life and left their mark on community life, ritual, fund-raising, and theology. In spite of media fascination with Jerry Falwell and Pat Robinson, it is women's support of conservative Protestantism that has enabled it to succeed.

James Dobson seems well aware that most of his backers are women. "Consider this evidence," he wrote in a 1982 newsletter. "Who reads books on family living? Eighty percent are known to be women. Who attends seminars on meaningful family life? The majority are women. Who enrolls in bible study classes devoted to Scriptural underpinnings of the family? Women outnumber men by an incredible margin. Who listens to family radio programs and cassette tapes on marriage and parenthood? Once again, they are likely to be female."[14] In 1992 Focus on the Family conducted a demographic survey and not surprisingly found that women between the ages of thirty and forty-nine who had two or more children made up the majority of its audience. Half of these women said they had a college or postgraduate degree.[15] A similar profile exists for those who frequent Christian bookstores.[16] Women are more active than men in Protestant churches, and they support parachurch organizations that supplement, and at times even replace, denominational life.

Women not only support parachurch organizations, but they are also employed by them. From its conception in 1977, James Dobson employed women in the evolving Focus on the Family ministry. Photographs of his early days in Arcadia, California, show him surrounded by a small staff of women. They answered his mail, typed his manuscripts, and, most likely, gave their opinions on raising children. Dobson's staff was typical of post–1930s evangelistic enterprises that needed workers to sell books, staff summer camps, and organize offices.[17] As in secular industry, women filled these positions because of their experience in pink-collar jobs and their willingness to work part time for minimum salaries. Like most American businesses, Focus on the Family has a gender-segregated workplace. Men pack books for mailing, keep the computers running, and occupy most of the policy-making positions. Women answer the volumes of mail, greet people at the door, and perform most of the clerical duties. Of the ten magazines that Focus on the Family prints, women compose slightly more than half of the editors or associate editors.[18]

Susie Shellenberger is the "thirty-something" editor of Focus on the Family's magazine for teenaged girls, *Brio.* She exemplifies women's professional involvement in parachurch organizations that exceeds that of clerical work. With degrees in communication and creative writing from a Christian college, Shellenberger has worked in teaching, youth ministry, and now publishing. A hip dresser who tries to keep up with current fashion, Shellenberger is far from the stereotype of the "church lady" worker. Yet she, *Brio*'s designer Jan Aufdemberge, and assistant editor Marty McCormack are all single women and highly involved with the ministry of Focus on the Family. Each month they meet the professional challenges of publishing a full-color, thirty-to-forty-page magazine. Shellenberger also writes advice books for teenagers, ranging from serious discussions of sexual abuse to light-hearted surveys of how to manage dating. She is a strong voice in *Brio,* and when she goes on lecture tours she arranges meetings with her *Brio* "sisses." There is no question that for many young Christian women she represents the possibility of not only having a career but also of having a career within a Christian organization. For women, parachurch organizations and Christian industries provide ministries that far exceed those of pastor, director of Christian education, church organist, or theology professor.

The Christianity that Focus on the Family articulates is a Bible-based, personalized faith that avoids theological disputes by flattening all denominational differences. Ideas or actions that might cause controversy or division among readers and listeners are rarely, if ever, introduced. That observation might come as a surprise to those familiar with what James Dobson calls his "fighting words."[19] I would argue, however, that the audience of Focus on the Family already believes what it preaches, and so fighting words are meant to rally the troops, not convince them. The retreat from controversy is clearly seen in how Focus on the Family treats women's reproductive rights.

Although Focus on the Family produces inexpensive booklets on topics as wide-ranging as menopause, addictive behavior, and safety tips for the home, there are no pamphlets that address family planning for a married couple. And yet families represented in Focus on the Family materials rarely have more than two or three children. James Dobson's mother was told after the birth of her son that "any attempt to have more children could be life threatening."[20] She had no more children. A sage Christian psychologist warned the young Dobson not to rush into marriage and family, and he and his wife Shirley complied. The couple married when James was twenty-four, and they postponed the birth of their first child until James was thirty. Although it is certainly possible that Christian couples through illness, abstinence, or infertility achieve small family sizes, a more plausible explanation is that they use condoms and other contraceptives.

When I asked about Dobson's attitude toward birth control, I was given three letters, all of which said that he found nothing morally wrong with the prevention of pregnancy. Although he condemns the use of the "morning after pill" (RU486) as an abortifacient, he leaves the question of vasectomies and tubal ligations up to individual judgment. In one of the letters, however, Clarence R. Holbrook, a correspondence assistant, explained why Focus on the Family does not engage in discussion of family planning: "The last time we offered such a broadcast [on birth control pills], the ensuing mail revealed how very wide is the array of opinions that exists among committed believers in this area. . . . It seems we are bound to offend someone as soon as we open our mouths, and we continue to receive criticism from listeners with differing perspectives despite our attempts to present a balanced treatment of the subject. This is why we have no plans for future programs of this kind."[21] To dwell on birth control is to spotlight one of the areas of division among supporters of "family values." Catholics, of course, have long divided over birth control. A vocal minority of conservative Protestants also rejects artificial birth control and promotes natural family planning. Unlike opposition to abortion, which has become an identity marker for conservative Christians, attitudes toward birth control do not forge the same unity. Reproductive freedom, as long as abortion is not an option, is assumed but not described.

Family planning is only one of many topics on which Focus on the Family is silent. *Brio* carries articles on Christian women musicians, gymnasts, actresses, soccer players, and rodeo riders but not on woman ministers. Girls in the stories go to church, not to a Baptist church or an Assemblies of God church. Likewise, teenagers are counseled that dating non-Christians is "risky business," but the reader is left to determine what exactly a Christian is. Do Unitarians or Episcopalians qualify?[22] Speaking in tongues, imagining what the Rapture might be like, being confirmed—none of these religious activities are described in print. *Brio* is not unique in this regard. Most Focus on the Family publications avoid mentioning denominational associations that would indicate that there is dissent within Christianity. The Bible-based piety of Focus on the Family shuns conflict, controversy, and division.

There is certainly truth to the frequently stated notion that conservative Christians see actions in the world as right or wrong, good or evil. They want truth with a capital T, and so they ignore evidence that might contradict the unity of God's world. Likewise, it is obvious that in order for Focus on the Family to appeal to the largest possible audience, it has to present a generic, some might say even "watered down" Christianity. The rejection of speculation, analysis, and argumentation is more than a fundamentalist retreat from modernity, however. Avoiding controversy and presenting a form of consensus Christianity may make the publications and media messages of Focus on the Family particularly appealing to modern women and girls. While debate and division might appear to be a sign of life to some, studies by feminist psychologists, educators, and linguists show that women and girls respond differently to conflict than men and boys.[23]

Studies of adolescents in the classroom show that assertive boys who demand, and receive, attention from teachers frequently overpower less-demanding girls. Boys feel more secure in experimenting with active, risk-taking learning styles, whereas girls value silence and compliance. Girls want to "get along" and strive to please others through consensus behavior. Developmental studies of college students have led some researchers to assert that when girls grow up, many feel uncomfortable with "separate knowing." "Separate knowledge" is a form of critical thinking that takes an impersonal stance and strives for unbiased reflection. It is the expression of "an objective, analytical voice, one that exercises care and precision." This way of knowing frequently takes an adversarial approach, with the primary mode of discourse being the argument. Feminist educators have noticed that women students are less comfortable and less adept in expressing separate knowledge than are men. While men like to argue and find argument useful in shaping their thinking, women prefer a more connected form of knowing. Psychologist Blythe Clinchy writes, "I am not saying that women will not or cannot think. I *am* saying that many women would rather think *with* someone than think *against* someone."[24] Many women—for reasons of nurture or nature—find analytical debate to be silencing.

Research on gender differences is in no way conclusive, and Blythe Clinchy admits that different modes of thinking are probably gender-related not gender-exclusive. I introduce gendered ways of knowing because I believe that idea helps explain not only why women prefer a Christianity that is not controversial but also why Focus on the Family magazines are surprisingly realistic. While Christianity must be presented as a truth all believers recognize and share, everyday life is permitted its blemishes and inconsistencies. Realism is not conveyed through careful analysis of theology or social policy but through discussions of mental and physical dysfunctions of particular families and individuals. Consequently, in spite of the tendency to idealize the "traditional" family in political rhetoric, magazines and books directed at Focus on the Family readers admit that the Christian family has real problems that vacillate between the catastrophic and the minor.

Developmental psychologists contrast "separate knowing" with "connected knowing." In connected knowing, a student learns not through detached debate but through collaboration and empathy. "Connected knowers," writes Clinchy, "deliberately bias themselves in favor of the thing they are examining. They try to get right inside it, to form an intimate attachment to it." In connected knowledge, emotion is not outlawed, and personal experience is used "as a means of understanding what produced the idea you are attempting to understand." Rather than bracketing personal feelings or experiences, a connected knower learns best when she can use her own life to make sense of another life.

Focus on the Family publications teach women and girl readers through realistic stories of modern life. Feature articles, fiction, and radio broadcasts give sensible descriptions of problems accompanied by suggestions for their remedy. Readers can relate their experiences to those described in the magazines or radio broadcasts. After this connection is accomplished, it is easier to give serious attention to the advice and strategies presented by Focus on the Family writers. Descriptions of realistic experiences and practical advice make up the bulk of Focus on the Family magazines. In the August 1997 "Money Talk" section of *Single-Parent Family,* a "single working mother" asks Mary Hunt: "Do I need disability insurance?" In the same issue articles point out the types of children in dysfunctional families ("the Placater," "the Responsible One"), suggest ways to cope with clutter in your home, and advise how to deal with a three-year-old who starts wetting the bed after a divorce ("Be patient, kind and loving. Offer him security, constancy, trust and lots of affection. If the behavior persists, ask your pediatrician what to do or get advice from experienced parents"). If a reader is touched by a story or advice column, Focus on the Family can then provide more discursive booklets and resource lists on topics ranging from how to escape anorexia to how to devise a family budget.

Tempered realism also pervades *Brio.* In one fictionalized story a teenager copes with her grandmother's Alzheimer's disease and in another a big brother is institutionalized for depression ("Doctors can often treat depression like other diseases"). In another short story, a girl confesses to her parents that her grandfather "touches me in places I don't like." At the end, readers are directed to the *Brio* publication *When Someone You Know Is Sexually*

Abused. Rather than sentimental morality fables, these stories show protagonists who become angry, frustrated, frightened, and embarrassed. At the same time, however, writers portray people who alleviate those problems through a combination of faith in God and psychological astuteness. Few articles end with the conflict or problem being fully resolved, but all end optimistically.[25]

The pages of *Brio* are sprinkled with the pictures of real sisses who have handicaps, wear braces, and inhabit messy bedrooms. Editor Susie Shellenberger and designer Jan Aufdemberge have made a conscious decision to provide readers with realistic role models who look and talk like *Brio* readers. While girls might fantasize about being an Olympic soccer star, they also are informed that Michelle Akers suffers from Chronic Fatigue and Immune Dysfunction Syndrome. When the editors ran a spread on back-to-school fashions, many *Brio* sisses wrote in that the clothing was too expensive. Who could spend $60 on a turtleneck? Readers wanted fashionable styles, but ones they could realistically afford. Focus on the Family appeals to women and girls because it acknowledges that Christians have problems, provides clear and reasonable advice, and continuously reminds them to rely on God's strength and love. Behavior changes are accomplished through an emotional connection with a common Christianity, not through reasoned, analytical persuasion.[26]

The tempered realism of Focus on the Family publications parallels the philosophy of their founder. From his earliest writings, Dobson has used anecdotes to illustrate problems and prove his points. Drawing from his own family experiences, his brief involvement in teaching, and his friends, Dobson is skilled at constructing short, descriptive narratives. In spite of media fascination with Dobson's acceptance of spanking, the stories he tells consistently urge readers to use understanding to cope with the behavior of their children and families. Empathy, far more than discipline, is Dobson's battle cry.

In 1974 James Dobson wrote that low self-esteem was a major problem in successful child-rearing. Like other psychologists of the time, he encouraged parents to counter feelings of inferiority in their children. "If we are to understand our children—their feelings and behavior," he wrote, "then we must sharpen our memories of our own childhood." It was sensitivity, not discipline, which Dobson preached in *Hide or Seek*: "Sensitivity is the key word. It means 'tuning in' to the thoughts and feelings of our kids, listening to the cues they give us, and reacting appropriately to what we detect there." Consequently, we should not be surprised that in many of Dobson's stories parents are asked to submit to the desires of their children. To the parents of a thirteen-year-old who wanted a brassiere (even though she was flat as a board), he explained, "Your daughter needs a bra to be like her friends, to compete, to avoid ridicule, and to feel like a woman." At other times, he chided a grandmother who expected her two-year-old grandson to be potty-trained. Later he disagreed with parents who wanted to get rid of their son's menagerie of snakes, wasp nests, plants, and insects ("bugs beat drugs as a hobby"). Although Dobson certainly believes in imposing limits on childhood behavior, when queried in 1993 on his support for spanking he responded much the same way as in 1974: "The key to raising healthy, responsible children," he told an interviewer for *Christianity Today,* "is to be able to get behind the eyes of the child and see what he sees, think what he thinks, and feel what he feels. If you know how to do that, then you know how to respond appropriately for him."[27] If there is any credence in the theory that women have a more connected way of knowing, it is not surprising that they would respond positively to Dobson's empathetic perspective.

Dobson's interest in modern life and his unacknowledged acceptance of many modern psychological traditions support what sociologist Mark Shibley calls, "the Californication of Conservative Protestantism." Shibley argues that as people moved out of the South and settled in other parts of the country, they brought with them southern styles of worship, values, and beliefs. Evangelical Christianity began to appear in the urban centers of the East and Midwest and eventually the West. Non-Southerners encountered these traditions and began to embrace southern styles of religion, leading to a resurgence of evangelicalism. Shibley calls this the "southernization of American religion." Southerners and their religion were also changing, however. Shibley contends that in California the more rigid southern faith had to bend to the openness of western living. Evangelicalism there would have a more democratic structure, stress religious experience, tolerate a certain level of difference among its members, and be oriented toward church programs. Shibley concludes, "Continued vitality of a religious institution is contingent on its achieving a 'cultural fit' between its constituents and the beliefs and practices it promulgates."[28] Evangelicalism in the West would not be as it was in the South.

James Dobson and his family are excellent examples of Shibley's thesis. In 1936 the depression was in full force when Dobson's father began his career as a Church of the Nazarene pastor and traveling evangelist. Like many who had difficulties finding work during the depression, Dobson frequently moved his family. His preaching jobs took them to Louisiana, Arkansas, Oklahoma, and Texas. After high school graduation in 1954, James Dobson, Jr., left San Bonito, Texas, to attend a Nazarene college in Pasadena, California. His interests were decidedly worldly: a passion for tennis and the humanities, a fondness for writing, and the desire to become a psychologist. If Dobson had a southern evangelistic spirit that "men rule, women submit, and children obey," it did not survive long in the orange groves and gentle climes of Los Angeles.

In 1967 Dobson received his doctorate, producing a dissertation on dietary treatment for phenylketonuria, a rare disease that if left unchecked leads to severe retardation. Dobson continued this work as a researcher at the Children's Hospital of Los Angeles. Along with the position came an appointment as a clinical assistant professor of pediatrics at the University of California Medical School.

Dobson seemed to be on a trajectory that precluded the Christian ministry, but at the same time he was researching his doctoral dissertation he was "mastering the art of public speaking." Dobson did not want to be an ivory-tower investigator but rather hoped to be a "public" psychologist and talk about "something with an immediate, practical impact."[29] In postwar America, James Dobson would be able to forge a career as a Christian psychologist who had the credentials of the secular world and the commitments of the religious.

Dobson's involvement in modern society is reflected in his use of popular psychology, his competitive sports spirit, and his successful construction of a multi-million-dollar organization. Focus on the Family publications continue this "Californication of Conservative Protestantism" by carefully adapting modern styles to Christian purposes. Susie Shellenberger and Jan Aufdemberge, for instance, do not read other religious magazines in order to get ideas for *Brio*. They instead read popular teen publications like *Seventeen* and the now-defunct *Sassy*. Although they reject what they deem as tasteless or overly sexual, they freely borrow format from popular magazines. *Brio* is filled with self-surveys ("How Good a Friend Are You?"), letters to the editor, biographical sketches of Christian music stars, and beauty tips. In her column "La Glamour" Andrea Stevens recommends facial hair removers, explains how to use blush, and warns against wearing pink lipstick with red clothes ("those two colors clash"). In Greg Johnson and Susie Shellenberger's *Getting Ready for the Guy/Girl Thing*, dating is an assumed norm. "Dear Susie," writes one fifteen-year-old, "my boyfriend of four months hasn't called me for two weeks. . . . Should I phone him again?" The answer: "Time to read the signs, Babe. If your boyfriend hasn't called, it's for a reason."[30]

Brio editors do not reject the female fascination with beauty, clothes, and the opposite sex. Instead, *Brio* shows that a middle ground exists between the rigors of religious faith and the delights of modern living. Faith in Christ does not entail a total rejection of contemporary life but rather a modification of teenage desires in ways that permit Christian youths to participate in consumer culture while holding steady on certain key religious issues. As one *Brio* reader observes, "As young Christian women, it is important to look nice and wear makeup but not to the point where it is our focus."[31] Wearing makeup, talking to boys on the telephone, holding a job at McDonald's—these activities are in and of themselves not problematic as long as the teen follows the dictates of her parents, refrains from sexual activity (anything past handholding and simple kissing), and maintains a personal relationship with Jesus. Indeed, the creation of a Christian consumer culture encourages her to continue to buy CDs of her favorite music, receive "chastity rings" as gifts from her parents, and go on "mission trips" during summer vacation. *Brio* provides Christian girls with a unique religious identity while supporting their interest in common teenage activities promoted by the general culture.

If Christian girls can participate in a consumer culture that mixes faith and fashion, Christian women should be able to manage the adult activities of work and religion. In most families in America, Christian included, women are involved in the workplace. Dobson has consistently supported women in their right to decide whether to work outside of the home. Consequently, when *Focus on the Family* did a story on "Motherhood in the Nineties," it included all types of mothers, including those who work. The article featured a single divorced mother on welfare, one who had a baby at thirty-nine, and another who ran a business out of her house. One mother stayed at home with her children, and another worked full time.[32] A short "portrait" in *Single-Parent Family* tells of a single woman who worked as a senior production manager for *Christianity Today* and who adopted three mixed-race children. None of the women in those articles have perfect lives, but all are committed Christians.

In another article, a mother of a nine-month-old baby discusses the issues of working mothers. Although Konny Thompson had hoped to be a "stay-at-home mom," she found her family not only needed the salary but also, "Over time I was glad to be involved in the working world. I welcomed the intelligent conversation of adults." While she honestly reflects on missing her daughter's daytime life, she also mentions the benefits of day care ("she certainly seems more social, verbal, more outgoing"). The article did not present Konny Thompson as unhappy and unfulfilled because she was breaking the natural order designed by God. As with many women's magazines, Focus on the Family points out the frustrations of women's employment without leveling judgment. Such articles encourage Christian women to acknowledge that their lives are difficult and to describe how a relationship with Jesus makes living easier.[33]

The reason that judgment is missing from such articles is that all these women have a sustained, intimate relationship with Christ. Konny Thompson is a Christian and works full time for the parachurch organization World Vision. She confesses she is in conflict over how to manage her home and career. She knows, however, that God will "pick me up when I fall," and so she has confidence in her decisions. What is abundantly clear from Focus on the Family publications is not that women should submit to God, their families, and their husbands but that women should create intense and stable relationships with these significant entities.

Focus on the Family taps into a long tradition in evangelical Protestantism that describes Jesus as a loving friend, companion, and supporter. As one *Brio* writer puts it, "Being a Christian means you've asked Jesus to come into your heart and be the most important Person in your life."[34] Focus on the Family does not spell out specific norms for teenage behavior, motherhood, or femininity. It assumes that if women and girls follow a few basic guidelines, their relationship with Christ will take care of the rest. Relationship rather than obedience is the foundation for success, both in faith and in life.

Focus on the Family has institutionalized the importance of communication and relationship into its organizational structure. When one takes a tour of the office building in Colorado Springs, guides lead visitors up a ramp to a glassed-off area. There the visitors peer out over a vast room full of small cubicles where numerous employees are answering mail, faxes, and e-mail. This is what tour guides call the "hidden ministry." In his radio broadcasts Dobson encourages listeners to contact Focus on the Family with questions and problems. All Focus on the Family publications, videos, and newsletters also encourage people to contact the organization. More than half of Focus on the Family's 1,300 employees have something to do with keeping up with constituent correspondence. If a listener merely wants a tape or a publication, agents in the teleservices department code the request, and eventually the material is packed and shipped. On any given day, Focus on the Family processes more than thirteen thousand orders and mails approximately six thousand parcels. It has its own postal Zip code and full-time postal worker. As a nonprofit organization, a suggested donation is requested, but materials are shipped regardless of payment.

Approximately 10 percent of the correspondence, "pain mail," is transferred to the correspondence and research department for a more thorough response. Using a sophisticated computer system that requires a staff of fifty to keep it going, correspondence assistants key information contained in a letter or call into a central system. This enables Focus on the Family to maintain a mailing list of four million names and addresses. By accessing a computerized database that covers more than 850 topics, correspondents then access "model" letters based on the issues discussed in the letter. Eight to ten "master writers" compose responses on topics not found in the model-letter database. The assistant may also search the computer's data banks or the books in reference areas for resources that might also address the query. All of Dobson's books, newsletters, and tapes are indexed and online. Slight adjustments in the model letter may be made, and then it is signed by the correspondence assistant and mailed. If additional pamphlets or books are to be sent, a notation is made for shipping. It takes the staff three or four days to process a letter and mail a response.

Telephone correspondence assistants handle between thirty-five and forty calls per day, using their desktop computers to record information on the caller and search for appropriate answers to queries or materials to send. Those in the "phone room" are something like reference librarians who have excellent listening skills and strong Christian commitments. Both telephone and mail correspondents have four-year college degrees and spend between six and eight weeks in training. If a call demands more psychological care than the correspondence assistant can furnish, it is "transferred upstairs." "Upstairs" is the counseling department, where seventeen licensed Christian counselors provide a one-time counseling session to the caller. They then refer the caller to Christian counselors located in his or her city.

The amount of correspondence that Focus on the Family processes and its use of technology to facilitate speedy responses are impressive. Yet it is quite common for people to write letters about personal topics to religious or social organizations. Catholics have a long tradition of sending to shrines letters that discuss problems, healings, and miracles. As early as the 1870s, American Catholics wrote letters about their illnesses and cures to priests at Notre Dame. The priests mailed small vials of Lourdes water to the devout, and in return those healed wrote letters of thanks. During the depression, thousands of letters were sent to Franklin D. Roosevelt. Likewise, Americans have sent letters to "Betty Crocker" and "Ann Landers." Sometimes asking for advice, other times using the letter as a means of making sense of a difficult experience, letter writing has a long tradition in American culture. In *Thank You, St. Jude,* Robert Orsi documents how women maintained their devotion to the patron saint of hopeless causes through their correspondence.[35] Marie Griffith indicates in this volume (chapter 9) that Pentecostal women during the 1930s also wrote of their illnesses and healing experiences.

In each of these cases, the writers created a relationship with a saint or president or priest by sending the letter. Reading a devotional magazine, listening to a radio broadcast, or seeing a column in a newspaper motivated writers to express themselves to someone who was there but not there. Focus on the

Family falls in this letter-writing tradition. Problems that occur in a family can be expressed to "James Dobson" in Colorado Springs. A week or so later a letter arrives, acknowledging the problem and making helpful suggestions. Easy-to-understand materials might accompany the letter. If the person cares to, he or she may call Focus on the Family and receive a quicker response to an issue. Alternatively, they may argue with whomever answers the telephone. In either case, there is a direct, person-to-person connection made between the "audience" and the organization. Through its use of up-to-date technology, Focus on the Family has created a way for large numbers of people to access information and gain a feeling that they count as individuals.

James Dobson continues to be a defining force in Focus on the Family, but the organization itself has a life of its own. Although Dobson may be increasingly involved with right-wing politics and more rigid in his opinions, what attracts women and girls to Focus on the Family is more than Christian certitude. Concern for home matters, a sense of personal caring, and a realistic attitude toward modern life keep women and girls listening to the Focus on the Family message. People do not flock to Focus on the Family and tour its facilities merely because of its Right to Life philosophy, anti-gay agenda, and Dobson's support of spanking. They come because their children have been enchanted by *McGee and Me* videos, their teenagers have learned strategies to "just say no," and their wives have read about other Christian women who balance work with family. Focus on the Family supports conservative Christians because it shows them how to be faithful and still enjoy the benefits of modern life.

Women and girls find in the Christianity of Focus on the Family a religion that is unified, connected, practical, and relational. Rather than engage in theological speculation or ethical argumentation, Focus on the Family is silent on any issue that would divide or demand an analytical response. Behavioral traits that already are identity-markers for Conservative Christians, such as the rejection of abortion and premarital virginity, do not provoke dissent among readers. Topics such as birth control or the ordination of women ministers are absent from their publications and broadcasts. Rather than engage in speculation, Focus on the Family publications and broadcasts try to provide practical advice and strategies. Readers and listeners are provided clues on how to "practice" Christianity in contemporary America.

The long-range goal of Focus on the Family is to integrate Christianity into every aspect of life—from child-rearing to entertainment to consumerism. Rather than seek the separation of good Christianity from bad modern culture, Focus on the Family assumes that faith must meet modern families where they are now. Women, who find that they cannot easily disconnect family lives from their working and religious lives, may find this type of Christianity more in tune with their emotional outlooks. Integration of faith with life, rather than separation of faith from life, may better parallel the connected knowledge of women and girls. The success of James Dobson's message and his organization may be more due to his emphasis on relationship and empathy than a fundamentalist wish for "clarity, certitude, and control."[36]

Notes

1. Carol Kreck, "Spoon Spanking Divides Experts; Bible Says Don't Use Hand, Some Experts Claim," *Denver Post*, Aug. 3, 1997.

2. Philip Greven, *Spare the Child: The Religious Roots of Punishment and the Psychological Impact of Physical Abuse* (New York: Vintage Books, 1990), 68.

3. John P. Bartkowski and Christopher G. Ellison, "Divergent Models of Childrearing in Popular Manuals: Conservative Protestants vs. the Mainstream Experts," *Sociology of Religion* 56 (1995): 30, 21.

4. This number, as with all the statistics in this essay, must be taken as unverifiable approximations provided by Focus on the Family. Focus on the Family is a dynamic organization. I gathered the information for this essay during the summer of 1997, so the statistics, publications, and staff that I mention may no longer reflect the current situation at Focus on the Family.

5. "Who We Are and What We Stand For," *Focus on the Family* (Aug. 1993): 10.

6. Michael Liensch, *Redeeming America: Piety and Politics in the New Christian Right* (Chapel Hill: University of North Carolina Press, 1993), 53.

7. I use the term *conservative Christian* to refer to those variously described as evangelical, fundamentalist, charismatic, holiness, right-wing Protestant, or born again.

8. Tom Neven, "A Day in the Life of Focus on the Family," *Focus on the Family* (March 1997): 9.

9. On domestic religion, see Colleen McDannell, *The Christian Home in Victorian America, 1840–1900* (Bloomington: Indiana University Press, 1986), and Colleen McDannell, "Parlor Piety: The Home as Sacred Space in Protestant America," in *American Home Life, 1880–1930: A Social History of Spaces and Services*, ed. Jessica H. Foy and Thomas Schlereth (Knoxville: University of Tennesee Press, 1992), 162–89. On fundamentalism and women, see Betty A. DeBerg, *Ungodly Women: Gender and the First Wave of American Fundamentalism* (Minneapolis: Fortress Press, 1990), and Margaret Lamberts Bendroth, *Fundamentalism and Gender, 1875 to the Present* (New Haven: Yale University Press, 1993).

10. On the evolution of postwar conservative Protestantism, see Colleen McDannell, *Material Christianity: Religion and Popular Culture in America* (New Haven: Yale University Press, 1995), 229–76, and Colleen McDannell, "Creating the Christian Home: Homeschooling in Contemporary America," in *American Sacred Space*, ed. Edward T. Linenthal and David Chidester (Bloomington: Indiana University Press, 1995), 187–219, as well as David Harrington Watt, *A Transforming Faith: Explorations of Twentieth-Century American Evangelicalism* (New Brunswick: Rutgers University Press, 1991).

11. McDannell, *Material Christianity*, 247.

12. Ann Braude, "Women's History *Is* American Religious History," in *Retelling U.S. Religious History*, ed. Thomas A. Tweed (Berkeley: University of California Press, 1997).

13. U.S. Bureau of the Census, *Census of Religious Bodies, 1936, Bulletin no. 1–78* (Washington, D.C.: Government Printing Office, 1939–40), 458.

14. James Dobson, *Focus on the Family Newsletter*, Nov. 2, 1982, 1.

15. The demographic survey is cited in Gustave Niebuhr, "Advice for Parents and for Politicians," *New York Times*, May 30, 1995, A10.

16. Thomas W. Gruen et al., *1992 CBA Christian Bookstore Customer Profile Expanded Statistics* (Colorado Springs: CBA Center for Research and Information, 1991).

17. Bendroth, *Fundamentalism and Gender*, 74.

18. As of July 1997, in senior editorial staff, editor, associate editor, or assistant editor jobs for *Physician*, there were two women; for *Single-Parent Family*, one man, one woman; for *Pastor's Family*, one man, one woman; for *Focus on the Family*, one man, one woman; for *Brio*, two women; for *Breakaway*, two men; for *Citizen*, two men; for *Club House*, one woman; for *Club House Jr.*, one woman; and for *Teacher*, one man.

19. James Dobson, "Why I Use 'Fighting Words': A Response to John Woodbridge's 'Culture War Casualities,'" *Christianity Today* 39 (1995): 27.

20. Rolf Zettersten, *Dr. Dobson: Turning Hearts toward Home: The Life and Principles of America's Family Advocate* (Dallas: Word Publishing, 1989), 33.

21. Clarence R. Holbrook to Colleen McDannell, July 31, 1997.

22. Kim Boyce, "Unequally Yoked: The Truth about Dating Non-Christians," *Brio* (Feb. 1997): 28.

23. Carol Gilligan, *In a Different Voice: Psychological Theory and Women's Development* (Cambridge: Harvard University Press, 1982); Mary Field Belenky et al. *Women's Ways of Knowing: The Development of Self, Value, and Mind* (New York: Basic Books, 1986).

24. All of the quotations on separate and connected knowing are taken from Blythe McVicker Clinchy, "Issues of Gender in Teaching and Learning," in *Teaching and Learning in the College Classroom*, ed. Kenneth A. Feldman and Michael B. Paulsen (New York: Simon and Schuster, 1994), 115–25.

25. On depression, see Margaret Lannamann, "Rumors about Rory," *Brio* (Dec. 1996): 28–30, and Jeenie Gordon, "Is Life a Bummer, or Are You Just Bummed?" *Brio* (Dec. 1996): 10–12 (a nonfiction discussion). On sexual abuse see Barbara King, "A Family Secret," *Brio* (March 1997).

26. The 1997 "Brio Girl" Lindy Morgan wears braces on the cover of the January 1997 issue, and Jill Battaglia is pictured in her wheelchair on the cover of the October 1996 *Brio*. On the Olympic soccer star, see Judith A. Nelson, "Gold and Glory through Pain and Tears," *Brio* (July 1997); on clothing, see "After Class," *Brio* (Sept. 1995), and author interview with Susie Shellenberger, July 29, 1997.

27. James Dobson, *Hide or Seek* (Old Tappan, N.J.: Fleming H. Revell, 1974), 43, 53. On brassieres, see Dobson, *Hide or Seek*, 58; see also *Newsletter* (July 1992[?]); *Focus on the Family* (July 1982): 4 (on "creepy things"); and "Interview: Dobson's New Dare," *Christianity Today*, Feb. 8, 1993, 69.

28. Mark A. Shibley, *Resurgent Evangelicalism in the United States: Mapping Cultural Change since 1970* (Columbia: University of South Carolina Press, 1996), 109.

29. Tim Stafford, "His Father's Son," *Christianity Today* 32 (1988): 20.

30. Greg Johnson and Susie Shellenberger, *Getting Ready for the Guy/Girl Thing* (Ventura, Calif.: Regal Books, 1991).

31. Stephanie Cheny, "Stephanie Says," *Brio* (Oct. 1996): 15.

32. "Motherhood in the Nineties," *Focus on the Family* (Jan. 1990): 9–17; Peg Roen, "Risking to Love," *Single-Parent Family* (July 1997): 3–5.

33. Konny Thompson, "Torn between Two Worlds," *Focus on the Family* (May 1983): 12–13.

34. Teresa Clery, "Pen Pals," *Brio* (Oct. 1996): 11.

35. On letters about healing from Lourdes water, see McDannell, *Material Christianity*, 132–62; on letters to pop culture figures, see Roland Marchand, *Advertising the American Dream: Making Way for Modernity, 1920–1940* (Berkeley: University of California Press, 1985), 353–56; on letters to President Roosevelt and St. Jude, see Robert A. Orsi, *Thank You, St. Jude: Women's Devotion to the Patron Saint of Impossible Causes* (New Haven: Yale University Press, 1996).

36. Karen McCarthy Brown, "Fundamentalism and the Control of Women," in *Fundamentalism and Gender*, ed. John Stratton Hawley (New York: Oxford University Press, 1994), 176.

PART 3

Constructing Women's Religious Experience

IN THIS SECTION we turn to essays that pay particular attention to how women as individuals and groups *construe* their experiences, especially through their texts. The authors of these essays explore the utterances of decidedly nonelite women—Chinese immigrant women in the case of Timothy Tseng, turn-of-the-century African American women writing for denominational journals in the case of Laurie Maffly-Kipp, and early female Pentecostals, black and white, in the case of Marie Griffith. Fortunately, these authors approach these rather humble texts at a time when literary canons are under attack, and so they hardly need to defend the legitimacy of their endeavors. They also write at a time when many scholars are preoccupied with how human beings "construct" themselves through language from diverse parts of their experiences. Chinese American women, for instance, built complex identities that drew from a multitude of sources: single white female missionaries, Chinese nationalism, civic activism in the Chinese American Christian community, Victorian domesticity, and Buddhist, Taoist, Confucian, and folk traditions. Finally, these essays respond to a recent renewed interest in popular religion—religion as lived and expressed by ordinary and usually silenced people.

In these essays we can enjoy a sense of "hearing" real voices of persons who are selecting their words and phrases, reflecting intense joys and fears and aspirations, and describing characteristic women's concerns and attitudes. To be sure, interpreters must use care; they cannot always be sure they are understanding words in the way writers were using them.

Moreover, the subjects of these essays operated under certain constraints. They were writing for certain readers, they had a certain defined vocabulary available to them, and all sorts of arbitrary factors determined whether their words would see the light of day. Griffith, for instance, is aware that male editors of Pentecostal publications made choices about which letters to print, which thus set a suggestive pattern for would-be writers to follow. Likewise, Maffly-Kipp reminds us that male editors oversaw what was published in most black denominational publications. Whatever cautions we approach these texts with, they are precious gifts from the past and ones well worth spending time on.

One of the virtues of these essays is that the writers manage to empathize with their subjects without valorizing them. That is no easy feat. At times, modernity can make late-nineteenth- and twentieth-century texts quite difficult to approach, especially the testimonies, prayer requests, and folk beliefs. No matter how open-minded most readers try to be, we come to those utterances with certain rational assumptions about the way things happen in the world and in history. If nothing else, we expect a certain level of theological sophistication and spiritual maturity. Most contemporary readers, for example, are skeptical about the healing power of anointed handkerchiefs and uncomfortable about a God who is addressed as a father or close friend. They cringe at suggestions of sentimentality, or, worse, signs that writers—often homemakers—acquiesce to, or even approve of, the gender arrangements of their era. Griffith acknowledges that "the language of divine appeal bespeaks a kind of desperation unfitting to women—a vulnerability that plays into gender stereotypes we would prefer to dismantle." We are used to making allowances for texts from distant times and places, of course, and from cultures radically different from our own. But the closer the text comes to the early-twenty-first-century, middle-class situation, the harder it is to be simultaneously critical and sympathetic and the more forcibly standards of literary and theological merit seem to impinge.

Here, we'd suggest, our postmodern imaginations can come to our rescue—our enjoyment of all kind of literary genres, from naturalism to magical realism to history in fictional form; our greater readiness to acknowledge that not only the rational and commonsensical govern experience; and our dawning recognition that the secular and the sacred, the natural and the supernatural may not be quite as separate as modernity once supposed. We think the following essays capture this postmodern sensibility admirably.

7. Unbinding Their Souls: Chinese Protestant Women in Twentieth-Century America

TIMOTHY TSENG

AFTER A DECADE'S WORK as superintendent and de facto minister of the Chinese Baptist Mission in New York City's Chinatown, Mabel Ping-hua Lee, Ph.D., decided to visit her birthplace.[1] The year 1937, as it turned out, was not a particularly good year for the Chinese in China or in the United States and Canada. The Japanese attack on Shanghai that summer sparked a bloody, prolonged conflict between the two East Asian nations. The Great Depression in North America reinforced an urban racial segregation that frustrated educated young Chinese Americans in search of professional careers outside of Chinatowns.[2] For Lee, these difficulties were compounded by the fact that she depended upon white Christians to vouch for her good character. "It is a pleasure to present Miss Mabel Lee, PhD," wrote the executive secretary of the New York City Baptist Missionary Society in a letter Lee was to keep in her possession while she traveled. Miss Lee, Charles Sears continued, was "leaving today for a trip to her old home near Canton, China, planning to return to America in about two or three months." Then he confirmed that Lee was employed by the missionary society, assuring immigration officials of her legal right of reentry into the United States. Finally, he added, "Any courtesy extended to Dr. Lee will be appreciated by this organization and by me personally."[3]

Lee was fortunate to return to the United States with her life and Sears's letter. Within the year, the Japanese Imperial Army had seized most of China's coastal cities and nearly trapped her in a messy conflict. Several years earlier, she had pondered a permanent return to China, but all hopes of establishing a future there were dashed by the war. Turning her attention to the Baptist mission on Pell Street in New York City, Lee decided to take the advice of her close friend, the eminent Chinese literary scholar Hu Shih, and transform the mission into a social service center.[4]

Since her student days at Barnard College and Columbia University, Lee had espoused the necessity of Christian social service and civic participation, along with Chinese nationalism and woman's suffrage. As she attempted to build such a center, however, the lingering effects of the economic depression and the reluctance of the New York City Baptist Missionary Society to yield control of the mission became major obstacles. Throughout her career, Lee was more preoccupied with her complex, often frustrating, interactions with white, male, Baptist executives than with the Chinese men and boys in her mission. She often expressed both resentment and appreciation—sometimes simultaneously—toward the mission's benefactors for their paternalistic control. Her ties with the Baptist sponsors gave her unusual authority over the Chinese mission, but they also kept her dependent upon the sponsors' goodwill. Caught between lost hopes of returning to China and a dependence upon white men, it is not surprising that Lee was perceived to be "temperamental" as she fought for full control of the mission.[5]

In 1950 she managed to wrest the mission away from the missionary society and reorganize it as an independent congregation. By then, however, years of struggle had caught up with a far less energetic Lee. The religious culture among Chinese Americans was also changing dramatically. The generation of American-born Chinese women that came after Mabel Lee's generation adopted a more secular and Americanized outlook and considered the mission outdated. Meanwhile, Chinese fundamentalists and evangelicals from overseas were gradually making their way to North America, ready to transform Chinese American Protestantism.

Mabel Lee's life illustrates a paradox in the history of Chinese Protestant women in North America. Many experienced social awakening and personal empowerment before 1950, when the number of Chinese women in the United States and Canada was a tiny fraction of the total Chinese population. At that time, Chinese women were stigmatized as prostitutes and victims.[6] Racial segregation directly affected the Chinese because immigration laws excluded all Chinese but those who were American-born, religious workers, students, or diplomats.[7]

That Chinese Protestant women of Mabel Lee's generation were able to assume active roles in church and civic life confirms Judy Yung's thesis that Protestantism was a significant catalyst in the awakening of Chinese women's consciousness in the United States before World War II.[8] The women were nurtured in an ethos of "civic" evangelicalism that emerged from urban Chinatown ghettos under the influence of the social gospel.[9] Chinese Protestants, particularly women, eagerly combined such public concerns as Chinese nationalism and the improvement of conditions in North American Chinese communities with a passion for evangelism that would have made John Mott and Sherwood Eddy proud.[10] Throughout the period, Chinese Protestants saw in Christianity the means by which China could overcome its patriarchy and backwardness and thus defeat racial discrimination and colonialism.[11] Since the 1950s, however, the role that Chinese churches play in women's lives has veered away from that empowering past. That was largely a result of the growth and dominance of "separatist" Chinese evangelicalism since World War II.[12]

The "separatist" ethos was a reflection of the social dislocation and psychological alienation of the Chinese diaspora during the postwar decades. More so than their "civic" predecessor, Chinese evangelicalism emphasized starting new congregations and organizations, nurturing individual piety, and a narrow focus on evangelizing Chinese people. Because of its origins in indigenous revival movements in China and the Chinese diaspora at the turn of the century, it resisted formal theological training and a professional clergy for some time. Its beginnings in the United States and Canada can be traced to a generation of sacrificial yet enterprising pastors and students who migrated to the United States between the 1950s and 1970s. Most toiled among a slowly growing urban Chinese population, some among Chinese college students.[13]

Since the 1970s, these pioneers have dramatically reshaped North American Chinese Protestantism, which is now more affluent and increasingly influenced by American evangelicalism.[14] Consequently, many Chinese congregations have resurrected more restrictive proscriptions toward women, even though women have been largely responsible for the Chinese church's growth in numbers and social status since World War II.[15]

That paradox notwithstanding, Chinese Protestant women have continued to retain a strong influence. In addition, they have gained greater leadership roles in Chinese churches. Throughout the twentieth century, Chinese Protestant women in North America have employed inventive ways to struggle through the paradoxes of their experiences and articulate their concerns. Since the 1980s, and in both mainline and evangelical settings, Chinese Protestant women have become even more conscious of gender inequality and the need to overcome it.

Chinese Protestant Women's Identity Construction in Twentieth-Century North America

In at least three ways, the construction of Chinese Protestant women's identities was synonymous with the creation of Chinese Protestantism in North America. Although outnumbered by men before World War II, it was women who most influenced the character of Chinese Protestantism. Most Chinese women found a new sense of identity in the examples set by women missionaries and volunteers who ministered to the Chinese community. These white women stepped outside of their domestic roles to teach and advocate for the Chinese. Indeed, one can argue that the Chinese church was born into a Victorian missionary culture that assented to the rhetoric of feminine domesticity while endorsing women's religious activism.[16] Consequently, the church has been one of the few places in Chinese communities where women could enjoy considerable influence and a variety of leadership roles.[17]

The construction of twentieth-century Chinese Protestant women's identities was also derived from women's traditions rooted in popular Chinese religiosity. "Wives' tales" pertaining to childbirth, child-rearing, marital relationships, and dietary advice still persist among Chinese Protestant women, particularly among immigrants raised in Asia. For example, as Evelyn Shih, wife of the founding minister of the Overseas Chinese Mission in New York City, described her daughter's appearance:

> The prettiest part of Joy is her eyes. She has a pair of big bright eyes with long lashes which are rarely seen among Chinese. As a result, many people thought she was "mixed blood." . . . When I had found out I was pregnant, my friend who was still teaching in Hong Kong sent me a picture of a pretty foreign girl. She knew that Torrey and I both wanted to have a daughter first; so she wrote on the back of the picture that she wished we would have a daughter as pretty as that girl. I put it under the glass of my dressing table. Each day I would look at it and wish my daughter would be like her. Is that the reason Joy has such beautiful eyes? I dare not say, but I can tell you that the other three children don't have them. Gloria, our youngest, still blames me for that.[18]

As light-hearted as such "explanation" stories were intended to be, they illustrate the persistence of indigenous women's traditions among Protestant women. Yet Shih also delighted in demonstrating how her Christian identity distinguishes her from traditional images of women. Raised in a minister's family, she considered herself a "strong-willed" girl, a sharp contrast with other girls who were "typically very sweet and obedient."[19] Unlike traditional Chinese parents, she and her husband wanted to have a daughter first. When they decided to feed their children processed baby food (a novelty in Singapore in the 1950s) and to build a playpen, they were criticized for being too Westernized. They ignored the criticism, however, and employed "modern" child-rearing practices.[20]

The persistence and trivialization of Chinese women's traditions illustrate how Chinese and Protestant sources are used to construct identities uninhibited by the constraints of a nineteenth-century Chinese gender and family system while allowing them to retain their Chinese and Protestant identities.[21] This strategy of identity construction is not unique to Chinese women.[22] Nicole Constable's study of contemporary Hakka Christians in Hong Kong yields similar conclusions for both men and women. She argues that the Hakka are not syncretistic. Rather, Christian "practices are maintained as strictly orthodox, and Chinese practices and festivals that have not been reinterpreted as secular are criticized, avoided, or deemed of little concern." As a result, a "dual system of belief" and a new ethno-religious identity are created.[23] The fact that male Chinese Protestants did not reproduce a totally traditional gender system hints at the possibility that Chinese women were central in defining twentieth-century Chinese Protestant identity.[24]

Finally, the impact of Chinese women's identity in the history of Chinese Protestantism can also be seen in its spirituality. As Kwok Pui-Lan notes, "In the process of adaptation to the Chinese context Christian symbolism was feminized in order to increase its appeal to both Chinese men and women."[25] Self-sacrifice, religious activism, piety, and the congregation as family became the marks of Chinese Protestant spirituality, not primarily correct doctrine. Watchman Nee's classic guide for church leaders, *The Normal Christian Worker,* contains, for example, echoes of Confucian concern for individual character formation, Taoist self-discipline, and the Buddhist ethos of voluntary suffering, although they are drawn exclusively from the Christian Scriptures.[26] Yet the selection of these characteristics mitigate against a domineering patriarchal spirituality. In Chinese churches, the authoritarian leadership and confrontative masculine preaching styles of revivalists such as John Sung, Andrew Gih, or Timothy Chao have been balanced by the gentler, self-sacrificing devotion of Chinese women, who are often viewed as better examples of Christian spirituality than the revivalists.

It was the venerated Christiana Tsai who best embodied Nee's ideal Christian worker. Born into a prominent official's family, Tsai was well known among Protestants for her skill as an evangelist. She was even better known for her devotion in the face of suffering. By 1931 her health had deteriorated, and she became bedridden for the rest of her life, as well as increasingly blind.[27] Nevertheless, she continued to evangelize everyone she could meet and rarely despaired about her physical condition. Between her move to Paradise, Pennsylvania, in 1949 and her death in 1984 she entertained Chinese students, military officials and soldiers-in-training from Taiwan, and advice-seekers—always exhorting them to become devout Christians.[28] She was instrumental in helping Ambassadors for Christ become a significant Chinese parachurch organization that evangelizes Chinese students and families.[29] Tsai embodies self-sacrificing Christian virtues so well that an entire generation of male pastors has adorned her with lavish praise.[30]

In spite of their influence in the church, Chinese Protestant women have struggled with its male-dominated leadership. Throughout the twentieth century, they have responded to the increasing proscription of their roles in North American Chinese churches in a variety of ways. Excluded from formal pastoral leadership, most women either acceded to the existing male-dominated church structure or found other outlets for their spiritual energies and gifts. Many deferred their callings by becoming homemakers while gaining influence by leading Christian education programs, Bible studies, and women's groups. Others became missionaries or served on the staffs of parachurch organizations. A few actually became ordained ministers of Chinese churches. In any case, contemporary Chinese Protestant women have no desire to return to the gender and family systems of nineteenth-century China and Chinatowns.

Conversion: Civic Evangelicalism and the Unbinding of Feudal Hierarchies (1900–1949)

At the turn of the century, the Chinese population in the United States and Canada was overwhelmingly male. The few women endured a repressive gender system transplanted from a feudal nineteenth-century Chinese society.[31] Many were prostitutes or servants—victims of the *mui tsai* system, a practice of selling and buying young girls from China to work as domestic servants in affluent Chinese homes or brothels. A few were wives of merchants and adhered to the gender protocols of foot-binding and/or shunning public appearances. Regardless of social standing, Chinese women in America had few options.

Chinese women in China and those who were a part of the Chinese diaspora could observe an alternative role for women when they encountered American missionary women. Single, free from familial obligations, and well educated, they demonstrated that Protestantism offered more options than traditional Chinese culture. Even though missionary women supported domestic roles for Chinese women, their religious activism was a model of female freedom to defer marriage and engage the public arena. Frequent contacts with missionaries and volunteers cultivated a public-minded religion in spite of Chinese Protestants' isolation from the American mainstream. Although the missionaries' message emphasized individual salvation and personal piety, their civic actions left a deep impression. They often publicly defended the Chinese against discrimination. Donaldina Cameron in San Francisco, for example, moved into the public arena to "rescue" Chinese women from prostitution rings.[32] Other volunteers from a nearby congregation helped Chinese immigrants acquire a working knowledge of English and taught Chinese children. The examples of these white Protestants helped converts gain a religious orientation that easily translated into civic engagement and revolutionary Chinese politics.[33]

Apart from a genuinely religious quest, the earliest Chinese women converts recognized an opportunity to be freed from traditional Chinese gender hierarchies.[34] Chinese congregations and rescue missions ("girls' homes") became sites for empowerment and the awakening of social consciousness.[35] The common belief was that "Christian civilization" would be a source of redemption for Chinese women.[36]

The reality was that women were oppressed in China. That fact allowed Chinese Protestants and American missionaries to explain and reject the weakness of the Chinese nation and its people. As a student at Barnard College, Mabel Lee argued that the "welfare of China and possibly its very existence as an independent nation depend on rendering tardy justice to its womankind. For no nation can ever make real and lasting progress in civilization unless its women are following close to its men if not actually abreast with them."[37]

Conversion from Chinese religious culture also implied conversion to new values. Some emulated their white missionary sisters and devoted themselves to a religious vocation or community service.[38] Wu T'ien Fu, for example, was sold by her father to be a *mui tsai* in a Chinatown brothel in 1893. A year later, she was "rescued" by Cameron at the Presbyterian Mission Home in San Francisco. Nurtured and raised there, T'ien Fu eventually received training at the Toronto Bible School and became Cameron's assistant and constant companion. She never married, and upon her death in 1975 she was buried beside Cameron, who had died seven years earlier.[39] Others took more conventional routes. Many women in Presbyterian and Methodist girls' homes in San Francisco had their marriages arranged by mission matriarchs. Such marriages, Peggy Pascoe observes, "established a core of middle-class Protestant Chinese American families in San Francisco and half a dozen other cities."[40]

Because Victorian notions of womanhood and family emphasized women's moral superiority and offered freedom from Chinese patriarchy in a male-dominated and racially segregated community, few Chinese Protestant women were willing to embrace explicitly feminist objectives.[41] Like her peers, Sophia H. Chen was critical of the constrictions of nineteenth-century Chinese family and gender systems and sought an enlarged role for women in society. Yet her vision of expanded opportunities for Chinese women was rather limited. Although social work, education, medicine, and literary activities were considered appropriate vocations, women's most important work was at home. As Chen observed:

> Since happy individuals make a happy nation, and since an unhappy home cannot produce happy members, it is therefore no small service that a woman can render to her country by removing the sources of domestic unhappiness, as well as by making herself an inspiring wife and a wise mother at the same time. Let therefore no woman ever regard marriage as a refuge from social responsibility, thereby hoping to lead a selfish and parasitic life; but let her remember that by marriage she has entered upon a new career whose significance to the nation cannot be over-emphasized.[42]

A traditional Victorian home was viewed as an improvement on a traditional Chinese family, and its elevation of the mother's role also tapped into a Chinese "motherhood cult." Stories of filial devotion to mother and familial tensions attributed to dominant mother-in-laws abound in Chinese literature. Thus, Victorian domesticity rejected much of the traditional Chinese family, but it also retained some continuity with the Chinese values surrounding motherhood.

These Victorian values contained inherent tensions that became more pronounced between the two world wars. It was often difficult to reconcile a belief in feminine domesticity with religiously motivated civic activism, although both were rooted in Chinese Protestant women's religious understanding. According to Victoria Wong, "Christianity offered women relative equality with men in the spiritual world, in that both women and men could go to heaven. Furthermore, the Christian emphasis on women's organizations brought Chinese American women together for the first time in the context of gender, encouraging them to develop a stronger gender-based identity. It implied that they, as women, could contribute to social change in their communities."[43]

The examples of women missionaries, the influence of social Christianity, and the post-suffrage notion of the ideal woman all converged to give greater weight to Chinese women's civic participation and social activism.[44]

Many who had been nurtured in Protestant churches during the 1920s and 1930s became respected leaders in North America's Chinatown communities. For example, one of the principal organizers of the first Chinese Christian Young People's conference at Lake Tahoe, California, in 1933 was Alice Fong, who was American-born. Fong later became very active in San Francisco's Chinatown. Like several other American-born Chinese Protestant women, she received a college education and was graduated from Teacher's College in New York in 1926. She attributed her education to her father's Chinese nationalism and progressive Christian outlook. She became the first Chinese hired by the San Francisco public schools, where she taught for thirty-one years.[45]

The civic skills acquired by this generation of American-born Chinese woman proved invaluable to Chinese missions affiliated with Protestant denominations. Through their efforts, these women helped Chinese congregations become self-supporting and helped prepare the next generation of Chinese to engage in public life during the 1950s and 1960s. Unlike their socially and politically apathetic counterparts in China and the Chinese diaspora, American-born Protestant women often equated their faith with social activism.

As they became more socially active, Chinese Protestant women seemed to experience little tension with the constraints of Victorian domesticity. One likely explanation can be found in Chinese Protestant nationalism. Chinese revolutionary politics in the twentieth century were in part derived from an iconoclasm found in most evangelical Christianity. A significant number of the early supporters of the 1911 revolution were Chinese Protestants in the diaspora.[46] After the Ch'ing Dynasty was toppled in 1911, China entered a decade of political fragmentation. The Chinese in North America were equally divided, although most Protestants supported Sun Yat-sen's objectives. After weathering a significant anti-Christian movement during the 1920s, they threw themselves behind the efforts of Chiang Kai-shek and the Kuomintang to unify the nation (although a few supported the communists).[47] So focused were Chinese in North America on building a new China that women, too, were urged to step out of traditional roles and take part. Things associated with feudal China were being discarded in favor of the modern and Western. That included family systems and gender roles. According to Tani Barlow, during these years the Chinese term for woman, *funü*, took on a new meaning—one no longer situated in the family kinship system but under a "patriotic inscription."[48]

Furthermore, Chinese Protestant women born or raised in North America in the 1920s were less constrained by Victorian definitions of womanhood.

Although they were equally committed to China's resistance against Japan in the late 1930s, they identified more with America than China.[49] Therefore, as North American public culture fled the grasp of Victorianism, so did many acculturated Chinese. Like their male counterparts, many Protestant women shared the relatively liberal religious ethos of the time and threw themselves into community service even though the doors to mainstream America were still closed.[50]

Nationalism and acculturation were limited vehicles for the development of Chinese Protestant women's consciousness, nevertheless. "Although Chinese nationalism, Christianity, and acculturation encouraged resistance to multiple forms of oppression," Judy Yung observes, "they also extracted a heavy price from Chinese women, calling on them to put aside feminist concerns for the sake of national unity and to go against their cultural heritage in favor of Western values."[51]

So long as Chinese men shared the common goal of modernizing the nation, women missionaries continued to exercise influence, and churches endorsed community service, gender conflicts were minimal. Chinese Protestant men and women both agreed that the nineteenth-century Chinese feudal system and the traditional family had to be done away with and the social standing of Chinese in North America elevated. Despite the clear gains in Chinese Protestant women's status, feminist consciousness and goals rarely were evident. But once China was lost and missionary control relinquished, Chinese Protestants in America turned away from civic concerns and toward questions of ethnic assimilation and the challenge of separatist evangelical growth. That limited the roles women could play in Chinese congregations but did not squelch their spiritual activism.

Confidence: Negotiating Space in the Chinese Church

The loss of China to the communists in 1949 greatly diminished the civic evangelical voice among Chinese Protestants and brought about an anticlimactic end to a generation of patriotic zeal. Furthermore, when the People's Republic became a cold war enemy, anticommunist intimidation from Chiang Kai-shek's regime in Taiwan and memories of Japanese American internment camps silenced many Chinese in North America.

Years of immigration exclusion had left their mark on the Chinese American population as well. Those born in America now outnumbered those from overseas, and they had little opportunity or desire to be active in Chinese politics. In their efforts to demonstrate their Americanism, many left the Chinese church; a few joined white congregations.[52] Although they continued to experience segregation after the war, many Chinese Americans were able to hurdle racial barriers in employment and home-ownership by quietly moving away from Chinatowns.

In the wake of the communist victory, mainline Protestants curtailed missionary efforts in China and lost interest in supporting or starting Chinese congregations in the United States and Canada.[53] Instead, a rising zeal for racial integration led many to question the relevance of Chinese congregations.[54]

As religious nationalism declined after World War II, women in Chinese mainline Protestant churches continued to express concern for the Chinese American community and ethnic identity. Having carved out a significant niche for themselves in their congregations, there appeared to be no overt concern about women's equality and ordination in the church until the 1960s. In separatist Chinese evangelical congregations antipathy toward feminist questions was even more pronounced. The question of evangelical piety took precedence over community and ethnic identity as well. For Chinese Protestant women, the issue of gender relations was again tabled until second-wave feminism made its impact felt during the 1970s. Since then, however, Chinese Protestant women have become more willing to demand equality and ordination.

Continuing the Civic Tradition in Mainline Chinese Protestantism

After World War II, a few Chinese congregations became self-sufficient. In some cities, Chinese missions sponsored by various denominations merged into a single congregation. Subsequently, several Chinese congregations became self-supporting and headed down the path of clerical professionalization. Yet as a new generation of church leaders came of age, it became evident that too few opportunities were available for Chinese pastors. Few Caucasian congregations were willing to employ graduates of Chinese seminaries. Mainline denominations were equally unenthusiastic about perpetuating "ethnic" congregations.[55] Thus the focus of the Chinese in mainline Protestantism shifted from the Chinese nation to the relevance and survival of the Chinese church in America.[56]

For many women nurtured in mainline Chinese churches during this time, participation in church activities became less appealing. Eventually, they redirected their energies toward the wider community. Uncomfortable with the separatist evangelical influence in Chinese congregations, they found homes in white mainline churches. Nevertheless, some women retained an emotional attachment to the Chinese church. In part, that was because they had been discriminated against in mainline denominations and were concerned for other Chinese in America. Ruth Hsiao, an English professor at a college in Boston, worships at a liberal United Church of Christ congregation and yet has a strong academic interest in Chinese American concerns.[57] Carole Jan Lee now worships at a multiethnic Episcopalian church in San Francisco but is active in Chinese and Asian American ecumenical Protestant organizations such as the National Conference of Chinese Workers in North America (CONFAB) and the Pacific and Asian Center for Theology and Strategy (PACTS) at the Graduate Theological Union in Berkeley, California. Emma Louie left the Chinese Presbyterian Church of Oakland because her husband had accepted a pastoral call to a white Presbyterian church in southern California. She had struggled with the "insularity" of the Chinese church in Oakland but became conscious of racial discrimination when housing covenants hindered her family's efforts to purchase a home in Los Angeles in the early 1960s. Only with the assistance of sympathetic church members was her family able to buy a home. Yet when the matter came up in a women's group at church, several white women dismissed or trivialized the Louies' experience. Although no longer involved with Chinese churches, Hsiao, Lee, and Louie all retain a strong symbolic attachment for them and embrace racialized ethnic identity. Among the Chinese women I interviewed, however, these three were the most conscious of social issues such as sexism, racism, and economic injustice.[58]

Those who remained active in Chinese churches believe that their congregations are vehicles for greater social and spiritual good. Helen Chun's decision to stay in the Chinese church came about by comparing Christianity to other organizations. She concluded that the church "was the best for involving people" and "was good for the community, family." Its ideals and faith were best for Chinese Americans.[59] Beneath this concern for the Chinese is resistance to assimilating into a mainstream church. Through CONFAB, for example, Chinese women joined male clergy to advocate ethnic-specific ministries within mainline Protestantism.[60]

The desire to retain a Chinese identity became even more pronounced when a new generation of predominantly American-born Chinese overtly rejected the assimilationist premise undergirding mainline Protestant policy. They joined other Asian Protestants to form caucuses in the early 1970s and draw attention to the rapid growth of the Asian population. Caucus leaders demanded greater Asian representation in their denominations and the diversion of more resources for racial and ethnic-specific ministries. Although the caucus movement was dominated by male leadership early on, many Chinese women were visible participants.

Also during this period, younger, more politically conscious women such as the Rev. Kathryn Choy-Wong wrestled with their racial and ethnic identities. As a third-generation, American-born teenager in San Francisco during the late 1960s, she was convinced that affirming her Chinese identity meant rejecting the dominant culture and casting all white people as evil.[61] During her seminary studies, however, and after a stint as the national director of Asian Ministries for the American Baptist Churches, she developed a more balanced perspective and could recognize the persistence of racism in American life without demonizing Caucasians. Choy-Wong attributes that shift in perspective to the universalizing aspects of Christian faith, which enabled her to rise above the excesses of extreme identity politics. Racial and ethnic identity concerns outweighed those of gender for Choy-Wong until later in the 1970s, when she could not find a pastoral position in a Chinese church after completing seminary. Although she eventually found a calling, she is aware that she may never have the opportunity to pastor a Chinese congregation. Yet Choy-Wong is hopeful that her leadership and example will "plant the seeds" for other women in the ministry.[62]

These are hopeful times for women within mainline Chinese Protestant churches. During the 1980s, they joined other women to advocate for equality and ordination. Furthermore, more mainline churches (and an increasing number of evangelical Chinese congregations) license and ordain women now then ever before. It is because women have served in the ministry of mainline Protestant congregations that mainline Chinese Protestants are slightly more open to them in positions of pastoral leadership.[63]

Women in "Separatist" Chinese Evangelical Congregations

On February 3, 1949, Christiana Tsai and her life-long companion Mary Leaman were welcomed at the port of San Francisco by Lorna Logan (Donaldina Cameron's successor) and Wu T'ien-fu. Already in her fifties, Tsai had come to America in search of better medical care and to escape the communists. Christiana Tsai epitomized the transformation of diasporic Chinese Protestantism since World War II. During her early years, she had valued the modernizing influence of missionaries in China.[64] Her civic evangelicalism, however, had narrowed by the time she settled in the United States. In part, the change could be attributed to trepidation about the impact of theological liberalism among many Chinese Protestants. Experience legitimized that concern. After a period of study in America, Tsai's one-time fiancé was so influenced by his liberal education that he eventually became skeptical of Christianity. Forced to choose between faith and the desire for a family, Tsai broke off the engagement and never married.[65]

Similarly, John Sung faced a crisis of faith during his studies at Union Theological Seminary in New York City. His mental breakdown and rediscovery of a separatist evangelical faith later propelled him into tireless evangelistic campaigns among the Chinese in Asia during the war years. For many Chinese Protestants, his notoriety and success created suspicion of liberalism, social engagement, and Union Theological Seminary in New York (or any "liberal" seminary).[66] When aspirations for a Christian China vanished, separatist Chinese Protestants filled the spiritual vacuum with a strident, apocalyptic message. This was especially strong among those in the diaspora who felt dislocated, particularly those who had fled China during the war with Japan and were stranded after the communist victory.[67]

Separatist evangelicals such as Christiana Tsai gradually made their way to North America after World War II. Until the 1970s, the majority of Chinese immigrants were Cantonese-speaking and originated from Hong Kong or Kwangchow Province. The trickle of Mandarin-speaking students began to increase during the 1950s and 1960s; some joined existing Chinese congregations, still others chose to form new ones. Because many mainline congregations had become predominantly English- or Cantonese-speaking, the newcomers were encouraged to start Mandarin-speaking churches or Bible study groups near universities. Since 1970 the trickle has turned into a tide of well-educated, highly skilled professional Chinese from several Asian countries, thus swelling the ranks of newer Chinese churches. Most evangelical women are immigrants, although a generation of American-born have been nurtured in these independent-minded congregations.

Immigrant Women

As young separatist evangelical congregations struggled to establish themselves they were rather pragmatic and rarely discussed gender roles. "It is interesting to note that ordinarily, the women's fellowship comes first in the church, but we were just the opposite," Evelyn Shih recalled about the formative years of the Overseas Chinese Mission in New York City. "I think there were two reasons for this: The first was that at the very beginning, our church was formed by a group of young people, just like the churches derived from Bible Classes, later developed in American universities and colleges. Secondly, our church had no tradition to follow, we just started a new work led by the Holy Spirit who urged us in our hearts to let us see the needs of each situation."[68] Without a tradition of women's leadership, the youthful founders of the largest Chinese church on the East Coast showed little awareness of (or interest in) the question of what roles women could fill in either church or society.

The appeal of the separatist evangelical church to immigrant women lay in a popular piety that blended Chinese and evangelical spiritualities. Lisha Li and husband Charlie Xiao came from Mainland China to study in the United States during the early 1990s. In China, she was cared for by her parents and in-laws and had servants. She enjoyed her work and lived in a prosperous and interesting city. Upon her arrival in Rochester, New York, however, things changed dramatically. "All of sudden, I have to take care of all matters at home," she noted. "Now I have to become a housewife, doing nothing at home and living in this isolated, snowy little town. . . . No one understood me and I had no one to talk to." Furthermore, her husband was under tremendous pressure because of his studies. Always nervous, he had "no time to sit down to talk to me," Li recalls:

> I always told myself to be patient. I waited and counted down the day until his graduation. I tried to be sensitive, but found myself complaining to him. That made our life very difficult and not peaceful. I could not find myself, neither could I see the future. So, after washing my face with tears many times, I knelt in front of the Lord. I began praying for His help. I prayed: "Lord, I come with a humble and thirsty heart to your throne of grace. In this last days of the world, all my thoughts are filled with sin. My own humanity and struggle can no[t] oppose the threat of Satan. So I want to turn my eyes upon You from the bottom of my heart. Only you are the source of life and the rock of my help. I pray that you would cleanse me with your precious blood. In Jesus Name I pray. Amen.

Everything changed dramatically after that: "The Lord became my strength and my salvation," she maintains. "I returned to school to a new environment so that I could study again and glorify His name. My fellow students appreciated me. My professor and boss praised me. All these make me feel God's power was surrounding me. As I was regaining my confidence, God also blessed my marriage."[69]

In such separatist evangelical congregations immigrant Chinese women found more than ethnic affirmation. The call to follow Christ in order to overcome a hostile world had tremendous appeal to those who felt lost in a foreign country. It certainly had greater appeal than the liberal Christian embrace of the world and agnosticism about the reality of supernatural intervention.

North American–Born Women

A generation of Chinese women born or raised in North American who came of age in the 1950s and 1960s were also heavily influenced by separatist evangelicalism. Bernardine Wong, who supervises Sunday school programs at the Chinese Cumberland Presbyterian Church in San Francisco, was raised in a civic Chinese Protestant setting in the Bay Area. Her conversion experience reflects a transition to a more clearly defined separatist religion. "That Jesus was the Son of God was something that I had always believed since I was a child," she says. "When I was seventeen, one night I was reading Psalm 139 aloud to myself. When I realized God was so personal to me, I believed in him. Then when I was twenty-nine, in preparation for my baptism, it was explained to me that Jesus Christ died for my sin (mine personally), so I accepted Christ as my savior and lord and committed my life to him."[70]

Although most of these women were raised in Christian families, they were often dissatisfied by what they perceived to be a lack of "biblically centered" piety in their upbringing. Thus, a deeper conversion experience was necessary—something they found in separatist evangelicalism from the Chinese diaspora and among white evangelicals. Most of the women eventually pursued homemaking and child-rearing while they moved into positions of influence in congregations. Once there, they provided congregations with a more distinct evangelical identity. For example, the Chinese Christian Union Church in Chicago—the result of a merger of mainline Chinatown missions during the 1930s—was a typical civic evangelical church in the 1940s, its members as politically and community-minded as they were religious. Shortly thereafter, students from Wheaton College and Moody Bible Institute started to teach in the church's growing youth ministry. By the late 1950s, one of the congregation's young women, Sylvia Wu, decided to study at Wheaton College. At about the same time, Wilberta Lei Chinn from the Chinese Baptist Church in Portland, Oregon, also came to study at Wheaton. Upon graduation, Wu taught in an elementary school for a few years while Chinn wrestled with a call to missions. Both chose to be wives and homemakers and demonstrate their gifts through voluntary activities in the Chinese Christian Union Church. As such, they were a significant part of a generation that transformed the church into one of the largest Chinese congregations in the United States.

Even though they became recognized leaders among Chinese Protestants, their views on gender have diverged. Sylvia Wu recalls a women's day at church in the 1960s, when the service was conducted by women and when the Rev. Philip Lee gave women missionaries opportunities to "share" (not preach). Nonetheless, Wu is not invested in feminism and expresses concern about the materialism and "un-biblical values" of many women. For her, God created relatively clear roles for males and females. Some church committees, therefore, would perhaps be better led by women.[71]

Although Wilberta Chinn followed a similar path as her friend and classmate, her missionary call pushed her beyond Wu's "domestic strategy." Like Bernardine Wong, she was raised in a Christian household but did not feel the need to receive Christ personally until after her family was stranded by the Chinese civil war and forced to stay in Portland in 1946. At fifteen, she felt a call to mission work and decided to study at Wheaton College, where she encountered the Chinese Union Church. Her marriage altered her original call, however, and she became a mother, Sunday school superintendent, and chemist. "One could be a missionary in the jungle of Burma and the asphalt jungle," she discovered.

After nineteen years of work at a chemical manufacturing company, Chinn finally faced the question of her call to the ministry. Women could not enter ministry in Chinese churches and were "at the most C.E. directors." But that was in name only, because, as she quipped, "Men turned them into secretaries." Influenced by Betty Friedan and feminism, she struggled to find the "woman's niche" and was "very combative at one time. . . . Eventually I was able to resolve this—went back to Scriptures—came to an equilibrium in my own thinking—really, I was mad, angry at the system—I fought that greatly." When her husband took an early retirement, Chinn seized the opportunity to respond to her calling. The Chinns moved to Los Angeles and joined the First Chinese Baptist Church, a Southern Baptist congregation that averages two thousand worshipers each Sunday. In 1991 she enrolled at Talbot School of Theology and was invited by the Rev. Herman Tang to join the church's staff. "I felt like Moses waiting in the desert. It was forty years from age fifteen to age fifty-five when God called me," she remarked.[72]

To assist other women in understanding their roles in the church, Chinn has written and published a study guide, *Finding My Identity as a Woman*. In it, she advocates a pragmatic "biblical feminism" that focuses on mutuality: "I am a woman, created to reflect God's image through exhibiting the fruit of the Spirit, not acting out a role, willing to set aside my selfish rights and desire to rebel for the purpose of glorifying Jesus Christ who is my first love."[73] True to her principles, Chinn, a licensed minister, is open to the prospect of ordination, provided her congregation calls her. She is also willing to serve in a denomination that recognizes woman's ordination, if God leads.

Most women of Chinn's generation have exercised their gifts through strategies of domesticity and/or deferment. Some, like Sylvia Wu and Bernardine

Wong, have found a calling by staying within "traditional" roles for women. Others, such as Wilberta Chinn, have pressed the Chinese church toward acceptance of women in the ministry. Some became ministers in mainline Chinese churches, although, like Chinn, they were ordained later in life. By deferring their ministerial vocation, they were able to undertake more accepted maternal roles in Chinese churches.[74]

Since the 1970s, gender equality has become an increasingly significant concern for many American-born evangelical women. Younger Chinese evangelicals, however, are attracted to mainstream evangelicalism and have inherited its debates over gender roles. Even congregations affiliated with mainline Protestantism have, for the most part, yielded to this new evangelical ethos. Consequently, for many younger evangelicals the doors to women's leadership appear to be inching shut.[75]

Given the history of postwar evangelicalism in North America and the desire by younger Chinese to be a part of it, attempts to circumscribe Chinese women's roles are not surprising.[76] Jeanette Yep, for example, lost her leadership role after her church called a pastor from a conservative, evangelical seminary to minister among its English-speaking members. After nearly completing a ten-week Sunday school class for college-age members, she was dismissed from teaching the course. "After class one day," she recounted, "a graduate student member came to me and said that I couldn't teach Sunday school anymore. He had chatted with the pastor and they agreed. [He] would be taking over, and he would finish out the quarter." The explanation given was a concern for consistency with biblical teachings about the role of women in the church. Through this painful experience, Yep realized that, as a woman, she "would not be allowed to teach, preach or have any authority over men in the context of the ministry of that church. And up until today, many years later, that church has been consistent in upholding that biblical interpretation on gender roles."[77]

Although many younger Chinese evangelicals have closed the door to women in church ministry or leadership, Yep and others have found some consolation in evangelical parachurch organizations such as Inter-Varsity Christian Fellowship and the Asian American Christian Fellowship, which tend to be relatively more open to women.[78] Nevertheless, today's evangelical women articulate themselves more confidently than their predecessors. Grace May, a doctoral candidate in theology, is coauthor of an article defending women's ordination for Christians for Biblical Equality, an evangelical feminist organization. Refuting J. I. Packer, May and Hyunhye Pokrifka Joe provide a comprehensive summary of biblical and theological arguments that support the ordination of women.[79] Cecilia Yau, the ministry ambassador of the Chinese Christian Mission, coauthored *A Passion for Fullness,* which, in Chinese, broadens the argument by incorporating historical and sociological studies.[80]

Although opportunities for Chinese women to assume pastoral leadership in evangelical churches are still limited, that may change as many who have responded to a calling become more gender-conscious and younger evangelicals begin to incorporate social realities with their theological outlook.

Conclusion: Gender Matters

In the twentieth century, Chinese Protestant women subordinated the development of women's consciousness and feminist hopes to the needs of the Chinese nation, the North American Chinese community, or a distinct separatist evangelical identity. Nevertheless, it is widely accepted that Protestantism's earlier role was as a catalyst for women's liberation from traditional Chinese patriarchy. But that was true only insofar as nationalism, concerns for social justice, and modernization were infused into the faith embraced by Chinese women. Consequently, Mabel Lee assumed an important position in New York City among supporters of the Baptist Missionary Society. Lee's civic evangelicalism thrived because of these external factors and despite the fact that she had submerged her feminist concerns into almost-forgotten years of teenaged suffragist activism. But once external factors such as nationalism were removed, many Chinese Protestant women felt compelled to subordinate their interests to the task of defining an evangelical identity that drew from indigenous Chinese revivalism as well as from mainstream evangelicalism in North America. Thus, the same religion that freed Chinese women from feudal Chinese patriarchy has, over the years, been used to squeeze them into a more restrictive evangelical framework. Twentieth-century Protestantism has unbound Chinese women's aspirations and then bound them yet again. Nevertheless, many Chinese Protestant women are seeking expanded roles and explicit gender equality. Unlike Chinese Protestant women of the early twentieth century, however, the new women's consciousness centers on the church itself rather than the Chinese nation or the Chinese American community. Whether it can be a vehicle for full equality in the church remains unclear, but there are signs of hope.

On Sunday morning, March 8, 1998, Herman Tang stepped up to the pulpit to preach. Although he had been called to serve at the Rochester, New York, Chinese Christian Church for less than a year, he felt confident enough to deliver a message from Galatians 3:28 in Mandarin Chinese: "There is no longer Jew or Greek, there is no longer slave or free, there is no longer male and female; for all of you are one in Christ Jesus." In the sermon, he rejected gender hierarchy by appealing to an egalitarian interpretation of the creation account in Genesis 1 and 2. He compared the female judge Deborah to the Chinese woman warrior Fa Mulan. He also pointed out how Jesus and Paul had treated women as partners and concluded with a call for those in the church to become partners as equals for the sake of the church's mission.[81] Perhaps not everyone present agreed with his message, but as I looked around the sanctuary there appeared to be consensus. After all, some of the most vocal and active leaders in that church are women.

Tang may have been an exception among Chinese male ministers, but he is one of a growing number who are committed to supporting women who are called into pastoral ministry. In spite of the efforts of many to circumscribe women's roles, Chinese congregations and leaders who are aware of the historical context of Chinese Christianity are, in general, becoming more receptive to women's equality and ordination. The stories of Chinese Protestant women in the twentieth century are becoming more familiar. Therein lies the hope that Chinese Protestantism will contribute to the unbinding of the souls of Chinese women.

Notes

I am indebted to the published works of Judy Yung, Kwok Pui-Lan, Peggy Pascoe, and Jane Hunter for my observations about the period before World War II. I have also found the Chinese Students Christian Association of North America's publications useful, as well as the collections of a few Chinese churches. For the post–World War II period, I drew heavily from interviews with more than forty Chinese Protestant women. The bulk of the interviews were conducted between 1996 and 1997, although I continue to interview individuals. I am grateful for the assistance of Min Min Lo and Carolyn Chen with these interviews. Finally, I drew upon a growing collection of writings by Chinese Christian women published by the Chinese Alliance Press and Chinese Baptist Press (both in Hong Kong).

1. Timothy Tseng, "Dr. Mabel Lee: The Interstitial Career of a Chinese American Woman, 1920–1950," paper presented before the annual meeting of the Organization of American Historians, Chicago, 1996.

2. Gloria H. Chun, "'Go West . . . to China': Chinese American Identity in the 1930s," in *Claiming America: Constructing Chinese American Identities during the Exclusion Era*, ed. K. Scott Wong and Sucheng Chan (Philadelphia: Temple University Press, 1998): 165–90; Sucheng Chan, ed., *Entry Denied: Exclusion and the Chinese Community in America* (Philadelphia: Temple University Press, 1991).

3. Charles H. Sears letter, July 12, 1937, general file C, folder 3, New York Baptist Missionary Society files, American Baptist Historical Society (ABHS) Archives (Rochester). White Protestant leaders in educational institutions and missionary societies and a few lawyers were often the only Americans who would lend assistance to or vouch for the Chinese.

4. For Hu, such a center would be "truly useful to the community and sufficiently inspiring to enlist the enthusiasm of the younger generation. In brief, it should not be mere evangelism and church-going. It should be education, social work, sanitation, culture, and civic life. That would be worthy of your work, your life-long devotion." Hu Shih to Mabel Lee, Nov. 19, 1936, folder entitled "No Value," New York City Collection, First Chinese Baptist Church, New York. The personal letters and papers of Mabel Lee and the church are held in the church but have not been organized.

5. As Sears noted privately, "The Chinese viewpoint and the Anglo-Saxon are so unlike that it is exceedingly difficult to get on without misunderstandings or at least with differences of opinion though I feel that you and I have succeeded rather well with her in this regard. . . . She is looking very, very tired, often-times more so than others. She is exceedingly temperamental in all her attitudes, but I need not tell you that." Charles H. Sears to E. L. Ballard, May 20, 1935, general file C, folder 3, New York Baptist Missionary files, ABHS Archives.

6. Sucheng Chan, "The Exclusion of Chinese Women, 1870–1943," in *Entry Denied: Exclusion and the Chinese Community in America,* ed. Sucheng Chan (Philadelphia: Temple University Press, 1991), 94–146.

7. These laws were not repealed until 1943, although the tinge of racial discrimination was not fully removed until 1965. The exclusion laws "ensured that most Chinese could enter America only by breaking its laws, a situation that had the effect of distancing Chinese even further from the mainstream white society as well as magnifying the importance of networking and secrecy within the Chinese community." Madeline Hsu, "Gold Mountain Dreams, Paper Son Schemes: Chinese Immigration Under Exclusion," in *Chinese America: History and Perspectives 1997* (San Francisco: Chinese Historical Society of America, 1997), 46; Judy Yung, "The Fake and the True: Researching Chinese Women's Immigration History," in *Chinese America: History and Perspectives 1998* (San Francisco: Chinese Historical Society of America, 1997), 25–56; Lucy E. Salyer, *Laws Harsh as Tigers: Chinese Immigrants and the Shaping of Modern Immigration Law* (Chapel Hill: University of North Carolina Press, 1995); Bill Ong Hing, *Making and Remaking Asian America through Immigration Policy, 1850–1990* (Stanford: Stanford University Press, 1993).

8. Judy Yung, *Unbound Feet: A Social History of Chinese Women in San Francisco* (Berkeley: University of California Press, 1995).

9. With the exception of college students and seminarians, few Chinese Protestants in North America embraced theological liberalism. In contrast to China, the fundamentalist-modernist controversy does not appear to have had any significant impact on Chinese Protestants in America during this period, although the North American–born generation was attracted to a world-affirming liberal Christianity. Timothy Tseng, "Religious Liberalism, International Politics, and Diasporic Realities: The Chinese Students Christian Association of North America, 1909–1951," *Journal of American-East Asian Relations* 5 (Fall–Winter, 1996): 305–30.

10. Norris Magnuson, *Salvation in the Slums: Evangelical Social Work, 1865–1920* (Metuchen: Scarecrow Press, 1977).

11. Timothy Tseng, "Chinese Protestant Nationalism in the United States, 1880–1927," in *New Spiritual Homes: Religion and Asian Americans,* ed. David K. Yoo (Honolulu: University of Hawaii Press, 1999), 19–51.

12. Daniel H. Bays, "The Growth of Independent Christianity in China, 1900–1937," in *Christianity in China: From the Eighteenth Century to the Present*, ed. Daniel H. Bays (Stanford: Stanford University Press, 1996), 307–16; Daniel H. Bays, "Christian Revival in China, 1900–1937," in *Modern Christian Revivals*, ed. Edith L. Blumhofer and Randall Balmer (Urbana: University of Illinois Press, 1993), 161–79.

13. Evelyn O. Shih, *Torrey Shih: The Lord's Servant* (Kowloon: China Alliance Press, 1994).

14. Since the liberalization of U.S. immigration policy in 1965, the tremendous influx of Chinese from Taiwan, Hong Kong, and other parts of the Chinese diaspora—many of whom are highly skilled professionals—has been greatly influenced by this generation of Chinese leaders. Thus, the continued domination of this strand of Chinese Protestantism seems assured. The *1994–95 Directory of Chinese Churches, Bible Study Groups, Organizations in North America* (Paradise, Pa.: Ambassadors for Christ, 1995) lists 986 congregations and organizations in the United States and 244 in Canada. Most are independent or evangelical. In 1955, however, only fifty-five Chinese congregations were recognized in a study conducted by the National Council of Churches. Horace R. Cayton and Anne O. Lively, *The Chinese in the United States and the Chinese Christian Churches*, abridged by Marjorie M. Carter (New York: National Council of Churches of Christ in the U.S.A., 1955).

15. Margaret Lamberts Bendroth, *Fundamentalism and Gender, 1875 to the Present* (New Haven: Yale University Press, 1993).

16. In China, single women missionaries from the United States did not exemplify Victorian domesticity despite their efforts to inculcate it among the Chinese women they sought to uplift. Ironically, it was their independence and freedom that Chinese women emulated in missions or girls' schools. Jane Hunter, *Gospel of Gentility: American Women Missionaries in Turn-of-the-Century China* (New Haven: Yale University Press, 1984).

17. Even among Chinese fundamentalists, women assumed a wide variety of roles, including those of school principal and preacher. For instance, Bethel Seminary, which trained hundreds of Chinese evangelists, was founded by Mary Stone and managed by "Betty Hu and another Miss Hughes." Samuel Ling recalls that "Betty Hu raised funds out of her Pasadena, California office for the Bible school, high school, elementary school, etc. selling Chinese dinners, etc. etc. etc. She was nicknamed 'silver tongue' for her gracious, charming speaking ability." Samuel Ling to Timothy Tseng, April 4, 1997 (e-mail correspondence).

18. Evelyn O. Shih, *Love Is Forever* (Hong Kong: Chinese Alliance Press, 1981), 76.

19. Shih, *Love Is Forever*, 19.

20. Ibid., 86–87.

21. Many Chinese Protestant women who were part of the post–1965 influx of immigrants from Asia appear to have retained this curious blend of traditional-Chinese Victorian religiosity. Carolyn Chen observed a selectivity of culture in her interviews with contemporary Taiwanese Protestant women in Southern California. Carolyn Chen, "Taiwanese Immigrant Women and the Home," senior honors thesis, Brown University, 1993.

22. Part of the strategy includes asserting Christian elements in Chinese culture or characters, as David Jordan notes in "The Glyphomancy Factor: Observations on Chinese Conversion," in *Conversion to Christianity: Historical and Anthropological Perspec-*

tives on a Great Transformation, ed. Robert W. Hefner (Berkeley: University of California Press, 1993), 285–304.

23. The Hakka, an ethnic minority group among the Chinese, retain a distinct identity while being very much assimilated into Chinese society. Nicole Constable, *Christian Souls and Chinese Spirits: A Hakka Community in Hong Kong,* (Berkeley: University of California, 1994), 98–99. Protestant religion as a central factor in ethnic identity formation among the subaltern has been explored in Stevan Harrell, see "Civilizing Projects and the Reactions to Them," in *Cultural Encounters on China's Ethnic Frontiers,* ed. Stevan Harrell (Seattle: University of Washington Press, 1995), 3–36.

24. Compare this with the experiences of Protestant Korean women. Jung Ha Kim, "The Labor of Compassion: Voices of 'Churched' Korean American Women," *Amerasia Journal* 22, no. 1 (1996): 93–105; Ai Ra Kim, *Women Struggling for a New Life: The Role of Religion in the Cultural Passage from Korea to America* (Albany: SUNY Press, 1996).

25. Kwok Pui-lan, *Chinese Women and Christianity, 1860–1927* (Atlanta: Scholars Press, 1992), 187.

26. Watchman Nee, *The Normal Christian Worker* (Kowloon: Church Book Room, 1965). Nee's writings are among the most influential in Chinese Christian literature. He was influenced by the Plymouth Brethren and higher-life Holiness movements.

27. Christiana Tsai, *Queen of the Dark Chamber: The Story of Christiana Tsai* (Chicago: Moody Press, 1953).

28. Christiana Tsai, *Christiana Tsai* (Paradise, Pa.: Ambassadors for Christ, 1988); Christiana Tsai, *Jewels from the Queen of the Dark Chamber* (Paradise, Pa.: Ambassadors for Christ, 1988).

29. Mary Leaman, who was Tsai's companion, and Tsai deeded their property in Paradise, Pennsylvania, to Ambassadors for Christ. *Ambassadors for Christ Thirtieth Anniversary* (Paradise, Pa.: Ambassadors for Christ, 1993). While AFC, founded in 1963, works primarily with Chinese students and families in the United States, the other major Chinese American parachurch organization, Chinese Christian Mission (established in 1961), sends missionaries to Chinese in Latin America and other parts of the Chinese diaspora.

30. Several Chinese male pastors (including my father) attest to Christiana Tsai's devotion and endurance through suffering as inspirations for their ministry. "Miss Tsai was an example to me of loving, persuasive evangelism. From her bed as a pulpit, she led countless people to accept Christ. Drawn by the Holy Spirit, people traveled from many parts of the world to visit her. She seldom refused to see anyone no matter how unwell she felt from the recurring symptoms of her illness," recalled Moses Chow in *Let My People Go! An Autobiography* (Paradise, Pa.: Ambassadors for Christ, 1995), 54; see also James Y. K. Tan, *Grace upon Grace* (Kowloon: China Alliance Press, 1993), 17–25.

31. I am indebted to Judy Yung for the conceptual distinction between a feudal Chinese gender system and Confucianism. It is somewhat convenient to place the blame for Chinese patriarchy upon Confucianism, but as Li Yu-ning, a historian, notes, "Confucian philosophy itself was not exclusively antiwomen. It has its favorable as well as its unfavorable consequences with regard to the position of woman." Li Yu-ning, "Historical Roots of Changes in Women's Status in Modern China," in *Chinese Women through Chinese Eyes,* ed. Li Yu-ning (Armonk: M. E. Sharpe, 1992), 112. This grounding in historical sensibilities allowed the Christian educator Pao-sun Tsang (1893–1978), great-granddaugh-

ter of the eminent statesman Tseng Kuo-fan, to avoid making patriarchy an innate Chinese cultural trait. See "The Chinese Woman Past and Present," in *Chinese Women through Chinese Eyes,* ed. Li Yu-ning, 72–86.

32. Charles J. McClain, *In Search of Equality: The Chinese Struggle against Discrimination in Nineteenth-Century America* (Berkeley: University of California Press, 1994); Peggy Pascoe, *Relations of Rescue: The Search for Female Moral Authority in the American West, 1874–1939* (New York: Oxford University Press, 1990). By the early decades of the twentieth century, Chinese prostitution was on the decline. Much of Donaldina Cameron's efforts, therefore, merely drew attention to an already dying institution. Chan, "The Exclusion of Chinese Women, 1870–1943," 94–146.

33. For instance, Helen Chun's father, who arrived in San Francisco in 1913, taught in the Chinese-language school of the Episcopal Mission and started a mission for the Chinese in Oakland. He was also involved with Sun Yat-sen's political goals and accompanied him on his travels across the United States. Both parents became Christians through their association with "revolutionists," who were deeply influenced by Christianity. Min Min Lo interview with Helen Chun, Oakland, Calif., July 10, 1996.

34. Kwok Pui-lan, *Chinese Women and Christianity;* Maria Jaschok and Suzanne Miers, ed., *Women and Chinese Patriarchy: Submission, Servitude, and Escape* (Hong Kong: Hong Kong University Press, 1994). As alternative communities in China, missions and girls' schools provided refuge and safe space where their personal potentials could be nurtured. Heidi A. Ross, "'Cradle of Female Talent': The McTyeire Home and School for Girls, 1890–1937," and Judith Liu and Donald P. Kelly, "'An Oasis in a Heathen Land': St. Hilda's School for Girls, Wuchang, 1928–1936", both in *Christianity in China: From the Eighteenth Century to the Present,* ed. Daniel H. Bays (Stanford: Stanford University Press, 1996), 209–27 and 228–42.

35. Judy Yung, "Unbinding the Feet, Unbinding Their Lives: Chinese Immigrant Women in San Francisco, 1902–1913," in *Asian Americans: Comparative and Global Perspectives,* ed. Shirley Hune et. al (Pullman: Washington State University Press, 1991), 69–85; Judy Yung, "The Social Awakening of Chinese American Women as Reported in Chung Sai Yat Po, 1900–1911," in *Chinese America: History and Perspectives, 1988* (San Francisco: Chinese Historical Society of America, 1988), 80–102; Victoria Wong, "Square and Circle Club: Women in the Public Square," in *Chinese America: History and Perspectives, 1994* (San Francisco: Chinese Historical Society of America, 1994), 127–53; Pascoe, *Relations of Rescue.*

36. Yuk Ying Lee, "Education of Chinese Women," in *Chinese America: History and Perspectives, 1988* (San Francisco: Chinese Historical Society of America, 1988), 106. Lee asserted that the degraded condition of Chinese woman—and, subsequently, the Chinese people—was a consequence of idolatry and superstition that prejudiced Chinese families against educating and Christianizing their daughters. Tradition and superstition were not entirely to blame, however. Lee also blamed American custom and prejudice for preventing women from stepping into public roles.

37. Mabel Lee, "China's Submerged Half," text of unpublished speech, 1915[?], and H. K. Chow to Mabel Lee, Oct. 12, 1915, both located in collections of the First Chinese Baptist Church, New York.

38. Even in the 1950s, the idea of the single missionary woman was strong enough to create uncertainty about marriage for Wilberta Chinn. She resolved this when she real-

ized that marriage, motherhood, and lay leadership were equally God's calling. Consequently, she married and raised a daughter before joining the staff of the First Chinese Baptist Church of Los Angeles in 1992. Author interview with Wilberta Chinn, Los Angeles, Calif., Dec. 6, 1996.

39. Yung, *Unbound Feet,* 39–40. Peggy Pascoe gives much attention to Wu (*Relations of Rescue,* 112–13, 122, 129–32, 137–38, 144–45, 155, 159, 200); an interview with her can also be found in "Lilac Chen," in Victor G. Nee and Brett de Bary Nee, *Longtime Californ': A Documentary Study of an American Chinatown* (Stanford: Stanford University Press, 1992), 83–90.

40. Pascoe, *Relations of Rescue,* 158.

41. Kwok Pui-Lan observes the same among middle-class, educated, Chinese Christian women in China as well (*Chinese Women and Christianity,* 108–9). Mabel Lee, however, was a suffragist.

42. Sophia H. Chen, "A Brief Survey of Women's Fields of Work in China," *Chinese Students Christian Journal* 5 (March 1919): 21. Pa Chin's classic novel *Family* (1931, repr. New York: Anchor Books, 1972), which severely criticized the traditional Chinese family, is representative of the sentiments of Chen's generation.

43. Wong, "Square and Circle Club," 137.

44. Honig's study of the China YWCA Labor Bureau head Deng Yuzhi (Cora Deng) reveals similar dynamics among some Protestant women activists in China during this period. Emily Honig, "Christianity, Feminism, and Communism: The Life and Times of Deng Yushi," in *Christianity in China: From the Eighteenth Century to the Present,* ed. Daniel H. Bays (Stanford: Stanford University Press, 1996), 243–62.

45. Yung, *Unbound Feet,* 131; author interviews with Helen Chun and Carole Jan Lee, San Francisco, Calif., July 5, 1996, and Rose Lee, San Francisco, Calif., July 3, 1996.

46. L. Eve Armentrout Ma, *Revolutionaries, Monarchists, and Chinatowns: Chinese Politics in the Americas and the 1911 Revolution* (Honolulu: University of Hawaii Press, 1990); Tseng, "Chinese Protestant Nationalism in the United States, 1880–1927."

47. Vera Schwarcz, *The Chinese Enlightenment: Intellectuals and the Legacy of the May Fourth Movement of 1919* (Berkeley: University of California Press, 1986). For a study of Chinese theological responses to the May 4 movement, see Wing-hung Lam, *Chinese Theology in Construction* (Pasadena: William Carey Library, 1983).

48. Tani E. Barlow, "Theorizing Woman: *Funü, Guojia, Jiating,*" in *Body, Subject, and Power in China,* ed. Angela Zito and Tani E. Barlow (Chicago: University of Chicago Press, 1994), 262–63.

49. Raised in a Christian household, Jade Snow Wong was able to settle into a life in which her dual cultural heritage could be affirmed. Jade Snow Wong, *Fifth Chinese Daughter* (1945, repr. Seattle: University of Washington Press, 1989).

50. Author interview with Edward Lee, Oakland, Calif., July 5, 1996.

51. Yung, *Unbound Feet,* 7–8.

52. "Civic" evangelicalism appears to have yielded to a more secular modernism among many American-born Chinese in the 1930s and 1940s. The Chinese Young People's Conference had lost its "theological" and religious base by the 1960s. Author interview with James Chuck, Berkeley, Calif., July 3, 1996.

53. For the impact of missionary romance of China on American foreign policy, see

James Reed, *The Missionary Mind and American East Asia Policy, 1911–1915* (Cambridge: Council on East Asian Studies, Harvard University, 1983), and T. Christopher Jesperson, *American Images of China, 1931–1949* (Stanford: Stanford University Press, 1996).

54. James F. Findlay, Jr., *Church People in the Struggle: The National Council of Churches and the Black Freedom Movement, 1950–1970* (New York: Oxford University Press, 1993).

55. Min Min Lo interviews with Paul Hom, San Francisco, Calif., July 14, 1996, and Alvin Louie, Oakland, Calif., July 2, 1996. Many Chinese Protestant leaders started independent churches as a result of a lack of mainline Protestant enthusiasm for planting new Chinese congregations.

56. Mainline Chinese pastors successfully gained support of the Home Missions Department of the National Council of Churches of Christ to hold the Conference of Workers among the Chinese in America (CONFAB) in 1955, which still continues.

57. Author interview with Ruth Hsiao, Boston, Mass., Feb. 7, 1997.

58. Author interviews with Carole Jan Lee, San Francisco, Calif., July 2, 1996, and Emma Louie, Los Angeles, Calif., June 26, 1996.

59. Min Min Lo interview with Helen Chun, Oakland, Calif., July 10, 1996. Chun was born in 1922 in San Francisco. As Chun observes of her parents, "Through their working together [they] became very concerned about the lives of the people of China and felt that the heart of their faith was that if people changed their thinking more in the Christian or from the heart, that they would eventually be able to succeed in the ideals—the original ideals—of the founding of the Republic of China, which they were at that time struggling to help bring about."

60. The Rev. Jenny Quey, the first women to head this conference, chaired CONFAB in 1996 and 1998.

61. Author interview with Kathryn Choy-Wong, San Francisco, Calif., July 1, 1996.

62. Author interviews with Amelia Chua, San Mateo, Calif., July 3, 1996, and Georgette Huie, Oakland, Calif., July 14, 1996.

63. As early as the 1960s, a few mainline Chinese Protestant congregations called ordained women ministers. See "Rev. Mavis Shao-ling Lee, Sixty-six," in Victor G. Nee and Brett de Bary Nee, *Longtime Californ': A Documentary Study of an American Chinatown* (Stanford: Stanford University Press, 1992), 133–35. For a discussion of women's status in mainline Protestantism, see Virginia L. Brereton, "United and Slighted: Women as Subordinated Insiders," in *Between the Times: The Travail of the Protestant Establishment in America, 1900–1960,* ed. William R. Hutchison (New York: Cambridge University Press, 1989), 143–67.

64. "Wherever the light of the Gospel shone, it enlightened that society so that it soon outstripped other places in the progress toward modern culture." Tsai, *Queen of the Dark Chamber,* 105.

65. Ibid. 99.

66. Leslie T. Lyall, *John Sung: Flame for God in the Far East* (Chicago: Moody Press, 1954). Liberal (or social) evangelists were also rejected for being "unable to satisfy the people's feeling of emptiness." During wartime, revivalists appeared to be better able to meet the "spiritual" needs of ordinary Chinese. Shih, *Love Is Forever,* 25.

67. The growth of independent Chinese Christianity in those parts of China and Asia occupied by the Japanese (and where relations with foreign missionaries had been sev-

ered) contributed greatly to the creation of this distinctively Chinese form of "separatist evangelicalism." Timothy Brook, "Toward Independence: Christianity in China under the Japanese Occupation, 1937–1945," in *Christianity in China: From the Eighteenth Century to the Present*, ed. Daniel H. Bays (Stanford: Stanford University Press, 1996), 317–37.

68. Shih, *Torrey Shih*, 155.

69. Lisha Li testimony in *Echo: Publication of the Rochester Chinese Christian Church* (April–May, 1997): 3.

70. Author interview with Bernardine Wong, San Francisco, Calif., July 1, 1996. Wong, born in Locke, California, in 1929, was nurtured in her faith by white Christians when she was a young adult. Her involvement in church leadership emerged from a concern for her children's development as Christians. As her teaching and evangelizing skills were encouraged, she returned to the Chinese church to support ministry to American–born Chinese. She believes that the Scriptures strongly support male preaching, and when women preach they do not "have the same impact." Wong represents a domestic strategy that is prevalent in her generation.

71. Author interview with Sylvia Wu, Chicago, Ill., Nov. 9, 1996. Sylvia Wu (b. 1938) directs the nursery school education program at the Chicago Chinese Union Church. One of her sons directs the church's social service program (Pui Tak Center), and the other is a pastor at Evergreen Baptist Church in Rosemead, California, which is the best-known pan-Asian American church.

72. Author interview with Wilberta Chinn, Los Angeles, Calif., Dec. 6, 1996. Chinn is director of English-speaking ministry at the First Chinese Baptist Church in Los Angeles. Wu and Chinn were born in China. Their families immigrated to the United States during World War II, shortly after the Chinese Exclusion Act was repealed in 1943. Chinn and Carole Jan Lee are cousins.

73. Wilberta L. Chinn, *Finding My Identity as a Woman: A Study Guide for Personal or Group Use* (Whittier, Calif.: Peacock Enterprises, 1987), 82.

74. The Rev. Mary Ling (an immigrant), for instance, became a minister after her husband (who pastored the Chinese Christian Church in Philadelphia) died. Author telephone interview with Mary Ling, July 28, 1998.

75. This point is confirmed by Fenggang Yang, who describes a Chinese-speaking pastor who advocated for the increased role of women in his church being forced out by younger, English-speaking members who objected. Fenggang Yang, *Chinese Christians in America: Conversion, Assimilation, and Adhesive Identities* (University Park: Pennsylvania State University Press, 1999).

76. The gradual circumscription of women in postwar evangelicalism is discussed in Bendroth, *Fundamentalism and Gender*, 99–117.

77. Jeanette Yep et al., *Following Jesus without Dishonoring Your Parents: Asian American Discipleship* (Downers Grove: InterVarsity Press, 1998), 110–11. She also recalled when she "reengaged the conservative Christian church's view of gender issues," she was so shocked, hurt, and angry that she had considered "'tubing' my faith because of the second-class treatment received by gifted and equipped women in the church." Author interview with Jeanette Yep, Chicago, Ill., Nov. 9, 1996.

78. Author interviews with Melanie Mar Chow, Rosemead, Calif., Dec. 8, 1996, Lisa Sung, Chicago, Ill., Nov. 9, 1996, and Lorraine Yuen, Vancouver, B.C., July 26, 1996.

79. Grace Ying May and Hyunhye Pokrifka Joe, "Setting the Record Straight: A Response to J. I. Packer's Position on Women's Ordination," *Priscilla Papers* 11 (Winter 1997).

80. Cecilia Yau, Dora Wang, and Lily Lee, *A Passion for Fullness: Examining the Woman's Identity and Roles from Biblical, Historical, and Sociological Perspectives* [in Chinese] (Hong Kong: China Graduate School of Theology, 1997); Carolyn Chen interview with Cecilia Yau, Petaluma, Calif., Dec. 18, 1997.

81. Herman Tang, "Co-heirs in Christ," sermon delivered (in Chinese) on March 8, 1998; Tang was filling in for a woman preacher who had fallen ill and could not speak that day. Herman Tang appointed Wilberta Chinn to be on the staff of the First Chinese Baptist Church of Los Angeles.

8. Writing Our Way into History: Gender, Race, and the Creation of Black Denominational Life

LAURIE F. MAFFLY-KIPP

IN 1869 FRANCES ELLEN WATKINS HARPER, one of the most prolific and best-known African American authors of the nineteenth century, published an epic poem entitled "Moses: A Story of the Nile." Neither the literary form nor the biblical content of "Moses" represented a departure for Harper. From the 1850s onward she had been publishing poetry, much of it containing explicitly religious imagery, in both book form and periodical literature.[1] Moses had long fascinated the ardent antislavery activist. In 1859 she commented admiringly on his ability to forsake the "glittering splendors" of Pharaoh in order to suffer with the enslaved.[2] But "Moses" was otherwise quite distinctive in its treatment of the Israelite hero. In Harper's hands, Moses' fate unfolds through a series of encounters with women. The poem opens as he informs Pharaoh's daughter, the Egyptian princess, that he is leaving the palace to "join / The fortunes of my race."[3] The account then backtracks and rehearses a history of Moses' earlier years, lavishing considerable attention on his Hebrew mother:

> From her lips I
> Learned the grand tradition of our race . . .
> She would lead us through
> The distant past: the past, hallowed by deeds
> Of holy faith and lofty sacrifice.
> How she would tell us of Abraham,
> The father of our race, that he dwelt in Ur.[4]

Harper's poem is intriguing in its reduction (or elevation) of one of the most powerful and politically potent biblical stories to a series of domestic encounters with maternal figures. Rather than narrating the story as a progression of Israelite patriarchs, Harper placed a racialized religious history squarely in the hands of women. Moses' mother is acknowledged as the curator of "the grand traditions of our race." While nodding to male religious leaders—the fathers—such as Moses and Abraham, Harper imbued women with the power of narrative (and thus of communal as well as individual creation), figures who

> would tell us
> Of a promise, handed down from sire to son,
> That God, the God our fathers loved and worshiped,
> Would break our chains, and bring to us a great
> Deliverance.

Despite the homage paid to men's roles as leaders of the community and conveyors of tradition, it is women who do the work of preserving cultural memory, of handing down "a promise" from mother to child.

In an important sense, this gendered dynamic of cultural creation also described Harper's own role as a female author within the male-dominated structures of African American Protestant culture. Like Moses' mother, she preserved communal identity—not only through oral tradition but also through her authority as a speaker and writer. An antislavery lecturer, a temperance advocate, and a contributor to religious periodical literature in a wide variety of genres, from essays to novels to poetry, Harper clearly viewed herself as the mother of a generation of female authors who could shape the future of the African American community. Yet unlike Harper herself, a widow left with means sufficient to publish her own books out of her Philadelphia home, most black women writers between 1880 and 1920 found themselves in a precarious and complex situation, one shaped by male authorities who controlled the content and production of women's writing.[5] "We can never tell what is in a race till it utters or expresses itself," wrote Harper to female colleagues in 1885, "and we cannot express ourselves without organs for utterance."[6] Those organs—primarily publishing venues controlled by male religious leaders—thus served as both the liberators and regulators of women's writing. The shadows of the fathers loomed large over the work of the mothers.

This essay explores the means by which African American women writers within the historically black mainline Protestant churches assumed religious authority between 1880 and 1920.[7] Scholarship on denominational or "church" history has most often focused attention on intellectual issues (theology) or religious sites and practices most closely connected with the work of the clergy and the institutional concerns of an organization. Denominations, in short, have been defined by what takes place within churches or by ideas and practices regulated by ordained ministers.[8] Those definitions, in large measure, impede full awareness of women's contributions to Protestant community life by defining "church" in exceedingly narrow ways. This essay also affords a window onto one aspect of black denominational life through a rethinking of how Protestant communities are constituted and sustained. Although scholarship has begun to acknowledge the full extent of tension and dissent within Protestant churches, be it between clergy and laity, men and women, or blacks and whites, it has been less often observed that what is at stake in these battles is the power of collective self-definition, the ability to define one's own contributions as central to the work of the church itself. Thus scholars have entered into the fray inasmuch as they, either overtly or implicitly, define "church" in particular ways.

One cannot understand black denominational life at the turn of the twentieth century without appreciating how women staked a claim to a public voice, and the power of definition, within religious communities. The pen and the press provided women with the means to shape a collective identity within Protestant denominations that often was denied within the space of the church itself. By now it is a truism that African American women historically have played an extremely important and still not fully recognized role in the strength and endurance of black Protestant church life. Numerous scholars have employed evocative structural metaphors, variously hailing middle-class women as the "arch," the "backbone," or the "glue" that binds the church.[9] Such insights have led to a number of studies that begin to reveal the wide range of leadership roles occupied by female church members from the heyday of organized black women's activism (1880–1920) to the present.[10]

In gauging the extent of women's participation in the church, most of these pioneering studies appropriately have made recourse to fairly standard notions of political power and participation. Women thereby succeeded inasmuch as they attained positions of leadership—as ministers, teachers, and missionaries—within organized religious life. For many, those achievements entailed considerable conflict with male-dominated church hierarchies and with other women. Yet typically these battles are presumed to have taken place within a communal arena and organizational structure whose parameters were already laid out for them. The sphere of the church was, in an important sense, already assumed to be a male construction, and membership within that community was governed by rules and norms laid down by male clergy and male-dominated traditions.

But the story of power, gender, and even race grows considerably more complicated if we consider the extent to which women served as agents in the construction of an African American "church" more broadly conceived as a religious community. In this essay, I discuss a facet of female power within the black church that is at once elusive and diffuse: the roles played by women authors in the shaping of a black Protestant culture in the late nineteenth and early twentieth centuries. Women are best seen not as agents reacting in opposition to, or working within, religious organizations, which were necessarily controlled and molded by men, but as agents of community formation whose work sometimes complemented, and at other moments competed with, that of male colleagues.

Using that definition of power, we discern women's agency in the extent to which they exploited available means in order to define the terms by which social and religious life was understood. They worked to persuade individuals—both men and women—that their carefully constructed conceptions of race, religion, and communal destiny were the "natural," or self-evident, characteristics of all American-born descendants of Africa. These constructions were, of course, necessarily limited by the socioeconomic, denominational, and regional positions that women occupied as well as by issues of gender. In this essay I also describe the production of a Protestant culture undertaken by middle-class African American women during this period and assess both the constraints placed upon them and the freedoms afforded by their work as bearers of cultural memory and religious identity.

For most African Americans who joined mainline Protestant churches during the last two decades of the nineteenth century, the notion of what it meant to be "religious" was entwined with understandings of race and history in complicated ways. Indeed, much of the rhetoric of the church encouraged people to accept that their destiny as believers in Christ coincided with their hopes and dreams as a racial community linked by a common heritage of ancient glory and subsequent enslavement. Although most would have acknowledged that Euro-Americans could also be true Christians (and many had demonstrated the sincerity of their religious beliefs during Reconstruction), the political climate of the day, with Jim Crow on the rise, made it imperative that black church leaders emphasize the importance of racial loyalty and "uplift." Conversely, African Americans, only one or two generations removed from enslavement and steeped in a culture replete with biblical imagery, articulated their history in terms of scriptural typology and allegory. The dissemination of collective histories that were at once sacred and secular—and that challenged the nature of these distinctions—had a century-long history within black churches.[11]

Although all members of the church community could imaginatively place themselves in these narratives, tacit assumptions about gender dictated their creation and articulation. As is true in all organizations, there were written as well as unwritten rules within the religious community that determined the ways participants could *not* speak as well as the ways that they *could.* "Race histories" were written almost exclusively by male religious leaders, clergy and laymen who wove together biblical interpretation and racial theory in order to locate African American Protestants in the world. Of the many book-length race histories, grand narratives of the origins and destiny of the Negro people written by African Americans in the last quarter of the nineteenth century, none were written by women.[12]

This discrepancy was not a function of formal male rule. Although the field of history technically was not closed to women, it was most often seen as the province of men. Differential instruction accounted for some of that gender imbalance. Although increasing numbers of black women obtained access to religious education through freedmen's schools after the Civil War, women's courses of study tended to emphasize themes such as "personal purity, consecration of life, the care of the home, the children and the sick, and work in the church" rather than the classical philosophy, theology, and history taught to aspiring male clergy.[13] Even after graduation, male intellectuals closed their doors to female colleagues. The American Negro Academy, for example, founded in the 1890s to promote the preservation of African American history, limited its membership to men.[14] Thus, many women did not learn the language of historical allusion that might have resulted from formal study and professional encouragement.

Churches also denied women access to the ritualized (and sacralized) presentation of history. Ordination, of course, was a matter of law within churches. As women sought access to the pulpit, which they did increasingly in the late nineteenth century, they were also requesting authority to interpret and expound Scripture, and thus sacred history, before the religious community. All the mainline black denominations denied that form of historical voice for women, battling against the growing number of females who sought official recognition as preachers in the decades after Emancipation. Typical was an assertion of AMEZ minister R. D. Davis, who stated that because Jesus did not call women as his apostles, so they should not be allowed to preach: "All the Hebrew cannons, Greek torpedoes and the thirteen inch English guns fired at the ministerial fort will not win a victory for female preachers."[15]

But if female church members did not write communal history or explicate it within the context of worship, they were expected to learn about it and pass it on. Their historical voices most often were channeled in ways thought to coincide with their "natural" roles as mothers and teachers of the young. Praised and even valorized within religious communities as the primary teachers of children, Protestant women were expected to inculcate a tradition established by male leaders and be the bearers, but not the authors, of history. Male religious leaders voiced assumptions about the circumscription of women's historical voices in easily penetrable code, often couching them in flattery. In 1889 one could have read an article in the *AME Christian Recorder* by I. D. Roes, who characterized women as a "gift from heaven" (presumably to men) and rhapsodized: "What is more lovely than a true, good woman, one who has the courage of her convictions and who having plenty to do for herself, can never find time to meddle in others' affairs?"[16] Those affairs included, presumably, those skills of leadership and interpretation belonging to male authorities.

The career of Hallie Quinn Brown illustrates the gendered politics through which women's voices in the religious community were caught up in a web of male leadership. Born in Pittsburgh and reared in the free black community in Chatham, Ontario, Brown graduated from Wilberforce in 1873. She then taught school in the Reconstruction South but was soon tapped as a skilled speaker to travel and solicit aid for her alma mater. Like Harper and several other female writers, Brown first gained fame as an outstanding "elocutionist," speaking in front of huge church audiences around the country. Significantly, however, she was not speaking her own words; she was a trained spokeswoman for her male superiors. Decades later, she gained fame as an author in her own right and was most renowned for *Homespun Heroines* (1926), a collective biography of notable African American women. Nonetheless, when a black male author heralded her in a book-length tribute to African American women he legitimated her skills through recourse to the opinions of AME church leaders, citing letters of commendation from Daniel Payne and Benjamin Arnett. Brown's talents and voice, it seemed, were linked inextricably to her position within a male church hierarchy.[17]

As women fought, often unsuccessfully, for a voice within the walls of the church, a new arm of denominational life simultaneously welcomed their contributions. In 1894 Gertrude Mossell, one of the most widely published female journalists of the day, observed the recent tremendous increase in work by women authors in black periodical literature: "The corps of lady writers employed on most of our popular magazines and papers is quite as large as the male contingent and often more popular if not as scholarly."[18] Nowhere was that more true than in the growing numbers of black, church-sponsored publications. Beginning in the 1880s, religious newspapers and periodicals, as well as other writings published, advertised, and/or distributed under denominational auspices, offered women another medium for self-expression, one not governed by the same ordering principles found within the church itself. Within the world of denominational publishing, women circumvented and even subverted the male monopoly on communal history. Couching their historical interpretations in "female" literary genres and shifting the content of the histories, women implicitly challenged the authorial voices of male clergy as the sole interpreters of collective identity.[19]

In order to assess the relationship between the growth of black Protestant culture and women's writing, we must first understand how and why so many black women joined the ranks of "scribbling women" in the late nineteenth century. The tremendous growth of female authorship was simultaneously enabled and constrained by a coincidence of ideological, social, and economic forces, some that pertained to American culture more broadly and others unique to the situation of African Americans in post-Reconstruction decades. Those forces included a rapid growth of periodical publishing, new marketing dynamics, denominational consolidation, and demographic trends among African Americans that elevated the importance of religious periodicals to collective identity.

By the 1880s, American periodical literature (including dailies and less frequently appearing journals and tracts) was enmeshed in a "revolution" precipitated by low prices, efficient mass circulation, and advertising revenues that transformed the industry and brought the literature to a large-scale reading public for the first time.[20] Although that was true for both black- and white-sponsored publications, its coincidence with the conscious attempt among middle-class blacks to forge a race-based African American community lent added significance to the emergence of black publishing as a major social force. Black writers wrote not simply to express their opinions but to provide a voice for a race that often lacked public and positive modes of expression in postbellum society. Indeed, it is not coincidental that black publishing became more active at the same cultural moment when the political and social status of blacks in the United States declined rapidly. Much of the energy of black authors was engaged in an effort to counteract the almost uniformly negative racial stereotypes placed upon them by whites.

Black Protestant denominations played a major role in this revolution. Although a number of church-sponsored periodicals had appeared before the Civil War, with the singular exception of the *AME Christian Recorder* it was not until after the war that churches built enough financial support and consolidated resources sufficiently to sponsor long-running, widely circulated publications. The *AME Church Review,* established in 1884, proved the most enduring—as well as the most financially solvent—black periodical of the nineteenth century.[21] Several, including the quarterly *Church Review* and *Christian Recorder* (the AME-sponsored weekly), *Star of Zion* (the AMEZ-sponsored weekly), and later the quarterly *National Baptist Magazine,* boasted both readerships and authors drawn from across (and occasionally beyond) the United States.

Distinctive features of African American life in this period also encouraged new emphasis on the links between reading and religion. In 1870 census statistics identified nearly 80 percent of the black population in the United States as illiterate; by 1910 that number had dropped to approximately 30 percent.[22] One of the many developments that the rapid rise in literacy enabled was a tremendously expanded market for literature of all sorts. Black denominations, among the best-capitalized organizations within African American communities, were some of the first to take advantage of the new source of income and outreach. By the 1890s, observers noted that reading had become a more common pastime among the black middle class and had even come to rival oral presentations and sermons for the attention of listeners. Gertrude Mossell remarked in 1891 that the press was encroaching on the power of the pulpit: "People are coming to prefer to sit by their own cosy firesides and read sermons at their leisure, to traveling in inclement weather to the house of worship." By 1897, a female contributor to the *National Baptist Magazine* placed the press alongside the pulpit as a primary shaping force in society: "I believe the press a divine institution," she noted.[23]

Indeed, the growth of periodical literature and the development of denominational consciousness among African American Methodists and Baptists enjoyed a symbiotic relationship that served both economic and evangelistic purposes. Religious publications also fostered racial loyalty. Although the AME Church had long billed itself as the "voice of the race," and the *AME Zion Quarterly* claimed to represent the general interests of "the Afro-American Race in America," the rapid rise of the National Baptist Convention in the 1890s provides a telescopic example of this pattern. Well into the 1890s, black Baptists (not yet nationally consolidated into a denomination) regularly used white Baptist Sunday school literature and were likely to have subscribed to one of the several white-sponsored Baptist periodicals of the day. But tensions began to rise as the movement toward race-based denominational consolidation began early in the decade. Richard Boyd, a prominent Baptist and entrepreneur who would later establish the National Baptist Publishing Board in Nashville, articulated the conjoining of religious identity and literary production by encouraging the creation of African American Sunday school literature, to be stamped with "Negro personality, thought, and feeling." Along with a growing number of black Baptists, Boyd believed that there could be no separate black Baptist denomination without its own self-produced religious literature. Between 1900 and 1903, less than a decade

after the founding of the National Baptist Convention and the Publishing
Board, the denomination claimed to have circulated more than thirteen
million tracts and booklets. Its national periodical, the *National Baptist
Magazine,* positioning itself in competition for the reading public with black
Methodist journals and white Baptist publications, claimed to be "devoted
to the interests of the Negro Race in general." It is fair to say that even as the
young Baptist denomination encouraged the production of "race literature"
the impulse toward literary production also shaped and even catalyzed religious identification with the Baptist church. Thus, not only did religious literature, particularly the new interest in race literature, contribute to the
growth of the black publishing industry, but competition for audiences also
strengthened denominational consciousness among black Protestants.[24]

As both readers and authors, black women gained from the growth of
publishing and its connections to black denominations. With the proliferation of black periodicals in the postwar decades came a concomitant interest in "women's issues." Appealing to the sensibilities of women aspiring to
middle-class notions of respectability, black magazines and periodicals actively solicited women's contributions and eventually instituted women's
departments within their pages.[25] Specialized magazines for women, some
of them connected to the emerging women's club movement, also grew in
number at the same time, including *Ringwood's Afro-American Journal of
Fashion* (established in Cleveland in 1891), *Woman's World* (Fort Worth, 1900),
and the *Colored Women's Magazine* (Topeka, 1907). In order to compete with
these publications, denominational periodicals, long the province of clergy
and predominantly male writing staffs, also added women's pages and departments and sought female contributors.[26]

Female representation within the world of print grew rapidly during the
ensuing decades, and women's voices came to play a larger role in the denominational press than they had within the ritual life of the church. Iconographic
presentations of the discrepancy between the pulpit and the religious press
bear out the growing divide between a male clergy and an increasingly feminized labor force in the religious press by the century's close. In May of 1900,
the *Star of Zion* presented, quite literally, the public face of the church when
it featured the "Bishops of the African Methodist Episcopal Zion Church,"
a gallery of portraits of nine male leaders, on its front page. The frontispiece
of the *National Baptist Magazine* of July 1897, conversely, pictured the staff
of the publishing house: three female and two male staff members, a more
gender-balanced image of a religious organization that still did not reflect
the many more women writers who contributed to its pages. As male church
leaders increasingly reacted to halt the contagion of legitimate female author-

ity in church management, the religious press welcomed the poetry, stories, and articles of female church members in ever-greater numbers.

Denominational publishing, then, somewhat ironically, empowered Protestant women in a variety of ways. Many who became noted journalists and writers, including Ida B. Wells, Frances Ellen Watkins Harper, Gertrude Mossell, Mary V. Cook, Victoria Earle Matthews, Kate Chapman, and Lucretia Newman Coleman, got their start in publishing through work on one of the many new religious periodicals. Most notable was the Louisville-based newspaper *Our Women and Children,* edited by William J. Simmons, a Baptist, which employed numerous accomplished women during the 1880s as department editors. Almost all of these contributors were actively involved in other sorts of Baptist church work as well. While some sought work on specific publications because of prior religious commitments, many others wrote for a number of church journals concurrently. These simultaneous commitments evinced a new niche for the kind of writing that black women could produce and also helped create a national stage for women's concerns.[27]

High-profile publications, in turn, opened other doors for many women. Economically, writing could supplement a livelihood outside the confines of domestic labor, teaching, and secretarial work. Socially, it brought women to the attention of prominent African American male leaders and even precipitated "good" marriages for enterprising women. Professionally, it introduced the work of female writers to other editors, who then vied for their talents. Unlike male contributors to religious periodicals, moreover, mostly clergy whose contributions were localized to the pages of specific denominational publications, women writers attained a status at once more prominent and more diffuse. Writers such as Ida B. Wells, Frances Harper, and Gertrude Mossell became national celebrities, correspondents for numerous publications, and authors of their own books as well; their words thereby carried a potential for influence unmatched by most of their male counterparts.

Those African American women who became journalists during this period represented a small proportion of the nation's black population, to be sure. They were members of a black middle-class that emerged in the post-Reconstruction era as educational opportunities proved more available. Some, including Mary Cook, had been born into slavery.[28] But most were born either in the North or as members of free black communities in the urban South.[29] As middle-class women dedicated to the "politics of respectability," they used their talent as writers to promote a decidedly genteel vision of black community life. In doing so, they strove to control and "correct" the behavior of the working classes in the name of racial and religious unity.[30] Their vision was also region-specific. Centered around Washington,

D.C., and other cities in New York and Pennsylvania, areas that gave birth to both the largest concentration of black publishing ventures and independent black churches, women writers articulated a communal identity at once cosmopolitan and urbane. As such, it was far out of step with the reality of the vast majority of black Protestants who remained in the rural South.[31]

Women writers capitalized on (and in turn promoted) a view of female cultural influence based on the biological fact of motherhood, which connected their experiences to those of southern blacks. In doing so, they established their own particular claims to religious authority within the church by subverting the proscriptions of male clergy. Like Frances Harper, black women authors continuously emphasized the links between communal history and female—particularly maternal—influence. Virginia Broughton, a Baptist, echoed and expanded upon Harper's sentiments in a discussion of "Woman's Work" (1894). As the first instructors of children, Broughton noted, mothers are critical to moral development: "The mother transmits her virtues or her vices to her children; in fact, she reproduces herself in her children." Unlike her male counterparts, who asserted that women should serve as the "elocutionists" of history scripted by male authorities, Broughton elevated the role of women within the story itself. She wedded maternal guidance to God's plan in the unfolding of Israelite—and, by extension, African American—history, which occurred primarily as a result of female influence. "In the deliverance of Israel from Egyptian bondage, it was the love and wisdom of woman that preserved, nourished, and trained the man child that God called to be the leader, judge, and priest for his people."[32] A year later, Mrs. C. H. Baxter summed up that commonly held view even more succinctly when she noted, "The influence of woman more or less affects for good or evil, the entire destinies of man."[33]

To some extent, this ideology of female cultural influence was not specific to the African American community but reflected pervasive American assumptions in the Victorian era about women's roles as nurturers, teachers, and moral paragons. For black authors, the interrelations of cultural inheritance, communal identity, and maternal influence assumed a distinctive and highly charged meaning, one best summed up in a poem published in the *Star of Zion* in May 1886. Written in commemoration of the author's mother's birthday, it described the collective history of slavery, Civil War, and Emancipation that only a mother could relate to her children:

> You have seen poor Afric's children,
> Struggling, groaning neath their load,
> You have seen those children flee to
> Where the North Star points the road.[34]

The mother is not the only witness to these events, but she is the most reliable vehicle of collective history in a period where families were torn apart and paternity was a precarious bearer of identity. The image of mother as the curator of communal history was repeated constantly by black authors at the turn of the century, and it helped female writers stake their claim to cultural authority.[35]

In reading through black women's writing of this period, the sometimes cloyingly romantic representations of ideal womanhood may cause contemporary readers to miss the political stakes at issue within a denominational setting. Increasingly able to draw African American Protestants into an "imagined community" of believers that extended beyond the walls of a local church, religious publications can be seen as an alternative sacred locale with the potential to complement—or compete with—the beliefs and behavioral norms promoted within the church edifice itself. Their messages, furthermore, could be communicated to a regional or even a national audience of believers and nonbelievers alike.[36]

As women increasingly articulated their roles as keepers of tradition and memory in print, then, they found ways to voice opinions that circumvented churchly dictates about appropriate female speech. Two strategies proved particularly common. First, women made use of traditionally female genres to narrate and interpret history. Second, they shifted the content of male historical accounts, often identifying women as the pivotal—and frequently unheralded—agents of sacred history and church life.

The late nineteenth and early twentieth centuries were the era of the "grand narrative" in male historical writing. But women found ways of writing history without announcing it as such. Often, they committed what Nina Baym has referred to as "historical acts" and alluded to history or narrated pieces of a larger story in such a way that they evoked an entire chronology.[37] In this way, history could be interpreted and recounted in a variety of literary forms, such as poetry or fiction. Thus Pauline Hopkins, an editor of the *Colored American Magazine,* could rewrite sacred history in her novella *Of One Blood* by reference to a forgotten civilization in Telassar, a city in the ancient Near East. In quoting Milton and the Bible, Hopkins drew these historical references into her fictionalized history of a sacred, African-descended people. Her story was not a formal history, but it made use of and revised history to stress the obligation of African Americans to a holy and transhistorical community.[38]

Writing about history also allowed women to interpret Scripture in ways that were forbidden within the church. Harper's "Moses," for example, functioned much like a sermon in its explication of a biblical text. Yet as poetry it fell within the formal purview of "women's writing," which thereby rendered its content legitimate. Similarly, Katherine Tillman, a frequent contributor to the *AME Church Review,* expressed her interpretation of sacred history within poems and occasional pieces. In *Heirs of Slavery,* a play published in 1901 in the *AME Review,* Tillman buoys the spirits of a disheartened black man by taking him back through the history of enslavement, from Miriam, to Moses, to an Anglo-Saxon slave. Tillman's message that everyone who aspires to progress must also suffer, her encouragement of racial uplift, and her use of biblical precedents as proof parallel thematically the themes articulated in black sermons of the day.[39]

If women used poetry, fiction, and even "women's columns" to interpret the past and "preach" in the present, the content of their narratives often revised male-authored accounts. One of the most frequent contributions made by female authors was the self-conscious inclusion of women in familiar stories. Certainly, Frances Harper's poetry, as was also true of her epic "Moses," frequently took up scriptural stories and themes and placed women squarely in the center of the historical frame.[40] But female authors also cited a litany of female social and religious leaders such as Joan of Arc, Sojourner Truth, Frances Willard, Harriet Beecher Stowe, and Florence Nightingale.[41] In 1894 Gertrude Mossell published a book-length study of black women that most closely approximated the male-dominated genre of the race history. In *The Work of the Afro-American Woman,* she lauded the accomplishments of women in business, art, law, medicine, journalism, and religion. One section, which she called a race history, covered the historical progress of black women up to the present and included women within traditional accounts of racial progress.[42]

But more than adding women to a preexistent (male-generated) historical record, some female writers shifted the focus implicitly—and occasionally explicitly—to challenge previous interpretations and restructure the public memory of the church. Some championed an alternative view of history in which the lowly, the quiet, and the obscure became the primary agents of moral and racial progress. As Sarah J. Dorset outlined the sacred work performed by women, "In the family she quietly labors for the children. . . . the outside world knows and thinks little of her trials and perplexities; but patiently and trusting in her God, she quietly discharges her daily routine of work."[43] The first woman's column published in the *Star of Zion* in the 1890s, written by Sarah Pettey (the wife of an AMEZ bishop), consistently touted the virtues of local churches and unseen workers, those "less noted but hardworking self-sacrificing Christian soldiers," as the backbone of the denomination. "The large churches stand as shining lights and towering sentinels to let Christianity and the world know that Zion is alive," she wrote in 1899.

"But it is to a certain extent the small churches and the country work producing the motive power propelling our great ship of Church."[44] For her, the church was a united community of humble servants and workers and extended beyond the bounds of worship and ritual life.

Female authors occasionally included subjects written out of male historical accounts. It is intriguing that African American enslavement, a subject frequently avoided or downplayed by male race historians because of its associations with religious degeneracy and black male powerlessness, figured differently for some women writers. Gertrude Mossell saw slavery as a time of heroism and argued that it should be included in historical accounts: "Let us see to it that we despise nothing—the croonings of our aged nurses, the weird monotone of the slave song, the folk-lore. These are our authors' first editions, the source of what will some day become the mighty rivers of our race literature. Let us not undervalue their worth, but gather and string them like pearls of great price upon the chain of memory."[45]

Miscegenation and the dilemma of the biracial heroine or hero also figured prominently in women's literature. Frances Harper, Pauline Hopkins, and other women associated with black Protestant life emphasized the religious dilemma of those figures caught betwixt and between the worlds of white and black Americans. Harper's only full-length novel, *Iola Leroy* (1893), features a heroine who discovers that her father was the white master of her mother.[46] The theme of racial intermixture has often been seen as a vehicle for discussing the precariousness of racial and moral identity during this period, but it is also significant that miscegenation represented a historical dilemma specific to black women: In a racist society, one's maternal racial status determined one's history.[47] Upon discovering her true paternity, for example, Iola Leroy is confronted with a dilemma, not of her own standing but concerning a problem of history. Her changed status alters her relationship to the past as well as to the present.[48] Therefore, the theme of racial mixing may have had a particular salience for black female authors as both the victims of white male domination and in their roles as the authors of a gendered black historical record.

Recasting history infrequently occasioned public confrontation with male clergy and their own historical narratives. In 1888 Catherine Casey contributed an article to the *AME Recorder* emphasizing the importance of race histories as a means of instilling pride in children, but she questioned the limitation of race literature to the work of black men. She described witnessing a sermon given by Levi Coppin (then an AME elder) in which he held up five books for presentation to a local church library, "calling them his 'black boys.' . . . While Elder Coppin was rejoicing over his 'black boys' I was wondering where the 'black girls' were. Why are not Mrs. Harper's poems bound in blue and gold and lying upon our library shelves?" Significantly, Casey did not confront Coppin within the church itself, but she did feel free to do so within the *AME Recorder*. Noting the genius of Harper's poem about Moses, she continued with a more general complaint: "Why is it always necessary when we want to quote a poetess to go all the way back to Phillis Wheatly, when we have such poems as those of Mrs. Harper's shining in our faces from the newspapers and the magazines of the present day?"[49] Other women, too, used the pages of religious periodicals to voice disagreements with clergy and bishops that most likely would not have been articulated within a church setting.[50]

African American Protestant women therefore found numerous ways to constitute religious authority. Most often, they interpreted and recast the tradition in ways that kept them within the bounds of "appropriate" gender roles and did not bring them into direct confrontation with male church leaders. Although it may be true that they did so because of their abiding respect for the clergy and for inherited patterns of male authority, it is important to remember that despite the newly won freedoms afforded by the printing press, women's literature was still embedded within a larger nexus of publishing controlled by men. The editors of religious publications invariably were male, men decided what constituted "suitable" work, and men even controlled what ended up on the women's page. Only a few intrepid women, including Pauline Hopkins and Frances Harper, gained access to the reins of their own literary destinies for any length of time. As Gertrude Mossell commented in the 1890s, despite all the strides women writers had made, they still played supporting roles: "They are admitted to the press association and are in sympathy with the male editors; but few have become independent workers in this noble field of effort, being yet satellites, revolving round the sun of masculine journalism."[51]

If male church leaders and publishers attempted to exercise control over the new generation of female authors, two additional features of denominational publishing after the turn of the century also may have worked to displace, if not silence, women's voices as the primary curators of collective memory. The first, paradoxically, was the advent of women's departments and columns in the denominational press. Although the creation of a special section of a publication geared toward women certainly reflected an attempt to attract a larger female readership, it did not necessarily amplify women's voices within periodicals. Once women's "concerns" were relegated to a separate section, female voices were less audible elsewhere. In 1901, for example, the *AME Church Review* established a women's department. But the pieces that ran there, edifying numbers such as "why women nag," were not on the whole written by women. They included snippets from other journals and short articles selected or written by the male editor and intended for the improvement of women.[52] A second development was the expansion of Sunday school curricula within mainline black churches during the first decades of the twentieth century. As denominations sought to provide race literature for children, some prominent female writers focused their literary efforts on works for youth in the church. It is difficult to say with certainty how many of those women might otherwise have written for a broader church audience, but providing a "naturally feminine" outlet for female authors channeled women's writing in directions acceptable to male religious leaders.[53]

Despite the structural limitations on women's religious voices, the advent of denominational publishing enterprises provided something new. It expanded opportunities for women to articulate and disseminate their understandings of the history and politics of black Protestant life. Because periodical literature in particular was a relatively new technology whose potential problems were all but unrecognized, publishing ventures allowed women to play by the rules of economics rather than those of traditional church authority, to speak in a wide variety of voices, and to shape understanding of the religious community in ways that had long ago been denied them within the context of church ritual life. They could not preach, but they could write. Thus, black women between 1880 and 1920 staked a claim to a public voice in the church, one that is overlooked if "church" is defined as the rites and practices that take place within worship services.

The constraints of the print medium, moreover, should not detract from female writing's potential impact on average readers and church members. Sacraments may have stayed the same, and men still gave the sermons. But for the reading public, which increasingly included more and more African American Protestants, religious identity was also shaped by a cadre of women who reconstructed collective identity through the written word. Women, in turn, gained a role in religious publishing that gave them access to church leadership in a new way, allowing them to exercise a distinct kind of cultural power.

Notes

1. Harper's first book, *Poems on Miscellaneous Subjects,* appeared first in 1854 when she was twenty-nine. Published under the sponsorship of antislavery advocates and with an introduction by the noted abolitionist William Lloyd Garrison, the book was reprinted at least five times before 1871, when it entered its twentieth edition.

2. Frances Harper, "Our Greatest Want," *Anglo-African Magazine* 1 (May 1859): 160.

3. F. E. W. Harper, "Moses: A Story of the Nile," in *Idylls of the Bible* (1901, repr. New York: AMS Press, 1975), 3.

4. Harper, "Moses," 9–10.

5. Joan Sherman, *Invisible Poets: Afro-Americans of the Nineteenth Century,* 2d ed. (Urbana: University of Illinois Press, 1989), 66.

6. Frances Harper, "The Ladies in the AME Review," *AME Christian Recorder,* Jan. 22, 1885, 1.

7. For the purposes of this essay, the mainline churches referred to include the three largest historically black denominations at the turn of the century: the African Methodist Episcopal Church (AME), the African Methodist Episcopal Zion Church (AMEZ), and the National Baptist Convention.

8. The literature on denominationalism is vast. As a starting point, one might consult the essays in *Reimagining Denominationalism: Interpretive Essays,* ed. Robert Bruce Mullin and Russell E. Richey (New York: Oxford University Press, 1994).

9. These metaphors can be traced back at least to the 1890s, when Victoria Earle Matthews described black women as the "arch" of the black church in *The Awakening of the Afro-American Woman* (1897; cited in Hazel Carby, *Reconstructing Womanhood: The Emergence of the Afro-American Woman Novelist* [New York: Oxford University Press, 1987], 117). See also Jacquelyn Grant, "Black Women and the Church," in *All American Women: Lines That Divide, Ties That Bind,* ed. Johnnetta B. Cole (New York: Free Press, 1986), 359–69; and Theressa Hoover, "Black Women and the Churches: Triple Jeopardy," in *Black Theology: A Documentary History, 1966–79,* ed. Gayraud S. Wilmore and James H. Cone (Maryknoll, N.Y.: Orbis Books, 1979), 377–88. I am indebted to Lynn S. Neal for the latter two examples.

10. Many of the pertinent secondary resources are available in the periodical literature. See Delores C. Carpenter, "Black Women in Religious Institutions: A Historical Summary from Slavery to the 1960s," *Journal of Religious Thought* 46 (1989): 7–27; Jualynne Dodson, "Power and Surrogate Leadership: Black Women and Organized Religion," *Sage* 5 (Fall 1988): 37–42; and Mary R. Sawyer, "Black Religion and Social Change: Women in Leadership Roles," *Journal of Religious Thought* 47 (1990–91): 16–29. Examples of excellent book-length studies include Evelyn Brooks Higginbotham, *Righteous Discontent: The Women's Movement in the Black Baptist Church, 1880–1920* (Cambridge: Harvard University Press, 1993), and Judith Weisenfeld, *African American Women and Christian Activism: New York's Black YWCA, 1905–1945* (Cambridge: Harvard University Press, 1998).

11. On this history, see Laurie F. Maffly-Kipp, *African-American Communal Narratives, 1780–1915* (in press).

12. On the writing of race histories, see Laruie F. Maffly-Kipp, "Mapping the World, Mapping the Race: The Negro Race History, 1874–1915," *Church History* 64 (Dec. 1995): 610–26.

13. W. H. Hartshorn and George W. Penniman, *An Era of Progress and Promise* (Boston: Priscilla Publishing, 1910), 116.

14. Mary Helen Washington, ed., *Invented Lives: Narratives of Black Women, 1860–1960* (Garden City: Doubleday, 1987), xviii.

15. R. D. Davis, "A Female Ministry," *Star of Zion,* Jan. 26, 1899.

16. I. D. Roes, "Woman," *AME Christian Recorder,* March 27, 1889, 1.

17. L. A. Scruggs, *Women of Distinction: Remarkable in Works and Invincible in Character* (Raleigh: L. A. Scruggs, 1893), 17–22.

18. Gertrude Mossell, *The Work of the Afro-American Woman* (1894, repr. New York: Oxford University Press, 1988), 98.

19. This production of texts was not merely a reflection of women's activities in other spheres of life but was in and of itself a conscious attempt to shape and define what it meant to be an African American church member. What Hazel Carby notes with respect to women's novels also pertains to the sphere of religious publishing. She astutely observes that early black women's novels are not merely "socially determined by the conditions within which they were created" but are "also cultural artifacts which shape the social conditions they enter." So, too, the writings of women in religious periodicals continuously created and replicated notions of black Protestant life. Carby, *Reconstructing Womanhood*, 95.

20. Ibid., 123. In Penelope L. Bullock's study of the black periodical press (in which she excludes daily newspapers), she counted ninety-seven titles appearing between 1838 and 1909. Of those, eleven appeared before or during the Civil War, and eighty-five in the three decades following the war, with the largest number appearing between 1900 and 1909. Bullock, *The Afro-American Periodical Press, 1838–1909* (Baton Rouge: Louisiana State University Press, 1981), 2.

21. Bullock, *The Afro-American Periodical Press*, 3, 71–72, 92.

22. Ibid., 9.

23. I. Garland Penn, *The Afro-American Press and Its Editors* (1891, repr. New York Arno Press and the New York Times, 1969), 487; Hardie Martin, "How the Church Can Best Help the Masses," *National Baptist Magazine* 4–5 (Oct. 1896–Jan. 1897): 281.

24. James D. Tyms, *The Rise of Religious Education among Negro Baptists: A Historical Case Study* (New York: Exposition Press, 1965), 153, 169; Higginbotham, *Righteous Discontent*, 12.

25. For an insightful discussion of the class- and race-based "politics of respectability," see Higginbotham, *Righteous Discontent*, ch. 7.

26. Bullock, *The Afro-American Periodical Press*, 167. According to Bullock (166), the AME Church even authorized publication of a "Ladies' Magazine" at the 1880 General Conference, but there is no evidence that the journal was ever published.

27. Gertrude Mossell was first encouraged as a schoolgirl to write by the editor of the *AME Christian Recorder*. By the 1890s she edited the women's department at the secular *Indianapolis Freeman*, served on the staffs of at least two other publications, and wrote for two more. Ida B. Wells had written for more than a dozen newspapers by 1891. While working as the assistant secretary and bookkeeper for the AME Church, Lucretia Newman Coleman wrote for *The American Baptist, Our Women and Children*, and the *AME Church Review*. Penn, *Afro-American Press*, 372–410.

28. Cook was born in Kentucky in 1862 and was later financed in her education by northern whites (Higginbotham, *Righteous Discontent*, 125).

29. Hallie Quinn Brown, for example, was born in Pittsburgh but grew up in the black community centered around Chatham in Canada; Pauline Hopkins came of age in the middle-class black society of Boston. Mary Church Terrell and Frances Harper, conversely, were products of the urban South and came north for educational reasons. Terrell grew up in Memphis and later graduated from Oberlin College in 1884. Harper, born in 1825 in Baltimore to free black parents, eventually moved to Ohio, and later to Pennsylvania

to teach, lecture, and write. Scruggs, *Women of Distinction,* 17, 227; Carby, *Reconstructing Womanhood,* 65.

30. Hazel V. Carby, "Policing the Black Woman's Body in an Urban Context," in *Identities,* ed. Kwame Anthony Appiah and Henry Louis Gates, Jr. (Chicago: University of Chicago Press, 1995), 124.

31. Bullock, *Afro-American Periodical Press,* 2–3.

32. Virginia Broughton, "Woman's Work," *National Baptist Magazine* 1 (Jan. 1894): 31.

33. Mrs. C. H. Baxter, "Woman's Sphere in Society," *National Baptist Magazine* 2 (Jan. 1895): 26.

34. Mrs. H. Brown, "To Mother," *Star of Zion,* May 7, 1886.

35. Emblematic was a passage included in Thomas Johnson's *Twenty-eight Years a Slave* that recalls the role his mother played in communicating information about religion, race, and family history. Johnson's mother taught him the little she knew about Africa and about heaven, where "God would think as much of the black people as he did of the white. . . . I cannot forget her tears as she looked upon me with a mother's love, more than sixty years ago, and told me what little she knew. To her, as to thousands of poor slaves, the Bible was almost a sealed book." Johnson, *Twenty-eight Years a Slave; or, The Story of My Life on Three Continents,* 7th ed. (Bournemouth, Eng.: W. Mate and Sons, 1909), 4.

36. It is important to note that many of these periodicals were read by people who were not members of the church or who belonged to other churches. The *AME Christian Recorder* was among the most widely circulated black periodicals in the South during the 1880s, and its pages contained letters and articles by members and nonmembers alike. Similarly, the *AME Church Review* and the *National Baptist Magazine* both featured pieces by unaffiliated African American readers.

37. Nina Baym, *American Women Writers and the Work of History, 1790–1860* (New Brunswick: Rutgers University Press, 1995).

38. Pauline Hopkins, *Of One Blood: Or, the Hidden Self,* was first excerpted in the *Colored American Magazine* (1902–3) and reprinted in *The Magazine Novels of Pauline Hopkins* (New York: Oxford University Press, 1988).

39. Katherine Tillman, "Heirs of Slavery," *AME Church Review* 17 (Jan. 1901): 199–203.

40. See, for example, "The Syrophenician Woman," in Frances Ellen Watkins Harper, *Poems on Miscellaneous Subjects* (1854, repr. Philadelphia: Rhistoric Publications, 1969).

41. See, for example, Mattie Roberts, "The Power and Influence of Woman," *AME Christian Recorder,* Jan. 28, 1886, 2.

42. Mossell, *The Work of the Afro-American Woman,* 21, 46. Shortly after its publication, the wife of an AME Bishop, Mrs. B. F. Lee, penned a poem dedicated to Mossell and published it in the *Recorder.* The book, she noted, "proves the mind / In womankind / It proveth too, / What she can do / The hopes and fears / Of her domesticity." Mrs. B. F. Lee, "To Mrs. N. F. Mossell on Her Book 'The Work of Afro-American Women,'" *AME Christian Recorder,* Jan. 10, 1895, 1.

43. Sarah J. Dorset, "Woman's Relation to the World," *Star of Zion,* Jan. 29, 1886.

44. Mrs. Pettey, "Woman's Column," *Star of Zion,* June 29, 1899.

45. Gertrude Mossell, "Life and Literature," *AME Church Review* 14 (Jan. 1898): 325.

46. See J. Lee Greene, *Blacks in Eden: The African-American Novel's First Century* (Char-

lottesville: University Press of Virginia, 1996), for a sustained analysis of this theme in African American literature before World War I.

47. The relationship between racial and religious history and the literary exploration of miscegenation is a complex subject taken up in more detail in Maffly-Kipp, *African-American Communal Narratives, 1780–1915*.

48. Carby, *Reconstructing Womanhood*, 90; see also Barbara Christian, *Black Feminist Criticism: Perspectives on Black Women Writers* (New York: Pergamon Press, 1985), 167.

49. Catherine Casey, "Our Woman's Column," *AME Christian Recorder*, Feb. 9, 1888, 5.

50. See, for example, Maggie Hood-Banks, "The Missionary Department," *Star of Zion*, April 19, 1900.

51. Penn, *Afro-American Press*, 490.

52. "Women's Department," *AME Church Review* 17 (Jan. 1901): 244–52. One might fruitfully compare this phenomenon to women's magazines, and now women's television stations, which invariably make decisions about what constitute "women's concerns," thus proscribing appropriate female roles.

53. It is also possible that this literature contains material potentially subversive of male religious authority. A topic for further research would include the content of Sunday school literature within black churches in the early twentieth century.

9. Female Suffering and Religious Devotion in American Pentecostalism

R. MARIE GRIFFITH

IN THE HISTORY OF Christian devotionalism, women play a vital role, a role far more lively, enduring, and tangible than they have played in most institutional church histories. Acts of devotion, after all, are not predicated on social authority but are accessible, according to scripture and tradition, to all. Even the quickest skim of American women's religious history uncovers pervasive female networks whose participants have sought spiritual and moral sustenance together in Bible study, hymn singing, discussions of church teaching, and earnest communal prayer. A plethora of women's diaries, letters, and recorded testimonies further reveals the centrality of more private forms of communion with God and gives eloquent voice to both the needs and the hopes that animate religious devotion.

But historians of American women and religion, particularly those focused on the twentieth century, seem more often than not to be both embarrassed and nonplused by the devotional lives of their subjects, as if the language of divine appeal bespeaks a kind of desperation unfitting to women—a vulnerability that plays into gender stereotypes we would prefer to dismantle. Perhaps these interpreters worry that close attention to female devotional experience carries the risk of infantilizing women, portraying them as victims of patriarchal theology rather than creative agents of their faith. It is far better, it might seem from one angle, to sweep women's prayers and testimonies under a grand historical rug and instead highlight the public action and religious activism of strong female leaders. It is better, that is, to depict women as courageous feminists or quasi-feminists even when disagreeing with their aims (such as converting the "heathen" or fighting for temperance). It seems, perhaps, more uplifting to observe them dynamically altering the world than to see them cloistered in the intimate seclusions of prayer.

Yet exploring the subjective side of religious belief—ground-level faith, religious experience, or what some call the religious imagination—is quite clearly a critical task for grasping the historical creation and reproduction of religious and cultural traditions generated in the interplay among individuals, communities, and social institutions. Just as one can only dimly perceive figures such as Frances Willard or Dorothy Day while ignoring their devotional lives as Christians, so are religious movements like temperance or the Catholic Worker obscured by inattention to the subjective beliefs and practices of participants. In other words, as historians David Hall, Dorothy Bass, and Steven Stowe have noted, the reciprocal dynamic between personal faith and communal religion—what Stowe eloquently calls the "refreshing of the subjective through common practice"—requires sustained analysis for interpreting how a particular tradition lives and evolves.[1] When those subjects are female, it seems all the more relevant to think about subjectivity and the ways in which those without full access to institutional power and authority have engaged their religion and shaped its contours for future devotees.

The relationship between subjectivity and religious practice is perhaps a specially intense one in traditions focused on personal salvation such as evangelicalism and its many offshoots: traditions that require individual conversion (and sometimes subsequent experiences of sanctification and Spirit baptism) and advocate "witnessing," that is, sharing these experiences with others in order to expand the Christian populace. These traditions have also caught the attention of historians of American women because they have appeared (from some perspectives at least) to offer greater opportunity for leadership and distinction than those traditions marked by constricting hierarchies of patriarchal authority.

Pentecostalism has been the focus of particular interest among theologians and folklorists as much as historians, with its focus on a spirit that topples earthly hierarchies by touching females, the poor, and persons of color as powerfully (if not more so) as males, the well-to-do, and white people. Yet very little of the growing literature on Pentecostalism addresses the formation of subjectivity among Pentecostal women. This essay attempts to do just that, exploring the testimonial writings of American Pentecostal women in order to highlight and decipher what has seemed so ordinary as to be overlooked in their lives: the language and practice of religious devotion.

Contextualizing Pentecostal Devotion

By the end of its first century of existence, denominational Pentecostalism claimed well over two hundred million adherents throughout the world.[2] If one adds to this the millions of "Charismatics" and "Third Wavers" from Roman Catholic, mainline Protestant, and especially Spirit-centered independent churches, the aggregate numbers of Pentecostal/charismatic worshipers is estimated at nearly half a billion people.[3] The success of modern Pentecostalism—materially represented in vast television ministries like that of Oral Roberts and the ever-growing mega-churches in metropolitan areas around the world—could hardly have been envisioned by the self-described plain and lowly folks, rural and urban, who were Pentecostalism's original constituents. Careful attention to these early Pentecostal adherents and their distinctive form of piety not only sheds light on a vast subculture, or cluster of subcultures, that otherwise remain largely invisible but also helps explain the persistent appeal of Pentecostal piety across cultures throughout the twentieth century and, doubtless, beyond.

The history of Pentecostal devotionalism overlays histories of gender and race, love and family and civic life, communication between and across geographic regions, and literacy and books and practices of reading. In this particular case the main characters of the story are women, the predominant writers of testimonies and prayer requests in early Pentecostal periodicals. (Men, too, were active participants in Pentecostalism during this period and beyond, but they wrote fewer and briefer personal accounts to the periodicals that are the main source of this analysis.) The characters in this study are of two distinct social groups. One is composed of mostly white Pentecostals from the Church of God in Cleveland, Tennessee, and the Pentecostal Holiness Church in Franklin, Georgia, who were largely southern, rural, and poor, reflecting a significant proportion of early Pentecostal converts (although by no means the total).[4] The other is composed of black Pentecostals from the Church of God in Christ in Memphis, Tennessee, who were largely urban and poor but scattered across a broad geographic area of the eastern and midwestern regions of the United States.

Although all three of these denominations were based in the South, by the 1930s Pentecostalism had gained as much a hold on northern and western urban areas as southern, rural ones. The risk of focusing on these relatively poor groups of people is to reinforce old stereotypes of Pentecostalism as a crude movement of hillbillies and bumpkins, attracting the lowly or "disinherited" who sought compensation for their poor lot on earth in a theology of divine reward.[5] Pentecostals have reacted in assorted ways to these stereotypes, struggling to present themselves as more cultured than their reputation while at the same time manifesting pride in the humble origins of their faith. Among other things, the sources analyzed here will perhaps provide a useful replacement for deprivation theory by focusing on the positive benefits made available through Pentecostal practices such as prayer and testimony.

Evangelical, Holiness, and Pentecostal women have long sought healing and happiness through the prayers of their Christian sisters. Denominational magazines and newspapers published in the first half of the twentieth century provided weekly forums where readers in need could ask for prayers and testify with exuberance to prayers divinely answered, sufferings alleviated, and lives restored. These sensational and often minutely detailed accounts required responsive action from Pentecostal readers, who were urged by writers as well as editors not merely to skim through the prayer requests sympathetically but to "tarry before the Lord" in diligent and prayerful supplication for all requests. The practices around prayer described in such accounts—praying for one another's needs, sending anointed handkerchiefs or other objects as signs of grace, and continually assuring one another of the ardent prayers sent out on their behalf—enabled formation of a Pentecostal community, composed predominantly of women, that transcended the ordinary bounds of geography and social location and imparted comfort, benevolence, and recognition to the suffering hopeful across the land.

The story of these particular practices and the formation of such a community of readers and writers during the early decades of the twentieth century needs to be contextualized within a much longer history of transatlantic evangelicalism, its practices surrounding divine healing, and the perpetual formation of women's prayer networks. A remarkable variety of localistic studies and more comprehensive surveys on the history of evangelicalism in the American and British contexts have impressed readers with richly evocative accounts of the devotionalism and discipline of evangelical piety, illuminating a broad range of practices pertaining to worship, Bible study, education, and mission work.[6] Somewhat less attention has been paid to devotional life by scholars of Holiness and Pentecostal movements, who, while ably demonstrating the continuities of Pentecostal piety with other strands within the Wesleyan tradition and beyond, have tended to focus more on social and denominational history than on the range and workings of practices among so-called Spirit-filled Christians.[7] Studies that analyze women's participation within Holiness and Pentecostal movements similarly tend to focus purposefully on female leaders—preachers, evangelists, educators, missionaries, and founders of religious organizations—and leave less influential women and their devotional lives unexamined.[8]

Although we know much about women's devotional narratives and prayer networks in the eighteenth and nineteenth centuries, we know far less about twentieth-century Pentecostal women's devotional lives and the printed texts that helped sustain and expand them, particularly after 1920. The dearth of attention to African American Pentecostal women (and to black Pentecostalism more broadly) has been particularly lamentable. Fortunately, several studies have been undertaken that examine both white and black women's devotional lives, taking account at last of the complex racial dynamics that accompanied the rise and trajectory of Pentecostalism in America as well as the dynamics of particular devotional practices.[9]

In this essay, I will examine the letters, testimonial accounts, and prayer requests printed in three Pentecostal magazines during the 1930s and 1940s, narratives written predominantly by women. Analyzing these materials will provide opportunity for scrutiny of what Susan O'Brien, studying evangelical publishing networks of the eighteenth century, has termed "a sense of the shared" among participants, created in the context of revival meetings and fervent worship services but sometimes maintained most effectively in printed texts.[10] Examining this "sense of the shared" described by Pentecostal women during the early decades of the twentieth century, and the ways in which published narratives occasioned and sustained a particular vocabulary of devotional experience, emphasizes ways in which women cut off from local networks of support found access to sympathy and healing from women known only through mediums of print. Such an analysis may also— although I do not explicitly attempt to do so here—begin to clarify the dynamic relationship between evangelical religion and therapeutic culture during the early decades of the century, elucidating the logic of Pentecostal women's resistance to emerging therapies of their day (along with all forms of modern medicine) in light of the wider cultural themes of pain and healing embedded in their narratives.[11] It is my hope, finally, that this study may lend support to emergent perspectives within the historiography of American religion pertaining to the examination of practices, locating and describing specific devotional activities within the broader context of religious histories in which they take part.[12]

"A Home beyond This Veil of Tears": Interpretations of Suffering

In 1910 the Church of God of Cleveland, Tennessee, began publication of the *Evening Light and Church of God Evangel* (shortened in 1911 to *Church of God Evangel*), a religious weekly brimming with joy over what appeared to be the "evening light" marking the long-anticipated return of Christ.[13] In 1917 the Pentecostal Holiness Church—a merger of B. H. Irwin's Fire-Baptized Holiness Church, the Holiness Church of North Carolina, and the Tabernacle Pentecostal Church of South Carolina began publishing its own weekly organ, the *Pentecostal Holiness Advocate,* from its Georgia headquarters.[14] By this time, the predominantly African American, Memphis-based Church of God in Christ (COGIC) had been publishing the *Whole Truth* for ten years. Similar in theology (derived from the Wesleyan/Holiness roots of the three churches with the addition of the tongues doctrine) and to some extent in form, these periodicals were widely circulated both among southerners who composed the majority of Pentecostalism's constituency until well into the 1940s and among believers scattered as far away as New Jersey, Chicago, and California. Throughout these decades and beyond, believers wrote frequent letters to the papers, sharing their burdens and sorrows even as they gave witness to the miraculous work of God in their lives and urged others to seek the joyous experiences of conversion, sanctification, and Spirit baptism.

More than the *Whole Truth*, *The Advocate* and *The Evangel* devoted considerable space to sections called "Testimonies" and "Requests for Prayer," and both printed far more contributions from women than from men. I have roughly calculated the female-to-male ratio of testimonies for *The Advocate* at approximately 4.5 to 1 and for prayer requests at 4 to 1. (That ratio does not include the number of people whom I could not identify as male or female, but even if all of those unknowns turned out to be male—which is highly unlikely—the number of testimonies and prayer requests would still be overwhelmingly written by women.) For *The Evangel*, the numbers are even more striking. Testimonies hold steady at about 4 to 1, but prayer requests were printed at an estimated ratio of more than seven women for every one man. Moreover, given the fact that these publications were edited by men who were concerned that the Pentecostal movement not become overly feminized, one wonders whether the ratio of letters received might prove to be even more overwhelmingly female. Although these numbers do not in any way demonstrate Pentecostal testimonies and prayer requests to be purely female genres, they certainly indicate women's particular enthusiasm for sharing their stories with the wider readership of these magazines.

In the *Whole Truth*, however, testimonies and prayer requests were somewhat overshadowed by the many notices of church news and reports of revivals, visiting preachers, and church conventions. Although these reports were often written by women ("reporters"), their names were frequently listed secondarily under the byline of the church pastor. Such reports sometimes included testimonial accounts from women or (less often) men in the congregation, but because these were transmitted third-hand they did not carry the same urgent immediacy as first-hand narratives. The personal testimonies that do appear in the *Whole Truth* seem also to have been overwhelmingly written by women, and they nearly always focus on physical healings; nearly absent are the expositions of continued suffering that were prominent

in *The Advocate* and *The Evangel*. Prayer requests also appear more explicitly filtered by the *Whole Truth*'s field editor, whose regular column, among
other things, advised readers what to pray for. A 1945 injunction that "prayer
should be made for the passing of the Anti-Lynching Bill" is a reminder that
this publication differed significantly from its predominantly white counterparts.[15]

Women's printed narratives in the latter periodicals centered on two basic emotional themes: sorrow and joy. Both testimonies and prayer requests
articulated the ravages of physical and spiritual pain while also professing
complete trust that relief was on its way, to be bestowed by a beneficent God.
Testimonies, which primarily informed readers of the many blessings received
by the one who wrote in, often began as Maggie Mosley, writing to *The Advocate*, did in 1935:

> I praise the Lord for being saved, sanctified and filled with the blessed Holy
> Ghost. I have no desire to turn back to this world, but have a strong determi-
> nation to go all the way with Jesus regardless of the cost.
>
> I praise the Lord for the many blessings He bestows upon me daily. I praise
> Him for touching my body when I was so sick, raising me up, and bringing me
> home safe from the hospital. I know if it had not been for the dear Lord I would
> not be here.

Yet in an instant, testimonies were often transformed into mournful appeals
for prayer. Mosley's continued in a new tone, contrary to her earlier delight:

> I am not entirely healed. I have a very bad stomach trouble, and my nerves are
> bad. It seems I have such hard trials, and sometimes I can hardly overcome, I
> am so weak in body. It seems that if I was well and strong my trials would not
> be so hard to overcome.
>
> I want all the Christians to pray earnestly that the Lord will completely heal
> my body for His glory. I feel so discouraged at times. I live too far from the
> Pentecostal Holiness Church to walk to the services. I have no way to go of my
> own. Pray for my husband to be saved before it is too late.[16]

Mosley's testimony encapsulates several of the critical elements of Pentecostal testimonies: praise, certainty of God's power and goodness, and an
account of a healing. It also typifies some of the particular features of the
women's texts: assertions of continued trials, sometimes perceived as "the
cost" of following Jesus; a sense of isolation from religious community; and
laments of emotional distance from a husband who remains unsaved. Ella
Taylor, writing to *The Evangel* in 1944, articulated her aloneness even more
starkly:

As I stand inside this morning and look out upon a dark and gloomy world, dreary and drooped in sin, my heart aches and I feel so homesick. I do know there is a guiding hand leading me on to a better day, to a home beyond this veil of tears, that Jesus went away to prepare for the few that hold out faithful to the end. On account of sin and uncleanness, my earthly home here was torn to pieces some years ago. Today as I stand alone Jesus is by my side and I can look to Him as my guide and director through this unfriendly world.[17]

Like Maggie Mosley, Ella Taylor struggled to praise God in the midst of her despondency, but she did not deny the reality of her mixed feelings. Like many other women who wrote letters to Pentecostal periodicals, Mosley and Taylor had essentially given up on this world of gloom and woe. Instead, they counted on a world of happiness beyond, "a home beyond this veil of tears."

The melancholy yearning for home that saturates these narratives, framed as the ardent expectancy for heaven and eternal communion with God, evokes the pain of broken relationships and a desire for them to be restored—or replaced with better ones—on earth. The idea of home in these accounts simultaneously suggests a haven from sorrow as well as a dwelling steeped in love, and both seemed to be in short supply for the women writing to Pentecostal periodicals during the Great Depression and World War II. "Home" also suggested relationships beyond the immediate family—whole communities bound by ties of affection, compassion, and common belief. Churches themselves were considered homes in that sense, and they also served some women as preferred alternatives to the literal homestead. Those whose families were divided or broken could hope to find a substitute family at the nearest Pentecostal prayer meeting.

In its idealized form, the home in these narratives also represented an emotional or spiritual purity, a thoroughgoing authenticity perceived as the antithesis of the fakery of the world. Rooted in Victorian depictions of the home and inflected with southern ideals of honor and domesticity, this Pentecostal depiction is kindred to American country music's enshrinement of home, which, in Cecelia Tichi's words, is counterposed to "materialism, social status, hurdles of hierarchy, and all sorts of false value systems."[18] There is no artifice in the homes these women longingly anticipate; all emotions and commitments are genuine, accepting, and predictable in their goodness. Yet letter-writers' unremitting complaints about wayward husbands, derelict children, and licentious neighbors bear harsh witness to the near-impossibility of maintaining a stable home on this earth, inspiring ever greater hopes for home in the world to come. The juxtaposition between the mundane abode of sorrow and the heavenly home of joy was voiced powerfully in one Pentecostal woman's poem:

I have a home, it's made of gold; Its wealth and grandeur is untold;
Eye hath not seen, ear hath not heard, To the heart of man it hath not
   occurred.
In that bright home no pain, no death, No poisonous air, no tainted breath,
No sin, no sorrow, want or care, But joys eternally are there.[19]

Recognizing the difficulty of building happy homes on earth served another and perhaps more critical function for the Pentecostal women of this era: It enabled them to redeem their suffering as part of the necessary cost of following Jesus and thus find meaning in daily experiences of pain. Over and over again, women testified to the ridicule they faced, even in their own homes, as Christians who rejected worldliness in favor of "holiness"; the latter, of course, carried with it expectations of behavior, hair length, and attire that worked to set Pentecostal women apart from all others. As Francis Brown wrote to *The Advocate*, "People think I am crazy for not partaking of everything of this world, and not dressing and acting like the world, but we know we are peculiar people, and we are not of the world."[20] At the level of narrative at least, the women were able to take pride in "the jeers of the world" and openly counted themselves as martyrs for the faith. Their "homesickness" or "homelessness" was refashioned as a source of pride and self-esteem. Feeling too at home in the world was a luxury indulged only by the wicked.

How much jeering these women actually encountered for their beliefs or their unusual appearance is, of course, impossible to determine. But there were undoubtedly other, very real troubles that they faced, and it must have taken great effort to turn these into occasions for Christian conceit. The most common grievance was the problem of wayward husbands, and female writers frequently urged readers to intercede prayerfully for the restoration of their marriages. In 1930 Mrs. J. L. Tolley of Purcerville, Virginia, wrote a series of anxious letters to *The Advocate* requesting "earnest prayer and fasting" for her husband, who was "deep in sin" and had abandoned her and their eight children. In a passage richly evocative of the anger and despair Mrs. Tolley must have felt toward her husband, other Christians, and possibly God for her continued suffering, she mused plaintively about the apparent failure of her requests for prayer: "Jesus says if we have faith and fast and pray He will do greater things than He did, but Christians are not doing it. What is wrong with them? We need more faith and to fast and pray more. . . . The Bible says if Jesus be lifted up He will draw all men unto Him, and we know it is true. There must be something wrong. I do wish I could be good enough to do these great things. Jesus told the disciples that for lack of faith that they couldn't cast out devils. Please pray for me."[21] Holding on desperately to the promises of the Bible and the Pentecostal community, Mrs. Tolley turned the blame for her broken home back onto herself and onto those Christians who seemed clearly to be neglecting their religious duties. She interpreted her continued suffering not as a blessing, a test of her endurance that would reap great rewards, but as a sign of spiritual bankruptcy, a constant reproach for sinful living and insufficient faith.

Wayward companions were a problem for many other women as well as Mrs. Tolley, although few voiced their exasperation so vehemently. In 1930 the editor of *The Advocate* asked readers, "Pray again for Mrs. Earnie Tumblin of Laurens, S.C., who is in trouble over her husband who has left her. She wants him to come back."[22] The next year, a North Carolina wife and mother, hospitalized for a year with what she called "sleeping sickness," told of her husband leaving her and their two young children; her wish, too, was for readers to "pray for him to come back."[23] In the same issue, *The Advocate*'s editor wrote of an Ontario, Canada, woman in "deep distress" and desiring prayer that her husband be healed of alcoholism.[24] Perhaps an even worse situation was endured by a South Carolina woman who beseeched prayers so "that her husband may get out of jail to earn bread for the home."[25] Aside from extreme cases of abandonment and imprisonment, countless husbands were simply "unsaved," and the plea to "pray for my unsaved husband" was included in a sizable proportion of testimonies from *The Advocate* and *Evangel* (although rarely seen in the *Whole Truth*). Although some of these accounts involved supposedly "backslidden" Christian men, the majority suggested that their husbands had never undergone conversion and were weary of their wives cajoling them to examine their sinful souls and attend church. We have no evidence on how these women interpreted their shared predicament, but it is clear that most assumed that the prayers of righteous Christians would ultimately cause their husbands to be transformed.

Women reduced to desperation over such plights could take heart in the frequent narratives printed in these periodicals detailing the transformation of a sinner into a respectable Christian. Latha Smith's 1930 account of a sot who had been recently redeemed was such a story:

> He is an old man who spent most all his days a bad drunkard. He would get drunk and lay out all night and his dear wife would not know where he was. He would lose his horse and buggy. But God had His hand on him. So one day he was arrested by the Holy Ghost. Sometime later, before he arose one morning, God forgave his sins and made him a child of the King. Praise His name. Now he goes to church, takes a front seat and doesn't mind getting up before the people who know the life he lived and telling how God in His mercy saved him from a drunkard's hell. Glory to God.[26]

Another dramatic story was recounted by a West Virginia woman, who noted that her last letter to *The Evangel* had requested prayer for her husband to be saved: "I made mention that I was ready and willing for God to take my life, if necessary, if that would cause my husband to be saved. I didn't have to give my life but I was willing to do it and God knew it. The day after I sent the request in my husband was saved. Thank God! It's wonderful what God can do when we get willing."[27] Such stories were presumably intended to raise the hopes of other wives who were yoked to heathen men, but many readers must have found them instead a discouraging contrast to their own dreary lots. An account of a husband who was apparently saved the very day after his wife sent in her prayer request surely provoked as much envy and disillusionment as encouragement.

Yearning for loving relationships and for a safe, affectionate home, many women delivered plaintive appeals for companionship. Onie Winn from Watonga, Oklahoma, who called herself "a cripple girl," wrote, "I would be glad if anyone would write me as I am lonely, no one to talk about Jesus with."[28] Minnie Coleman of McKenzie, Alabama concluded her otherwise cheerful letter with a similar entreaty for a Christian pen pal: "Will some one who read [sic] this please write to me as I live in a place where there are no Pentecostal people. I would be glad to get letters, also pictures of some of the young Christians. I get lonesome sometimes, so please write me."[29] Mrs. R. A. Flurrty, a "shut-in" from Perkinton, Mississippi, thanked fellow readers of the *Church of God Evangel* for their comforting testimonies and then asked, "Dear Christians—unseen friends—keep praying for me—this old grandmother in a wheel chair."[30] Such women as these, isolated from companionship by location, religion, or illness, sought to cure their "lonesomeness" through a community of people to whom they had access only through prayer columns of weekly magazines.

Even those who regularly participated in a local Pentecostal church considered the readership of these periodicals to be an extended community, at times substituting for local churchpeople. "As I sit here in my room all alone this rainy Sunday A.M.," Martha Cabe began in 1930, "I feel impressed to send in my testimony as I will not get to be in service today. I live seven miles from our church and have to go by train or bus, and the weather is rainy and bad. . . . As I sit alone [Jesus] speaks to my heart to be of good cheer. I don't feel like I could stay here if I didn't have Him to talk to my heart. I know I would be miserable without Him."[31] Other women noted that "there are no holiness people in this place," a lack that marked not only their own loneliness but also, and perhaps more important, the writers' high status as brave pilgrims traveling alone on the narrow path. Although they would receive no earthly glory for this arduous journey, their privileged rank was sure to be recognized by other wayfarers in distant places.

The community of Pentecostal sisters strove to assure the lonely that prayer requests were heeded. In 1935 Sister Berta Maxwell, leader of a women's prayer group that received frequent mention in *The Advocate,* wrote, "On each Thursday afternoon the meeting of Mizpeh Prayer Band is held at Falcon, N.C., at four o'clock. At this hour letters with requests are read, and we pray for each one separately. After all written requests are prayed for other requests are presented, and we pray for them one by one. We then read the requests printed in The Advocate, and pray for each one separately. We also pray for any others we hear of needing help, far or near."[32] Maxwell's letter confirmed that no matter how isolated the individual reader, all were enclosed in the embrace of Christian kinship and surrounded by fervent prayer. Writers were strengthened by such assurances and periodically updated the readership on their progress, thanking them for continued prayers.

Pentecostal women made a variety of petitions in these periodicals, but nearly all contained a powerful desire for "a home beyond this veil of tears." Many sought to recreate the ideals of home through the magazine itself, finding there a compassionate fellowship of female testifiers who seemed to care deeply about the trials of suffering sisters elsewhere. Together, these women struggled to praise God's presence in their lives, but words of praise were inevitably framed by confessions of persistent misery, regret, and occasional anger. The ideal home remained far from reality, and Pentecostal women perpetuated and deepened their disappointment by staking all their hopes on prayer, believing that the cure for unhappiness essentially lay in the hands of pious Christians. Theirs was a theology of prayer that professed to know God's will, even while making protestations of humility, and that sought to nudge God into fulfilling scriptural promises of happiness and healing. Rather than abandoning religion when their ideals failed to materialize, Pentecostal women shored up their faith by means of ceaseless denials of the pain to which they simultaneously confessed. This practice provided the essential structure of the testimony, so the contradiction between its avowal of perfect happiness and its disclosure of utter despair remained unidentified and unspoken. Likewise, all religious ambivalence was erased, and the repeated shattering of women's hopes by prayer requests that seemed forgotten or ignored was thoroughly concealed.

"In a New World and a New Body":
Testimonies of Religious Experience

Although the perfect home remained largely unattainable on earth, many women wrote of God giving them a kind of foretaste of the world to come. The account of Mimi Thurman is particularly vivid: "No tongue can tell the thing I went through with last night. I was in glory, and saw the beautiful city. Jesus was standing over me. I felt so good that I don't think I was on earth nor in glory. The Lord came down and baptized me with the Holy Ghost, and today everything seems so much brighter than ever before. I felt like I was in a new world, and in a new body."[33] Another woman, a former Roman Catholic, described receiving a new body when, after dying and remaining dead for twenty-four hours, she was miraculously raised from the dead—an occurrence that understandably shocked the undertakers in the process of embalming her.[34] More often, letter-writers dramatized the gift of a new world and a new body by means of comparatively ordinary healing narratives, describing in often excruciating detail the healings they had witnessed or experienced from broken bones, chronic diseases, burns, mental illness, and lifelong disabilities. Because such healings often had the alleged effect of persuading wayward family members (usually husbands or children) of God's awesome power and Pentecostalism's validity, these healing narratives were also beacons of hope to those in search of a home beyond the veil of tears.

Even when a healing did not induce the conversion of a loved one, writers sought to create hope and expectation among readers about God's willingness to answer prayer. The testimony of Sister Mattie Daniels, printed in the *Whole Truth* in 1934, recounted a wrenching case of appendicitis, a failed operation, and gallstones. When her doctor told her that she would have to have another operation, Daniels wrote, "I did not consent, for I had made up my mind that I was not going to the hospital again, but was going to put my trust in the Lord." Her pastor and the members of her church prayed and fasted for her for five weeks, until "the Lord did wonderfully heal me and oh how I love him today." Daniels ended her testimony with a resounding word of encouragement for readers: "The saints here are on the firing line for God, truly He has some people living one hundred per cent for Him. . . . I want everyone to know that I'm a witness that the Lord is yet healing and that there is nothing too hard for Him to conquer."[35]

Other writers sought to frighten readers into realizing the serious consequences of neglecting God's will in their lives. Sister Amenthia McCoy, also writing to the *Whole Truth*, described being awakened one morning by the "death chorus singing, 'You better get ready, for you've got to die.'" When she inquired of God the reason for her impending death, she learned that it was because she had "neglected my work for Him." Immediately she grew weaker, and her "flesh began to consume away." Over the next few days, as she alternately prayed and slept, she saw someone measure her body, and "with a spiritual eye" she glimpsed her own wooden casket at her bedside. But after her pastor came and prayed for her, she wrote, "My bones got happy. I got up and went into a dance. O! how I danced and spoke in tongues. My mind was changed. I wanted to stay and work for the Lord. . . . I began to improve and get in line to work for Jesus." Having been given a second chance to fulfill God's plan for her life, McCoy concluded with a dire warning: "I hope this testimony will help those whom the Lord has called to do service for him. God does not want any slackers. He will take you out of the way. The servant who knows to do His Lord's will and does it not, shall be beaten with many stripes."[36]

A common practice reported in the letters printed in Pentecostal devotional materials, whether the audience was predominantly white or black, was the use of "anointed handkerchiefs" in procuring physical healings. This practice found scriptural basis in the nineteenth chapter of Acts (11–12): "And God did extraordinary miracles by the hands of Paul, so that handkerchiefs or aprons were carried away from his body to the sick, and diseases left them and the evil spirits came out of them." In a typical narrative, Blanche Guthrie from Lepanto, Arkansas, gave an account of receiving one such handkerchief from a Church of God evangelist, placing it carefully upon her ailing lungs, and being healed of tuberculosis.[37] Mrs. Frank Colville from Erwin, North Carolina, told a similar story. She had been healed from phlebitis and "untold agonies" after wearing "an anointed handkerchief that Sister Maxwell sent" her.[38] Such handkerchiefs, always at hand and easily transported, might be monogrammed, embroidered, or plain; people used whatever they happened to have at the time.

If one did not own handkerchiefs, she could obtain them from special services. An advertisement in the *Whole Truth* reads: "For olive oil and anointed cloths, Write the Field Editor . . . send a donation to keep a supply."[39] Sister Maxwell offered readers the cloths for free, asking only for the cost of mailing: "Many write us that they have been wonderfully blest by application of the anointed handkerchiefs. Please remember to send stamps to pay for mailing same. It is not necessary for you to send handkerchiefs, as we have the thin soft material cut in sizes suitable for mailing. We can put a dozen of these in a letter if needed."[40] The simplest of items, usually associated with wiping away tears or sweat or mundanely blowing one's nose, a handkerchief's cleansing function was easily extended into the realm of divine healing.

Sometimes writers described sending their own ordinary handkerchiefs to powerful Pentecostal preachers and evangelists, who would anoint these cloths with oil and prayer and send them back. At other times writers such as Della Tuttle begged readers, "Will somebody send me a handkerchief?"[41] One woman sent a letter to *The Advocate* directed to the "Falcon Prayer Band," noting, "I received the letter with the anointed handkerchief and wonderful blessings I received after I placed one to my body. . . . I surely do feel so much better."[42] Sister L. Banks from Fresno, California, likewise wrote to the *Whole Truth:* "I received the letter and anointed cloths from you, for which I thank the Lord. My heart rejoiced and the power of God came upon me as I applied the cloth to my breast. I could feel the affected part being drawn, and when I applied the second cloth it completely left. I have not felt the hurting any more. I thank the Lord for being healed."[43] As sacramental objects saturated with fervent prayer, anointed handkerchiefs could substitute for the physical presence of one whose prayers were sought, healing the sick when there was no one there to lay hands upon her.

The power of the anointed handkerchiefs was so strong, in fact, that healing could apparently occur even before the cloth was placed upon one's body. Two separate accounts in a 1944 issue of *The Evangel* described such an event. Mrs. Joe Jones, ill with "heart trouble," sent to Sister Mary Tidwell her own handkerchief to bless and anoint, and, she wrote, "I praise His name because my body was touched before I got it back." Likewise, Mrs. Paul Reath, suffering from a nervous breakdown, was healed "before I got the handkerchief" back from Sister Helman.[44] In a letter to *The Advocate,* Mrs. A. W. Hardee managed to slip in a veiled critique of a male pastor when she wrote that she had requested a handkerchief from Brother Culbreth to heal her eye trouble: "I didn't hear from him, but my eyes began to get better from that time."[45] Whether a sign of divine grace or human kindness and generosity, handkerchiefs were important material articles in the economy of Pentecostal emotion and held tremendous healing power for those who obtained or just requested them.

In other cases, Pentecostal letter-writers reported using the devotional newspapers themselves as sacramental prayer objects. Sister Happy Smith testified to the power of the *Church of God Evangel,* saying that "every member of our family has been healed by laying on the Evangel." Once, apparently dying from an asthma attack that even a "room full of people . . . praying" could not avail, Smith testified, her pastor "laid the Evangel on me and God wonderfully came on the scene."[46] A Louisiana woman similarly described how only the night before her young son "took real sick and I took the Evangel and laid it on him and asked Jesus to heal and let the child rest and, glory to His name, the work was done."[47] These magazines, filled with testimonies of divine healings and with promises of prayer, became carriers of hope and so, too, of healing. Women unable to receive personal prayer from magazine writers could secure some of that healing power from the material substance in which the testimonies were printed, transforming the magazines, like the anointed handkerchiefs, into sacramental objects. They became suitable tools that could be used to impart divine healing power to those with faith.

God is no abstract, transcendent being in these narratives but a living, immediate presence; likewise, Jesus plays an intimate role in the lives of believers, conversing with them upon the most ordinary of subjects and acting as a sympathetic, affectionate companion in time of loneliness. Like later Pentecostal women who have interpreted Jesus quite literally as a lover, husband, or friend, these women intentionally cultivated a daily relationship with him, one they believed could be damaged by betrayal, bolstered with gifts, and nurtured through communicative prayer. Their interpretation of this relationship emerged out of their experience of earthly kinship, particularly familial ties, and represented an ideal by which they could measure those earthly relationships and a standard of affinity that they hoped these could attain.[48]

Usually, of course, earthly relationships did not measure up, and intermittent letter-writers used the perfection of Jesus' love to condemn the failures of human beings. In one protracted testimony, for instance, Mrs. Thomas Buchanan complained, "During my husband's sickness I looked for my brothers and sisters in the churches where I had worked to visit us, but only two . . . came and stayed a short while with us. Others stopped a few minutes, but none of them stayed long enough to pray. Jesus is the only true friend that we have on earth. He will never leave nor forsake us." Her bitterness remained palpable at the end of the letter: "I love everybody. I can feel the love of Jesus abounding in me. If any of my brothers and sisters in Christ get sick I sure will visit them if I have to walk. God will make a way for me."[49] Pentecostal worshipers like Mrs. Buchanan clung to the intense feeling of God's tenderness toward them, hoping that love would color their dreariest moments with joy and propel them forward in selfless service to less virtuous beings.

The women who wrote testimonial letters to the *Pentecostal Holiness Advocate,* the *Church of God Evangel,* the *Whole Truth,* and a wide variety of similar publications prayed for the same things Christian women have long prayed for, although in forms and rhythms bequeathed to them by their particular Holiness/ Pentecostal heritage and the pages of Pentecostal periodicals. For many, congregational life was at best fragile and more often unavailable. Like later generations of Pentecostal women, the letter-writers focused their prayer narratives on illness, wayward husbands, and feelings of loneliness; they reached out for solace, healing, and sympathetic kinship through the prayers of women near and far. Narrating their lives not primarily in terms of their own sin, which was most often relegated to accounts of the past, but more in terms of undeserved pain and illness, the women assured one another that healing was obtainable through faith (if not absolutely predictable), that sufficient prayer worked miracles, and that the ultimate earthly result of their petitions would be a passionate, emotional closeness with the loving God.

Conclusion

The rhythms of devotion evident in Pentecostal texts from the early decades of the twentieth century have hardly faded in subsequent years; if anything, they have become thoroughly established in ever more therapeutically tinged narratives. Devotional accounts published by such groups as Women Aglow Fellowship, a contemporary organization of Pentecostal and charismatic Christian women, demonstrate a yearning for home and the fulfillment of relationships that is strikingly similar to that of earlier Pentecostal women.[50] Like their spiritual forebears, latter-day Pentecostal women have described coming to feel healed, inwardly transformed, and outwardly "set free" from suffering through the power of the Holy Spirit. Recounting, in far more explicit detail than earlier Pentecostal narratives, events such as physical or sexual abuse that left them, in their terms, angry, disappointed, despairing, fearful, ashamed, self-hating, and even suicidal, these women have similarly articulated twin desires: the desire for God's loving presence on the one hand and the longing for affirming familial relationships on the other. Although modern Pentecostal women generally find the world outside the church less repellent than did their foremothers, they too articulate the search for "a home beyond this veil of tears."

A conspicuous evolution has taken place in the testimonial form since the 1930s, as evidenced in the slick, professionalized testimonial magazines that emerged in the final two decades of the twentieth century—from *Guideposts* to *Aglow* to *Today's Christian Woman*—as well as the contemporary versions of older Pentecostal magazines. Significantly, written testimonies no longer allow for confessions of continued pain but relegate suffering to accounts of the past. Testimonial writers now seem required to tie up the loose ends of their experience and profess perfect, unadulterated joy in a "happily ever after" scenario. It would now be unthinkable to begin a testimony as Ella

Taylor did in 1944: "As I stand inside this morning and look out upon a dark and gloomy world, dreary and drooped in sin, my heart aches and I feel so homesick." Or to complain angrily, as Mrs. Tolley did some years earlier, that Christians were not doing enough to save her sinful husband and demand, "What is wrong with them?" However scripted Pentecostal testimonies from the 1930s and 1940s may appear, they are paragons of spontaneity and complex emotional ambivalence next to their modern-day counterparts.

Like other contemporary Christian periodicals, Pentecostal magazines have been compelled to add zip, color, and polish to their traditional formats in order to compete in a rapidly growing market of spiritual literature and cybernet prayer groups. *The Evangel,* still being published from Cleveland, is today a "splashier, more perfect (also less read) periodical" in the words of the archivist at the Church of God's Dixon Pentecostal Research Center.[51] Although full of inspirational articles and church news, *The Evangel* contains only occasional testimonies, and those that do appear are rather more formulaic than their predecessors (or are formulaic in a different way). Although they include graphic details of pain and subsequent healings from diseases such as leukemia, breast cancer, and pneumonia, they do not admit to continuing troubles with family members or persistent unhappiness over other life circumstances. A 1997 testimony by Donna Marrs, instantly healed of suicidal depression after a pastor's prayer, ends on a typical note: "My advice is this: Stop dwelling on physical or emotional disorders; instead, focus your mind and heart on Jesus." To even speak of present suffering would strike Marrs as a sign of the same affliction that she says led to her mental illness: self-pity.[52]

The Advocate continued to be published until the end of 1996, when it was discontinued in favor of a new magazine, this one aimed solely at church leaders rather than the laity. The new magazine, the *IssacharFile: Keeping Church Leaders in Touch with the Times,* alerts pastors to world issues and discusses current events but contains no testimonial materials.[53] Testimonies for Pentecostal Holiness Church members are now tellingly limited to the magazine for women's ministries, *Helping Hand,* and two newsletters aimed at overseas and domestic evangelization. Moreover, the occasional testimonies that are printed do not include admissions of prevailing sorrow or prayer requests for anything other than mission success, and they are relentlessly upbeat. As the former editor of *The Advocate* admits, there has been a significant decline of interest in testimonies within the Pentecostal Holiness Church—and within Pentecostalism more broadly.[54] Personal stories are apparently passé, whether because people no longer need the community of periodical readers or because they are too busy to care about the sufferings of people far away.

The Church of God in Christ has gone even further in its evolution of the written testimony. Current issues of the *Whole Truth* have done away with letters and testimonies altogether, replacing these with sermonic articles by paid staff members and photo advertisements of church conventions. One item close to a testimony, a brief blurb from 1996 on "Getting through Difficult Times," hardly compares to the detailed accounts of suffering and hard-won return to joy that appeared in the periodical's pages fifty years earlier:

> Difficulties have always plagued the saints, but through them all, they have become established in their faith, strong in their commitment, mature in their experience, tempered in their souls, and developed in their patience. They have powerful testimonies because they do not allow problems, difficulties, adversities, afflictions, trials, temptations or troubles to deter them. God brought them through their difficult times. But thanks be to God, which giveth us the victory through our Lord Jesus Christ. . . . Let me encourage you to praise God through your difficulties and make the tough times count.[55]

The fact that this passage was written by a woman, Emma J. Clark, heightens the salience of this dramatic historical mutation. Like Donna Marrs's testimony in *The Advocate*, the message here is simple: buck up, praise God for everything, and keep your problems to yourself.

Making the tough times count was always a strategy of Pentecostal women, but most women who wrote to earlier periodicals were attentive toward describing their suffering in detail, whether to evoke sympathy in readers, elicit prayers and letters of condolence, or try to fit their experience into a much needed interpretive pattern. Few would have accused themselves of self-pity for telling their stories, nor would they have considered it their duty to "praise God through [their] difficulties" without giving an explicit account of what those difficulties were. Now, however, explicit accounts of anything other than total victory seem grossly out of fashion in Pentecostal literature.

Although numerous factors have undoubtedly contributed to this displacement of the written testimony in contemporary Pentecostalism (at least in the professionalized materials that highlight its public face), two stand out as particularly salient. The first is the massive transformation in social and economic class that has taken place in American Pentecostalism since the end of World War II. Latter-day Pentecostals are far more educated, affluent, and (by their own standards) "worldly" than their prewar ancestors; most have relaxed earlier proscriptions against modern dress and hair fashions and have exchanged plainness for style and comfort with nary a backward glance. Not content to wait for the millennium, Pentecostals have poured energy and resources into building colleges, seminaries for training religious workers, and handsome new structures of worship and Christian education. No longer composed wholly or predominantly of the economically disadvantaged or "disinherited," Pentecostals are now as mainstream as Episcopalians. Indeed, given their fast-growing numbers, they are by most accounts pushing Episcopalians, Presbyterians, and other so-called mainliners to the margins and are numerically if not culturally dominant.

The reserve of modern Pentecostal testimonial records is consonant with this broader class shift toward greater wealth and growing status. As their financial burdens have lightened and their contact with the wider worlds of business and culture has increased, ministers and ordinary believers alike have yearned for acceptance by America's mainstream establishment. With an eye to once deplored bastions of commerce and prestige, Pentecostals have sought to show that they understand the rules of the game and so have trimmed and tamed the wilder vocabulary of their tradition's youth. Retaining their hold on the miraculous and their belief in the power of prayer, they have nonetheless exchanged a highly emotional style for one less friendly toward excess and utterly intolerant of the plaintive begging and clear-eyed misery so characteristic of earlier testimonial accounts. Pain, like death, is set at a polite distance and given an appropriately cheerful gloss.

A second and related factor that has helped give rise to this profound stylistic transformation in the written testimonial form pertains to early attempts by male leaders to infuse Pentecostalism with a heavy dose of masculine energy in the hope of reducing Pentecostalism's association with feminine piety. In line with their increasing hopes for higher status, male ministers were surely concerned about the disproportionate gender ratios of printed testimonies. The abundance of women's testimonies closely linked Pentecostalism with women's concerns, a source of great potential concern for an anxious and ambitious male ministry. Branded with what was perceived to be a weak and "feminine" emotional style, and thus giving witness to what was most excessive and least mainstream about Pentecostalism, such testimonies likely prompted male denominational leaders to edit, ignore, and at times even eliminate them from publication, at the same time extending their control over oral testimonies that remained central to congregational life. In this way, the decline of the written testimonial form signals the recurrent attempt by religious authorities to "re-masculinize" their churches and buttress their own power.

The capacity for feeling saved, sanctified, baptized in the holy spirit, and healed in all of these settings was a capacity cultivated within the Pentecostal networks that thrived on testimony. However natural and authentic these experiences and their accompanying emotions may have felt to those who recounted them, they were patterned after testimonial accounts told by other women and so were generated out of a social context that defined authentic experience, cutting off some experiential possibilities while sanctioning and ultimately mandating others. Women who have participated in the highly expressive practices of Pentecostal worship have been compelled to reconstruct their life stories and refashion themselves according to the available vocabulary of experience. Although this vocabulary was supple enough to allow variant interpretations of pain and sickness, it remained sufficiently restricted to sustain the authority of Pentecostal theology, elicit correct attitudes and feelings, and produce disciplined religious selves.

Although not completely homogenized, Pentecostal religious experience became ever more predictable in twentieth-century narratives. In part, of course, this uniformity has upheld critical distinctions between the "cold" and the "hot," the order of God's plan and the disorder of the world, between saints and sinners, the saved and the damned. The narratives have created and sustained expectation of relief from the burdens of everyday life and hope in the paradisiacal world—the ideal home—to come. For women, they have opened the way for triumph over illness, incorrigible husbands, and grueling loneliness and have ensured "victory over sin and shame." Now, however, the shame is apparently felt as too scandalous to describe, and victory relies less on the "shouting of the saints" than on their silence.

Notes

1. David Hall, *Lived Religion in America: Toward a History of Practice* (Princeton: Princeton University Press, 1997); Dorothy Bass, ed., *Practicing Our Faith: A Way of Life for a Searching People* (New York: Jossey-Bass, 1997); Steven Stowe, review of Christine Heyrman, *Southern Cross: The Beginnings of the Bible Belt* (New York: Alfred A. Knopf, 1997), in the on-line *Journal of Southern Religion* 1 (Jan.–June 1998) at http://jsr.as.wvu.edu/.

2. On the history of Pentecostalism, see Robert Mapes Anderson, *Vision of the Disinherited: The Making of American Pentecostalism* (New York: Oxford University Press, 1979); Edith L. Blumhofer, *Restoring the Faith: The Assemblies of God, Pentecostalism, and American Culture* (Urbana: University of Illinois Press, 1993); Donald W. Dayton, *Theological Roots of Pentecostalism* (Grand Rapids: Zondervan, 1987); and David Edwin Harrell, Jr., *All Things Are Possible: The Healing and Charismatic Revivals in Modern America* (Bloomington: Indiana University Press, 1975). The most recent and comprehensive account of early Pentecostalism is Grant Wacker, *Heaven Below: Early Pentecostals and American Culture* (Cambridge: Harvard University Press, 2001), which was published after this essay was completed.

3. These are the figures cited by Vinson Synan, himself a member of the Pentecostal Holiness Church. Synan, *The Holiness-Pentecostal Tradition: Charismatic Movements in*

the Twentieth Century, 2d ed. (Grand Rapids: Eerdmans, 1997), ix. The figure of half a billion is likely inflated by, including many worshipers, who, although practicing a Spirit-centered religion, do not see themselves as Pentecostal or charismatic as such.

4. An occasional letter from the *Church of God Evangel* identified its writer as "colored," but the fact of that identification presumes a mostly white readership. The Church of God has always had African American members but separated them into segregated churches for most of the denomination's history and published a separate periodical for its black membership. There appear to have been few or no African Americans in the Pentecostal Holiness Church for much of its history. On the failure of white Pentecostal historians to deal adequately with issues of race and racism, see Anthea Butler, "Walls of Division: Racism's Role in Pentecostal History," paper presented to the American Society of Church History, Atlanta, Ga., Jan. 1996.

References to African Americans were rare in the early pages of the *Church of God Evangel* and the *Pentecostal Holiness Advocate*, save for an occasional article along the lines of one that praised God for, in the author's words, sending "His angels to shield me from some negroes" (*Pentecostal Holiness Advocate*, May 3, 1934, 2).

5. This notion held long sway in studies of Pentecostalism, capped by Anderson's *Vision of the Disinherited*. A classic version of this argument is Liston Pope's *Millhands and Preachers* (New Haven: Yale University Press, 1942), a sociological study of cotton mills and churches in Gaston County, North Carolina. Historians such as Edith Blumhofer have begun to refocus attention on Pentecostalism in urban settings, especially New York, Chicago, and Los Angeles.

6. An exhaustive list of these sources is impossible, although some exceptional examples are Edith L. Blumhofer and Randall Balmer, eds., *Modern Christian Revivals* (Urbana: University of Illinois Press, 1993); Randall Balmer, *Mine Eyes Have Seen the Glory: A Journey into the Evangelical Subculture in America* (New York: Oxford University Press, 1989); Margaret Lamberts Bendroth, *Fundamentalism and Gender, 1875 to the Present* (New Haven: Yale University Press, 1993); Joel A. Carpenter and Wilbert R. Shenk, eds., *Earthen Vessels: American Evangelicals and Foreign Missions, 1880–1980* (Grand Rapids: Eerdmans, 1990); Betty A. DeBerg, *Ungodly Women: Gender and the First Wave of American Fundamentalism* (Minneapolis: Fortress Press, 1990); Nathan Hatch, *The Democratization of American Christianity* (New Haven: Yale University Press, 1989); Evelyn Brooks Higginbotham, *Righteous Discontent: The Women's Movement in the Black Baptist Church, 1880–1920* (Cambridge: Harvard University Press, 1993); Mark A. Noll, David W. Bebbington, and George A. Rawlyk, eds., *Evangelicalism: Comparative Studies of Popular Protestantism in North America, the British Isles, and Beyond, 1700–1990* (New York: Oxford University Press, 1994); Leigh Eric Schmidt, *Holy Fairs: Scottish Communions and American Revivals in the Early Modern Period* (Princeton: Princeton University Press, 1989); and Leonard I. Sweet, ed., *The Evangelical Tradition in America* (Macon: Mercer University Press, 1984).

7. See, for instance, Anderson, *Vision of the Disinherited;* Blumhofer, *Restoring the Faith;* Dayton, *Theological Roots of Pentecostalism;* and Harrell, *All Things Are Possible.*

8. An issue of *PNEUMA: The Journal of the Society for Pentecostal Studies* (Spring 1995) is dedicated to the topic of "Women and Pentecostalism" and exemplifies this perspective. The collection of essays deserves praise for bringing Pentecostal women's lives to the fore, yet the solitary focus on women in ministry and evangelism leaves out the stories of

ordinary women. Attention to laywomen's devotional lives is needed to enrich current accounts of women's participation in American Pentecostalism.

9. Studies of black Pentecostal women undertaken by Cheryl Townsend Gilkes and Felton O. Best are welcome examples, although Best focuses primarily on women in leadership roles. Cheryl Townsend Gilkes, "'Together and in Harness': Women's Traditions in the Sanctified Church," *Signs: Journal of Women in Culture and Society* 10 (Summer 1985): 678–99; Cheryl Townsend Gilkes, "The Role of Women in the Sanctified Church," *Journal of Religious Thought* 43 (Spring–Summer 1986): 24–41; Felton O. Best, "Loosing the Women: African-American Women and Leadership in the Pentecostal Church, 1890–Present," in *Affirming Diversity: Twenty-fourth Meeting of the Society for Pentecostal Studies* (Toronto: Society for Pentecostal Studies, 1994).

10. Susan O'Brien, "Eighteenth-Century Publishing Networks in the First Years of Transatlantic Evangelicalism," in *Evangelicalism: Comparative Studies of Popular Protestantism in North America, the British Isles, and Beyond, 1700–1990*, ed. Mark A. Noll, David W. Bebbington, and George A. Rawlyk (New York: Oxford University Press, 1994), 38–57.

11. The rise of therapeutic culture and its relationship to American religion has been the subject of much discussion. See, for example, E. Brooks Holifield, *A History of Pastoral Care in American: From Salvation to Self-Realization* (Nashville: Abingdon Press, 1983); T. J. Jackson Lears, "From Salvation to Self-Realization: Advertising and the Therapeutic Roots of the Consumer Culture, 1880–1930," in *The Culture of Consumption: Critical Essays in American History, 1880–1980*, ed. Richard Wightman Fox and T. J. Jackson Lears (New York: Pantheon Books, 1983); T. J. Jackson Lears, *No Place of Grace: Antimodernism and the Transformation of American Culture, 1880–1920* (Chicago: University of Chicago Press, 1981); Donald Meyer, *The Positive Thinkers: Religion as Pop Psychology from Mary Baker Eddy to Oral Roberts*, 2d ed. (New York: Pantheon Books, 1980); David Harrington Watt, *A Transforming Faith: Explorations of Twentieth-Century American Evangelicalism* (New Brunswick: Rutgers University Press, 1991), esp. 137–54; and Robert Wuthnow, *Sharing the Journey: Support Groups and America's New Quest for Community* (New York: Free Press, 1994).

12. Dorothy C. Bass, "Congregations and the Bearing of Traditions," in *American Congregations*, vol. 2: *New Perspectives in the Study of Congregations*, ed. by James P. Wind and James W. Lewis (Chicago: University of Chicago Press, 1994), 169–91; Bass, ed., *Practicing Our Faith;* Hall, *Lived Religion in America*.

13. On the history of the Church of God, see Mickey Crews, *The Church of God: A Social History* (Knoxville: University of Tennessee Press, 1990); see also Charles W. Conn, *Like a Mighty Army: A History of the Church of God, 1886–1976*, rev. ed. (Cleveland, Tenn.: Pathway Press, 1977).

14. On the history of the Pentecostal Holiness Church, see A. D. Beacham, Jr., *A Brief History of the Pentecostal Holiness Church* (Franklin Springs: Advocate Press, 1983), and Vinson Synan, *The Old-Time Power: A History of the Pentecostal Holiness Church* (Franklin Springs: Advocate Press, 1973).

15. *Whole Truth* 10 (Feb. 1934): 18.

16. Maggie Mosley in *The Advocate*, March 7, 1935, 13.

17. Ella Taylor in *The Evangel*, June 10, 1944, 13.

18. Cecelia Tichi, *High Lonesome: The American Culture of Country Music* (Chapel Hill: University of North Carolina Press, 1994), 35.

19. *Word and Work,* 1915.

20. Francis Brown in *The Advocate,* Aug. 14, 1930, 11.

21. Mrs. J. L. Tolley in *The Advocate,* July 10, Aug. 14, and Dec. 4, 1930 (quotation). Letters from Tolley to her sympathizers were printed several more times during the next few years, keeping the community up to date with her situation and thanking them for their constant prayers.

22. *The Advocate,* June 19, 1930, 13.

23. *The Advocate,* May 28, 1931, 15.

24. Ibid.

25. *The Advocate,* June 5, 1930, 15.

26. Latha Smith in *The Advocate,* Dec. 4, 1930, 13.

27. *The Evangel,* April 9, 1938, 7.

28. Onie Winn in *The Advocate,* June 5, 1930, 14.

29. Minnie Coleman in *The Advocate,* Sept. 4, 1930, 15.

30. Mrs. R. A. Flurrty in *The Evangel,* Sept. 12, 1942, 9.

31. Martha Cabe in *The Advocate,* Dec. 18, 1930, 8.

32. Berta Maxwell in *The Advocate,* May 23, 1935, 7.

33. Mimi Thurman in *The Advocate,* Aug. 14, 1930, 1.

34. "[T]hen death struck me and I passed away," the author reported. "The doctors pronounced me dead. I was dead twenty-four hours; at the end of twenty-four hours I was removed to the undertakers establishment. They began to embalm me; at this time the Lord raised me up. . . . My husband was at home waiting for the undertakers to return me as a corpse, but instead of a corpse I returned very much alive. Now I am still praising the Lord for healing me, and also raising me from death." *The Advocate,* Oct. 17, 1935, 12.

35. Mattie Daniels in *Whole Truth* 10 (March 1934): 17.

36. Amenthia McCoy in *Whole Truth* 10 (Feb. 1934): 18.

37. Blanche Guthrie in *The Evangel,* Dec. 17, 1938, 13.

38. Mrs. Frank Colville in *The Advocate,* March 22, 1934, 15.

39. *Whole Truth* 10 (Feb. 1934): 18.

40. Berta Maxwell in *The Advocate,* May 23, 1935, 7.

41. Della Tuttle in *The Advocate,* May 7, 1931, 13.

42. Mrs. Minnie Johnson in *The Advocate,* Nov. 9, 1933, 15.

43. L. Banks in *Whole Truth* 9 (May 1933): 2.

44. Mrs. Joe Jones in *The Evangel,* May 13, 1944, 12; Mrs. Paul Reath in *The Evangel,* May 13, 1944, 12.

45. Mrs. A. W. Hardee in *The Advocate,* May 23, 1935, 14.

46. Happy Smith in *The Evangel,* Dec. 5, 1942, 12–13.

47. *The Evangel,* April 8, 1944, 12.

48. For parallels with contemporary Pentecostal women, see R. Marie Griffith, *God's Daughters: Evangelical Women and the Power of Submission* (Berkeley: University of California Press, 1997). On Catholic women's relationship with humanized saints, see Rob-

ert A. Orsi, *Thank You, St. Jude: Women's Devotion to the Patron Saint of Hopeless Causes* (New Haven: Yale University Press, 1996).

49. Mrs. Thomas Buchanan in *The Advocate* Nov. 7, 1935, 14.

50. Griffith, *God's Daughters.*

51. David Roebuck to author, March 11, 1998 (personal correspondence).

52. Donna Marrs in *The Evangel* 87 (Jan. 1997): 33.

53. The name of this periodical is taken from 1 Chronicles 12:32: "Men of Issachar, who understood the times and knew what Israel should do" [NIV]. The reference is to men who joined David in battle against Saul, soldiers who composed "a great army, like the army of God" (v. 22).

54. Author telephone interview with Shirley Spencer, Oklahoma City, March 11, 1998.

55. Emma J. Clark in *Whole Truth* (Spring 1996): 45 (limited ed.).

PART 4

Women and the Professionalization of Religious Work

PROFESSIONALIZATION IS INTRINSIC to modern life. In the late nineteenth century, many occupations—medicine first, then law, business, social work, and the ministry—began to restrict the work of "amateurs." The concept, built on the prestigious medical model, has come to mean the organization of an occupation into a body of practitioners who, having passed through a rigorous educational credentialing process, possess expert knowledge and skills and agree to abide by a set of ethical principles. Professionalization usually involves the existence of a formal organization that operates more or less autonomously, apart from government regulations. The organization depends on its ability to exclude those considered unqualified, in part for the welfare of the profession and its clients and in part for the financial well-being of the professionals, whose earning power depends on limiting the total number of practitioners.

In the twentieth century, women's advances in economic and social status have naturally depended upon their entry into the professions—first, their access to schools that have acted as gatekeepers and, second, their acceptance by male colleagues and eventually by the public as true professionals. Professionalization has not been easy for women to attain, but by the end of the twentieth century they have managed to surmount most barriers.

Their very success, however, has involved them in contradictions. Middle-class women in the nineteenth century were taught self-denial and selflessness, and although professionals talk frequently about service, self-denial is not normally part of their vocabulary. Their expertise, they assume, ought to earn them a high degree of respect, honor, and certainly respectable recompense. Their discourse, although hardly devoid of ideals and dedication to a calling, has tended to emphasize a more neutral language of efficiency and social science—not always the preferred language of women. Finally, the tendency of professions to draw boundaries violates the inclination of many women for building inclusive, democratic communities and for leveling hierarchical relationships between the expert and the ostensibly uninformed.

Another complication of professionalization for women is that it has tended to lower the value ascribed to unpaid volunteers. In a culture where most things have a price, people often assume that the time and skills contributed by someone who does something for nothing can hardly be worth very much. For a time that attitude was offset somewhat by the wealth and upper-class status of many volunteers—who clearly did not need an income—but that was less and less the case as the century went on. Even the well-off, it is assumed, deserve to have their value to an organization reckoned in dollars. The lowered status of volunteers has, of course, affected women disproportionately, because they have traditionally done much of the volunteering. It has also greatly weakened churches, which have long depended upon the free labor of women.

One of the professions women have sought to enter has been the ordained ministry. Although the ministry has been widely regarded as a profession in the twentieth century, its practice does not precisely conform to the medical model. There has been less consensus about what body of knowledge and skills every minister needs to possess and a persisting conviction (in some groups) that a minister needs only to be "called" by God rather than educated and credentialed by human beings. Some of the skills typically needed by a modern ministers—counseling, community organizing, and administration—seem better exemplified by psychologists, social workers, and corporate executives. Ministers as a body have enjoyed less autonomy than doctors and lawyers. In the end, they are far more answerable to their congregations and/or to the officialdom of their denominations than doctors or lawyers to their clients. Thus, as professionals ministers have been less than certain about their status, and the entry of women in substantial numbers has threatened to render their standing even more problematic.

For all these reasons, the fit between religious women and professional roles has been far from smooth. Susan Yohn's missionary organizers attempt to be "modern" and adopt efficient fund-raising methods; they appear to buy into the corporate model of capitalism. Yet not only have they been raised on notions of benevolence and self-sacrifice, but they are also running a business that is not really about profit—at least not worldly profit. The women Mark Chaves discusses present a useful contrast. They followed some of the classic strategies of professionalization, favoring education, credentialing, and a middle-class style. And yet, as Chaves demonstrates, when women really entered the profession of the ministry in large numbers during the 1970s, the organization declined or at least failed to play a forceful role. Chaves's insightful case study points out some of the structural barriers that even a self-consciously professional women's organization could not overcome, including the fact of denominational control over jobs. The story of the International Association of Women Ministers also suggests that professionalization is at its core configured as masculine and therefore is not particularly amenable to gendered forms. Not all women involved themselves as much as these in standards of professionalization. The faith healers whom James Opp discusses have offered both an implicit and explicit critique of the most hallowed of the professions, medicine. They also created alternative paid professions for themselves.

Like many other aspects of modernity, professionalization has brought both benefits and curses—and ambiguous consequences—and this ambiguity has been magnified in the case of women who have religious goals.

10. "Let Christian Women Set the Example in Their Own Gifts": The "Business" of Protestant Women's Organizations

SUSAN M. YOHN

WHEN SHE CONSIDERED more than forty years of women's missionary activity, Helen Barrett Montgomery, long the president of the Woman's American Baptist Foreign Mission Society, noted with great satisfaction that the millions of Protestant women who donated their pennies to the effort had "astonished the world with their success."[1] What had started in 1861 with one mission society that supported one woman in the field had grown by 1909 into an enterprise composed of forty-four societies supporting 4,710 unmarried women in the field. Collections for the effort had risen from a modest $2,000 in 1861 to $4 million in 1909. The women's mission enterprise built colleges, orphanages, asylums, training schools, and industrial plants and created organizations "from which they could reach from headquarters to the remotest auxiliary, with appeal and information."[2]

The literature discussing the various denominational organizations that composed the Protestant women's mission movement has focused attention on the ways in which women used mission work to move into the public arena and extend their influence to matters that were also social and political.[3] With the mission movement as a base, women pursued work and politics, which put them squarely in the midst of debates concerning various social and political policies. In the process, they called into question popularly held ideas that limited or confined women to a domestic role.

What has been largely overlooked, however, is the role these organizations played in American women's economic history. Barred from many kinds of economic activity, either by law or by custom that questioned the respectability of women engaged in business, women in the nineteenth century turned their attentions to the "business" of social reform. They did so at a time of national economic transition, when businesses were growing ever larger and more complex and there was increasing emphasis on rationalization, efficiency, and scientific method. Cognizant of these developments, women adapted the language and methods of the for-profit business sector to build innovative, vibrant organizations that raised millions of dollars to provide much-needed social services. They marshaled the limited resources of members, whom they thought of as investors, and in the process promoted strategies of philanthropy that would ensure a steady flow of income. Protestant women active in the mission enterprise generated social capital and engaged in social entrepreneurship; they also built institutions that increased the capacity of the nation to respond to the country's needs. They cared for the needy, worked to foster goodwill, and generally reminded people of their membership in an interdependent community. What resulted was a network of organizations that were built largely with the money raised by Protestant women and that provided a variety of services with, as Helen Montgomery pointed out, international scope and appeal.

The strategies and methods the leaders used generated donations that supported their efforts and fueled the growth and expansion of their enterprises. This associational experience, which historians and sociologists, Max Weber among them, have identified as an important springboard to greater economic success for men, proved more limited for women. So successful were women in raising money and expanding their enterprise that they became take-over targets for the men who ran parallel church organizations. In what was also a period of business merger and consolidation, mission organizations were not exempt from pressures to do the same. Beginning early in the twentieth century, men in Protestant churches sought to gain control of the mission enterprise by merging and consolidating parallel male and female organizations. In the process, they raised a host of questions about the efficacy of women's endeavors, not the least of which called into question women's motivations in building an enterprise and their ability to administer the funds they raised.

At the heart of the struggle was an inability on the part of both men and women to acknowledge that women, in creating these organizations, wielded a degree of economic power they had never before imagined. Women gained invaluable economic experience but could not think of the profits they reaped as that, nor did the nature of the enterprise—social service—allow them to. When they spoke of what they had accomplished, they did not highlight their business acumen or sensibility but focused instead on the social gains the enterprise had made. The mission movement served principle before people. It served God, and in the case of African American women it served both God and race.

When women gave way to the demands of men and consolidated their efforts, they lost control over the enterprise they had created. In mainline Presbyterian and Baptist churches, for example, women gave way to men in positions of leadership. Where they did not, as in the case of Nannie Helen Burroughs of the National Baptist Convention (NBC), they fought an ongoing battle against charges, intended to undermine their work, that they were personally profiting from their church association. Mission activism opened new political and social arenas to Protestant women, but the ethic underlying the work—self-denial and self-sacrifice—limited its economic and political impact. Here women were allowed to embrace the business practices and philosophies of their day and test entrepreneurial skills. The reaction to their success, however, shows the limits (the "glass ceiling" of the era) they encountered as they pursued social entrepreneurship.

Women's mission organizations were built upon the small donations of millions. With relatively few large donations, leaders came to stress a high rate of member participation rather than the amount they gave. They were also concerned about developing strategies to ensure regular giving. Tithing and systematic or proportionate giving were encouraged, even if a woman gave only a few cents a week or a dollar a month. What may have appeared "inefficient" to those who sought to rationalize giving in the late nineteenth century was in fact highly effective in tapping women's very limited resources. Mission leaders insisted that every woman could and should participate, no matter how small her donation. Christian stewardship was not just the province of men. The secret, as one observer noted, was "plodding perseverance. . . . not waiting for great windfalls, bequests, the gifts of millionaires, but picking up the pennies and trudging on."[4] The goal was to instill regular giving—an idea that later efforts such as the Community Chest and United Way would come to depend upon.

For Protestant women, there was a dual message in the appeals made by mission organizations. They were encouraged to participate and develop an ethic of stewardship—to contribute in a regular, systematic, and rational fashion, whether by tithing or proportionate giving. They were never to forget, however, that they were God's messengers and that their donations constituted acts of self-sacrifice and selflessness. The profits generated were measured in the numbers of people converted or the lives helped. Individual contributions yielded no tangible returns except the emotional and spiritual satisfaction of having participated in a good cause.

Typical of the earliest fund-raising appeals made by the Presbyterian

Church's Woman's Board of Home Missions (PCWBHM) was that of president Mary James, who, as she addressed the annual convention in 1877, in-
toned, "Let us pray for money." In her efforts to raise money for mission
purposes, James railed against the "rust of hoarded wealth," warning that the
nation's wealth would be a "curse if spent upon ourselves while souls are
perishing without knowledge." Recognizing that most women did not "hold
the purse," James encouraged followers to exert influence on those who did.
Equating donations to the board to "offerings," she called upon those who
supported the enterprise to tithe the first tenth of their incomes.[5]

As James's comments suggest, the PCWBHM was engaged in a constant
fight against what it called "spasmodic" giving.[6] As it expanded activities,
hiring additional women and opening new missions, the board found that
it had to inculcate an ethic of stewardship among supporters. With many
different charities competing for women's limited funds, the board championed a system whereby women divided their money, allocating it to a variety of causes. That strategy was uniformly pursued by groups across all
denominations. Women were encouraged to begin their training in stewardship by keeping a mite box in their kitchens, depositing whatever extra pennies and nickels they could save. The next step was to pledge a certain amount,
either on a monthly or annual basis. The organizations broke down, by
month, what the money might be used for. In the Woman's Home Missionary Society of the Methodist Episcopal Church (WHMSMEC), September
was dues paying month, November was for a thank offering, May was mite
month, and April and October were for student aid.[7]

Regularity was stressed over the amount given. Indeed, all donations were
applauded, no matter what size. Mission boards were acutely aware that many
contributors depended upon husbands who gave them little, if any, allowance. Women were encouraged to save their pennies and hoard small
amounts to be offered monthly during a mission society meeting. The ex-
cuse of an "empty purse" or a lack of money was not accepted. Published
testimonials told of poor and widowed women who gave what little they had
and then encouraged others to give more. In one such account, readers were
introduced to a mine laborer's wife, who, over the objections of her husband,
endeavored to save her pennies: "Tempted often by strenuous times to give
it up, but persevering and repeatedly testifying to its blessing, she not infrequently lays upon the collection plate of the class a dollar, and sometimes
brings the teacher two dollars, with the words, 'Give it to someone who needs
it more than I do.'" To shame those more wealthy who hesitated to contribute, the author added about this woman, "Always has her church envelope
been ready for the annual collection for the Boards, and it contains more than

many members of prominence subscribe." By way of conclusion, readers were admonished, "We shall never know how much we can give till we try the systematic way."[8]

The "third class passenger," the small donor, was celebrated as the one who "gets out and pushes." When times are difficult, noted one observer, "it is the third class passengers that we want not only in this, but in every department of mission work, for there is many an upgrade which calls for vigorous pushing, if we would keep things moving."[9] Mission organizations were acutely aware that women's limited economic resources circumscribed the scope of mission work. They championed "allowances" for wives, suggesting that every married woman should have one. As one correspondent wrote in favor of allowances, "It causes embarrassment to listen to stirring appeals and to make no response by a contribution, and it is still more humiliating to say that one has no money to call her own, and her husband disapproves."[10] The benefits of allowances would come not just to the mission enterprise. A wife who had an allowance would be encouraged to "budget" and in the long run save her family's money as well.

Mission leaders argued that the impact of these small donations, when totaled, would be to reinvigorate Protestantism. By using a variety of plans—a voluntary pledge system, an envelope system, systematic gleaning, or a freewill gift—Presbyterian women, for example, could pool their money and make their impact felt.[11] The PCWBHM warned against thinking of oneself as autonomous but rather considering individual contributions in combination with others. "If $18 a year seems little for one to give let us look at it in this way," wrote the treasurer, "suppose fifty women in our church can each give that amount." Such donations would not be "despised" by the church.[12] Methodists employed the metaphor of a quilt to describe the process involved in this enterprise; pennies multiplied into dollars as "she hath done what she could." An "indispensable factor in any gathering of woman's product," they reported, was that "heritage from our grandmothers—a quilt," which "bears 1200 names, and each name is worth, in ready currency, ten cents—an easy calculation making the quilt thus transformed into a roll of profit, if not of honor."[13]

By collecting money in this fashion, women's mission societies experienced continual growth. Although technically subordinate to male mission boards and subject to their final authority, women's societies designated that the funds they raised be used to support schools and community centers employing women missionaries. Within the Presbyterian church, for example, women were not allowed to serve as elders until the late 1920s and were not ordained as ministers until the early 1950s. Nevertheless, as fund-raisers they came to wield considerable economic influence, so much so that during the early 1920s the male hierarchy moved to consolidate all church mission boards. The men hoped that women would maintain high levels of giving, even though there was no longer an autonomous women's organization. What women who ran the board expected was for regularized contributions to sustain the growth of the organization and become the "vertebrate system" of the organization's treasury.

Katharine Bennett, who took over as president of the PCWBHM after Mary James, was guided by a corporate model. As the board employed more missionaries and new fields of work were added, the organization grew more complex and bureaucratic. Located in New York City, the Woman's Board's purpose was twofold. First, it set policy and provided support to women missionaries in the field. Second, it promoted philanthropy among the women who stayed at home. It also brought together women who were geographically separated so they could exchange information and resources in a common cause. As the leader of an organization that was national in scope and private (although in the public service), had a centralized authority, and focused largely on one product—in this case the development of a national culture—it is perhaps no wonder that Bennett took to comparing the organization with other major corporations of the day.[14]

Bennett moved the board to institute more businesslike procedures. Whereas James had likened contributions to "offerings," reiterating the evangelical nature of the project, Bennett employed more secular language. Likely influenced by the growing emphasis on "scientific philanthropy," she saw her role as board president to institute "planned growth." Even as the board was critical of the social dislocation caused by corporate capitalism, Bennett likened her organization to the powerful railroad industry. Gone was the emphasis on teas, fairs, and luncheons—staples of fund-raising during the mid-nineteenth century that were referred to in 1890 as the "lazy way" of giving.[15] Much-heralded "business methods" replaced them as the PCWBHM took every opportunity to impress upon its supporters that it was running a "business operation." That "business of benevolence," reminded the board, involved women in financial and legal matters beyond their domestic roles. Because the treasury often found itself without funds to cover operating expenses while it awaited contributions to come in, it borrowed money from banks to tide it over and thus became involved in dealings of the national banking community. Women who ran the PCWBHM did not hesitate to tell supporters that they were well informed about the ups and downs of financial markets.[16]

The leaders were very careful, however, to temper the rhetoric of business with reminders of the spiritual motives underlying the enterprise. The secretary of home affairs of the Woman's Missionary Society of the Methodist Episcopal Church, South (WMSMEC, South) warned in 1893 that there was danger to the spirit of the enterprise in "pushing forward business methods." "While the work must be based upon solid business principles," she cautioned, "it should never be prosecuted with unsanctified hearts, unconsecrated hands." The Missionary Society should not let success be a "snare" or be tempted to expand "beyond our financial strength" and take on debt.[17]

These appeals for money made women more conscious of how much (or how little) financial control they exercised within their families and churches. When mission organizations found that the amount a woman could contribute depended on how much she was able to hoard from money given to her by her husband for household expenses, leaders pushed for allowances for women, one part of which would go toward donations of their own determination. Indeed, mission literature was replete with stories of women who, emboldened by their desire to more actively participate in mission fundraising efforts, had gone home to their husbands and demanded allowances. In one story, the main character relates that her husband "never seemed to understand that a woman needed a little money of [her] very own." She describes herself as "proud-spirited," so "the question of finance at our house was like an electric battery, and neither of us knew how to manage it." When she finally did bring herself to broach the topic with her husband, it was not in a "proud-spirited" manner, however. She "went home as *meek* as you please, and told John all about it." They "talked" the issue through, and she then "had" her allowance every month.[18] The very act of raising money for missions changed the way women thought about money; their need was legitimated, and their credibility established—or so thought the women active in the mission movement.

Male counterparts discussed the women's efforts with disdain and envy, however. Although the leadership of the women's organizations presented a heroic front, it masked a deeper debate of a gendered nature about the role of the church in the production of social capital. All churchgoers agreed about the need for evangelization. They also celebrated the successes women had in generating millions of dollars for the mission cause. What they could not agree upon was who would control those dollars and the activities they funded. Although most correspondence between the men and women engaged in these struggles was cordial (they were, after all, trying to be "Christian"), the antagonism is best represented in a letter from the Rev. R. B. Dunmire to G. Pitt Beers, executive secretary of the American Baptist Home Mission Society in 1941. Dunmire wanted to know the details of a proposed merger between Beers's male-controlled society and the Woman's American Baptist Home Mission Society. He was perfectly willing to allow women to raise money for mission societies ("let the women go to it and raise *all* the money if they can beat the men") but drew a line at how those funds would be administered. "Two bosses on the same job?" he commented. "It is a bit hard for a missionary or anyone else to serve two Masters." Dunmire spoke, he said, from experience. In Alaska he had worked with women missionaries who were managed and financed by the New England Ladies from Boston but could not *"even hold their own. . . .* I think kindly," he wrote sarcastically, "of those Boston ladies giving of time, effort and money, meaning so well, and yet pouring most of it as 'Mark Twain' said, just down a 'rat hole.'"[19]

Historians of philanthropy have described the latter part of the nineteenth century as a time when charities came under increasing pressure to put their activities on a more "businesslike basis." The Civil War proved a tremendous impetus for the proliferation of new organizations and for formal giving, which continued to increase as opportunities for giving grew. Some have suggested, moreover, that most of these fund-raising efforts were decidedly inefficient, uncoordinated, and unbusinesslike. Robert Bremner notes, for example, that fund-raising efforts of benevolent groups were in a "chaotic condition," with "duplication or overlapping of effort, rivalry for public favor, [and] competition for funds."[20] It took the massive fund-raising efforts during World War I and the rise of the Community Chest movement, he argues, to bring some order and a sense of professionalism to the activity of fund-raising. Perhaps in part as a response to this seeming "chaos," the period also saw the rise of "scientific philanthropy." From it came large, general-purpose foundations that set a criteria against which to judge the effectiveness of charity and social service organizations.[21]

Not insulated from these developments, church organizations found themselves being influenced by the wider movement as they engaged in debates about the purpose of philanthropy and voluntarism. As organizations that occupied a central position in debates about social service and the delivery of social services, and as the recipients of millions of dollars in contributions from American men, women, and children, they were aware of and affected by discussions of how to make philanthropy more effective. Leaders of the women's mission enterprise, women such as Baptists Helen Barrett Montgomery and Nannie Helen Burroughs and Katharine Bennett, who was Presbyterian, for instance, were acutely aware of the need to bring some order to their efforts. Their attempts to do so and systematize fund-raising indicate their commitment to making their respective organizations more efficient and instilling discipline in supporters.

Furthermore, a survey of the administrative records of mainline Protestant (primarily Baptist, Methodist, and Presbyterian) women's mission organizations indicates the extent to which women who founded and ran those groups viewed such efforts as educations in entrepreneurship. They believed themselves to be in the "business" of promoting social and moral reform and took their lessons on how to run these organizations from male colleagues. They wanted very much to administer their organizations in a "business-like" fashion. Presbyterian women were thankful to the male mentors who served on the Board of Home Missions, acknowledging that the PCWBHM was "comparatively a small undertaking and simple in management, but it was before the days when there were many organized efforts by women and few women had business experience." As they grew more successful, their dependence lessened and their relationship to the men's board evolved into something much more akin to one between "client and attorney."[22]

What women learned in the early years was the art of running a business. They familiarized themselves with the legal niceties of incorporation and expanded control over their finances (the extent to which they did so varied from denomination to denomination), taking over the collection and disbursement of receipts, the administration of bequests and annuities, and worrying about how much money they had to borrow against future receipts to meet their debts. They also became proficient in investing and money management, whether extolling the virtue of buying annuities or explaining the complications of international currency exchange. By the high point of the mission enterprise, the female leadership oversaw financial portfolios worth millions.

Proud of their achievements, Katharine Bennett compared her organization to the railroad companies of the day: "It is as if a railroad were all surveyed, graded, track laid, stations built, trains running, business flourishing, credit sound."[23] Not only was this an expanding enterprise, but it was also an efficient one. The leadership liked to point out that it operated with a low overhead, thanks to the dedication of a largely volunteer staff. "It would, no doubt, surprise many business men to know," wrote one supporter of the Woman's Foreign Missionary Society of the Methodist Church (WFMSMC), "that there is an organization with a total membership of over three hundred fifty thousand people, carrying on activities in all parts of the world, with a yearly turnover of approximately one and a third million dollars, with as low an overhead as this Society has."[24]

The rapid growth of Protestant women's organizations, and their ability to attract members and volunteers and show consistent economic growth, was envied by the men who dominated parallel church groups. They had allowed, even encouraged, the organization and proliferation of women's mission groups during the late nineteenth century as a way to raise extra money in support of activities not readily funded by established, male-dominated, mission boards. Women's fund-raising activities were clearly defined as "extra," above and beyond those ordinarily undertaken. The constitution of the WFMSMC, for example, stipulated that "funds of the Society shall not be raised by collection or subscriptions taken during any church services or in any promiscuous public meeting, but shall be raised by securing members . . . and by such other methods as will not interfere with the ordinary collections or contributions for the treasury of the missionary society of the Methodist Episcopal Church."[25]

Women soon discovered that such funds were the wedge by which to expand participation in mission activities and earmarked the money they raised specifically to support female missionaries. By all measures they were tremendously successful. Revenues increased annually, as did the scope of the activities they undertook. Most important, women were distinguishing themselves as the financial backbone of the church. Not only did they give to women's mission organizations, but they also played a critical role in supporting local parish activities. In the Episcopal church, for example, the Woman's Auxiliary began in 1875 by raising one-third of the amount raised by parishes for the support of missions. Thirty years later, their fund-raising efforts yielded $100,000 more than parish contributions.[26]

Early in the twentieth century, moves were made to consolidate women's groups and integrate, merge, or unify them (the wording changes depending on the denomination as well as the decade) with the respective denominational men's groups. Many women involved in these groups perceived these moves as attempts to usurp the power they had gained. Others feared that consolidation would lead to fewer opportunities for women within church administration. Still others argued that integrating parallel efforts of men and women would dampen the enthusiasm of the female constituency that had generously supported the movement's work.

In an exchange of letters with Evelyn Nicholson, president of the WFMSMC, William Shaw, corresponding secretary for the Board of Foreign Missions, went out of his way to "remind" her of his personal commitment to the women's work. His sister, after all, had been a missionary, and his mother and wife were active members of women's mission societies. As a pastor, he had given twenty "Thank Offering Addresses" for the Woman's Foreign Missionary Society. What Shaw proposed was a United Board of Missions, which would enlarge, not reduce, the scope of women's work. His intention was to secure a wider base of support for the "General World Service program," for which women did not feel a responsibility. He described men as feeling "overburdened" and expressed frustration that the women's missionary group had not created "an interest and sense of responsibility in the entire membership for the total missionary task." Although it is not completely clear what Shaw meant by women feeling a lack of "responsibility," what he implied was that women's societies were neither sharing resources nor encouraging members to give to other, more general, missionary causes. Shaw proposed that a united board would also allow women to be brought into the "councils of general missionary work."[27]

Evelyn Nicholson was not so easily flattered. "I know that you desire to be cooperative," she wrote to Shaw, "and to see the largest possible number of individuals, men and women, so related to this missionary enterprise as to be able and glad to make their contribution freely. I know the attitude of the women in this section of the country. They have given themselves without stint or limitation to the work for which they feel responsible. They desire to continue working according to their own plans and under their own administration." Certainly, women would expect to be given the opportunity for "autonomy, initiative and administration" should the boards be united, contended Nicholson, but she was skeptical about women being given equal representation in a united governing council. Furthermore, she doubted whether the matter could be addressed satisfactorily at a "United Conference," because "the women will have inadequate representation because of their lesser numbers and because of their reluctance to take the floor."[28]

Although it is difficult to pinpoint just what kind of impact these discussions about unification had on the larger population of women who worked for and supported missions, it is true that women's support for mission efforts declined during this period. That was precisely what Evelyn Nicholson feared. In an especially biting letter to Shaw on the subject of unification, she apologized for appearing "contentious." "Above all things," she said, "I do want to have right attitudes and to stand for what is most likely to enlist the service and loyalty of the women of the church. Too many secular channels and other activities and interests are luring them away as it is."[29]

The move toward merger or unification, however, was as much welcomed by women as it was feared. Evelyn Nicholson insisted, for example, that she wanted to have the "right attitudes." By the twentieth century, records indicate that administrators and executives of the women's mission enterprise were very much concerned with getting the most for their money. They, too, believed that merging men's and women's groups could lead to greater efficiency, allow a greater range of services to be offered, and make better use of mission resources—all of which would strengthen the church. They wanted to centralize both mission services and administration. Here they were echoing the corporate ethos of the day, that bigger was better. At the same time, however, female administrators feared for their jobs and were concerned that women's power and influence would be diminished.

That concern seems to cross denominations and time. The first effort at consolidation came with proposals that the multiple women's boards within denominations merge. This was generally a proposal made by male leaders and was seen as the first step toward administering all disparate mission organizations under one umbrella (generally a male-dominated board of missions). The WMSMEC, South was one of the first denominations to discuss consolidation. At its 1906 General Conference a union with women's societies was proposed without first consulting those women involved. Unable to speak at the conference, they chose not to argue against a closer relation but rather to seek equal representation on the general board that was to oversee the work. "So foreign was the idea of equal representation to the time-honored policy of Methodism," reported one female observer of the proceedings, "that the formal announcement of the bill met with a good-humored ripple of laughter."[30]

When the men of the WMSMEC, South ultimately succeeded in merging mission boards, women maintained some financial autonomy but were not equally represented on the governing board. It is no wonder that Evelyn Nicholson grew suspicious and defensive when William Shaw pointed to the example of the WMSMEC, South. Merger might enhance evangelization efforts, but the benefits women working in mission societies would gain were not clear. When considering whether to merge in the early 1950s, the Woman's American Baptist Foreign Mission Society pointed to the history of other Protestant women's groups and noted that similar developments earlier in the century had left women in denominations such as the Presbyterians and Congregationalists with little power. From the Congregationalists came a comment: "There is a feeling that we have lost in this merger."[31]

The women's concerns seem to have been justified. Where integration did take place, women's divisions remained, although under a male-dominated administration. In addition, women sat on executive boards (or boards of directors), although they were generally guaranteed only a minority (often no more than a third) of the seats. When women raised concerns about what was to happen to female leadership in the process of integration, it was generally too late. Such was the case of Margaret Wenger, the executive secretary of the Woman's American Baptist Home Mission Society, who protested as plans for a merger with the male-dominated mission society were almost complete, "Probably it is time to ask what the title means in relation to other staff. Am I some kind of Executive in more than name only."[32] From the Congregationalists came the comment that "some of the best women workers are not at their best working with men, and vice versa." Added as a note was the information that the Woman's Home secretary of the American Board (Congregational Church) had resigned, saying, "I have come to feel, because of difficulties inherent in the organizational machinery as well as for personal reasons, that I can no longer render the most effective service in an official capacity."[33]

The merger process varied across denominations. In every case, women approached the new relationship with some trepidation. "Be sure if you unite that all matters which you want to guard are written in the plan of union," Presbyterians cautioned the Baptists.[34] Among Presbyterians, plans for merger generated a flurry of letters, most of which expressed concern that women's interests be safeguarded. "Why should the women of the church who are loyal faithful supporters of our Woman's Work have this taken from our hands, and given to management of men who can't begin to do it well?" one supporter asked the Presbyterian Woman's Board of Home Missions in protest of the merger and reorganization of mission boards. "I note that fifteen women are to be placed on the Foreign Missions Board but learn nothing of the fate of Mrs. Bennett, Miss Dawson, yourself and others [directors of the Woman's Board of Home Missions]—who have showed such efficiency, devotion and enthusiasm in the Christianizing of America. What is to become of the Synodical and Presbyterial Machinery of the Women's Societies? No men can match the unselfish unpaid work of these organizations."[35] They feared—and rightfully so—that their successes, apart from those in fund-raising, would go unappreciated and that women administrators would be relegated to lesser roles. In 1969, when she reflected on what had been the gradual incorporation of the Woman's Auxiliary of the Episcopal Church into the National Council, Avis Harvey remembered that women active in the auxiliary had initially thought integration a "good thing." "We believed that it [integration] would give greater representation to the women in all aspects of the church's work. We thought we were doing something good," she commented. What they did not realize was that it would "mean less women's work throughout the church and in the mission field."[36]

However positive the gains women made through the mission enterprise—establishing independent mission boards, proving their abilities in administrating and fund-raising for a growing organization, and, on a more personal level, learning to be philanthropists—this was also a movement that promoted an ethic of self-denial. The very same woman who was able finally to confront her husband and request an allowance also related that she would "always believe that there has been something miraculous about our funds [meaning mission funds]."[37] Whatever benefits women realized, either as individuals or as a class, were to be subordinated to the needs of the church and, ultimately, to the word of God. That ethic led those in positions of administrative power, for instance, to reserve comment about fears for their own jobs when mergers were discussed. If merger or unification meant a stronger church, women felt compelled to support the initiative. Protest was muted, checked before their piety could be questioned. They wanted, after all, to be seen as having the "right attitudes." The church could never be more than only a training ground for economic independence, a place where women could be educated about how to run a successful institution. Those who wanted to realize a different kind of economic power or independence, who looked to run an organization that was truly autonomous, or who desired a business partnership that was more egalitarian had to look beyond mainstream Protestant denominations or to the secular world. For many, it was very likely a frustrating experience. The church had provided access but then limited what women could accomplish. Others were to follow the same model during the twentieth century, particularly white Anglo-Protestants, who developed a contradictory relationship to capitalism in general.

The Anglo-Protestant wives, sisters, and daughters of the emerging entrepreneurial and managerial class were the beneficiaries of the wealth generated by corporate capitalism. Yet they were building organizations that exposed and attempted to redress the worst abuses of that same system. Mission societies were their attempt to bridge class differences, put the wealth of the period to good use, and in some small way redistribute that wealth. They celebrated self-denial. What they recommended as the "heroic way" was to "limit our own expenditures to a certain sum, giving away all the rest of our income."[38] This model of economic behavior was suited for homemakers of privilege and means. Women such as Helen Barrett Montgomery were celebrated. She and her husband, a successful businessman, were regarded "as exemplary trustees of personal resources." Montgomery was also remembered as "careful" with her money and one who "avoided all display and extravagance."[39] What is not so clear, however, was how that ethic benefited poor widows or the struggling "business woman" (salaried employees or proprietors of small businesses)—those, that is, who could not count on a husband or some other male relative to support them.

Because they were married to affluent businessmen, Katharine Bennett and Helen Barrett Montgomery had no financial worries.[40] That they were so determined to "grow" their organizations was a testament to their religious zeal as well as to entrepreneurial acumen for which there was no other suitable outlet. Although men such as R. B. Dunmire might belittle women's efforts as "pouring money down a 'rat's hole,'" his charges did not reflect personally on the leaders of women's mainline denominational groups. Women like Bennett and Montgomery, insulated by their privileged class position, could easily deflect such accusations as the words of a bitter man.

For mission leaders whose economic position was more precarious, however, charges of acting in a selfish manner or for personal gain could be devastating. Such was the case with Nannie Helen Burroughs, who had built the National Training School for Women and Girls under the auspices of the Woman's Convention Auxiliary to the National Baptist Convention (the Woman's Convention). For decades she battled charges that she had abused her relationship with the Woman's Convention to build the school, an institution that brought her prominence and provided her with a small personal income.

The example of the African American Woman's Convention illustrates just how broad and inclusive the Protestant women's mission enterprise was. It also suggests how the gendered struggles found in mainline Protestant denominations take on added dimension when issues of race and class intervene. The Woman's Convention faced many of the same problems as its white counterparts, including male ministers who resented the money women were able to raise and tried on numerous occasions to reign in their autonomy. Like their white counterparts, Woman's Convention leaders also employed a variety of strategies to educate members about the importance of systematic giving. It, too, relied upon money raised in small amounts from a great number of women.

What set the Woman's Convention apart was its celebration of successful businesswomen. Female entrepreneurs such as Madame C. J. Walker (a manufacturer of hair products) and Maggie Lena Walker (president of the St. Luke Penny Savings Bank of Richmond) were invited to address annual meetings. The organization also consulted Maggie Walker for financial advice. These women served as models for others to follow. They embodied what was the primary goal of the Woman's Convention: the uplift of the race. They understood that the organization provided a means for achieving social mobility. As Anna Cooper stated, "When and where I enter . . . then and there the whole Negro race enters with me." The emphasis on uplift and self-determination for the race tempered concern with self-denial.[41]

African American women may have celebrated individual entrepreneurial successes, but like their white counterparts they viewed such successes through gendered lenses. They, too, juggled a desire to build successful institutions (and achieve a certain measure of recognition) with an ethic that judged those desires in a woman as suspect. The personal papers of Nannie Helen Burroughs in the Library of Congress chronicle a decades-long struggle with National Baptist Convention leaders over control of the National Training School for Women and Girls. Because the papers relate to her professional and her private lives (although she did not make a distinction between the two), they allow a much fuller picture of the conflicts and dilemma faced by a mission leader who was a servant of God and church and also had entrepreneurial ambitions.[42] Burroughs was an enormously competent businesswoman who ran her National Training School on a shoestring, traveling throughout the country to raise funds for its support.[43] She also owned several pieces of property and had investments.[44] What kind of living these afforded her remains unclear, however. She lived, it seems from her correspondence, hand to mouth, yet she managed to maintain the school through years of adversity and near-bankruptcy.

Burroughs first proposed the National Training School and was elected corresponding secretary of the Woman's Convention in 1900. The school was officially incorporated in 1907, and Burroughs and two others acquired property in Washington, D.C., for an institution, which, she envisioned, would provide young black women "first class training for missionary, Sunday School and Church work." In addition, the school would provide lessons in "household arts, such as cooking, sewing, housekeeping, nursing and . . . horticulture."[45]

As incorporated, the institute was the property of trustees who served under the auspices of the Woman's Convention. The project began with a $500 donation from Maggie L. Walker. Walker, whose bank was one of the most successful African American enterprises at the turn of the century, intended her donation to inspire the contributions of many other, poorer, black women.[46] By 1922 the Woman's Convention's annual report was showing that the school was valued at more than $80,000. The majority of the money collected was earmarked for the National Training School. Burroughs's intent was to build a "great national institution for our girls . . . at the Nation's Capital, a great Christian University for women—a university that will be as sacred to the Negro race as Holyoke or Vassar or Wellesley is to the Anglo-Saxon race."[47]

The school was to be Burroughs' life-long endeavor, but by 1917 she was confronting charges from the male-dominated National Convention (as well as from women within the Woman's Convention who opposed her) that she was personally profiting from the school.[48] Her refusal to support a revision in the school's charter so the institution would fall wholly under the control of the National Convention further fueled the attacks. In 1938, after years of controversy, the National Convention moved to disassociate the institute with the NBC. Burroughs remained a corresponding secretary of the Woman's Convention, but she was largely exiled by both the male and female leaders of the National Convention and the Woman's Convention and her school received no funding. She remained popular with the rank and file, however, and they continued to send letters of support throughout the long battle. In 1948 she was made president of the Woman's Convention, and the school reaffiliated with the National Convention.

Burroughs was especially incensed at attempts by men in the National Convention to take over the efforts of women. It rankled her that the Woman's Convention was not autonomous of the NBC and that the charter of the NBC denied women the right to manage and control their own institutions. The NBC, she argued, was a "man's organization." Although she did not challenge that as illegitimate, she did note that "Negro Baptist women should have a parallel national organization just as distinct and powerful." If men would not grant the Woman's Convention autonomy, then the Training School would remain a "woman's institution . . . conceived, developed, managed, owned and controlled by Negro Christian women." As for charges that she had somehow profited from the school, she wholeheartedly denied a personal interest: "There was never any thought of personal ownership or personal glory."[49]

Burroughs went to great lengths to defend herself against attacks that she was somehow abusing her connections to the National Convention. "Nothing but love for the advancement of Negro women and girls has actuated me," she wrote. "I have no selfish motive." She also reiterated her loyalty to the church:

> I think more of the National Baptist Convention than Dr. Williams can ever think of it, because I have worked harder and longer and have made more sacrifices to build it up than he has. I have scrubbed floors, edited papers, washed windows, written books, produced supplies and literature of all kinds, directed and instructed women, developed leaders, sold my little substance to help the Cause, pled the Cause of Missions. I have stood by the Secretaries of the Boards, worked for the Convention for seventy-five dollars a month—practically nothing—and I'll be blessed if I'll let Dr. Williams run me out of a Convention for which I have worked like a galley slave, not for pay and honor but for the Cause.[50]

Over four decades, Burroughs reiterated time and again that her motives were "pure" and that she did not seek personal profit. One supporter who wrote to Burroughs in 1924 noted that she did not understand why the "brother's board" wanted to change the charter. But, she added, "That is the way with most all things, the beginner has the work and all the trouble and after getting things in running order the looker on comes in and wants the job of bossing."[51] Unlike many of her white counterparts, Burroughs was not going to give way. She chose to be cut off first.

Perhaps her ability to withstand the pressures exerted by the National Convention was a function of her forceful personality (one supporter called her "our Moses"), but Burroughs's personal papers show a woman as adept at raising money and conducting business as she was dedicated to the cause.[52] Although it was a major asset to the Woman's Convention, the Training School survived on a prayer and a promise in addition to a lot of hard work and constant effort on Burroughs's part. She invested substantial money in the project. Although she was granted a salary as its executive, it seems not to have been paid in full or very regularly. Her financial records reveal that she struggled to keep the school going, collecting rent from properties she owned to pay (although rarely on time or in full) unending bills. By 1930, struggling to keep up with payments on the school's mortgage, she was negotiating with the mortgage-holder, the Columbia Building Association, for more time. Burroughs assured John Harrell, the association's president, that she had been "working earnestly to get the money to put our loan in satisfactory condition."[53] To repay these debts she spent many months on the road, fund-raising.

Burroughs had many different business personas. She could be tough and unforgiving, as when she ordered the agent who managed her properties to evict tenants for nonpayment.[54] She could also dissemble and appear apologetic, as she did with Harrell. She could even make herself out to be pitiable if the occasion called for it. At the height of the depression, when a creditor wrote to ask that she send payments on a more regular basis because he had just lost a substantial amount of his own in a bank failure, she responded that she could not. She had "been sick and afflicted and am still poor and needy." She was, she added, making a "heroic effort to keep my word and to keep the most important things going."[55]

Although she never gained any real measure of wealth (perhaps not even comfort), Burroughs was flexible and persistent in her efforts to maintain the Training School. That, she would argue, reflected her commitment to the cause, but the point should also be made that the cause in this case defined her life, spiritually, practically, and materially. To give the Training School to the National Convention would be to give up power—including what little bit of economic power she wielded. Perhaps it was not coincidental—it might have been a show of her support—that when Helen Barrett Montgomery died in 1934 she left $1,107 to Burroughs's Training School, even though she must have known about the controversy in which Burroughs was embroiled.[56]

Max Weber suggested that religious associations in the United States were the "vehicles of social ascent into the circle of the entrepreneurial middle class."[57] Religious affiliation and the expression of faith guaranteed creditworthiness. As Weber argued, "Admission to the congregation is recognized as an absolute guarantee of the moral qualities of a gentleman, especially those qualities required in business matters. Baptism secures to the individual the deposits of the whole region and unlimited credit without any competition. He is a 'made man.'"[58]

Working within and through Protestant churches offered women a kind of moral guarantee as well. Their affiliations secured their reputations and the small donations of the women who joined their organizations. But a gendered reading of church history suggests that Weber's understanding of the results of this process must be qualified. My intention in this essay has been not to celebrate the capitalist and corporate ethos that mission women embraced when they built these organizations nor to lament their exclusion from the larger marketplace and their relegation to the production of social capital. It is more important to understand the limitations of the economic experience and vision of the women whose work was integral to the creation of the modern welfare state. They recognized and were critical of what they believed to be the excesses of corporate capitalism, but they did not, by and large, challenge its underlying economic ideas.[59] Indeed, they hoped to make their own organizations more dynamic and powerful by embracing as their model the corporate structures of their day. They may have succeeded in their religious mission, but as individuals, and collectively as women, they were simultaneously limited by the popular belief that entrepreneurial success was best left to men. In most cases, the result was that mission women lost control of the institutions they had created. Ironically, it seems that black women (members of communities trying to build economic foundations after the Civil War) best fit the model Weber envisioned, although not—as the example of Burroughs suggests—without generating controversy within those communities. For many other women—especially white women—who so desired, the church and church work did not provide the experience nor the network by which they would enter the "entrepreneurial" middle class. They were not to grow rich in the fashion envisioned by Weber; the profits they generated were not to be monetary ones but rather social. In the developing economic order, these women were the producers of "social capital," a category of economic activity that would continue to be undervalued and overshadowed. As the struggle between the men and women who are the subjects of this discussion suggests, women's power and authority were challenged even in the arena of social capital.

Notes

1. Montgomery also served as the president of the National Federation of Women's Boards of Foreign Missions, as well as president of the Northern Baptist Convention. Helen Barrett Montgomery, *Western Women in Eastern Lands* (New York: Macmillan, 1911), 38. The quotation found in the title is from a speech given by Mary James, first president of the Presbyterian Church's Woman's Board of Home Missions. See "Address of the President," *Home Mission Monthly* 1 (July 1887): 199.

2. Montgomery, *Western Women in Eastern Lands,* 243–44, 38 (quotation).

3. See, for example, R. Pierce Beaver, *American Protestant Women in World Mission: A History of the First Feminist Movement in North America* (Grand Rapids: Eerdmans, 1968); John P. McDowell, *The Social Gospel in the South: The Woman's Home Mission Movement in the Methodist Episcopal Church, South, 1886–1939* (Baton Rouge: Louisiana State University Press, 1982); Peggy Pascoe, *Relations of Rescue: The Search for Female Moral Authority in the American West, 1874–1939* (New York: Oxford University Press, 1990); Patricia Hill, *The World Their Household: The American Woman's Foreign Missionary Movement and Cultural Transformation, 1870–1920* (Ann Arbor: University of Michigan Press, 1985); Susan M. Yohn, *A Contest of Faiths: Missionary Women and Pluralism in the American Southwest* (Ithaca: Cornell University Press, 1995).

4. Mrs. J. Fowler Willing, "I Can Plod," *Heathen Woman's Friend* 25 (Feb. 1894): 226.

5. Mary James, "Address of the President," *Home Mission Monthly* 1 (July 1887): 198–99.

6. The reference to "spasmodic" giving comes in "A True Story; Or, Aunt Margaret's Experience," *Home Mission Monthly* 4 (Oct. 1890): 268.

7. "Report of the Corresponding Secretary, Delia Lathrop Williams," *Twenty-eighth Annual Report, Woman's Home Missionary Society of the MEC,* Oct. 1909, 5, General Commission on Archives and History, United Methodist Church, Drew University, Madison, N.J. (hereafter UMCA).

8. May D. Strong, "Systematic and Proportionate Giving," *Home Mission Monthly* 22 (Sept. 1908): 265–66.

9. *Home Mission Monthly* 11 (July 1897): 201.

10. "The Problem of the Empty Purse," *Home Mission Monthly* 20 (March 1906): 112.

11. "Best Plans for Giving," *Home Mission Monthly* 14 (Sept. 1900): 257.

12. "The Treasury," *Home Mission Monthly* 15 (March 1902): 106–7.

13. *Fourteenth Annual Report of the Woman's Foreign Missionary Society of the MEC,* 1883, 62, UMCA.

14. See Alfred Chandler, *The Visible Hand: The Managerial Revolution in American Business* (Cambridge: Harvard University Press, 1977), for a discussion of the corporate model of this period.

15. "Seven Ways of Giving," *Heathen Woman's Friend* 22 (Sept. 1890): 63. The lazy way was third on this list. The list included, in the following order, the careless way, the impulsive way, the lazy way, the self-denying way, the systematic way, the equal way, and the heroic way.

16. "Treasury Notes," *Home Mission Monthly* 22 (July 1908): 219; Mary Bennett, "The Art of Giving," *Home Mission Monthly* 23 (March 1909): 113–14; Mary Torrance, "The Hungry Gap," *Women and Missions* 3 (Jan. 1927): 376.

17. "Report of the Secretary of Home Affairs," *Fifteenth Annual Report of the Woman's Missionary Society of the MEC, South,* 1892–93, 81, UMCA.

18. Mrs. O. W. Scott, "A Reminiscence Meeting," *Heathen Woman's Friend* 25 (March 1894): 258.

19. Rev. R. B. Dunmire to G. Pitt Beers, May 8, 1941, in Beers, G. Pitt File no. 52–22, American Baptist Archives Center, Valley Forge, Pa. (hereafter ABAC). For a more focused discussion of Protestant men's fears of the church becoming feminized and their attempts to reassert masculine dominance, see Gail Bederman, "'The Women Have Had Charge of the Church Work Long Enough': The Men and Religion Forward Movement of 1911–1912 and the Masculinization of Middle-Class Protestantism," *American Quarterly* 41 (Sept. 1989): 432–65.

20. Robert Bremner, *American Philanthropy* (Chicago: University of Chicago Press, 1960), 123–24.

21. Thomas H. Jeavons. *When the Bottom Line Is Faithfulness: Management of Christian Service Organizations* (Bloomington: Indiana University Press, 1994), 16.

22. "An Appreciation," RG 305, box 1, History of Incorporation File 20, Presbyterian Historical Society, Philadelphia.

23. Katharine Bennett, "Annual Address of the President," *Home Mission Monthly* 25 (July 1911): 200.

24. Ruth M. Wilson, "Membership and the Modern Woman," *Woman's Missionary Friend* 71 (Feb. 1938): 43.

25. Quoted in Patricia Hill, "Heathen Women's Friends: The Role of the Methodist Episcopal Women in the Women's Foreign Mission Movement, 1869–1915," *Methodist History* 19 (March 1981): 147.

26. In 1875 the Woman's Auxiliary raised $75,524 to the $226,472 raised in parishes. By 1905 those figures were $452,835 for the Woman's Auxiliary and $346,800 for the parishes. Mary S. Donovan, "Women as Foreign Missionaries in the Episcopal Church, 1830–1920," *Anglican and Episcopal History* 61/62 (1992): 21.

27. William Shaw to Evelyn Nicholson, Feb. 9, 1939, Admin. vol. 3, folder 1109-1-1:21, UMCA.

28. Evelyn Nicholson to William Shaw, Jan. 6, 1939, Admin. vol. 3, folder 1109-1-1:21, UMCA.

29. Evelyn Nicholson to William Shaw, Sept. 6, 1938, Admin. vol. 3, folder 1109-1-1:20, UMCA.

30. Quoted by McDowell, *The Social Gospel in the South,* 127.

31. Data Regarding the Merger of Congregational Foreign Boards, and Data Regarding the Merger of the Foreign Board of the Presbyterian Church in the U.S.A., memos, AB/WABFMS Merger, 1933–35 File, ABAC.

32. Jewel Asbury, "Integration of the Woman's American Baptist Home Mission Society and the American Baptist Home Mission Society from a Feminist Perspective," 19, unpublished paper, ABAC. See also Margaret Wenger to a Miss Hazzard, Jan. 23, 1954 (Integration 1945–54, Committee Reports Background File, 35–37, ABAC), wherein she spells out her dissatisfaction at finding herself stripped of many of her duties.

33. "Synopsis of Information from Two Women's Boards which Have Merged," 1, AB/ WABFMS Merger, 1933–35 File, ABAC.

34. Ibid., 2.

35. Katherine Williams to the Board of Directors of the Woman's Board of Home Missions, June 11, 1922, RG 305, box 1, file 37, Presbyterian Historical Society, Philadelphia.

36. Quoted by Ian T. Douglas, "A Lost Voice: Women's Participation in the Foreign Mission Work of the Episcopal Church, 1920–1970," *Anglican and Episcopal History* 61 (1992): 54.

37. Mrs. O. W. Scott, "A Reminiscence Meeting," *Heathen Woman's Friend* 25 (March 1894): 258.

38. "Seven Ways of Giving," 63.

39. Helen Barrett Montgomery, *From Campus to World Citizenship* (New York: Fleming H. Revell, 1940), 240.

40. Helen Montgomery's husband, William, was a businessman whose venture, the North East Electric Company, became the Rochester Products Division of General Motors Corporation. Katharine Bennett's husband Fred listed his occupation as a manufacturer. In 1915 he was an officer in the William L. Burrell Company of New Jersey.

41. My discussion of the Woman's Convention Auxiliary to the National Baptist Convention is drawn largely from Evelyn Higginbotham's *Righteous Discontent: The Women's Movement in the Black Baptist Church, 1880–1920* (Cambridge: Harvard University Press, 1993).

42. Unable to locate personal papers or correspondence of Katharine Bennett or Helen Barrett Montgomery, I have relied primarily on the institutional records found in the archives of the mainline Baptist and Presbyterian denominations.

43. For biographical sketches that focus primarily on her politics, feminism, or offer a more general overview of her life, see Higginbotham, *Righteous Discontent;* Casper LeRoy Jordan, "Nannie Helen Burroughs," in *Notable Black American Women,* ed. Jessie Carney Smith (Detroit: Gale Research, 1996), 137–40; and Evelyn Brooks Higginbotham, "Burroughs, Nannie Helen," in *Black Women in America: An Historical Encyclopedia,* ed. Darlene Clark Hine (Brooklyn: Carlson Publishing, 1993), 201–5.

44. For a full picture of Burroughs's financial dealings, see Administrative and Financial File, 1900–63, Nannie Helen Burroughs Papers, Manuscript Division, Library of Congress (hereafter NHBP). This file contains papers dealing with her personal financial affairs and the financial records of the National Training School for Women and Girls, as well as the Woman's Convention Auxiliary to the National Baptist Convention.

45. Minutes of the Corresponding Secretary's Report for the Executive Committee, Woman's Convention, 1904, 346, file 2 "Controversy," container 310, NHBP.

46. *Circular of Information for the Seventeenth Annual Session of the National Training School for Women and Girls, 1925–26,* 9, Miscellany—National Trade and Professional School Brochures and Catalog, container 310, NHBP.

47. "You Can't Have My Baby She Cries: Nannie Burroughs Gets Militant," *Black Dispatch* (Oklahoma City), Jan. 12, 1928, 2, Speeches and Writings File, container 46, NHBP.

48. About these charges one supporter observed, as to the motivations of the leaders of the national convention, that in 1907 when only worth $7,000 the convention had cared nothing about the training school. Not until 1917, when the school was worth more than

$200,000, did the convention look to intervene. Undated and anonymous article, file 4, "Controversy," container 310, NHBP.

49. Statement Made by Miss Burroughs at the Close of Her Annual Report to Woman's Convention, at St. Louis, Sept. 1938, Speeches and Writings, 1918–60, container 46, NHBP.

50. "Eight Allegations of Dr. L. K. Williams, Not Founded in Fact," 8, file 4, "Controversy," container 310, NHBP.

51. Mollie Nugent Williams to Burroughs, Feb. 22, 1924, Controversy over Status of National Training School, file 1, container 310, NHBP.

52. Fannie Carter Cobb to Burroughs, Nov. 29, 1932, General Correspondence, Carter, Fannie Cobb, 1930–57, container 5, NHBP. After she became president of the Woman's Convention in 1948 she apparently set about to reorganize the fiscal operation of the convention. One thing she did was to institute a plan whereby members were authorized to raise funds for specific categories of activities—something that had gotten her into trouble with the auxiliary and NBC earlier. "Scope and Content Note," Finder's Guide to the Papers of the Nannie Helen Burroughs, 5, NHBP.

53. Burroughs to John Harrell, Oct. 23, 1930, Harrell to Burroughs, Nov. 6, 1930, and Burroughs to Harrell, Nov. 7, 1930, all in Administrative and Financial Records, Correspondence Oct.–Dec. 1930 File, container 56, NHBP.

54. Burroughs to Arthur Carr, Feb. 6, 1931, Administrative and Financial Records, Correspondence Jan.–May 1931 File, container 56, NHBP.

55. Burroughs to Charles Cole, Nov. 30, 1933, Administrative and Financial Records, Correspondence 1933 File, container 56, NHBP.

56. National Trade and Professional School Legacies File, Administrative and Financial Records, container 114, NHBP.

57. Max Weber, "The Protestant Sects and the Spirit of Capitalism," in *From Max Weber: Essays in Sociology,* ed. H. H. Gerth and C. Wright Mills (New York: Oxford University Press, 1958), 308.

58. Weber, "The Protestant Sects," 305.

59. In *Poor Richard's Principle: Recovering the American Dream through the Moral Dimension of Work, Business, and Money* (Princeton: Princeton University Press, 1996), Robert Wuthnow suggests (202–4) that this may be an ongoing problem for voluntary or charitable organizations in the United States that try to balance the need to raise money for activities with a mission to shape the social "values" of the larger society. He argues that the donations given to charitable organizations are an "ambiguous commodity." We prefer to think of them as "gifts" and the organizations that solicit them as untainted by money and the marketplace. Reluctant to discuss the issue head-on, contemporary voluntary associations do much as their predecessors did when they embraced the popular corporate models of the day: They justify their programs "much as a business would, in terms of cost-benefit analysis." That, Wuthnow argues, is unfortunate, because "much of the public views these as service organizations, functioning mainly to perform some unprofitable social function, rather than recognizing their potential to instruct the public in how better to think about values."

11. Healing Hands, Healthy Bodies: Protestant Women and Faith Healing in Canada and the United States, 1880–1930

JAMES W. OPP

> BEELER: Doctor says it's a natural cure. Says the new medical books explain it.
>
> RHODA: Do you think, because they give it a name, that they explain it?
>
> BEELER: *Bursts out petulantly.* You women don't want things explained! You prefer hocus-pocus. Take Martha there. Forty-four years she waddles around without an idea in her noggin but house-work, then all of a sudden she ups with—(*imitates her*)— "You can't keep a spirit in its grave, not when it's a mind to come out." Mystery! Lolly-pop. You women would live on it if we'd let you.
>
> RHODA: Whether you let us or not, we do live on it, and so does the rest of the world.
>
> BEELER: What the world lives on is facts. *He points at the books.* Hard-boiled sci-en-ti-fic facts! With a few jokes thrown in for seasoning.
>
> —William Vaughn Moody, *The Faith Healer,* act 4 (1909)

Moody's insightful portrayal of an argument between Matthew Beeler and his niece Rhoda exposes many of the gendered tensions surrounding the subject of divine healing in North America at the turn of the century. In the play it is the women of the household who support the efforts of the newly arrived faith healer, while the male characters with whom he associates are feminized by virtue of their age and race or both. Even the hesitant, halting actions of the faith healer himself do not inspire much masculine confidence from the "real" men with whom he comes into contact. Masculinity instead arrives in the guise of professionalism: the doctor, the cleric, and Matthew Beeler's proud collection of scientific books.

Like Beeler, many historians have regarded faith healing as more of an historical joke than a serious topic of inquiry. Of the few studies that exist on the divine healing movement, none consider the role of gender in their analysis despite the fact that the practice of faith healing centered around women's bodies.[1] A cursory glance at a few of the religious periodicals promoting divine healing reveals that first-person testimonials written by women accounted for more than 80 percent of the healing narratives printed.[2] At a Vancouver campaign in 1929, the Pentecostal faith healer Charles S. Price collected 102 first-person testimonials to healing, ninety-five of which were from women and only seven from men.[3] Women were not simply a part of the divine healing movement, their bodies were the movement.

Like the female defenders of Moody's faith healer, women found themselves arraigned by a masculine professionalism that came in a variety of forms: the cleric, the doctor, and the scientific knowledge within Beeler's books. Faith healing provided an interface through which women engaged this professionalism on a variety of levels: leading as healers, subverting the control of physicians by seeking healing, reconceptualizing the body, and questioning the epistemological basis of scientific medicine itself. The first part of this essay explores the role of women as healers in the divine healing movement, tracing their initial prominence in the late nineteenth century and their gradual decline over the first half of the twentieth century. The second section inverts this historical perspective to examine faith healing from the position of those who sought it. Their narratives reveal how apprehensions regarding medical control, professionalization, and the nature of the body were interwoven with devotional concerns. Personal experience was the basis of authority for the majority of these testimonials, but for a small group of women who had been trained as physicians the adoption of divine healing meant confronting their own identity as professionals.

No single voice can fully encompass the diversity of meanings embodied within the narratives of the thousands of women who claimed healing through faith. Nevertheless, these texts share the basic assumption that physical healing was intimately related to a bodily experience of the divine. God was given credit for healing, but the unspoken premise was that the body had the capacity—indeed, was actually designed—to receive such a dispensation. By claiming "the Lord for the body," women mediated multiple discourses surrounding the nature of religion, medicine, and the body. The individual experience of a faith cure was intensely personal, but the practice of divine healing was profoundly shaped by its cultural context.

Healing Hands

One of the most important texts of the early divine healing movement concerned the recovery of Carrie Judd. After a severe fall on a stone sidewalk, inflammation in her spine left the eighteen-year-old student prostrate and suffering from "hyperaesthesia." On the basis of a local newspaper's report of a "faith cure," Judd's sister wrote to Sarah Mix, an African American from Connecticut who had been healed of tuberculosis. Mix detailed how faith healing could be achieved, even at a distance:

> Whether the person is present or absent, if it is a "prayer of faith" it is all the same, and God has promised to raise up the sick ones. . . . Now if you can claim that promise, I have not the least doubt but what you will be healed. You will first have to lay aside all medicine of every description. Use no remedies of any kind for anything. Lay aside trusting in the "arm of flesh," and lean wholly upon God and His promises. When you receive this letter I want you to begin to pray for faith, and Wednesday afternoon the female prayer-meeting is at our house. We will make you a subject of prayer, between the hours of three and four. I want you to pray for yourself. . . . It makes no difference how you feel, but get right out of bed and begin to walk by faith. Strength will come, disease will depart and you will be made whole.[4]

Following Mix's directions, Carrie Judd felt a change in her body and sat up in bed for the first time in two years. As word of her healing spread, she found herself being propelled to the forefront of the divine healing movement. In less than four years, she had published her account of healing, launched a monthly journal, and established her own "Faith Rest Cottage" in Buffalo. Judd's growing prominence was augmented by her personal and professional association with A. B. Simpson and the Christian Alliance, an interdenominational fellowship for which she served as a vice president and its first recording secretary.[5]

The healing of Carrie Judd in 1879 occurred just as the divine healing movement in North America was emerging as a major phenomenon. The new interest in faith healing was built on the theological foundation of the Holiness movement.[6] Drawing upon Wesleyan notions of Christian perfection, the Holiness movement in North America exhorted believers to seek the "second blessing" of sanctification, a purification from sin in order to lead a consecrated life on earth. The divine healing movement extended perfectionism, whether designated as a separate, distinct experience or a gradual process, beyond the redemption from sin to include the restoration of the body. As such, atonement encompassed not only salvation from sin but also freedom from sickness and disease, afflictions that were themselves the product of sin. A number of key figures within the Holiness movement were introduced to divine healing by Charles Cullis, a homeopathic physician and philanthropist who had been inspired by the story of the Swiss healer Dorothea Trudel. W. E. Boardman, A. B. Simpson, A. J. Gordon, and R. Kelso Carter were all influenced by the Boston doctor, and their writings formed the basis for a systematic theology of divine healing.[7]

As important as these theological expositions were in giving the divine healing movement a secure foundation, the emphasis traditionally placed on male theologians has tended to overshadow the role of women in defining the broader practice of divine healing. As Judd's narrative reveals, faith healing took place within a larger framework that involved simultaneously coordinating her own prayer with that of Mix's "female prayer-meeting." Women like Judd were regular speakers at Christian Alliance conventions and camp meetings, but most faith healing took place within more informal networks that carried the message of healing directly to the bedside. Blind and bedridden from serious injuries sustained in a carriage accident, Mrs. C. B. Newcomer recounted how she was visited by an African American woman who "remarked that it was her chief work to visit and pray with the sick and invoke God's healing power to rest upon them that they might be restored to health." The healer was an unknown stranger to Mrs. Newcomer, but "her gentle, unassuming manner attracted me, and the clear and convincing way in which she set forth the promises of God's Word . . . together with her fervent prayer for my restoration to health, seemed to inspire in me a faith and hope that I had never realized before."[8]

These informal and often localized activities were projected onto a continentwide audience through published personal accounts of healing. Judd's healing narrative *The Prayer of Faith* was published in 1880, and the following year she launched a monthly journal, *Triumphs of Faith,* appropriately subtitled "devoted to the promotion of Christian Holiness and to Divine Healing." Women would read such accounts at bedsides or distribute them through the mail to relatives or friends when they heard of a sickness. Isolated on a farm outside Martintown, Ontario, Maggie Scott recalled that the arrival of Judd's *Prayer of Faith* "caused me to feel not quite so much alone" in seeking divine healing. Scott wrote to Cullis, Judd, and Mix to arrange for special times of prayer. A testimonial to her recovery was published in the *Pacific Herald of Holiness,* which in turn inspired another healing in California.[9] These print and publishing efforts extended the support of women's networks and played a significant role in spreading the divine healing movement across the continent.

In urban centers, "faith homes" became the central focus of divine healing, and it was within these homes that women's leadership was most apparent. The maternal domesticity offered by faith homes was presented as a spiritually enriching alternative to the sterile atmosphere of hospitals or rest homes. Founded by Rebecca Fletcher and a Miss Griffiths, Bethany Home in Toronto was opened in order to offer "Christians suffering in mind and body, who instead of going to some health resort or to a hospital would prefer a quiet home . . . surrounded by Christian influence and kind sympathetic friends, they could be directed to the Lord Jesus Christ Himself as the Healer of all their diseases."[10] The theme of the sacred home, what Colleen McDannell has termed "domestic religion," defined the ideal social space for both spiritual and physical recovery.[11] Before the establishment of the Faith Rest Cottage, a parlor in the Judd home became a "Faith Sanctuary" that was furnished "not in any style of severe solemnity, but with reference to a home-like beauty and graceful simplicity, which would make us feel that this hallowed spot was indeed a part of our home, and that our Lord, in a special manner, had taken up His abode within our humble dwelling."[12] Even in homes founded by men, the daily management and operation of these institutes usually lay in the hands of women "matrons."

For some critics, the female-controlled space of faith homes posed a serious threat to the traditional family. J. M. Buckley charged, "Certain advocates of faith-healing and faith-homes have influenced women to leave their husbands and parents and reside in the homes, and have persuaded them to give thousands of dollars for their purposes." The fear that women could use faith homes as a space through which to escape the traditional bonds of domesticity was apparent in a "heartrending letter" Buckley received from a "gentleman whose mother and sister are now residing in a faith-institution of New York, refusing all intercourse with their friends, and neglecting obvious duties of life."[13] Despite occasional opposition, R. Kelso Carter could identify more than thirty faith homes in North America in 1887, the majority of them run by women. That number would continue to grow over the next decade.[14]

Through these networks the divine healing movement developed an infrastructure that operated outside the denominations, allowing women to assume positions of leadership that were less likely to upset ecclesiastical sensibilities. Nevertheless, the role of the healer required careful negotiation at certain points, such as the invocation of James 5:14, which called for the "elders of the church" to anoint the sick with oil. Cullis, a lay Episcopalian, had freely anointed his patients, but Judd, also an Episcopalian, was more reluctant to assume a position of ecclesiastical power. Instead she had a male "elder" known as "a man of piety and faith" perform this sacramental duty.[15] Judd was well aware, however, that other women, including Sarah Mix, had anointed the sick.[16] In 1885 the *Triumphs of Faith* reprinted an article by Charlotte Murray, a matron at the Bethshan faith healing home in London, England, who openly supporting women's right to administer anointings with oil. Murray argued that the "elders" were "whosoever has received light from God on this part of His word, and is prepared by the Holy Ghost to pray the prayer of faith, is an Elder in the truest sense of the word."[17] From the testimonials printed in *Triumphs of Faith*, it is clear that women were taking on this role, and Judd overcame her reluctance.[18]

Women's activities as healers within their own households could also lead to gendered tensions. Many men supported faith healing, but within families that were divided over the appropriate method of treating illness it was far more common for women to endorse the practice of divine healing. When M. B.'s young son Arthur contracted a severe fever, she "begged [God] to let the fever go down before his father came home, so that he would not have to take medicine." The fever seemed to lessen, but during the night Arthur woke up screaming and delirious. When Mr. B. went to retrieve the medicine, M.B. recounted, "I laid my hand on Arthur's head, and praised the Lord that He had promised a restful night for the child, and I knew He would put the enemy to flight. . . . When Mr. B. came back with the medicine Arthur was sound asleep."[19] Nellie Fell similarly trusted in faith for the recovery of her infant daughter from constipation, but eventually the condition "became so alarming, that it seemed like insanity not to resort to something for relief." Her husband, who was "of like faith," finally could not stand his daughter's suffering any longer, declaring "I shall have a doctor, this can not go on any longer." Nellie responded by "[asking] the Lord not to let him go for a doctor" and after a great deal of prayer their daughter was eventually healed.[20]

As the divine healing movement entered the twentieth century it was profoundly altered by the advent of Pentecostalism. The Pentecostal emphasis on the gifts of the spirit drew upon faith healing from the beginning.[21] Many women associated with the divine healing movement received the "latter rain" of glossolalia, including Carrie Judd Montgomery and Maria Beulah Woodworth-Etter. For those who remained within traditional Holiness organizations, however, the emergence of Pentecostalism produced bitter divisions. In response to Pentecostal congregations leaving its fellowship, the Christian and Missionary Alliance adopted a stricter denominational form, which resulted in a significant decline in the number of women occupying leadership positions.[22] Faith homes were also affected by these developments because the debates over tongues divided loyalties and disrupted the spirit of interdenominationalism that had provided them with a broad basis of support. Homes that became Pentecostal often shifted their emphasis toward training workers in the absence of Bible institutes.[23] Although Montgomery's Home of Peace continued to operate outside Oakland, most faith homes gradually disappeared during the first few decades of the twentieth century.

Many of the women faith healers who traveled the road from Holiness to Pentecostalism continued to have successful healing ministries. As the social space of faith healing shifted from faith homes to evangelistic campaigns, however, women found themselves competing with men for their share of the stage. Inspired by the success of Billy Sunday, large-scale evangelistic campaigns became increasingly professional and carefully managed in the twentieth century and required substantial resources to mount.[24] That style of urban evangelism emphasized the masculine characteristics of the ministerial vocation, where vigor, energy, and athleticism were the proper tools with which to battle sin.[25] The new generation of faith healers included such noted evangelists as F. F. Bosworth, Smith Wigglesworth, and Raymond Richey. Women remained in the campaigns, but unlike the early days of the Christian Alliance conventions they were serving less as evangelists and more as assistants, both behind the scenes and onstage.

The extraordinary exception to this pattern was Aimee Semple McPherson, whose success as an evangelist and faith healer was unrivaled. The Canadian-born Aimee Kennedy, together with her new husband Robert Semple, were involved in itinerant evangelism with William Durham of Chicago when Aimee broke her ankle. Initial prayers to heal her were unsuccessful, and she returned to Chicago on crutches, her foot in a cast. After a week, she asked Durham to "lay hands" upon her, which produced a healing experience that felt "as if a shock of electricity had struck my foot. It flowed through my whole body causing me to shake and tremble under the power of God."[26]

McPherson made her mark as a healer with a series of phenomenal campaigns in 1921. Starting in San Diego in January, she preached to enormous crowds, an outdoor healing service drawing an estimated audience of thirty thousand to hear her. Equally successful campaigns in San Jose and Denver enshrined her celebrity status as a faith healer despite her insistence that healing was only part of her message. McPherson skillfully adapted healing to the changing environment of the twentieth century, placing it firmly onstage. One observer described a healing meeting in Montreal just before the San Diego campaign that launched her career:

> The piano and stringed instruments played softly "My faith looks up to Thee" as the prayer of faith was ascending. . . . Quietly and softly the music floated over the air, suddenly all eyes were turned on a young girl who ascended the platform with crutches, with great difficulty. . . . Prayer was offered, she arose

to her feet and to the amazement of the crowded house she walked across the platform with Mrs. McPherson's aid but no crutches, suddenly she started out alone and by this time there was no longer silence but great exclamations of joy and praises to God arose all over the congregation. Shortly she ran like a child of ten throwing herself into the outstretched arms of Mrs. McPherson. The people could no longer keep their seats but stood to their feet and in one volume there rose the sound of many hands clapping together for what God had wrought among them.[27]

Healings were clearly integrated into the coordinated performance of music, exhortation, and invitations that had become a part of modern revivals.[28]

McPherson was certainly influential, but her career was not representative of the healing roles most women played. Upon her death in 1944, there were practically no women to take her place. When faith healing was resurrected after the war, the banner was carried by a group of men: William Branham, Oral Roberts, T. L. Osborn, Jack Coe, and A. A. Allen.[29] Despite the success of McPherson, the social geography of faith healing in the twentieth century was far less hospitable to most women compared to the close network of friends, family, and prayer circles in a domestic setting that had characterized the early divine healing movement.

While the public role of women as healers gradually decreased over the twentieth century, women continued to promote divine healing on a local scale. In place of faith homes, many single women such as Dorothy Ruth Miller turned to a growing number of Bible schools for support. A graduate of Simpson's Missionary Training Institute in Nyack, New York, Miller taught at a variety of Bible schools across the United States and Canada. Her diaries from the 1920s illustrate that women (both Pentecostal and non-Pentecostal) continued to perform many of the same duties they had in faith homes: holding prayer meetings for the sick, visiting hospitals, encouraging students not to use medicine, and often answering requests for aid in healing by praying over handkerchiefs and returning them to the beneficiary. Despite this activity, Miller clearly distinguished such endeavors from more formal positions of leadership. When a female colleague sought ordination, Miller worried about the potential consequences: "I realized how much harder it would make my work, a part of which was to influence the girls of the school to find places where they could work under the leadership and protection of men and without being made prominent."[30] The fears of a "feminized" church that accompanied the rise of fundamentalism in the 1920s made women conscious of how being "prominent" was no longer an acceptable role in conservative evangelicalism.[31] Women continued to serve as heal-

ers within the new network of Bible institutes, but the "public" face of healing shifted to male evangelistic healing campaigns. Even while the role of
healer was being negotiated, however, women's bodies remained central to
faith healing.

Healthy Bodies

"Men don't want to be sick. Women want to be well," observed one commen-
tator about Aimee Semple McPherson's campaign in Dayton, Ohio.[32] The gendered body signified a particular relationship between illness and health. Victorian medicine entrenched the popular notion that women were physically
weaker than men and therefore more susceptible to disease.[33] In particular,
the female sexual organs were deemed to be responsible for the majority of
women's illnesses, because "woman's entire being . . . mental and moral, as
well as physical, is fashioned and directed by her reproductive powers."[34] The
universal ideal of health was defined according to male standards, implying
that women could never really achieve a "true" state of health. Well into the
twentieth century, popular home-remedy books reinforced this understanding of women's bodies: "Physically and mentally, woman is man modified."[35]

Faith healing intersected a central paradox in late-Victorian perceptions
of gender and the body. Women were "naturally" deemed to be both more
inclined to religion and more susceptible to disease. It is not surprising that
many of the female testimonials reflected the prevailing Victorian perceptions
of "fashionable diseases" linked to various forms of "neurasthenia" and "hysteria." One sufferer, who endured seventeen years of a wide variety of illnesses, complained that she was "so weak most of the time I could not turn over
without assistance and for two months was utterly helpless, unable to turn
my head or body the least bit, and could bear no one in the room only long
enough to do what was strictly necessary, owing to extreme nervousness,
which was nearly nervous insanity."[36]

The very conditions that made it socially acceptable for women to engage
in discourses on the body, disease, and religion produced an environment
in which men, particularly those who were not clerics, would be reluctant
to offer their own narratives of illness. The cultural associations of sickness
and frailty with femininity stigmatized and emasculated men who had less
than perfect health; male testimonies rarely admitted such "utter helpless-
ness" and practically never employed such terms as "nervous prostration."
When male narratives were printed, it was far more likely to find men discussing their "bondage" to vices such as tobacco and alcohol or describing
accidents they had sustained while working.

Establishing the "reality" of illness is less important than understanding how women ordered their own personal experience of pain, illness, and healing. Testimonials to faith healing both reflected and challenged dominant medical paradigms present at the turn of the century. The rhetoric of the divine healing movement drew heavily upon the mid-nineteenth-century "crusade" for health. Where Christianity had traditionally treated the body as carnal, sinful, and ultimately a temporary vessel before death, the health reform movement redeemed the body's natural state as one of health. The body was made whole by following the "laws" of health such as diet, exercise, and sexual purity, which offered a means of self-prevention instead of medical intervention.[37]

The perfectionism of the Holiness movement was grafted onto these new ideas of health. The "natural" state of the body was to live within God's laws and maintain God's consecrated presence in daily life. Therefore, divine healing was not just a miraculous cure but a state of preservation: "The body is constantly undergoing decay, but 'the life also of Jesus' . . . counteracts the forces of disease and decay."[38] Montgomery referred to the "indwelling Health" that "abides within, to spring up continually with rejuvenating power in every organ and nerve, in every tissue and fibre of this wonderful physical organism."[39] Divine health collapsed the typical dualism surrounding the body (matter/spirit or natural/supernatural) and instead emphasized an ever-present divine state. In rejecting parts of the medical paradigm while investing in health reform, faith healing subverted cultural constructions of femininity and women's bodies, offering a means by which women could obtain a state of wellness otherwise denied them by conventional medicine.

The adoption of "divine health" as a discursive strategy was also part of a larger concern regarding the manner in which women engaged medical culture. The transformation of late-nineteenth-century therapeutics offered medicine unprecedented levels of control over the body, altering the relationship between patients and doctors. Within the divine healing movement, the reaction to these changes varied enormously. John Alexander Dowie, the Scottish-born Australian evangelist who converted Chicago's seven-story Imperial Hotel into the Zion Divine Healing Home, was embroiled in a series of legal battles with the city's doctors over allegations that he was practicing medicine. Never one for subtlety, Dowie labelled physicians, surgeons, and druggists a "banded trinity of poisoners and murderers." This anti-medical assault was based on more than metaphysical debates over the nature of the body and medicine. Dowie attacked medicine as a profession, echoing popular fears about the development of gynecology and other areas of medicine that left a doctor's morality open to question. To confirm such suspicions, women's letters denouncing the licentiousness of physicians were read from the platform at Zion: "When I lay upon that man's dissecting table, helpless, naked well nigh, he stole my virtue and defiled my body."[40]

Dowie's sensational battles were exactly what other faith healers tried to avoid. Most protested that they had no quarrels with doctors, and the scandalous accusations of Dowie never reached the pages of more respectable divine healing journals. Underlying the discourse of faith healing, however, was a clear and definite challenge to medical control on a variety of levels.

The professional authority of medicine was based on its claim to represent objective scientific principles in diagnosing and explaining the etiology of disease. This epistemology was questioned by advocates of faith healing, who suggested that the practice of medicine appeared to be far from the mark. Sarah Bush, for example, had "thirteen physicians, but my disease baffled their science." Through the use of the possessive, scientific objectivity is qualified and compromised as a limited, inherently inferior, scope of knowledge. The *Christian Alliance and Foreign Missionary Weekly* reported a "pathetic story" going around in daily newspapers about a girl suffering a headache. She was successively diagnosed by different physicians as having "impoverished blood and shattered nerves," neuralgia, malaria, and "love sickness."[41] Aimee Semple McPherson made a similar point about how malleable the "science" of medicine appeared to be:

> A short time ago a pneumonia patient was kept in a warm room, all the windows closed so that no chance draft of cold air might reach him. Today the room must be open, fresh, cool air, constantly circulating. . . . Ten years ago most of us didn't even give a thought to the glands of our body. In fact, the doctors didn't just know what they were all for, anyway. But today they tell us we can't live without gland treatments of first one kind and then another. . . . Operations have changed; serums have changed; electrical treatments have changed. . . . But . . . He is as eternal as the mountains.[42]

Rhoda's rejoinder to Matthew Beeler, "Do you think, because they give it a name, that they explain it?" reflects how the discursive ground for establishing a medical diagnosis was far from settled at the turn of the century. Proponents of divine healing recognized that a professional demeanor and attaching a Latin name to an illness did not necessarily represent a fixed medical reality.

Dissatisfaction with the medical community went beyond simple frustration with its inconsistencies. It was also a reaction to the expansion of medical interventionism. Observational control in dedicated spaces such as hospitals and asylums was rapidly increasing in the late nineteenth century, as was physical manipulation of the body through operations. As often as prayers were lifted in expectation of healing, the accompanying hopes of preventing medicine from "touching the lips" or keeping bodies safe from the hands of surgeons were usually not far behind. Issues of control were evident in the case of a young Armenian girl taking a medical course in Boston who developed an abscess behind her ear. The Apostolic Christian Assembly prayed "let no surgeon's knife touch her" while "those who thought they had authority" hurried her to the hospital. By the time the operating room was prepared, the girl had been cured.[43] Less fortunate sufferers often described their treatment at the hands of physicians in great detail. These narratives rarely criticized physicians openly, but they effectively represented doctors as little more than torturers of the body who left the patient in an even worse condition.

Medical control through the use of drugs raised different issues. The development of anesthetics and painkillers allowed increased surgical practice, but the corresponding loss of self-control through the loss of consciousness introduced new moral questions. Mrs. E. M. Whittemore was "filled . . . with repugnance" at the thought of a hypodermic, fearing the "risk of losing that sweet conscious sense of my Saviour's presence, for even a short while, by consenting to stupefying my brain just in order to dull the pain."[44] For proponents of divine healing, even supposedly curative agents were actually little more than temporary alleviations that could lead to "constant bondage to the medicine." The common references to bondage held a double meaning. As a rhetorical device it alluded to the bondage of sin, but "bondage" also referred to the addictive nature of remedies that relied upon opiates or a high alcohol content. Because women were the major consumers of these medications, confronting the therapeutic use of drugs was a frequent theme in many testimonies.[45]

No issue has animated historical debates regarding the growing medical control over women's bodies more than the question of childbirth. Dowie proudly published the pictures of hundreds of children, born where "no murderous physician with unclean breath and heart and hands stood near with dread instruments all in readiness."[46] A large network of former doctors, midwives, and maternity "nurses" were associated with Zion's activities in encouraging natural childbirth, both in Chicago and across the continent. For Dowie and for the many women who testified about childbirth, the two most reprehensible features of modern obstetric practice were the use of forceps and pain-relief drugs. One of Zion's elders, Dr. J. G. Speicher, confessed to having "used the accursed instruments in the delivery of children with unreasonable frequency" and during the delivery of his own eldest child he had placed his wife under chloroform for six hours, an experience from which she only recovered upon arriving in Zion.[47]

Outside of Zion, it is more difficult to trace the employment of divine healing in childbirth, but the practice clearly spread to many different corners of the Pentecostal movement, including a unique faith healing home outside Los Angeles known as Pisgah. Dr. Finis E. Yoakum had founded the Pisgah Home Movement after his miraculous recovery from injuries sustained when he was struck by a buggy. In 1911 the Pisgah Home provided housing for 175 regular workers and had provision for nine thousand clean beds to serve the urban homeless and poor.[48] When cases of childbirth began to appear around 1905, an inexperienced Lizzie Stone served as one of Pisgah's first midwives. Self-conscious about her lack of training, Stone assisted in three deliveries attended by physicians, but her experience did not endear her to the medical profession: "The last [physician] used instruments,—the little one's face was paralyzed,—the mother all torn,—then I knew what the Lord had been doing for me."[49] It was the first-hand encounter with "professionals" using forceps that convinced Stone of the superiority of faith healing in maternity cases.

Like Zion, Pisgah served as both a base for childbirth and as an outreach whereby workers could travel to attend women in their own homes. One mother had assumed that "according to the law" she would be required to have a physician in attendance "although I did not wish it," but Yoakum informed her that she was under no legal obligation to do so. Instead, Sister Lizzie arrived at her house. Four hours later, "my eight and one-half pound baby was born without a pain or the least effort on my part, for which I thank God as the dread of child-birth has been taken away."[50]

Both Zion and Pisgah attracted widespread attention over the issue of divine healing and childbirth, with many mothers from across the continent and overseas writing to request prayers and anointed handkerchiefs. Yoakum received this testimonial from a vicarage in London, England:

> My husband requested your prayers and a handkerchief for me in regard to the birth of our expected little one. The midwife (I of course had no doctor) who last attended me having asserted that a certain dangerous complication . . . would attend the birth. Your prayers were answered. Thanks and Glory be to God! I had a beautiful time, and no complication, nor hemorrhage, nor ailment of any sort. In fact the midwife (who was not a believer) remarked upon the strength and remarkable health of my uterus, and needless to say I had no "after pains."[51]

Against the medical definition of childbirth as a site of potential disease, faith healing offered the preservation of health for mother and child and even suggested that labor pains could be relieved without resorting to drugs. Not all births entrusted to faith healing could fulfill this ideal. Agnes Meredith, for example, endured severe pain during fifteen hours of labor but believed that "had I had more faith in God I should have suffered less."[52]

The discourse of divine healing in childbirth embodied how women renegotiated their relationship with medical culture. Moral concerns were interwoven with fears regarding specific therapeutic practices. Taking the "Lord for the body" was powerful statement set within the context of professional claims for control over the body and competing definitions of health. If different quarters of the movement reacted with varying degrees of hostility toward physicians, the underlying concerns remained strikingly similar.

Physician Heal Thyself

Occasionally, male medical doctors such as Cullis and Yoakum turned their attentions to faith healing. More frequently, however, the physicians attracted to the divine healing movement were women. For Dr. Jane Baker, it was the discovery of her own breast cancer that led to a spiritual crisis that turned her to faith healing, and when the healing took place, "It seemed as if some one had heated irons red hot and thrust them through my breast."[53] For Dr. Elizabeth Keller, injuries sustained from a carriage accident were cured after a group of believers spent the night praying for her.[54] Dr. Florence Murcutt, who had fallen from a veranda and suffered both internal injuries and a fractured arm, found that anointing and prayer effected a healing that was confirmed by X-rays.[55]

The most famous woman physician to join the divine healing movement was Lilian B. Yeomans. The Canadian-born daughter of a Civil War surgeon, Yeomans received her medical degree from the University of Michigan in 1882. Her recently widowed mother, Amelia, also took up medicine and graduated from the same school the following year. Together the Yeomans went into practice in Winnipeg, where Amelia soon became occupied with temperance and suffrage activities and Lilian concentrated her efforts on her professional career.[56] The strain of medical practice took its toll, and Lilian found herself dependent upon a daily combination of morphine and chloral hydrate. For years she searched for a cure to her addiction, trying everything from Christian Science to the Keeley Institute's gold cure, until she was finally healed at Dowie's Zion Home in 1898.[57] Declaring never to use medicine again, Yeomans returned to Canada to serve as a missionary in the north; she later moved to Calgary and eventually settled in California. Like many women healers in the twentieth century, Yeomans leaned upon the infrastructure of the Bible institute movement for support, teaching at McPherson's L.I.F.E. Bible College. A prolific author, Yeomans wrote numerous articles and books on the subject of divine healing.

Although Yeomans had been healed by Dowie, she refrained from adopting his denunciations of her former profession: "The worst thing I would say about physicians, and the entire medical fraternity would perforce agree with me, is that they are men, and not God, and their activities flesh, and not spirit."[58] The professional position of women doctors bestowed them, however, with authority to undermine the very idea of medical professionalism. Yeomans reflected on how as a doctor she could talk with a "commanding voice to the submissive patient trembling before me, with possible castor oil, calomel, rigid dieting, perhaps even fasting, looming darkly in their horizon, with all proper professional dignity."[59] Dr. Mina Ross Brawner used her professional authority to provide a stark appraisal of the nature of disease:

> Oh, if disease is only a matter of germs I am not afraid of germs. I know their names, their habits of life and mode of reproduction. I'll just put on a cap and long white surgical gown, and rubber gloves, and then sail right into the battle with lance and disinfectants! But when I see that back of those death dealing germs stands the devil as the first cause I will not undertake to deal with him. So I take off my gown and rubber gloves, make one heap of all my weapons of warfare, my years of study and credentials, and carry them all to the foot of the Cross where I see the bleeding, mangled body of my Lord.[60]

Brawner might have laid her credentials "in a heap," but the initials "M.D." remained vitally important in establishing and maintaining a professional level of credibility. Yeomans did not publish a single article or book without her well-earned initials trailing closely behind her name. It was easier to escape the practice of medicine than it was to leave behind the credibility and status bestowed by professional association.

If medicine was not as efficacious as prayer in making the body healthy, at least it provided a stock of useful metaphors to encourage spiritual healing. Even such technically sophisticated topics as modern germ theory could be used to promote spiritual ends: "Human blood defends the body by actually conquering deadly microbes when they get into the circulation. The soldiers of the blood, tiny white corpuscles, called leucocytes, stand up and fight them to the death. So the blood of the Lamb overcomes all Satan's power of sin, sickness, and death."[61] The power of a medical vocabulary was not always so malleable in its application. Yeomans herself admitted that the structures of knowledge produced by her medical training could pose difficulties. A bout with pneumonia in 1923 produced an inner dialogue between her entrenched

medical rationality and her religious belief: "The enemy said, 'You have pneumonia of the right lung, with some involvement of the left; it is complicated
by pleurisy, which causes that intolerable agony when you cough. Look at your
blue face! See how motionless your right lung is! Notice your rapid, shallow
respiration, feeble pulse and laboring heart.' But I refused to note the 'lying
symptoms' and just reiterated, 'None of these diseases.'"[62]

If it was easier for former doctors to criticize some elements of professionalism, extricating themselves from the mental framework of medicine was
more problematic. Sarah Bush could posit that "their science" was not hers,
but physicians who turned to faith healing were once part of the scientific
machinery. Removing the "gown and rubber gloves" entailed confronting
one's own identity both as a physician and as a professional.

Conclusion

Professional authority can be embodied within a wide range of loci, and faith
healing intersected many varieties of professionalism. Women had to negotiate their role as healer between the growing professionalization of evangelism and changing expectations surrounding gendered social roles. The rhetoric of health served as a bulwark against interventionism and provided a
vocabulary to reconstruct the body as more than a discrete, autonomous
collection of organs and tissues. The divinely consecrated and restored body
offered women a state of wholeness denied them by the medical definition
of health based on universal male norms. If suspicions regarding the "science" of medicine were not enough to question its claims to professional
authority, a small group of women doctors could use their own credentials
to undermine such pretensions.

A central concern for women who confronted the varieties of professionalism was the issue of control. Ann Braude has observed, "If women are to
be the main characters, then, power must be the subplot, whatever the main
events."[63] For women in the divine healing movement, "power" existed on
multiple levels simultaneously, and the question of "empowerment" through
religion is complicated by the competing sites of power within the structures
of both religion and medicine. In faith healing, the body itself becomes a focal
point of control. For some women, exercising control meant simply praying
for healing before a doctor could arrive. When M.B. prayed for her sick son,
she noted that "the secret of strength and power is to be perfectly passive, to
lie in His will and to have none of our own."[64] For others, exercising control
involved expelling physicians from the realm of childbirth or accepting the
status of an "elder" by anointing the sick. Binary distinctions of resistance

versus submission cannot adequately represent the wide range of women's encounters with professional authority. Nor were the women who turned to faith healing simply liberal health reformers in disguise. Divine healing was foremost an intense religious experience; the redemption of the body as sacred bestowed an authority to receive a physical, bodily expression of the divine. In faith healing, the therapeutic and the devotional are intimately related. It was only through the epistemological space that constructed the body as divine that a social space for challenging modern medicine could be created. Conversely, the divine healing movement itself was profoundly shaped by the "therapeutic revolution" of the nineteenth century.[65]

In *The Faith Healer*, professionalism arrives on the scene in the form of a cleric, a doctor, and as a body of knowledge hidden within Beeler's scientific books. Rhoda's devastating rejoinder that giving something a name does not explain it encapsulates how women were able to rescript their experience of illness and recovery. It was in opposition to professional authority that women wrote personal narratives defining their understanding of how the body served as a site of religious experience and claiming a metaphysical ground that preempted "belief" in science or medicine. Women's bodies were not a series of passive constructions; rather, they were actively negotiated as women lay claim to faith healing. For Beeler, such "hocus pocus" illustrated that women did not "want things explained." In fact, the voices raised by women in favor of divine healing explain a great deal about the relationship between religion, medicine, and women's bodies at the turn of the century.

Notes

I wish to thank Janet Friskney and Joanna Dean for their invaluable comments on earlier drafts of this essay. In addition to a research grant provided by this project, the Social Sciences and Humanities Research Council of Canada has supported this work through a doctoral fellowship.

1. Donald Dayton, "The Rise of the Evangelical Healing Movement in Nineteenth-Century America," *PNEUMA: Journal of the Society for Pentecostal Studies* 4 (Spring 1982): 1–18; Paul G. Chappell, "The Divine Healing Movement in America," Ph.D. diss., Drew University, 1983; Raymond J. Cunningham, "From Holiness to Healing: The Faith Cure in America 1872–1892," *Church History* 43 (Dec. 1974): 499–513. There are two notable biographies of prominent women healers: Edith Blumhofer, *Aimee Semple McPherson: Everybody's Sister* (Grand Rapids: Eerdmans, 1993), and, on Maria Beulah Woodworth-Etter, see Wayne Warner, *The Woman Evangelist* (Metuchen: Scarecrow Press, 1986).

2. *Triumphs of Faith* (hereafter *TF*) and the *Christian Alliance and Foreign Missionary Weekly* (hereafter *CAMW*) carried separate sections reserved for healing testimonials. Notably popular throughout the 1890s, both journals consistently had figures of female

first-person narratives well over 80 percent. That figure does not include third-person testimonials or cases where the gender of the writer could not be identified, but those numbers were relatively small.

3. Price Testimonial Cards in file 4/3/4, Assemblies of God Archives, Springfield, Mo. A total of 112 testimonial cards survived, but it unknown whether those represent all or only a portion of the total cards received. Seven of these could not be classified according to gender, and two were third-person accounts of the healing of children. A sample of more than two hundred testimonials from Price's periodical, *The Golden Grain,* taken from the active campaign years of 1927, 1929, and 1931, suggests that 85 percent of first-person testimonials were from women.

4. Carrie F. Judd, *Prayer of Faith,* 2d ed. (Chicago: Fleming H. Revell, 1902), 14–15; Mrs. Edward [Sarah] Mix, *Faith Cures and Answers to Prayers* (Springfield, Mass.: Springfield Printing, 1882), 39. Mix noted that because of stormy weather, the only people able to pray for Carrie were she and her husband. I am grateful to Nancy Hardesty for pointing out this source.

5. "All the Way," *TF* 42 (1922): 34–38; Carrie Judd Montgomery, *"Under His Wings": The Story of My Life* (Oakland: Office of Triumphs of Faith, 1936), 98–101. In 1890 Simpson was part of the wedding ceremony when Judd married George S. Montgomery, a California businessman who had been healed of diabetes in the early ministry of John Alexander Dowie. The couple moved to Oakland, California, and founded their own temperance town, Beulah, just outside the city limits.

6. On the Holiness movement, see William Kostlevy, *Holiness Manuscripts: A Guide to Sources Documenting the Wesleyan Holiness Movement in the United States and Canada* (Metuchen: Scarecrow Press, 1994).

7. Charles Cullis, *Dorothea Trudel; or, The Prayer of Faith,* 3d ed. (Boston: Willard Tract Repository, 1872); W. E. Boardman, *The Great Physician* (Boston: Willard Tract Repository, 1881); A. B. Simpson, *The Gospel of Healing* (New York: Christian Alliance Publishing, 1896); A. J. Gordon, *The Ministry of Healing* (Boston: H. Gannett, ca. 1882); R. Kelso Carter, *The Atonement for Sin and Sickness; or, A Full Salvation for Soul and Body* (Boston: Willard Tract Repository, 1884).

8. Mrs. C. B. Newcomer in *TF* 6 (1886): 46–47.

9. Alexander Scott, *Ten Years in My First Charge* (Toronto: Hart, 1891), ch. 4; *CAMW,* June 19, 1895, 382.

10. *CAMW,* Feb. 14, 1890, 107.

11. Colleen McDannell, *The Christian Home in Victorian America, 1840–1900* (Bloomington: Indiana University Press, 1986).

12. Montgomery, *Under His Wings,* 78.

13. J. M. Buckley, *Faith-Healing, Christian Science and Kindred Phenomena* (New York: Century, 1892), 57.

14. R. Kelso Carter, "Divine Healing; or, 'Faith Cure,'" *Century Magazine* 33 (March 1887): 780.

15. "Faith-Work," *TF* 4 (1884): 268; Montgomery, *Under His Wings,* 80.

16. Mix, *Faith Cures,* 67, 161; Mrs. M. Baxter, "Deliverance from Sin," *TF* 1 (1881): 114.

17. C. C. Murray, "Anointing Him with Oil," *TF* 5 (1885): 99.

18. *TF* 7 (1887): 216, 284; *TF* 8 (1888): 92.

19. M.B., "???," *TF* 11 (1891): 240.

20. Elizabeth Baker et al., *Chronicles of a Faith Life* (ca. 1926, repr. New York: Garland, 1984), 92–93.

21. Donald W. Dayton, *Theological Roots of Pentecostalism* (Metuchen: Scarecrow Press, 1987); James R. Goff, Jr., *Fields White unto Harvest* (Fayetteville: University of Arkansas Press, 1988).

22. Wendell W. Price, "The Role of Women in the Ministry of the Christian and Missionary Alliance," D.Min. diss., San Francisco Theological Seminary, 1977, 45–47. Four of the eight vice presidents of the Missionary Alliance in 1887 were women, as was a third of the executive board. By 1919 only Mrs. A. B. Simpson held a position on the board of managers.

23. Edith Blumhofer, "Life on Faith Lines," *Assemblies of God Heritage* 10 (Summer 1990): 10–12, 22.

24. The classic work on twentieth-century revivalism is William G. McLoughlin, Jr., *Modern Revivalism* (New York: Ronald Press, 1959), esp. ch. 8.

25. Margaret Bendroth, *Fundamentalism and Gender, 1875 to the Present* (New Haven: Yale University Press, 1993), chs. 1 and 4.

26. Aimee Semple McPherson, *This Is That* (Los Angeles: Bridal Call Publishing, 1919), 72–75; see also Blumhofer, *Aimee Semple McPherson*, 83.

27. *Pentecostal Testimony* (Ottawa) 1 (Jan. 1921): 2. On McPherson's rise to fame, see Blumhofer, *Aimee Semple McPherson*, ch. 4.

28. Blumhofer emphasizes the differences between McPherson and Billy Sunday, contrasting her "gentler persuasion" to Sunday's "stern denunciations" and arguing that McPherson lacked the organizational apparatus of the Sunday campaigns (*Aimee Semple McPherson*, 169, 203). From the point of view of divine healing, however, McPherson employs techniques much closer to her contemporaries than to nineteenth-century precedents.

29. For the post–World War II healing movement, see David Edwin Harrell, Jr., *All Things Are Possible* (Bloomington: Indiana University Press, 1975). Kathryn Kuhlman is often considered McPherson's successor, but she remained marginal to the movement until the late 1960s. Wayne Warner, *Kathryn Kuhlman: The Woman behind the Miracles* (Ann Arbor: Servant Publications, 1993).

30. Miller Diaries, Aug. 2, 1923, Prairie Bible Institute, Three Hills, Alberta.

31. On fundamentalism and gender, see Bendroth, *Fundamentalism and Gender*; Betty DeBerg, *Ungodly Women* (Minneapolis: Fortress Press, 1990).

32. "A Further Report of the Dayton Revival," *Pentecostal Evangel*, July 24, 1920, 11.

33. Wendy Mitchinson, *The Nature of Their Bodies: Women and Their Doctors in Victorian Canada* (Toronto: University of Toronto Press, 1991), 51; John S. Haller, Jr., and Robin M. Haller, *The Physician and Sexuality in Victorian America* (Carbondale: Southern Illinois University Press, 1974).

34. Henry M. Lyman, et al., *Twentieth-Century Family Physician*, rev. ed. (Chicago: Charles C. Thompson, 1917), 883.

35. R. V. Pierce, *The People's Common Sense Medical Adviser*, 78th ed. (Buffalo: World's Dispensary Medical Association, 1914), 737.

36. *TF* 24 (1904): 209. For two examples of the many different approaches to hysteria,

see Elaine Showalter, *The Female Malady* (New York: Pantheon, 1985), and Francis G. Gosling, *Before Freud: Neurasthenia and the American Medical Community, 1870–1910* (Urbana: University of Illinois Press, 1987).

37. James C. Whorton, *Crusaders for Fitness: The History of American Health Reformers* (Princeton: Princeton University Press, 1982). As a form of "physical Arminianism" (5), the health reform movement had been inspired by Christian perfectionism, so it is not surprising that its rhetoric was appealing to the divine healing movement.

38. "How to Keep in Health," *Pentecostal Evangel*, July 23, 1921, 5.

39. "God's Temple, the Body," *TF* 27 (1907): 73.

40. "Doctors, Drugs and Devils," *Leaves of Healing*, Aug. 28, 1897, 697–98. For a sampling of perspectives on women and doctors, see Ann Douglas "'The Fashionable Diseases': Women's Complaints and Their Treatment in Nineteenth-Century America," and Regina Morantz, "The Perils of Feminist History," both in *Women and Health in America*, ed. Judith Walzer Leavitt (Madison: University of Wisconsin Press, 1984), 222–38 and 239–45. On Dowie, see Philip L. Cook, *Zion City, Illinois: Twentieth-Century Utopia* (Syracuse: Syracuse University Press, 1996), and Grant Wacker, "Marching to Zion: Religion in a Modern Utopian Community," *Church History* 54 (1985): 496–511.

41. *TF* 16 (1896): 163–64; *CAMW*, Jan. 3, 1890, 8.

42. Aimee Semple McPherson, "Divine Healing—Ancient and Modern," *Foursquare Bridal Call* 10 (Oct. 1926): 33.

43. Emma L. MacDonald, "God, or Surgeon's Knife?" *Word and Work* 24 (Feb. 1912): 41.

44. *CAMW*, Dec. 30, 1892, 425. On Whittemore, see *Mother Whittemore's Records of Modern Miracles*, ed. F. A. Robinson (Toronto: Missions of Biblical Education, n.d.). On the development of anesthetics, see Martin S. Pernick, *A Calculus of Suffering: Pain, Professionalism, and Anesthesia in Nineteenth-Century America* (New York: Columbia University Press, 1985).

45. *TF* 8 (1889): 141; Haller and Haller, *The Physician and Sexuality*, ch. 7.

46. The words were Speicher's, but they reflected Dowie's sentiment. John G. Speicher, "Happy, Healthy Zion Babies," *Leaves of Healing*, Feb. 15, 1902, 798–99; see also "Zion Babies," Dec. 29, 1900, 292–94. Mary B. Speicher, one of Zion's deaconesses and Speicher's mother, claimed that even before she came to Zion she had been called to help mothers during childbirth. *Leaves of Healing*, Sept. 9, 1899, 892–93.

47. *Leaves of Healing*, Sept. 9, 1899, 892–93. On childbirth, see Mitchinson, *The Nature of Their Bodies*, ch. 6; Judith Walzer Leavitt, *Brought to Bed: Childbearing in America 1750 to 1950* (New York: Oxford University Press, 1986); and Richard W. Wertz and Dorothy C. Wertz, *Lying-In: A History of Childbirth in America* (New York: Free Press, 1977).

48. "F. E. Yoakum" and "Pisgah Home Movement," in *Dictionary of Pentecostal and Charismatic Movements*, ed. Stanley M. Burgess and Gary B. McGee (Grand Rapids: Zondervan, 1988), 907–8 and 717–18.

49. *Pisgah* 1 (Nov. 1909): 6.

50. Ibid.

51. *Pisgah* 1 (April 1913): 8.

52. *Leaves of Healing*, June 24, 1905, 329.

53. Jane M. Baker, "Is Cancer Curable?" *CAMW*, Sept. 23, 1892, 201–2.

54. Elizabeth Keller, "An Experience," *TF* 30 (1910): 129.

55. *TF* 42 (1922): 117–18.

56. On the suffrage activities of Amelia Yeomans, see Catherine Cleverdon, *The Woman Suffrage Movement in Canada* (Toronto: University of Toronto Press, 1950), 50–53.

57. *Leaves of Healing,* Feb. 5, 1898, 350–51.

58. Lilian B. Yeomans, *Resurrection Rays* (Springfield: Gospel Publishing House, 1930), 36–37.

59. Lilian B. Yeomans, "He Brought Me Through," *TF* 43 (1923): 54–57.

60. Mina Ross Brawner, "Jesus Destroys the Works of the Devil," *TF* 46 (1926): 55–56.

61. Lilian B. Yeomans, *Balm of Gilead* (Springfield: Gospel Publishing House, 1936), 26.

62. Yeomans, "He Brought Me Through," 55.

63. Ann Braude, "Women's History *Is* American Religious History," in *Retelling U.S. Religious History,* ed. Thomas A. Tweed (Berkeley: University of California Press, 1997), 90.

64. *TF* 11 (1891): 240.

65. Charles Rosenberg "The Therapeutic Revolution: Medicine, Meaning, and Social Change in Nineteenth-Century America," in *Explaining Epidemics,* ed. Charles E. Rosenberg (New York: Cambridge University Press, 1992), 9–31. Rosenberg uses this term to refer to both medical techniques and the social relations between doctors and patients.

12. The Women That Publish the Tidings: The International Association of Women Ministers

MARK CHAVES

WOMEN'S ORDINATION and the twentieth-century experiences, struggles, and triumphs of female clergy have received a fair amount of scholarly attention.[1] A little-known part of this story, however, concerns the International Association of Women Ministers (IAWM), an interdenominational professional association that has been in continuous existence since 1919.[2] From one perspective, the lack of attention to the IAWM is understandable. It is and has always been a small organization, it has not been particularly visible in recent decades in the various denominational struggles for gender equality, and its earlier position as the professional association for women ministers has been largely eclipsed by groups for female clergy that now exist within virtually every denomination.

From other perspectives, however, the IAWM warrants attention. Its annual assemblies provided social support, affirmation, and sustenance that, before the emergence of women's ministerial groups within denominations, was perhaps the only such support available for otherwise relatively isolated women ministers. In addition, since 1922 it has continuously published a periodical, the *Woman's Pulpit* (*WP*), which until the post–1970 burst of interest in female clergy constituted the most comprehensive repository of information about the status of gender equality in religious denominations around the world. Moreover, it is one of the very few national, interdenominational professional associations of clergy—male or female—that has ever existed in the United States. Examining the IAWM's history thus provides an opportunity to document its personal significance to members and its significance as disseminator of information about gender equality in religion, as well as an opportunity to reflect on the relative importance of gender and denomination as bases for professional identity among female clergy.

The IAWM was organized in 1919 in St. Louis as the International Association of Women Preachers; it began publishing the *Woman's Pulpit* in 1922. The organization's founder and driving force during its first several decades was M. Madeline Southard (1877–1967), a Methodist preacher from Kansas. Southard earned a master's degree from Garrett Seminary in 1919, and her thesis, "The Attitude of Jesus toward Women," was published in 1928. She also taught at Taylor University and published another book, *The White Slave Traffic versus the American Home.*[3] Southard worked as a lay evangelist in the United States and as a missionary in the Philippines and India, and she was a delegate to the 1920 and 1924 General Conferences of the Methodist Episcopal Church. She was president of the IAWM from 1919 until 1939 except for the four years she was overseas, and she spoke at the association's annual assembly until well into the 1950s.[4]

This essay is based primarily on a close reading of seventy-five years of *Woman's Pulpit.* The periodical, published between four and six times a year during that period, includes profiles of women clergy; letters from members; book reviews; announcements of meetings of women clergy and reports about those meetings; articles on topics and events of interest to women ministers; listings of "resources for ministry"; sermons, poems, essays, and meditations; brief announcements of important events, both personal and professional, in members' lives; and, occasionally, job opportunities. Two features occupy much space: reports on the status of women in denominations around the world and announcements or reports about the association's annual assembly.

The Social Base of the IAWM

Throughout the association's history, the vast majority of IAWM members have been functioning female clergy. In its early days, most members were Methodist, midwestern, college-educated, and progressive. There were strong ties both to the Woman's Christian Temperance Union (WCTU) and to the world of foreign missions. Many early members were conscious of being part of an elite vanguard and concerned with maintaining standards of excellence and respectability.

Over time, the group has become more denominationally and regionally diverse. Its temperance emphasis has faded, but its ties to worldwide ecumenism and missions remain strong. Its geographical base has shifted eastward to Pennsylvania and has become more international. Its denominational base is no longer as Methodist, but membership remains predominantly liberal Protestant, whether Presbyterian, Methodist, or United Church of Christ. The group of educated, accomplished, and progressive women is now self-consciously part of a larger women's movement.

Geography

During the 1920s, almost half of the association's 150 to 200 members were from Kansas, Illinois, and Nebraska. A strong midwestern base was still evident during the 1970s. In 1975 almost one-quarter of the group's approximately four hundred members lived in Illinois, Indiana, and Ohio, but membership had begun to spread out. No one state had more than 9 percent of the membership in 1975, and a fifth of the membership was from California, New York, and Pennsylvania. Also noteworthy is that 8 percent of the membership lived outside the United States by 1975. By the late 1990s, the IAWM had a solid base in Pennsylvania (18 percent of the approximately 250 members), and 21 percent of its members lived outside the United States. Never had there been more than a smattering of members from southern states.[5]

The shifting geographical base of the association can be seen in other ways. State auxiliaries were formed in Nebraska, Kansas, and Illinois by 1922. The practice of organizing regional units seems to have declined but was revived in 1974, when "the first two regional members of the association, Ohio and Indiana," were received. Since then, regional associations have been organized in Delaware, southwestern Pennsylvania, Iowa, Vermont, Western Canada, England, and Australia. In 1977 a historian of the New England Association of Women Ministers (NEWMA) noted that until the 1950s the IAWM "was essentially a mid-western fellowship as ours is a New England group." Beginning in 1953, and especially during the 1960s and early 1970s, the membership and leadership of NEWMA and the IAWM overlapped substantially. Still, the New England group voted in 1977 not to join the IAWM as a regional association but rather to retain its autonomous existence.[6]

The increasing internationalization of the IAWM is evident in where the group chose to meet as well as its membership figures. The first meeting outside the United States was in Canada in 1971. Since then, the association has met outside the United States six times, four of them—in England (1974, 1987), Scotland (1991), and Hungary (1996)—outside North America.

Although the internationalization of membership seems a real post–1970 change, the IAWM has had an international focus from its beginning. The *WP* has always covered developments in the ecclesiastical status of women around the world, and the association has had ongoing relationships with analogous groups in other countries. The IAWM, for example, has been in contact with the comparable British association, the Society for the Minis-

try of Women, at least since the 1930s. When IAWM member Florence
Schleicher Teed visited Europe in the fall of 1937, she met with the leaders of
groups of women ministers in England, Switzerland, and the Netherlands.
Moreover, the association and its members always have had ties to international organizations of various sorts. IAWM member Annalee Stewart led the
U.S. delegation to the International Congress of the Women's International
League for Peace and Freedom held in Luxembourg in 1946. After 1948 WP
closely followed developments in the World Council of Churches (WCC), and
the association twice—in 1954 and 1983—arranged its annual assembly to coincide with that group's meetings.[7]

The IAWM's international ecumenical focus took root in the missions
movement. Many of the group's early leaders were involved in missions and
spent time overseas. Eighteen of the thirty-three prominent members profiled
in 1945 (55 percent) were active in missions work, and brief WP biographies
of other members throughout the period often indicate the same connection. In its early years, the association "commissioned Dr. Ruth Kroft Hol-
man as a missionary to Guam, where she served in medical and evangelistic
work for two years." As time went on, mission connections developed into
close ties with the international ecumenical movement. As Zikmund notes,
"The group was always aggressively ecumenical." In addition to arranging
assemblies and devoting substantial attention to the WCC in the pages of WP,
the association sent two delegates to the council's meetings in 1991; at least
seven other members were present at the same meetings. The association's
roots in the missions movement explain its early international focus, and its
missions legacy is evident in the group's post–1970 internationalization of
membership, programming for assemblies, and continuing ties to worldwide
ecumenism.[8]

Denomination

More than 40 percent of the IAWM's early members were Methodist Episcopal. Although sixteen different denominations were represented among
members in 1923, no other denomination had more than 10 percent of the
membership in that year. The Methodist dominance of the association during its early decades can also be seen in WP's detailed reporting of the struggle for gender equality within that denomination. Madeline Southard was
actively involved—speaking on the floor of the General Conference—in the
1920 struggle that resulted in women winning the right to be granted licenses
to preach. Florence Resor Jardine, the association's president from 1939 to
1943, presented the minority report that recommended full clergy rights for

women at the uniting conference of the Methodist Church in 1939. The prominent roles that Southard and Jardine played in Methodist developments were proudly recounted in *WP* throughout the 1950s; no other denomination's events received so much first-hand attention. As a 1947 resolution memorializing the Methodist General Conference to "give qualified women ministers equal status with men ministers" began, "Since a considerable proportion of our members are Methodist women ministers."[9]

The IAWM's early connections to Methodism also are evident in its close ties to the temperance movement; it continued to pass anti-liquor resolutions into the 1950s. Madeline Southard "swung an ax with Carrie Nation," and the founding assembly of the association occurred immediately after a WCTU meeting that several of the original members had attended. An early Southard biographer reports that the IAWM was formed "after consultation with Miss Anna Gordon, National and World President of the [WCTU]." Many early members were active in the WCTU, and WCTU leaders, including Ida Wise Smith, were also members of the IAWM. In 1944 it had passed a resolution "deploring the lowering of our country's morale, especially as connected with our youth, by the liquor traffic." By 1947 the group was still prohibitionist: "As total abstainers from the use of intoxicating liquors," the IAWM went "on record as favoring legislation to prohibit the manufacture, use and sale of intoxicating liquor in all of its forms." In 1957 members resolved that the association should "stand for the Christian principle of total abstinence from the use of alcoholic beverages" and in addition oppose "interstate advertising of alcoholic beverages." Members were to "call upon the women of America to reject any recipe which requires the use of alcoholic beverage."[10] This part of the association's roots, although visible and important during its first several decades, seems not to be part of the contemporary IAWM.

By the 1990s, the IAWM was not quite so Methodist in orientation, although it was still dominated by mainstream Protestants. Its officers and executive board included four Presbyterians, two Methodists, two Baptists, two Lutherans, one each from the United Church of Christ and the Disciples of Christ, and representatives from denominations in England, Canada, Scotland, Hungary, and Switzerland. Still, more than half the U.S. membership was from just three denominations: Presbyterian, Methodist, and United Church of Christ.[11]

Social Class

The IAWM has always been an organization of well-educated, accomplished women, particularly its early leadership. *WP* reported in 1923 that "a large proportion of our women are college graduates, some holding Master's and Doctor's degrees. The women who led in forming our Association were college women." The 1939 executive board included Hazel Foster, who held a doctoral degree from the University of Chicago and was administrative dean of the Presbyterian College of Christian Education, and Iva Durham Vennard, a graduate of Wellesley College and the president of the Chicago Evangelistic Institute. Seven of the twenty "well known members" profiled in *WP* in 1945 had attended elite schools, earned a doctorate degree, or written books: Lucy Ayres, Victoria Booth Demarest, Elizabeth Wilson, Florence Schleicher Teed, Iva Vennard, Hilda Ives, and Georgia Harkness. Only Demarest and Harkness did not serve as officers of the IAWM. "A number of our members have written books of interest" *WP* noted in 1944, and it encouraged them to send in the books for review. A 1945 issue listed thirty-eight publications by fifteen different members. As Zikmund observes, the association "has aggressively supported the highest standards of education for ministry."[12]

Throughout its history, the IAWM has been a professional association whose leadership is well connected to the organizational centers of American and international Protestantism. In 1960 the association acted as an "advisory patron" of *Who's Who of American Women,* and at least nineteen IAWM members are listed in the volume. During the mid–1960s, its president was among the thirty-five national presidents of women's professional organizations invited to an annual Congress of American Women Leaders called by the National Business and Professional Women's Clubs. It was also represented at the National Council of Churches Commission on Women in Ministry in 1974. The association was co-sponsor of the conference "Two Hundred Years of Feminism in Religion in the United States" in 1976 and co-chaired the National Council of Churches Consultation of Ethnic Women in Ministry in 1977. Moreover, several IAWM members attended World Council of Churches meetings in 1991.[13]

Exclusiveness and Inclusiveness

One manifestation of the IAWM's social class composition has been its culture of educated respectability, which at times took the form of self-conscious exclusiveness. That culture—and its decline—is evident in several aspects. From the association's origins, full and "active" membership has been limited to "women licensed, ordained, or otherwise authorized as preachers." Others could join by means of various additional categories. In 1932, for example, one could be an active, associate, affiliated, fraternal, supporting, or memorial member, although only active members were able to vote or hold office. The criterion for being an active member is still the same, and additional membership categories (retired, student, fraternal, and sustaining) also remain basically unchanged. In 1985, however, the association voted to allow members from any category to hold office. It was a "basic change in the philosophy of IAWM membership."[14]

The process of joining the association also became less exclusive. In 1932 the rule was that "application for membership shall be accompanied by payment of the annual dues, and names of two suitable references." By 1947 three new members were said to "come to our Association recommended as sincere, charming, refined, and intensely Christian." Another was recommended as "one who has done hard and good work in the churches to which she has ministered." She was described as a "woman of excellent character, fine ability and devotion, and a minister of good standing in her own brotherhood." Among the business conducted at the 1957 assembly was "consideration of seven applicants for membership . . . and two applicants for associate membership." Membership in the IAWM still required recommendation as late as 1973. Only after that year was it possible to join by clipping a form published in *WP* and mailing it in along with dues. The requirement that membership applications include the names of two references was finally dropped from the constitution in 1986.[15]

That the association was concerned with respectability during its first several decades is evident in other ways. There seems to have been debate in 1923 concerning whether to make the membership criteria more stringent by limiting full membership to women who were fully ordained, college-educated, or who met some sort of doctrinal standard. Southard resisted that effort. "Any doctrinal test [for membership] other than evangelical faith," she wrote in 1923, "would seem impossible." Similarly, admitting only those who are ordained "would defeat one of our purposes in organizing. There are several denominations represented in our membership that give no recognition whatever to women as preachers, yet individual members are preaching with power. . . . We advise them to remain in their own churches and pioneer the way for ecclesiastical recognition." Following Southard's preferences, membership remained unencumbered by "doctrinal, educational, and various other tests." At the same time, Southard had reassurance about standards: "We have been very careful in our membership. Some applicants have had to be rejected. Some have been so clearly eligible that it has not been considered necessary to write to the references given. When there was any doubt we have so written and made other investigation. And personally we feel very happy to be in touch with such a company of refined, efficient, intelligent and spiritual women as compose our Association." This theme—

that members of the IAWM were a select group of "refined, efficient, intelligent and spiritual" women—was present throughout the 1950s. As the group was described in 1941, "The membership of our association is necessarily small. Our standard is a high one, as we aim for quality rather than quantity." In 1953 it was called "an organization made up of a *carefully screened* membership of ministers, evangelists, missionaries and theologians."[16]

The significance of the insistence on respectability appears to be that it differentiated IAWM members from Pentecostal women preachers and from feminist "fanatics." The boundary was occasionally explicit. Florence Teed opened a 1938 report on her European travels by reflecting on the differences between the situation of women ministers in the United States and those in Europe:

> One of the greatest anticipations of my trip to Europe last Fall was that of meeting women ministers in the various countries visited. Now that I am back and can reflect there is one thing in particular they and we here in the states do not have in common: they have no "Aimee" nor any of her school. And before one gets an entree with these well trained women of serious mien one must give evidence that she is "schooled" and a bona-fide minister and not a mere sensationalist seeking headlines and hiding behind the prefix "the Reverend" to gain admission to their august assemblies, or bidding for entertainment by them at some social function.[17]

That sentiment was reflected by the IAWM's membership, which did not—and still does not—include Pentecostal preaching women.

The salience of the other side of the boundary is evident in a column written by a new member of the association after she had attended the assembly in 1925:

> Earnest friends tried to discourage me from joining any organization which encouraged women preachers, fearing lest I became entangled with fanatics and cranks. Indeed from a few contacts with certain women, I am aware there are grounds for considerable caution . . . I went [to the IAWM assembly], very cautious, a trifle apprehensive, and with a double armour around my conservatism. . . . No, you are not fanatics; no, you are not cranks; far from it! . . . You are true women, womanly women, all of you are mothers in spirit, most of you are mothers of living children. . . . It was encouraging to ascertain that our association is being carried forward by the highest type of high minded cultured educated consecrated evangelical Christian women.[18]

The IAWM was an association for "high minded cultured educated consecrated evangelical Christian women." In this way, they carved out a space in the 1920s and 1930s between Pentecostal preaching women on the one hand and feminist "cranks" on the other hand. The IAWM, in this sense, was a manifestation of liberal feminism within American religion—the emphasis was on equal opportunity for women within existing organizations (including religious denominations), not on radical transformation of those organizations.

The IAWM as an Organization

Size, Prominence, and Member Recruitment

The IAWM has always been a small organization. From the original group of twenty-nine charter members, it grew rapidly during its first few years and reached a membership of 187 in 1923. After that it grew more slowly, reaching a peak of nearly four hundred during the 1970s. Then membership began to decline. In 1996 its membership was 268. Active membership was even smaller. Only one-half to two-thirds of the listed membership paid dues in any given year, and the pages of *WP* constantly contained pleas for members to pay up. The core membership included those who attended the annual assemblies, usually between thirty and forty individuals. Assembly reports in *WP* often carry the comment that "our numbers are never large."[19]

By any measure, the IAWM is a small organization that is apparently in decline. During the 1920s, approximately 10 percent of the female ministers in the country belonged.[20] Given that almost half of the membership was Methodist in those early years, it is likely that the IAWM contained a reasonably large proportion of Methodist female ministers. By the 1970s, the proportion of active female ministers was much smaller. More important than a numerical decline, however, was what appeared to be a decline in the association's prominence as a representative organization of women ministers.

Until the 1950s, the IAWM had been recognized as *the* organization of women ministers and *the* authority on the subject of female clergy. Even if *WP* exaggerated in 1923 that, because of the "Associated Press on our tail," thousands of items concerning women's preaching have been published," it is clear that IAWM assemblies during the 1920s received wide press coverage, particularly from the wire services. The association also contributed to the Federal Council of Churches' *Women in American Church Life* (1949) and to a WCC publication, *Summary of Facts about the Ordination of Women* (1958). Hazel Foster was asked to write the "Ordination of Women" entry for the *Schaff-Herzog Encyclopedia of Religious Knowledge* (1955) and reported that, as director of research for the IAWM, "again this past year [she had] been asked for information by persons working on papers in the field of women in the ministry." Such recognition continued at least into the early 1960s. The association's 1955 annual assembly was reported in *Time* magazine, and a *Newsweek* article in 1965 on women ministers quoted the association's president, Eva Henderson.[21] With the rise of denominational associations for women ministers after 1970, the IAWM seemed to lose its position as the most prominent organization of female clergy.

Although there were periodic calls for focused effort at new member recruitment throughout the IAWM's history, they became more frequent after the 1960s. More significantly, the calls revealed increasing awareness that potential new members were now more likely to be found in seminaries rather than pulpits.

Early efforts at member recruitment focused on informing practicing female ministers about the work of the association. One recommendation urged in 1930 "that a letter be prepared by the President, stating the object of this organization, the same to be sent to all ordained Evangelical women by the denominational representative, to the end that all women ministers may become acquainted with this Association." Similar efforts were initiated in 1940 and again in 1957, this time directed at the "great many women ministers, especially those in isolated areas, [who] do not know that there is an Association of this type to which they may belong."[22]

By the late 1960s, it became clear that something new was happening. Women began to attend seminaries in larger numbers, and the IAWM consequently directed more of its attention toward them. Although encouraging young women called to the ministry has been an explicit goal of the association from its beginning, after the mid–1960s that objective received even more attention. The association received a Lilly Endowment grant in 1965, for example, to support "the development of a program of internships for young women interested in entering the ministry." A 1971 *WP* article noted that "beyond the bounds of the denominational organizations, there are various developments of which the IAWM should be aware, and with which we should find means of co-operation. There is a movement toward organization among women students on Seminary campuses." A report of the 1972 assembly highlighted four female seminarians, who, as a headline put it, voiced "Hopes, Views, [and] Protests."[23]

Such efforts notwithstanding, the most significant aspect of the association's post–1970 membership history was its inability to connect in meaningful ways to increasing numbers of women seminarians. Membership began to decline during the mid–1970s, exactly when the female population of seminaries began to increase dramatically. The decline was especially striking when compared to the signs of organizational vitality elsewhere among women ministers and seminarians. Women United in Theologizing and Action, for example, emerged in 1978 from a group of female seminarians and faculty that met annually "to explore theology from the ground of their experience and work toward developing more fully their own ability to shape religious and social institutions to which they belong."[24]

Most striking in this regard, however, is the obvious vitality of the female clergy who organized within denominations after 1970. Three hundred attended the National Consultation of Ordained Women in the United Methodist Church in 1975, seven hundred in 1983, and nine hundred in 1992. In 1979, 130 Disciples of Christ women met in connection with the denomination's General Assembly. Fifty United Church of Christ clergywomen met in 1980 and organized their own national association in 1983. In 1982 fifty women attended a meeting of Friends Women in Public Ministry. Sixty African Methodist Episcopal women met in 1983 for a women's conference on ministry, and National Baptist women organized nationally in 1984. The National Association of Presbyterian Clergywomen had 485 members in 1990—one of every four Presbyterian clergywomen—and 120 attended that year's meeting. Four hundred Wesleyan-Holiness women met at the first International Wesleyan-Holiness Women Clergy Conference in 1994.[25] Comparing such organizational vitality with the IAWM's post–1970 membership decline raises a question: Why did the association remain small and even decline during a period of growth in the numbers of female clergy?

Purposes

Throughout its existence, the IAWM's central concerns have been to publish *WP* and organize an annual assembly. Its stated purposes have also remained constant. In 1922, "The primary purpose of the Association of Women Preachers [was] to develop the spirit of fellowship among women who are preaching." In 1923 Southard reported: "Another purpose that developed as we planned and prayed was to secure equal opportunity for women in the ecclesiastical world. Our Association can honestly claim the obtaining of the license for women to preach in the Methodist Episcopal Church as a direct result of its work, and it is working toward some other things that will be revealed later." In addition, the association was "to encourage young women whom God has called to preach." Although not wholly unattended in the group's history, that goal seems to have been of a lower priority than the others. All continue to remain important and have been joined by two others: "to urge women to grow as women in ministry" and "to urge women to participate in continuing education for efficiency in Christian ministry."[26]

Of these stated purposes, the first—fellowship—has been most fully realized in practice. Throughout *WP*'s first several decades, its pages were often filled with letters that testified to the group's significance in providing support for women otherwise isolated in their work. After the 1942 assembly, for example, readers reported:

> Who has more in common than lone "Women Preachers?" What a delight to get together and share our natural woes and interests—also ambitions for the advancement of Women's ministry.

> Dear Member Who Has Never Attended Assembly: How I wish I could find words to make you understand why I think it is worth any sacrifice to be able to attend! This is no mere convention. It is a spiritual feast.

> When one has spent all of one's ministerial life among the opposite sex, being politely (and sometimes not so politely) put in one's place by the male of the species, it is indeed a joy to be in a meeting where one is a preacher among preachers.

> I went to the Assembly broken hearted and discouraged—I came away with a joy and peace in my heart such as I had never experienced before and a new determination to live and work for my Master with renewed trust and faith knowing that His way leads on to victory.

A current member adds:

> It is not possible to understand unless you've been there how desperate one becomes for the company of just one other individual in the struggle. I read about IAWM in an ad in Christian Century when I was in my first pastorate . . . a church of sixty-five members in a town of six hundred people in Iowa farm country, fifteen miles from the Missouri line. Seeing the ad was like a drowning person spotting a life raft.

As Zikmund puts it, the IAWM "provided some very simple things for people who felt isolated and unsupported in their work." The group's significance as a source of social support for a small group of core members should not be underestimated.[27]

The significance of the association's other major purpose—advocacy—is more difficult to assess. On the one hand, it is clear that IAWM members, as individuals, have been activists in denominational conflicts over gender equality throughout the association's history. On the other hand, the group's collective action appears primarily limited to passing resolutions and sending letters to denominational leaders and assemblies in support of increased gender equality. That pattern was established early. Southard's claim in 1923—"the obtaining of the license for women to preach in the Methodist Episcopal Church [is] a direct result of [the association's] work"—probably should be understood as referring to her individual actions at the 1920 General Conference rather than to any collective and organized action of the IAWM. Beginning with Southard, several individual members have had distinguished records of activism. In addition to Florence Resor Jardine's efforts at the 1939 Methodist General Conferences, Hazel Foster, long the author of *WP* reports on the eccesiastical status of women, helped initiate an eventually successful effort during the 1940s that established the status of "commissioned church worker" within the Presbyterian church. More recently, Betty Bone Schiess, one of the eleven women "irregularly" ordained in the Episcopal church in 1974, was president of the association from 1985 to 1987.[28]

Collectively, the IAWM's support for gender equality in religion and other spheres has been unequivocal. Southard, who considered the group to be in the vanguard of a progressive movement for such gender equality, set the tone in 1924: "Pioneers in any movement for righteousness are always of finest calibre, the hardships are too severe for others to endure. This new outreaching of evangelical women toward the ministry is undoubtedly the greatest pioneer movement of the present age. The annual assembling of ourselves together to rightly guide such a tremendous force as we are destined to become is a mental and spiritual necessity." It is in that spirit that the IAWM has directed resolutions and correspondence at denominational assemblies throughout its history. Among many issues on which it has taken a stand have been to ask the Methodist General Conference in 1944 "to grant women an ecclesiastical status equal to that of men"; to pass resolutions in 1955 calling for gender equality in the Presbyterian Church USA and in the Methodist church; and to encourage the ordination of women in the Reformed Church in America in 1976.[29]

The IAWM's progressivism extended beyond a single issue, however. In addition to involvement in temperance and alcohol-related causes, during World War II the association "started a campaign for the appointment of women chaplains." It was, it declared, "a great injustice which affects every woman preacher." The group encouraged writing to Congress about the issue, even providing names of appropriate legislators. At the same time, the association supported the efforts of female doctors to secure medical commissions in the army and navy. In 1947 the association expressed support for jailed conscientious objectors and opposition to universal military conscription. Several IAWM leaders were among the members of the national Woman's Committee to Oppose Conscription. In addition, the association has been consistently and explicitly opposed to racial discrimination. In 1949 it resolved that it is "contrary to every Christian principle to entertain any race

prejudice or discrimination," and antiracist resolutions were passed throughout the 1950s and 1960s. Before 1961 the IAWM also passed resolutions supporting the Equal Rights Amendment and the United Nations and opposing nuclear tests.[30]

The IAWM spoke out on an even broader range of issues during the 1960s.
In addition to resolutions calling for greater gender equality in church and
society, it called for banning nuclear weapons (1960), supported the seating
of China in the United Nations (1962), deplored U.S. involvement in the Viet-
nam War (1967), and urged accelerated withdrawal of U.S. troops (1969).
Resolutions on issues other than gender equality seemed to lessen during the
1970s, perhaps reflecting a backlash among the membership.[31] They resumed
during the 1980s, however, and still continue. The association has endorsed
the boycott of California grapes (1985), supported restoration of the Civil
Rights Act (1985), urged sanctions against South Africa (1986), affirmed the
Sanctuary movement (1986), opposed the build-up of nuclear arms (1986),
deplored the Supreme Court's decision upholding laws against sodomy (1986),
and opposed legislation revoking or limiting access to safe and legal abortions (1989). Although the IAWM has always firmly supported gender equality and been on the progressive side of other social issues, during the 1960s
(and again after 1980) it seemed to devote more attention to a broader range
of concerns. By the 1970s, the association was no longer anxious to differen-
tiate itself from feminism. On the contrary. As Zikmund puts it, since the
1970s the IAWM "has considered itself part of the contemporary women's
movement."[32]

Beyond passing resolutions, the IAWM has only rarely organized or engaged in collective political action. On occasion, *WP* exhorted readers, for
example, to "seek to open wide the doors of opportunity for coming generations."[33] The only direct efforts at mobilizing the IAWM membership for
political action, however, were a World War II campaign in favor of female
military chaplains and a "Message for Methodist Women" of 1948 that encouraged them to send a memorial asking the General Conference "to consider admitting women as full members in the annual conferences."[34] Effective advocacy associated with the IAWM was almost always that of individual
members rather than collective organization via the association. That is not
surprising given the association's chronic lack of funds and the logistical
difficulties, especially earlier in the century, of organizing collective action
among a small, scattered membership.

The IAWM has served another purpose, perhaps its most important collective contribution to the broader struggle for gender equality in religion.
The association in general, and the *WP* in particular, have been, at least un-

til a post–1970s' growth of scholarly attention to female clergy, a major repository of interdenominational information about the status of women in U.S. religion. The fact-filled, wide-ranging reports in *WP*—especially Hazel Foster's, which appeared from the late 1930s through the early 1960s—extensively document the ecclesiastical status of women. Now, after several decades of historical and sociological research on women and religion, it may be difficult to appreciate the importance of the association's efforts to gather and disseminate information about women's access to religious leadership.

Conclusion

In this chapter, I have attempted to provide a basic descriptive introduction to the IAWM, an organization that until 1970 was the primary manifestation of collective identity for women ministers. If there is a puzzle in the IAWM's history, it lies in the fact that the association did not grow in numbers and prominence as the number of women ministers grew after 1970. The post-1970 emergence and strength of denominational organizations of female clergy indicate that there was and is no shortage of demand for a professional association. Well before denominational organizations arose, the IAWM was there and, presumably, could have been strengthened by the influx of women into seminaries and remained the primary organizational vehicle of female clergy in the United States. But that did not happen. The social movement for gender equality in religion overtook and bypassed the association. The movement and the organization crossed but did not join paths.

Occasional calls for widespread member recruitment notwithstanding, it seems that throughout the association's history what recruiting that did occur was almost completely by way of the personal ties of current members. A chronic shortage of funds and the fact that its leadership was almost always composed of women ministers who had demanding, full-time jobs placed real limits on the IAWM's organizational activities, including new member recruitment. Consequently, recruitment occurred mainly through personal connections and did not reach much beyond the personal networks of core members. Friendship networks tend to be age-segregated, and it is difficult to cross generations by means of recruitment that relies on such networks. Hence, overreliance on members' personal networks hampered the association's ability to recruit members from seminaries and from younger generations of women ministers after 1970. Membership patterns followed the contours of the core membership's social networks rather than the contours of the broader movement of women into the clergy.[35]

There also appears to have been a broader generational shift. Although waning by the 1970s, the association's continued emphasis on qualifications and standards likely did not help efforts to attract post–1970 seminarians. The serious, legitimate concerns of a previous generation of women ministers striving for the respect of a suspicious world have not, since the 1970s, been widely shared by female seminarians. *WP*, for example, in 1970 published the "Guidelines for Proper Use of the American Association of Women Ministers Pin." The pin could be "purchased on the authority of the emblem permit card received by each new member." In addition, it could be "pinned on a suit coat when it substitutes for a dress [but it] should not be worn on an academic gown or clergy robe [nor] used as jewelry on a lapel, on a chain around the neck, as a charm on a bracelet, or in any utilitarian manner."[36] It is not difficult to see how such generation-specific concerns could have undermined the association's sincere efforts to find recruits among recent cohorts of women ministers and seminarians. The generational shift in the carriers of the movement for gender equality in religion was evident more generally during the conflicts of the 1970s over women's ordination.[37]

Moreover, and perhaps most important, it seems likely that the denominational structuring of American religion is partly responsible for the IAWM's inability to attract more recent cohorts of women ministers. As Zikmund observed of the 1970s, "What seems to be happening is that the long-awaited response of denominational structures to women in ministry has captured the loyalties and energies of the younger women. As special commissions, offices and task forces on women are created by major denominations, women in ministry caucus and work within denominational judicatories."[38] To put the point slightly differently, clergy careers still occur largely within denominational boundaries, which poses a huge obstacle to organizing a national professional association of clergy. Given the scholarly emphasis on the declining significance of denominations for laity, however, it seems worth pointing out that denominational identity, for better or worse, is alive and well among U.S. clergy.

The small size of the IAWM thus indicates a more general phenomenon that is partly responsible not only for the shift to denominational associations for female clergy but also for the declining status of clergy in the "professional system" of the United States. There is no national professional association of clergy analogous to the American Medical Association, the American Bar Association, or the American Sociological Association. The continuing salience of denominations seems to hamper not just gender-based professional organizing but any sort of interdenominational professional organizing among clergy. It is ironic that the more genuine career opportunities there are for women within denominations, the less interest there appears to be in an interdenominational professional association. Consequently, the IAWM began to decline just as it might have been expected to expand.

From that perspective, the association's more than seventy-five years of continuous existence as a national, interdenominational, professional association for women ministers seems a significant accomplishment. There is, after all, no vibrant national, interdenominational, professional association of clergy—male or female—other than the IAWM. The degree to which it, for a time, successfully overcame denominational boundaries is perhaps more impressive than its inability to overcome them even more. The association's history points to the continuing importance of denomination as a basis for the professional identity of clergy, male or female. At the same time, it is equally important that only on the basis of gender has a national, interdenominational, professional association of clergy had any degree of success.

Notes

Thanks to Margaret Bendroth, Virginia Brereton, Elizabeth Sykes, and members of the *Women in Twentieth-Century Protestantism* working group for helpful comments on a draft of this chapter.

1. For representative historical work, see Virginia Lieson Brereton and Christa Ressmeyer Klein, "American Women in Ministry: A History of Protestant Beginning Points," in *Women in American Religion*, ed. Janet Wilson James (Philadelphia: University of Pennsylvania Press, 1980), 171–90; Rosemary Radford Ruether and Rosemary Skinner Keller, eds., *Women and Religion in America*, vol. 3: *1900–1968* (San Francisco: Harper and Row, 1986); Catherine Wessinger, ed., *Religious Institutions and Women's Leadership: New Roles inside the Mainstream* (Columbia: University of South Carolina Press, 1996); and Carl Schneider and Dorothy Schneider, *In Their Own Right: The History of the American Clergywoman* (New York: Crossroad, 1997). For representative sociological work, see Jackson W. Carroll, Barbara Hargrove, and Adair Lummis, *Women of the Cloth: A New Opportunity for the Churches* (San Francisco: Harper and Row, 1983); Sherryl Kleinman, *Equals before God: Seminarians as Humanistic Professionals* (Chicago: University of Chicago Press, 1984); Edward C. Lehman, Jr., *Gender and Work: The Case of the Clergy* (Albany: SUNY Press, 1993); Paula Nesbitt, *Feminization of the Clergy in America: Occupational and Organizational Perspectives* (New York: Oxford University Press, 1997); Barbara Brown Zikmund et al., *Clergy Women: An Uphill Calling* (St. Louis: Westminster/John Knox, 1998); and Mark Chaves, *Ordaining Women: Culture and Conflict in Religious Organizations* (Cambridge: Harvard University Press, 1997).

2. The only extant scholarly essay on the IAWM is Barbara Brown Zikmund, "The International Association of Women Ministers: Half a Century of Professional Solidarity," unpublished manuscript, no date. An appendix to Elsie Gibson, *When the Minister Is a Woman* (New York: Holt, Rinehart, and Winston, 1970) provides a brief history of the association.

3. The association has changed its name five times: Association of Women Preachers

of the United States of America (1922); Association of Women Preachers (1933); American Association of Women Preachers (1936); American Association of Women Ministers (1943); and International Association of Women Ministers (1970).

4. M. Madeline Southard, *The White Slave Traffic versus the American Home* (Louisville: Pentecostal Publishing, 1914); M. Madeline Southard, *The Attitude of Jesus toward Women* (New York: George H. Doran, 1928); *Woman's Pulpit* (hereafter *WP*), Jan.–Feb. 1940, Oct–Dec. 1994. Southard would make an interesting historical subject, and her three thousand journal pages, which cover the period from 1892 to 1967, are being edited by Carol Lynn Yellin. An assessment of Southard's individual reasons and goals for starting and pouring so much of her energy into the IAWM will have to await the publication of those journals. *Woman's Pulpit* is a newsletter, usually of eight pages, in which specific items do not always have either titles or named authors. The notes that follow will cite the specific issues of *WP* from which factual material has been drawn, and page numbers are provided for direct quotations.

5. *WP*, April 1923, July–Sept. 1975; IAWM 1997 Prayer Calendar.

6. *WP*, no month, 1922, Oct.–Dec. 1974, 8 (first quotation), April–June 1977, 6 (second quotation), Jan.–March 1978, Oct.–Dec. 1992.

7. *WP*, Nov.–Dec. 1936, March–April 1938, May–June 1938, July–Aug. 1946, April–June 1954, Jan.–March 1983.

8. *WP*, March–April 1945, July–Aug. 1945, 4 (first quotation), July–Sept. 1991; Zikmund, "International Association of Women Ministers," 9 (second quotation).

9. *WP*, April 1923, May–June 1939, Oct.–Dec. 1947, 3.

10. Author telephone interview with Carol Lynn Yellin, Jan. 9, 1997 (first quotation); *WP*, Jan.–Feb. 1940, 2 (second quotation), Nov.–Dec. 1944, 1 (third quotation), May–June 1945, Oct.–Dec. 1947, 3 (fourth quotation), Jan.–March 1958, 2 (fifth quotation), Oct.–Dec. 1994.

11. Author telephone interview with LaVonne Althouse, Jan. 9, 1997; IAWM 1997 Prayer Calendar.

12. *WP*, April 1923, 3 (first quotation), Nov. 1939, Sept.–Oct. 1944, 4 (second quotation), May–June 1945; Zikmund, "International Association of Women Ministers," 15 (third quotation).

13. *WP*, April–June 1960, Oct.–Dec. 1963, Jan.–March 1967, July–Sept. 1975, Jan.–March 1976, April–June 1977, July–Sept. 1991.

14. *WP*, Jan.–Feb. 1932, 4 (first quotation), March–April 1938, April–June 1986, 5 (second quotation).

15. *WP*, Jan.–Feb. 1932, 4 (first quotation), May–June 1947, 2 (second quotation), Oct.–Dec. 1957, 12 (third quotation), Oct.–Dec. 1973, April–June 1979, April–June 1986.

16. *WP*, April 1923, 3 (first quotation), July–Aug. 1941, 3 (second quotation), April–June 1953, 2 (third quotation, emphasis added).

17. *WP*, March–April 1938, 1.

18. *WP*, Dec. 1925, 3.

19. *WP*, Sept.–Oct. 1926, 1.

20. *WP*, Oct. 1923.

21. *WP*, April 1923, 3 (first quotation), Jan.–March 1950, Oct.–Dec. 1952, 2, Oct.–Dec. 1959; Inez M. Cavert, *Women in American Church Life: A Study Prepared under the Guid-*

ance of a Counseling Committee of Women Representing National Interdenominational Agencies (New York: Friendship Press, 1949); World Council of Churches, *Summary of Facts about the Ordination of Women in the Member Churches of the World Council of Churches* (Geneva: World Council of Churches, 1958); Lefferts A. Loetscher, ed., *Twentieth-Century Encyclopedia of Religious Knowledge: An Extension of the New Schaff-Herzog Encyclopedia of Religious Knowledge* (Grand Rapids: Baker Book House, 1955); "Words and Works," *Time,* Aug. 22, 1955, 42; "God—Male or Female?" *Newsweek,* July 12, 1965, 60.

22. *WP,* Sept.–Oct. 1930, 1 (first quotation), May–June 1940, Oct.–Dec. 1957, 2 (second quotation).

23. *WP,* April–June 1965, 4 (first quotation), July–Sept. 1971, 8 (second quotation), April–June 1972, 1 (third quotation).

24. *WP,* Jan.–March 1979, 5.

25. *WP,* Jan.–March 1975, Oct.–Dec. 1979, July–Sept. 1980, Oct.–Dec. 1982, April–June 1983, July–Sept. 1983, Oct.–Dec. 1984, July–Sept. 1990, July–Sept 1992, Oct.–Dec. 1994.

26. *WP,* Sept. 1922, 1 (first quotation), April 1923, 3 (second quotation); *The International Association of Women Ministers,* brochure, 1996 (third quotation).

27. *WP,* Nov.–Dec. 1942, 1–2; Elisabeth Sykes to author, Feb. 11, 1997 (personal correspondence); Zikmund, "International Association of Women Ministers," 4.

28. *WP,* April 1923, 3, March–April 1944, Oct.–Dec. 1980, July–Sept. 1996.

29. *WP,* June 1924, 4 (first quotation), Sept.–Oct. 1926, Jan.–Feb. 1944, 2 (second quotation), Oct.–Dec. 1955, July–Sept. 1976.

30. *WP,* Nov.–Dec. 1943, March–April 1944, 3 (first quotation), Jan.–Feb. 1943, 1 (second quotation), July–Aug. 1945, Oct.–Dec. 1947, Jan.–March 1949, 3 (third quotation), July–Sept. 1958, April–June 1960.

31. A 1967 letter to the editor notes, "Some of us were very unhappy about the political trend introduced by [the recent president]. . . . Some of us could never agree with admitting Red China to the United Nations and we didn't feel this had any place in our assemblies" (*WP,* July–Sept. 1967, 8). It is impossible to assess how widespread this sentiment was among the membership, but political resolutions seem to occur less frequently during the 1970s.

32. Zikmund, "International Association of Women Ministers," 9.

33. *WP,* Oct.–Dec. 1947, 7. Similar appeals appear in Oct.–Dec. 1952 and Jan.–March 1954.

34. *WP,* Jan.–March 1948, 7.

35. The practice by which current members recruit new members (mainly through preexisting social ties) also explains the somewhat idiosyncratic geographical bases of the membership over time. The shift from a strong base in Kansas to a strong base in Pennsylvania seems primarily a result of the location of leaders at different times.

36. *WP,* April–June 1970, 2.

37. For more detail on this generational shift, see Chaves, *Ordaining Women,* ch. 7, and Mark Chaves and James Cavendish, "Recent Changes in Women's Ordination Conflicts: The Effect of a Social Movement on Intraorganizational Controversy," *Journal for the Scientific Study of Religion* 36 (1997): 574–84.

38. Zikmund, "International Association of Women Ministers," 16.

PART 5

Women and Modernity

IT IS IMPOSSIBLE to write about women and religion in the twentieth century without engaging one of those grand concepts called variously (although not synonymously) "secularization" or "modernity" or the "disenchantment" of the world. In fact, it is hardly possible to speak about twentieth-century history more generally without invoking these terms and perhaps debating their provenance. But the issue is that much more pressing in regard to women, who all through the nineteenth century, and well into the twentieth, were construed as more religious and certainly more moral than men. As public life is more taken up with issues of technology, mass culture, and the trading of commodities, the question of women's special religiosity has become more pressing, interesting, and sometimes more poignant. To critics of the modern, Woman (the "good" woman at least) has sometimes seemed to be the embodiment of the traditional, of the organic community, and of ancient moral values.

Clearly, many factors operated during the twentieth century to contradict the feminine ideal and make women appear less connected to life of the spirit and more like men. We might say that in the twentieth century we witnessed a progressive disenchantment of women analogous to the disenchantment of the world that sociologists of religion have long talked about. There are all sorts of reasons for this. Thanks to Freud (and his interpreters, for example, Havelock Ellis in Ann Taves's essay), women, defined in the nineteenth century as lacking sexual feelings, have emerged as sexual beings. Even conservative evangelicals have come to acknowledge that women can and should enjoy their sexuality, albeit carefully confined within the bounds of marriage. Aspects of women's personalities that used to be seen as symptoms of their sinfulness—anger, ambition, desires, and jealousies—have come to be regarded as characteristics of well-rounded humanity—needing to be understood, expressed, and channeled in constructive ways but not suppressed or abolished. Women have become public persons, not only in the workplace but also in sports, in the media, at places of amusement, and even in war. They have become consumers par excellence. In many ways it seems as if women have become more like men (and vice versa) and as if the distinctions that still linger as a result of socialization might disappear after a generation or two of changed upbringing of daughters and sons.

The process of disenchantment continued throughout the twentieth century, hastened by men and women themselves and by forces beyond their control. In part the essays of this section document that disenchantment and move us beyond the clichés about women and modernity. They also raise questions about the "straight line"—almost predetermined—nature that is often ascribed to the disenchantment process. Writing from the vantage point of her familiarity with Catholic and Jewish leaders, Maureen Fitzgerald doubts whether Protestantism disappeared from women's reform efforts just because they switched to social scientific language to describe what they were doing and why. Taves deconstructs the notion of a "feminized religion" of the nineteenth century, upon which our arguments of disenchantment depend. She argues that there were (and are) as many varied meanings for feminized religion as there have been speakers. One result of these essays—although not necessarily intended by the writers—is to scramble the old nineteenth-century construction of two more or less distinct worlds: the secular, inhabited mainly by men (and working-class women and women of color), and the sacred, inhabited by middle-class white women. Modernity worked enormous changes in the twentieth-century religious history of American women, but it was not always easy to predict what those changes would be or what directions they would eventually take. Nor are we as ready as we once were to assume that modernity is, in any simple way, disenchanted.

13. Losing Their Religion: Women, the State, and the Ascension of Secular Discourse, 1890–1930

MAUREEN FITZGERALD

> We have recently grown accustomed to the realization that there is no purely human space which stands disclosed once we are free of the burden of religious illusion. However a more important consideration may be that there is no purely *secular* space, outside the constitutive opposition of this term to that of "the sacred." . . . On the contrary, the secular as a self-regulating, immanent space . . . is something sustained only by a conventional symbolic coding, and only . . . by imaginary identification do we take this space for the real itself.
>
> —John Milbank, "Problematizing the Secular"

IN A COURSE I TEACH each year on race and ethnicity in American history, I ask students on the first day to talk about how they define themselves ethnically or racially. Responses vary from "Mexican American," "Jewish," "Native American," "African American," and "Irish Catholic" to (sometimes in fun) "Mutt," meaning a distinct blend of Chinese, Italian, Polish, or other influences. Always fascinating, however, are the few who define themselves as "nothing." These students are invariably and visibly white and vaguely middle class. Their response is often a lament, because it distinguishes them from peers who have, in the estimation of the nothing group, a much more interesting personal and cultural history. An important part of the course that follows, however, encourages students to recognize that one could only claim "nothing" if one was squarely situated in the dominant racial or ethnic group, an identity so naturalized and normative in American society that it is not visible as a distinct racial or ethnic identity. It is also a position of extraordinary power. Other students claim the label of Mexican American or African American because they are well aware that they are viewed as outside the dominant culture. "Nothing," therefore, is really quite something.[1]

I use this story as an analogy in trying to introduce a very difficult topic, the study of the substantive content of the secular, particularly as female activists incorporated it into what we call the welfare state in the early twentieth century. In the minds of many Americans, the secular is nothing; it is not talk about God; one does not go to a church or synagogue or mosque to participate in it; and priests, ministers, and rabbis do not have cultural authority in defining it.[2] It is simply "not religious." In late-twentieth-century America, Christian fundamentalists often defined the liberals and leftists with whom they vied politically as secular humanists. At base in fundamentalist definitions of humanism is an accusation—that secular humanists look to the fallen, or human nature, in order to discern ultimate truth. This is a label many secular activists resist embracing, because it implies a conscious commitment to a specific ideology they are not sure exists, never mind deliberately espouse. That secular humanism drives their activism in ways comparable to fundamentalist Christianity's undergirding of the Christian Coalition's agenda, for instance, seems absurd. How could nothing influence them to a degree similar to the very substantial something of Christian fundamentalism?

Historicizing how predominantly white-middle-class, elite female activists incorporated some of the tenets of mainstream liberal Protestantism into the welfare state in the early twentieth century might help us acknowledge that a particular religious influence was important in American welfare-state formation and became so naturalized as to not be visible except to those self-defined as outsiders. In the Progressive Era (1890–1930), many "outsiders," including Catholics, Jews, conservative evangelical Protestants, and African American Protestants, identified the moral and political values being inscribed in the welfare state as at odds with their own religious traditions. Yet Progressive Era activists tended to deride those who were explicitly religious as "backward" and as retarding American "progress." They often assumed that their own reluctance to employ explicitly religious rhetoric was a mark of their liberation and tolerance, and heralded the advent of a better and more just society.

In the essay that follows, I will analyze secular thought, especially that apparent in women's Progressive Era social work, as having substantive content that was derivative of, if not identical to, mainstream Protestantism through the nineteenth century.[3] I will focus on the religious presumptions in two aspects of this work, the perfectionist ethos implicit in social science and social work thinking and the praxis evident in casework. "Casework," as it came to be called in the Progressive Era, was most intensively used in the female trajectory of the welfare state, predominantly in programs that focused on women and children. As a social work term and methodology, casework derived from both a social science perspective that emphasized investigation of social conditions and also from an individualist approach to the problems of poverty in America.

Women and the State

Identifying the religious and/or secular components of state ideology is particularly difficult when employing gender analysis. The primary methodological challenge for scholars of women and the state is to identify what the state *is*. For historians of women, moreover, the first question begs the corollary: What *was* the state? Historians concerned primarily with men, and uninterested in the gendered nature of state development, often characterize the state as an entity whose boundaries and scope are obvious: It is associated with the public sector rather than the private.[4] For historians of women, the existence of the public/private distinction is made endlessly complicated by our understanding that the dichotomy has been constructed and used to limit women's collective participation in the public, however "public" may be defined historically and across cultures.

Historians of women in nineteenth-century America have long held that the Anglo, Protestant, middle-class promotion of a newly emergent normative culture was heavily dependent upon the ideological gendering of public and private spheres.[5] In industrializing urban areas, white men and women of the Protestant middle class constructed figurative boundaries that clearly delineated appropriate forms of male and female work and masculine and feminine nature. Male work patterns in urban areas shifted as factories took both middle- and working-class men away from home and left women, especially middle-class women, consigned exclusively to the domestic sphere. The "home as haven" was defined by its difference from the public market, where worldly corruption, competitiveness, and chaos reigned. In turn, conceptions of normative femininity and masculinity were increasingly defined by the attributes of these ostensibly distinct spheres. Masculinity was associated more emphatically with market attributes, including individualism, competitiveness, aggression, and rationality. In contrast, femininity was increasingly defined as a balance to market attributes. Women were to be nurturing, warm, selfless, irrational, and the moral guardians who, especially through mothering, would provide stability against an outside, public world seemingly devoid of the moral principles Americans were thought to value. Women's exclusion from the public sphere was considered by many, including many women, to be necessary to protect them from the moral contagion of life outside the domestic haven and therefore ensure their own, and their families', moral and sexual purity.[6]

Moreover, this model of public and private was at least vaguely Protestant, even if the actors did not recognize it as such. Before the Protestant Reformation, a variety of European women had access to the public, including prostitutes and Catholic nuns. The presumption that women should be subordinate to an individual man in a private household, and that this was the only option available to adult women, was a new concept tied to the Reformation. As Lyndal Roper argues in her study of Reformation Augsburg, Protestantism was inseparable from a new emphasis on the household as the primary institution through which a gendered distribution of civic and moral authority was ordered. Women were integrated into Protestant societies as mothers, daughters, wives, and aunts—or in other words through their relationship to the male head of household. Nuns were characterized as disorderly because they claimed a home in the public sphere and sexually suspect because they refused to be defined through a male head of household. As Roper points out, Protestants publicly derided convents as institutions analogous to brothels, and women within convents were characterized as a special brand of prostitutes organized for Catholic priests' use. Protestant leaders, including and perhaps especially Martin Luther, held that women were naturally less rational and more vulnerable to temptation than men. He and others then cast convent life as an institution at odds with female salvation in that too much independence from men cast nuns down dangerous paths of temptation and irrationality. Throughout Reformation Europe, convents were closed, nuns' property was seized, and former nuns were "rescued" and then encouraged or forced to marry.[7]

In nineteenth-century America, especially the Northeast, the dichotomization of public and private at the advent of industrial capitalism not only ideologically relegated all adult women to the private sphere but also invested that sphere with increased religious significance. This shift, moreover, was consistent with what Clarissa Atkinson has termed the "sacralization of motherhood," a new emphasis on mothering as the primary means through which children learned the moral and religious values of Protestant middle-class culture.[8] Male ministers and institutional churches, although important links between the public and private, became far less important in this system than the growing collective influence of mothers throughout the nation. Protestant Americans were to learn moral and religious values less through institutional church structures and more through mothering within the home, thereby feminizing the reproduction of religious culture and sacralizing the nature and perception of motherhood itself.[9]

It was but a short step, although a significant one, for many white, middle-class, Protestant women to argue that such responsibility should be enhanced by corollary rights to influence the public. Women's role as moral guardians of the home, and, collectively, of the nation, legitimated their movement into the public sphere so as to lead and direct the clean-up of capitalism's excesses through charities, moral purity, and temperance. The relegation of Protestant women to motherhood and domesticity was not only a proscription that denied women social, political, and economic power comparable to men but also a rationale for demanding unprecedented political, economic, and social power. The insistence on a separation of spheres, and women's role in morally compensating for the havoc wrought by capitalist men in their unbridled search for profit, provided Protestant, female, middle-class women's rights activists, charitable workers, missionaries, and reformers with claims to a new type of public authority. Drawing on the traditions of "Republican Motherhood," middle-class Protestant women argued that the widespread poverty, prostitution, vice, and general suffering that had grown in tandem with urbanization and industrialization required that mothering be extended beyond the bounds of home so that the public, as well as the private, be endowed with the moral influence of women. Compassion, nurturance, and "mother love" were to balance the ruthless competition that had left so many victims, especially women and children, in its wake.[10]

Throughout the late nineteenth century, many middle-class and elite Protestant women's groups that influenced the development of the welfare state were nonprofessional and explicitly religious. The Woman's Christian Temperance Union, which grew enormously in the decades after the Civil War under the leadership of Frances Willard, provided a rationale for movement into the public sphere through a terse statement of principle, "For God, and Home, and Native Land."[11] The WCTU's "do everything" policy served as an umbrella for activisms as diverse as temperance prayer vigils, suffrage agitation, and countless small charities dedicated especially to relieving the suffering of women and children. Other white, Protestant, middle-class women increasingly shaped local and state laws on social purity and divorce reform; derived public funding for their work; and pushed for the expansion of government oversight and regulation of charities, industry, and food production. More elite Protestant women often played significant roles in urban Charity Organization Societies, which were composed almost exclusively of Protestants until the 1890s. As Paula Baker has observed, the myriad social movements constituting white, middle-class women's politics through the nineteenth century changed the nature of what we call the state.[12]

Without these women's movements, feminist scholars argue, the welfare state as we know it would not exist. Women therefore were not incorporated into a male conception of the state but instead shaped the nature of what "public" and "private" meant and therefore what the state was. The prescription that relegated middle-class white women to the private sector was therefore neither a reflection of their experience nor a static boundary line that represented physical space.[13] As Seth Koven has noted about similar movements in Britain, women's "voluntary activities depended upon but ultimately challenged the distinction between the state as the site of public political life and civil society as the location of private productive and reproductive activities. . . . [W]omen moved between the supposedly discrete spheres of public and private, revealing the artificiality of bipolar constructions of these categories."[14]

It is all the more curious, therefore, that historians of American women seem to accept uncritically a sharp break in the religious and secular content of this state formation. The field of American women's history tends to characterize women's public activism as religious in the nineteenth century, then abruptly and absolutely secular in the twentieth. Historians discussing the "do-everything" policies of the Woman's Christian Temperance Union in 1885 emphasize the Protestant evangelical membership, ethos, and ideological underpinnings of the group's work in myriad reforms.[15] Historians discussing the Mothers' Congress or General Federation of Women's Clubs at the turn of the century begin to drop analysis of religion per se despite the overlap with the WCTU in membership and political agendas. More prominent and elite female activists, such as Florence Kelley, Jane Addams, and those firmly situated in the "female dominion" so influential in Progressive reform movements, become entirely unhinged from religious movements or activism.[16]

There are, of course, some important differences in the self-identification of these groups and their willingness to ally themselves with specifically religious organizations. The Woman's Christian Temperance Union identified itself as Christian, whereas the General Federation of Women's Clubs did not. Moreover, it was the work of groups such as the WCTU that enabled the latter groups to drop the religious label. Having fought the battle to legitimate their right to public sphere activities by using Christian rhetoric, the WCTU carved a path through which their daughters and protégées could claim access to public space without a religious rationale at all.

Yet self-chosen labels should not be taken at face value; they are but the tip of the iceberg. The much larger dynamic of the social movements discussed is that white, Protestant, middle-class, and elite women were first invested with religious and moral authority over both children and men and then their activities, begun and shaped in accordance with religious values, were incorporated into what constituted the emerging welfare state. That is evidence not of the lack of religious influence on state formation but rather points to the religious roots of the ostensibly secular thought that shaped welfare-state policies, bureaucracies, and practices. The relative invisibility of the religious in this transition, moreover, constitutes secularization's most powerful contribution to a hegemonic state ideology. If it cannot be named, it cannot be contested. Embracing a social science perspective by which experts validated their work through claims of objectivity, Progressive Era–reformers used the relative invisibility of religious language and ideology in their work to compare themselves favorably to their predecessors, those they thought to be too quick to promote explicitly anti-Semitic and anti-Catholic policy.

Such claims of objectivity, however, should not stop us from examining the relationship between the ideological premises of ostensibly secular Progressive reform and the more explicitly religious Gilded Age charities. I will therefore focus on perfectionism and casework as a means of further defining what became the substantively religious nature of social work thought, or at least the source from which the scientific premises of social work derived. Inherent in much of the rhetoric and behavior of Progressive reformers was a deeply felt but not explicitly expressed belief in perfectionism. The attainment of knowledge, both to aid individuals and to steer movements for reform, was premised on the belief that knowing the "natural laws" that guided human behavior and society would lead ultimately to humanity's betterment—the creation of the "kingdom of God" on earth. Casework, although an apparently self-evident term that conveyed nothing more profound or threatening than a rather tedious compilation of facts and figures necessary to properly certify a social worker's expertise, was actually derived from ideological premises unique to liberal Protestant charitable work since the mid-nineteenth century. We can see that most clearly in the resistance of Catholics and Jews of the period to incorporating casework into their own charitable work. In both cases, the opposition to such secular reform was characterized by state activists as religious and therefore different from, and more self-interested than, those who eschewed religious labels entirely.

Perfectionism(s) and Casework

An essential idea in Progressive thought was a firm belief by a wide spectrum of activists that they could, especially by influencing social policy and influencing state formation directly, eradicate the causes of poverty and therefore end poverty itself. At root in this thinking was a fundamentally religious concept, the belief that the perfection imagined in heaven, the kingdom of God, was attainable on earth and that one's moral obligations entailed pursuing that perfection. This was, moreover, not a distinctly Protestant concept.

Rather, Catholics, Jews, and Protestants fought within their respective traditions and communities over the extent to which perfection could or should be pursued on earth. Most religious traditions have historically acknowledged the disparity between women's collective condition on earth and the promise of full equality in salvation, for instance, or the poor or sick's suffering on earth as a penance to be endured in the world but eradicated in the afterlife. Perfectionist movements go further and contend that the disparity need not exist and that it is possible to attain the conditions of heaven while still on earth. Perfectionist reformers, moreover, assume not only that the kingdom of God can be created on earth but also that there is a moral imperative to work toward that goal. The orthodox within each group, however, saw perfectionism as evidence of the fall.[17]

As Margaret Bendroth has argued, it was precisely the perfectionist strain in social science thinking and the state that so alarmed Protestant Christian fundamentalists in the early twentieth century. Bendroth holds that fundamentalists claimed as a "fundamental" principle that perfection on earth was ontologically impossible. Far worse, secular reformers looked to the human rather than the divine to discern basic truths. For conservative Protestants, therefore, work by such activists to attempt to achieve perfection in this world was actually evidence of the fall itself because it signified a falling away from God. Secular reformers, they argued, were carving a path through the morass by looking only to the fallen and not the divine, thereby leading humankind en masse to the cataclysms and Armageddon preceding the end of all time, the Second Coming, and ultimate judgment.[18]

Fundamentalist Protestants were substantially correct in noting that the expanding state of the Progressive Era was rooted in a perfectionist ethos. Perfectionism is implicit in the entire social science project, including work in the state or social work. Yet much of what is implicit in social science thinking and terminology accepts these premises but rarely identifies or defines them, so fundamental is the perfectionist ethos to this worldview. A primary concern of liberal Protestant charitable and social work activists from the mid-nineteenth century through the Progressive Era was the eradication of poverty, not just aid to the poor. This was, from its inception, a markedly religious project led first by evangelicals and buttressed later by the more elite, and rational, Unitarians. In her discussion of the historical influences on social work and casework, Mary Richmond claimed that "child-saving," the work of Charity Organization Societies, and medical diagnosis were each critical historical influences leading to social work's development in the Progressive Era. Medical diagnosis was most important in pointing to the primary goal—a cure. Child-saving and Charity Organization Societies, however, were central to the philosophical discussion of poverty by naming its causes and therefore pointing to its remedies. Social work was distinctive from its forebears not because it identified different problems or worked toward different goals, but because its rationalized methodology provided a system to do such work more efficiently, scientifically, and comprehensively.[19]

In the child-saving movement organized at mid-century by middle-class, white, and predominantly evangelical Protestants, religious values were central to discourse justifying the saving of children and to the rhetoric legitimating women's increasingly visible leadership in this work. From the early 1850s through the mid–1870s, Protestant middle-class and elite reformers removed tens of thousands of poor immigrant children from seaboard cities such as New York and sent them to Protestant homes in the Midwest.[20] Protestant female reformers were prominent in the movement, and their maternalist politics were central in constructing policy. The practice of taking urban poor children away from their natural parents rested on the normative belief that the Protestant nuclear family, guided by the devotion of a Protestant mother, was the only proper setting for child-rearing in the American republic. Arguing that, if left undisturbed, the mothering of poor immigrant women would result in the reproduction of a permanent dependent class, male and female native-born Protestant activists ("child-savers") legally transferred the rights to mother from poor, immigrant, Catholic and Jewish women to Protestant mothers. By century's end, hundreds of thousands of predominantly immigrant, and Catholic and Jewish, children had been taken from parents and placed in Protestant homes in the Midwest.

Who American society defined as secular in the twentieth century was closely related to who was considered "nonsectarian" in the nineteenth century, including those leading the child-saving and charity organization movements. In the placing-out movement, for instance, all children who were taken from immigrant parents, predominantly Catholics and Jews, were "placed out" in Christian homes, meaning Protestant ones. These activists, moreover, were not picky about which Protestant denomination claimed the children. Methodist or Anglican, Baptist or Presbyterian, Unitarian or Quaker, all were accepted as rightful parents for children of the state. Protestant churches were thought by their nature to encourage individualism, a reverence for American institutions, and a distaste for claiming minority status and allegiance to a nondominant group. No placing-out society run by Protestants in New York would agree to place a Catholic or Jewish child in a Catholic or Jewish home, even if those homes were solidly middle-class or elite, until after the turn of the twentieth century. Protestant homes and families were to serve as the settings, and Protestant women as the redemptive agents, in poor immigrant children's reform.[21]

The most vulnerable immigrant parents were destitute mothers. Because poverty was conceptualized as a moral problem, middle-class Protestant reformers saw intervening in motherhood so as to alter the reproduction of moral traits associated with poverty as the best strategy for eradicating poverty itself. According to the logic of Protestant reformers, Catholicism either exacerbated or was wholly responsible for the tendency toward dependency, and even alcoholism, so evident in the behavioral patterns of Irish Catholic poor. The sooner children could be removed from the influence of such a mother, community, and religion, the better the chances for thwarting the reproduction of a dependent class in America.[22]

Female and male child-savers were nonetheless indignant when Catholics and Jews argued that the system was anti-Catholic, anti-Semitic, and at odds with the principles separating church and state. As others were to argue throughout the century, the American Female Guardian Society, the Children's Aid Society, and later the State Charities Aid Association and the Charity Organization Society, although composed only of Protestants and not Catholics or Jews, claimed they were not sectarian organizations because they represented many Protestant groups and agreed on broad-based Protestant principles for rearing and reforming children. Catholic and Jewish groups, Protestants argued, were sectarian because they represented the views of only one church or sect. In contestation over the century about the content of religious teachings in state-run reformatories or placing-out societies, no one argued that children should be brought up without religious training, but rather that the training should not lead to conversion to any particular sect, including and perhaps especially Catholicism or Judaism. In 1873 one Catholic leader voiced his considerable frustration, "[W]hilst we cannot yield our rights to any one sect of Protestantism, we are equally determined . . . not to yield our constitutional rights to all . . . sects of Protestantism combined."[23]

Charity Organization Societies, established in the 1870s and 1880s, had similar pan-Protestant, ostensibly nonsectarian roots but also moved to a more explicit embrace of science. One of the many results of Catholic and Jewish resistance to the placing-out system was that by the late nineteenth century many native-born, white, elite, Protestant female charitable activists moved away from both religious labels and discourse, emphasizing their increased use of utilitarian science in charitable work by organizing under the rubric of "scientific charity." Critical of the explicitly anti-Catholic and anti-Semitic policies of the antebellum period, these activists warned volunteers against "proselytization," which they understood as the attempt to convert clients to specific Protestant religions. The "friendly visitor," who would dispense little actual cash, was encouraged to "lift up" the poor to the superior moral system of the elite and to encourage hard work, thrift, and abstinence. Josephine Shaw Lowell, for instance, was one of the most important and powerful of scientific charity leaders in the late nineteenth century. In contrast to the "indiscriminant aid" given by religiously motivated charity workers of the antebellum period, the Charity Organization Society over which she presided would thereafter trace with precision those individuals who received aid from any public or private source. At base in her thinking was not just that some poor people cheated the system but that poverty was caused by moral failings, a framework that for all its new scientific pretensions still held the destitute individually and collectively responsible for their own poverty. And as Mary Richmond discussed in *Social Diagnosis*, the premier textbook on casework methodology, casework was built from the experience of Charity Organization Societies: "In this new discipline, . . . discoveries that were made with pain and difficulty by the pioneers of one generation have become commonplaces of our thinking in the next. There is a half century of hard social endeavor between Edward Denison's despairing exclamation—'Every shilling I give away does fourpence worth of good by helping to keep their . . . miserable bodies alive, and eightpence worth of harm by helping to destroy their miserable souls.'"[24]

Scientific charity workers and social workers, although moving to use terms such as *character* and *personality,* were also comfortable inserting *soul* more explicitly to talk about the individual at base in all strategies of reform. Similarly, Lowell was prone to calling indiscriminate aid an "evil" because of its presumed corruption of the soul itself. Moral failings, including laziness and intemperance, were more likely to be exacerbated when regular aid was given. Thus, Lowell herself was convinced that scientific management, and decidedly not empathy with the poor as individuals, could counteract the tendency of the well-off to help too much and therefore to harm. Enlisting the emerging social sciences in her vision, moreover, Lowell, a Unitarian from a prominent abolitionist family, believed that science would unveil the "natural laws" governing earthly existence and reveal to reformers exactly what caused poverty. By encouraging individuals to behave with that knowledge in mind, they could eradicate poverty entirely.[25]

This perfectionist vision was incorporated into social work as a field at the turn of the century, especially into the arm of social work constituting programs for women and children and run predominantly by female reformers. Casework, the method of social work taught at Columbia University and the University of Chicago, for instance, incorporated the belief that poverty could be eradicated through the application of scientific principles and methodologies. As Linda Gordon explains, moreover, "Effective casework required individual treatment of each client, not simply across-the-board relief."[26] To be sure, such treatment was not about simple stinginess. As Richmond observed:

> To step between a man and the spur to purposeful action is to do something a good deal worse to him than what we meant when we used to talk about the danger of "pauperizing" him. That term had always a materialist slant. What we really were in danger of doing was not merely pushing him down by the careless giving of alms, but cutting him off from further social development at some one or more points. This danger has never been confined to the giving of material relief; many who have never lacked for material things as well as the destitute have been exposed to the more subtle danger of other forms of service . . . which are without reverence for the recipients own powers and latent possibilities.[27]

At base, the premises of social workers entailed the acceptance of society's structures, and, as Michael Katz argues, "Social workers joined other contemporary experts who tried to teach people to adjust to their environment, not to change it."[28] Reform was best expressed in expanding resources provided by the state to better help that adjustment. Mary Richmond contended that "the central aim of social case work is the maintenance and development of personality" and also held that social workers had a responsibility to agitate for "the social resources and expert services of many kinds" that individuals would need in their journey.[29] Further, individuals must be encouraged to restore social relations that had become strained by flaws of character and personality, thus linking "the interdependence of individual and mass betterment." In this sense, she argued, "social reform and social case work must of necessity progress together."[30] Citing the perfectionist roots of such a perspective, Richmond maintained that "if we would understand *what* social case work is we must realize *why* it is, and push that why beyond the accidents of civilization to its main stream of advance . . . a permanent part in making this world a better one to live in."[31]

Resistance to Richmond's perspective was widespread and varied. Many Protestant, or Protestant-born, women did not accept the terms of the social work profession or its underlying perfectionist vision, the most conspicuous of them being either from the fundamentalist right or the social justice left wing of female reform.[32] Even more conspicuous historically were Catholic and Jewish charitable activists, who as groups were likely to characterize their work in charities and welfare activism as deriving from religious traditions and ideologies that rejected the premises of casework methodology. Catholic and Jewish resistance to casework in the Progressive Era reflected their historical resistance to child-saving and Charity Organization Societies since the mid-nineteenth century and to the alternative perfectionist visions upon which such work rested. Although a very few Catholic and Jewish women entered the social work field during the Progressive Era, most Catholics and Jews did not follow the alternative trajectory.[33] Catholic and Jewish activists did not just complain of religious sectarianism; they claimed that their most fundamental notions of what caused poverty, and how to relieve it through charity, were absolutely at odds with Protestant liberal thinking and social work strategies.

Catholic and Jewish resistance to such work was buttressed by alternative perfectionist visions, each of great popularity among the Jewish and Catholic poor. Implicit within Marxism, for instance, is a perfectionist ideal to be realized through the collective efforts toward an egalitarian state and redistribution of wealth. As Eve Tavor Bannet writes, "By the time Marx wrote *On the Jewish Question* and *Contribution to the Critique of Hegel's Philosophy of Law* in 1843, he spoke of 'truly implementing' religion by 'realizing' the universal and human basis of religion 'in a secular manner,' or joining 'the heaven of (man's) generality' to the 'earthly existence of his actuality,' and of binding the 'heaven of the political world' to the 'earthly existence of society' . . . the project remains . . . : to unite heaven and earth, spirit and matter, idea and reality *in* reality."[34] Bannet further maintains that Marx's particular brand of perfectionism was deeply influenced by Jewish tradition. The Jew, Bannet argues, does not seek personal salvation or what Marx calls "'the Christian egoism of heavenly bliss'; his goal is to make today the day when 'the idols will be utterly cut off,' and when 'the world will be perfected under the kingdom of the Almighty.'" Marx "criticized all religious, quasi-religious, political and philosophical positions which understood the two worlds to be removed and cut off from each other, and insisted that the worlds are one in their ground, and can become one in their reality."[35] Marx's often-quoted sloganistic assertion that "religion is the opiate of the masses" is reflective of a more specific critique than of religion in its entirety. Only insofar as religious tradition supported a radical break between worldly oppression and a heavenly vision of social justice could it be termed an opiate. Marx would likely find fundamentalists, whether Christian, Jewish, or Islamic, as similarly threatening to social justice.

Consider as well the sermons of Catholic Father Edward McGlynn, founder of the Anti-Poverty Society in the 1880s after excommunication from the Catholic church and expulsion from a working-class parish in New York

City. Wildly popular among the city's poor, especially Irish Catholics, Mc-
Glynn held that he was "intensely convinced that poverty is not a law of God,
but a violation of God's law. Poverty arises from inability to get work. Inability
to get work arises from that fact that the general bounties of nature are ap-
propriated as private property by a few, and the masses are deprived of their
divine inheritance."[36] Poverty, therefore, was not due to individual failings
but to the appropriation of resources and labor by the rich. McGlynn thrilled
the poor with his attack on the rich in general and orthodox Catholic church
officials in particular, who held that perfection on earth was not possible and
that movements for social justice were the work of the fallen. "There is an
old Latin saying, 'Let justice be done though the heavens fall.' But let justice
be done and the heavens will not fall to our ruin. Then the heavens will stoop
to embrace of earth and the earth will be lifted up to the kiss of heaven, and
then on earth shall be at last fulfilled the Savior's Prayer, the prayer that all
His children everywhere are reciting with yearning hearts: 'Thy kingdom
come, Thy will be done *on earth* as it is in heaven.'"[37]

Such perfectionist visions were apparent in Catholic and Jewish charitable
work from the mid-nineteenth century, and both groups at first refused to
incorporate a social science conception of casework into their charitable activities. Catholics and Jews could and did instead turn to traditions that reflected debates about the remedies for poverty much before industrial capitalism.
By using a much longer, more versatile tradition associated with taking care
of the poor in societies (and the world itself) that were stratified, Catholics
and Jews refused as groups to blame the poor for poverty. We should not, however, pretend that something essential about Catholic and Jewish ideology and
practice was at work. Rather, in a specific historical context in which Catholics and Jews were overwhelmingly poor and white Protestants predominantly
middle class and elite, each tradition was used in creative fashions to either
support struggles for social justice or legitimatize the well-being of a particular group. Cognizant that a substantial part of their population lived in des-
perate poverty, they were more likely to see poverty as deriving from specific
political and religious persecutions—the Irish famine and British colonialism and the anti-Semitism and pogroms of Eastern Europe.[38]

Catholic objections to the practice of individual investigation and supervision were apparent in the antebellum period and continued through the
Progressive Era. In the Catholic community, asking endless questions about
personal reasons for "misfortune" was considered a cruel harassment of poor
people already demoralized and vulnerable. Even more important, there was
no point to it when the Catholic ethos about charity derived from a medi-
eval worldview whereby some people did well and others did not. One was

not better morally because one had power and money, and neither was one lesser morally because one was poor. Rather, "Christian charity," as Catholics understood it, was to alleviate the suffering of those who found themselves in destitution. Although recognizing that some recipients might cheat by taking more than a fair share, Catholics did not imagine that poverty sprang from the poor's dependence on aid. They therefore championed the expansion of public welfare provisions to a far greater extent than their native-born counterparts. Indeed, attributing the potato blight to the supernatural but the famine itself to British poor-law policies, Irish Catholics shifted the blame for Irish poverty from the Irish to the Protestant elite in Ireland and America. British poor-law officials who withheld aid to the starving so as to encourage the Irish to improve their characters through hard work were characterized by Irish nationalists as deliberately genocidal. John Stuart Mill's support of the Poor Law of 1834, under whose auspices the famine thrived, was characterized by one Catholic writer as just one example of the absolute contrast between Protestant and Catholic thinking. Mill argued that the poor law "prevents any person, except by his own choice, from dying of hunger" and "leaves their condition as much as possible below that of the poorest who find support for themselves." Such reasoning, one Catholic charged, "seems to arrive at the *reductio ad absurdum;* for the state of these poorest of the working poor . . . is too distressing for charity, acting below that level, to be of any avail. Usually inclined to the most liberal and humane views, Mr. Mill has here given way to a Protestant prejudice, which regards as ill-advised the more whole-souled Catholic style of charity."[39]

Unlike Protestant reformers' strategies, which focused on a top-down elevation of the poor morally through contact with the elite, Catholic theology emphasized instead that the elite must learn from and embrace the struggles of the poor. Catholics deemed religious orders, not friendly visitors, as providing a model of interaction between classes. Through all nuns' voluntary assumption of poverty, "poverty itself becomes ennobled by the assumption, and its degradation disappears."[40] By virtue of the fact that convents were increasingly the province of women from poor and working-class backgrounds, the cooperation between classes necessary for the everyday interactions in each sisterhood exemplified Catholic visions of social harmony. The centrality of ascetic selflessness in Catholic ideology also helped nuns remove themselves from the values and prejudices of the society in which they worked. Poverty may not have been shameful, according to Irish Catholics, but the lack of charity evident in Protestant reformers' efforts to deprive the poor of the most meager material aid derived from the greed and materialism to which Protestant individualism inevitably led.

At the turn of the century, Jewish activists questioned the basis of case-work. Morris Goldstein noted that Jewish activists were more likely to characterize "poverty a misfortune [than] . . . a fault," in contrast to their native-born Protestant colleagues.[41] Harold Silver pointed out that for the orthodox especially, "The principle of investigation . . . was alien to his philosophy and repugnant to his 'Jewish heart.'"[42] Abraham Cronbach, in a 1930 article entitled, "What Makes Jewish Social Work 'Jewish'?" held that "the bible seems, on the whole, more inclined toward what we call social justice than what we call charity." In his understanding of Jewish charitable work, he argued that Jews participated in only limited investigations, a characteristic he discussed as "far from the 'social diagnosis' of Mary E. Richmond." Cronbach, moreover, noted that the more progressive of Progressive reformers' legislation was hardly new if one considered Jewish tradition. "Such protective measures as mothers' pensions, . . . have their talmudic analogue in the *ketubah,* a written document which safeguarded the right of the wife . . . and [was] intended to care for the woman in the event of widowhood or divorce." Rather than alms-giving, Jewish activism in support of such "social legislation" was an entirely understandable attempt to "align tradition on the side of progress."[43] The Talmudic tradition of the regular sharing of crops, land, and community resources with the poor of any society bespoke of social justice rather than charity, entitlement rather than alms.

Many Catholic and Jewish activists in the early twentieth century therefore held that it was precisely their distinctive religious perspectives that enabled them to champion not only the labor movement but also an expanded welfare state. Cronbach observed that "statistics indicate that . . . Jewish relief allowances are higher than the non-Jewish," which he attributed to "Talmudic principle that relief be generous and liberal."[44] The statistics upon which he relied, however, likely did not include those of Catholics, because they refused overall to keep statistics on individuals they aided, believing that such investigation, or even the keeping of the historical record, constituted a serious infringement upon the rights and privacy of the poor. In 1914 the New York State Commission for Relief of Widowed Mothers, researching whether private charities gave sufficient aid to mothers for them to keep children at home, asked Catholics and Jews to send it records of charitable dispersement. Catholics submitted nothing. This was despite the fact that it was assumed that Catholics gave more aid than either Protestants or Jews combined, in part for philosophical reasons and in part because the majority of New York City's poor population was Catholic. The investigation was therefore pointed at ostensibly secular groups such as the Charity Organization Society, which, along with Richmond, argued against the pensions, believing that the concept of regular payments to poor women threatened the premises of the emerging social work profession.

Both Jewish and Catholic female activists also protested against the presumption that only "good women," as defined through social work investigation, deserved funding to support their mothering. In 1916, for instance, a fleet of investigators trained by Mary Richmond and Edward Devine of the Charity Organization Society descended upon the Foundling Hospital run by the Sisters of Charity since 1869.[45] Sheltering infants as well as women who were either poor or estranged from their families for sexual transgressions, the work of the sisters at the Foundling Hospital reflected an ethos common to all nuns' charities for women—that no investigation be made of their background. To do so would be to subject women to the kind of public shaming from which nuns were committed to protecting them. The investigators nonetheless maintained that "[n]o child or mother shall be accepted as a city charge, unless an investigation of the mother's statement establishes her claim to such support."[46] As one city investigator lamented, "There is no effort made to find out or record any family history. Even when the mother remains for months in the institution, no record is made of the names, the addresses of friends or relatives who may visit her. Sister Mary Fidele said that the reason no record was kept or information sought was because 'our object is to shield the girl and her family.'"[47] One Sister of Charity's defense of the practice was deceptively simple in its concept of poor women's struggles: "I consider that all women who have babies are good women. . . . The mothers who come to us are just poor girls. Some of them want to keep their story from their parents. Or they may have brothers and sisters to shield. We let them stay here and take care of their babies."[48]

Hannah Einstein and Sophie Irene Loeb were each leaders in organizing the research and activist labor that led to the 1915 legislation insuring widows' pensions in New York state. Loeb and Einstein used Jewish traditions that emphasized women and children's entitlement to such funding, as well as the presumption that funding be generous, to structure their participation on the Commission for Relief of Widowed Mothers. Acting as an inveterate moral prosecutor when questioning the relief policies of the Charity Organization Society, Loeb continued her activism by pushing for state legislation that would extend the aid to deserted and divorced women and ensuring that pensions be allotted through a bureaucratic body entirely separate from investigators whom Richmond and Devine had trained.[49]

In their opposition to casework, however, Catholics and Jews became much more visible as sectarian or religious, refusing, at least through the Progressive period, to either change their self-identification or, more important, downplay the substantive differences in their analysis of poverty, its causes, and its remedy. Catholics, Jews, and Protestant African Americans, for instance, each formed their own national organizations, including the National Conference for Catholic Charities and the National Conference for Jewish Charities in the United States, to discuss charitable work and activism apart from the National Conference on Charities and Corrections, the ostensibly nonsectarian national conference that was nonetheless dominated by white Protestant elite and middle-class activists.[50]

Such separatism embarrassed some Catholics and Jews because their collective resistance to casework training seemed a refusal to accept the realities of the "modern age." Catholic and Jewish communities contained elements that celebrated, and elements that felt disgraced by, religious distinctions evident in their charitable work. As one activist complained in an anonymous article published in 1930, "One of the great handicaps from which Jewish social work is suffering, which is retarding the raising of proper standards, and which is keeping it on a level inferior to non-Jewish social work, is the Jewish community itself. Ignorance, adherence to vague tradition . . . characterize the behavior of practically all boards of Jewish social agencies . . . [and] are not conducive either to progress or to satisfactory social service."[51] Instead, the author maintained, the "vestigial remains of a bitter ghetto past" continued to retard the "progress" of the community in social work, its distinctiveness betraying a refusal to embrace the modern social work perspective.

It would be somewhat absurd to survey the organizations and decide that white, elite, Protestant women were underrepresented in welfare-state activities because they had no organization explicitly limited to their own group. To do so would be to claim that they had "nothing." Returning to my initial story about my course on race, white Protestant women's ability to lead national groups, including the National Mothers' Congress, the Children's Bureau, and the General Federation of Women's Clubs, without naming their distinctive religious underpinnings was evidence not of their lack of visibility or power but of their normative stature. Catholics and Jews had to name themselves as distinct, conscious as they were not only that Protestants saw them as outsiders but also that national groups dedicated to debate about welfare activities did not reflect their viewpoints. That Protestant women did not claim this to be a "Protestant" state is indicative less of the absence of Protestantism than of the unquestioned dominance of mainstream Protestant thinking in what constituted the bulk of what we now call the "women's trajectory" of the welfare state.

In part because this literature on women and the state rarely investigates the religious underpinnings of social work, secularization as a process is naturalized and unquestioned. To characterize Catholics and Jews as "religious" and sometimes ignorant in regard to presumably more enlightened social work was among the most powerful tools the white, Protestant, native-born, middle class used to construct a hegemonic discourse about the welfare state. To the degree that Catholics and Jews assimilated to this perspective, particularly as they threw off the "vestigial remains of a bitter ghetto past," they also impeded their ability to contest hegemonic discourse from a standpoint outside the dominant culture. To state, moreover, that their contestations were about "religious" issues was to trivialize the fundamental ideological differences apparent in each group's thinking about the causes of poverty, the rights of the poor, and the obligations of the state.

And yet the perfectionist vision of nineteenth-century liberal Protestantism still shapes the state and discourse about poverty profoundly. The welfare debate of the 1980s and 1990s is more accurately an extraordinarily narrow discourse, in contrast to historical moments when resistance to dominant modes of welfare provision were contested overtly. New programs offer the tidbits Mary Richmond advocated, as liberals attempt to make the poor's ostensible journey to the middle class easier and resist dismantling the safety net entirely. Conservatives fear that liberal welfare provision will lead to greater dependence and therefore greater poverty, thereby mimicking scientific charity rhetoric from industrial capitalism's inception. At base, this debate is most powerful in accepting as a premise that individual character, or now sometimes culture, is causal in creating poverty in America.[52] It also reifies the centrality of controlling the mothering of poor women as the primary means of diminishing poverty, because such control over mothering is deemed the best method of controlling the formation or reproduction of character in their children. Through everyday practice, the framework of caseworkers' reports, and the ongoing demonization of the "welfare mother," most Americans, whether from Protestant, Catholic, Jewish, or Islamic backgrounds, reaffirm continually the religious premises of nineteenth-century liberal Protestantism without recognizing the religious underpinnings of such powerful state and secular ideology. "Nothing" is therefore really quite something.

Notes

The epigraph comes from John Milbank, "Problematizing the Secular: The Postmodern Agenda," in *Shadow of Spirit: Postmodernism and Religion*, ed. Philippa Berry and Andrew Wernick (London: Routledge, 1992), 37.

1. I have offered this course at the University of Arizona. "White," or "whiteness," as we discuss, is also a historically constructed category, and its normative stature in the late twentieth century was quite different than the use of "Anglo-Saxon," for instance, at the turn of the twentieth century.

2. Historical discussions of secularization and Progressive Era mainstream Protestantism include, for instance, T. J. Jackson Lears, *No Place of Grace: Antimodernism and the Transformation of American Culture, 1880–1920* (New York: Pantheon Books, 1981), and Richard Fox, "The Culture of Liberal Protestant Progressivism, 1875–1925," *Journal of Interdisciplinary History* 23 (Winter 1993): 639–60. On the various sociological traditions defining the "secular" and "secularization," see, for instance, Mark Chavez, "Secularization as Declining Religious Authority," *Social Forces* 72 (March 1994): 749–74.

3. For the purposes of this essay, I distinguish between *secular* and *secularist* thought, the former meaning only an absence of explicitly religious rhetoric, the latter a commitment ideologically to secularism as a closed thinking system distinct from the religious. I use the term *secularization,* moreover, to describe the historical process analyzed here, whereby "the religious" or supernatural increasingly drops out of Protestant women's discourse as they participate in state formation. In Harvey Cox's formulation, secularization "represents 'defatalization of history,' the discovery by man that he has been left with the world on his hands, that he can no longer blame fortune or furies for what he does with it. Secularization occurs when man turns his attention away from worlds beyond and toward this world and this time." Harvey Cox, *The Secular City: Secularization and Urbanization in Theological Perspective,* rev. ed. (New York: Macmillan, 1966), 1–2.

4. Mark Carnoy, *The State and Political Theory* (Princeton: Princeton University Press, 1984), 3.

5. I use the terms *Anglo* and *white* to racially tag the Protestant, native-born, middle-class group I discuss throughout and distinguish them from African American middle-class Protestants or, for example, German middle-class Protestants. Hereafter, reference to Protestant middle-class Americans should be assumed to mean white and native-born unless otherwise noted.

6. Nancy Cott, *The Bonds of Womanhood: "Woman's Sphere" in New England, 1780–1835* (New Haven: Yale University Press, 1977); Ann Douglas, *The Femininization of American Culture* (New York: Avon Books, 1977); Linda K. Kerber, *Women of the Republic: Intellect and Ideology in Revolutionary America* (Chapel Hill: University of North Carolina Press, 1980); Jeanne Boydston, *Home and Work: Housework, Wages, and the Ideology of Labor in the Early Republic* (New York: Oxford University Press, 1990); Paula Baker, "The Domestication of Politics: Women and American Political Society, 1780–1920," *American Historical Review* 89 (June 1984): 620–47.

7. Lyndal Roper, *The Holy Household: Women and Morals in Reformation Augsburg* (New York: Oxford University Press, 1989).

8. Clarissa Atkinson, *The Oldest Vocation: Christian Motherhood in the Middle Ages* (Ithaca: Cornell University Press, 1991).

9. Douglas, *The Feminization of American Culture.*

10. Elizabeth B. Clark, "Organized Mother Love and the Maternal State," unpublished essay in author's possession; Kerber, *Women of the Republic;* Baker, "The Domestication of Politics"; Barbara Leslie Epstein, *The Politics of Domesticity: Women, Evangelism, and*

Temperance in Nineteenth-Century America (Middletown: Wesleyan University Press, 1981); Ruth Bordin, *Woman and Temperance: The Quest for Power and Liberty, 1873–1900* (Philadelphia: Temple University Press, 1981); Carolyn De Swarte Gifford, *Writing Out My Life: Selections from the Journal of Frances E. Willard, 1855–1896* (Urbana: University of Illinois Press, 1995).

11. Carolyn De Swarte Gifford, "For God and Home and Native Land," in *Women in New Worlds: Historical Perspectives on the Weslayan Tradition* ed. Hilah F. Thomas and Rosemary Skinner Keller (Nashville: Abingdon Press, 1981), 310–27; Bordin, *Women and Temperance;* Epstein, *The Politics of Domesticity.*

12. Baker, "The Domestication of Politics."

13. For an especially good overview of this literature, see Seth Koven and Sonya Michel, "Introduction: 'Mother Worlds,'" in *Mothers of a New World: Maternalist Politics and the Origins of Welfare States,* ed. Seth Koven and Sonya Michel (New York: Routledge, 1993), 1–42. See also Linda Gordon, "The New Feminist Scholarship on the Welfare State," in *Women, the State, and Welfare,* ed. Linda Gordon (Madison: University of Wisconsin Press, 1990), 9–35; and Anne Showstack Sassoon, ed., *Women and the State: The Shifting Boundaries of Public and Private* (London: Routledge, 1992).

14. Seth Koven, "Borderlands: Women, Voluntary Action, and Child Welfare in Britain, 1840–1914," in *Mothers of a New World: Maternalist Politics and the Origins of Welfare States,* ed. Seth Koven and Sonya Michel (New York: Routledge, 1994), 96.

15. Baker, "The Domestication of Politics"; Epstein, *The Politics of Domesticity.* Clark's work ("Organized Mother Love and the Maternal State") is an exception in discussing the religious roots of state policy.

16. The very best work on women and the American state might sometimes allude to an individual's religious background, but the field as a whole rarely connects religious orientation with the kinds of public policy these historical actors advocated. Robin Muncy, *Creating a Female Dominion in American Reform, 1890–1935* (New York: Oxford University Press, 1991); Molly Ladd-Taylor, *Mother-Work: Women, Child Welfare, and the State, 1890–1930* (Chicago: University of Illinois Press, 1994); Linda Gordon, *Pitied but Not Entitled: Single Mothers and the History of Welfare, 1890–1935* (New York: Free Press, 1994); Theda Skocpol, *Protecting Mothers and Soldiers: The Political Origins of Social Policy in the United States* (Cambridge: Harvard University Press, 1992); Gwendolyn Mink, *The Wages of Motherhood: Inequality in the Welfare State, 1917–1942* (Ithaca: Cornell University Press, 1995). Kathryn Kish Sklar does note Florence Kelley's background and hints at its importance. See Sklar, *Florence Kelley and the Nation's Work: The Rise of Women's Political Culture* (New Haven: Yale University Press, 1995), 86–88.

17. Robert Abzug is particularly good at analyzing how antebellum reformers had a "tendency to apply religious imagination and passion to issues that most Americans considered worldly," a "sacralization of the world, where sacred and profane were of a piece." Abzug, *Cosmos Crumbling: American Reform and the Religious Imagination* (New York: Oxford University Press, 1994), 7.

18. Margaret Lamberts Bendroth, *Fundamentalism and Gender, 1875 to the Present* (New Haven: Yale University Press, 1993); George Marsden, *Fundamentalism and American Culture: The Shaping of Twentieth-Century Evangelicalism* (New York: Oxford University Press, 1980).

19. Mary Richmond's texts for the emerging social work profession illustrate in a succinct manner the major philosophical tenets and methodologies central to casework of the period. Mary E. Richmond, *Social Diagnosis* (New York: Russell Sage Foundation, 1917), and Richmond, *What Is Social Case Work? An Introductory Description* (New York: Russell Sage Foundation, 1922).

20. In discussing the placing-out movement, especially Catholic and Jewish resistance to it, I rely on my dissertation and unpublished manuscript, which analyze its change in New York City from 1850 through the Progressive Era. Thus my sources privilege the debates in New York City. Maureen Fitzgerald, "Irish-Catholic Nuns and the Development of New York City's Welfare System, 1840–1900," Ph.D. diss., University of Wisconsin-Madison, 1992, and Fitzgerald, "Charity, Poverty, and Child Welfare," *Harvard Divinity Bulletin* 25 (Summer 1996): 12–17.

21. For a discussion of the larger literature on the placing-out movement and its relation to industrial urban reform, see Fitzgerald, "Irish-Catholic Nuns," passim; see also Paul Boyer, *Urban Masses and Moral Order in America, 1820–1920* (Cambridge: Harvard University Press, 1978), and Christine Stansell, *City of Women: Sex and Class in New York, 1789–1860* (Urbana: University of Illinois Press, 1986), 193–96.

22. *Annual Report of the New York Association for the Improvement of the Condition of the Poor* (1851), 19.

23. Rev. Isaac Hecker, "Public Charities," *Catholic World* 17 (April 1873): 4.

24. Richmond, *Social Diagnosis,* 27.

25. See, for instance, Josephine Shaw Lowell, *Public Relief and Private Charity* (New York: G. P. Putnam's Sons, 1884).

26. Linda Gordon, "Putting Children First," in *U.S. History as Women's History: New Feminist Essays,* ed. Linda K. Kerber, Alice Kessler-Harris, and Kathryn Kish Sklar (Chapel Hill: University of North Carolina Press, 1995), 72.

27. Richmond, *What is Social Case Work?* 167.

28. Michael Katz, *In the Shadow of the Poorhouse: A Social History of Welfare in America* (New York: Basic Books, 1986), 165–66.

29. Richmond, *What Is Social Case Work?* 144, 115.

30. Richmond, *Social Diagnosis,* 365; Richmond, *What Is Social Case Work?* 115.

31. Richmond, *What Is Social Case Work?* 128.

32. Kathryn Kish Sklar, for instance, distinguishes the social justice wing of female Progressive Era reformers such as Florence Kelley from maternalists. "Keynote Address," Women in Twentieth-Century Protestantism Conference, April 24, 1998, Chicago.

33. As elite white Protestant women gained access to college education and then to the professional schools associated with the emergence of social work as a profession, this professional claim to expertise and authority severely undercut the explicitly religious argument that women should bring religious and moral influence to the public and eventually the state. As Molly Ladd-Taylor has argued (*Motherwork,* 6, 74–75), the movement to professionalize these fields at once promoted some women as potential experts who had intellectual and administrative capacities equal to men and simultaneously undercut the value of an exclusively female perspective on this work historically.

34. Eve Tavor Bannet, "Marx, God and Praxis," in *Shadow of Spirit: Postmodernism and Religion,* ed. Philippa Berry and Andrew Wernick (London: Routledge, 1992), 125, 123–34.

35. Bannet, "Marx, God and Praxis," 126, 125.

36. Edward McGlynn, reprinted in Stephen Bell, *Rebel, Priest and Prophet: A Biography of Dr. Edward McGlynn* (1941, repr. New York: Robert Schalkenbach Foundation, 1968), 108.

37. Edward McGlynn, speech at Chicago Central Music Hall, June 22, 1887, reprinted in Bell, *Rebel, Priest and Prophet,* 108.

38. I emphasize "historical context" because the versatility of the Catholic and Jewish traditions was extensive, and various aspects of those traditions could be and would be reevaluated as the more substantial middle-class and elite contingent in each group came to dominance in charitable work.

39. Anon., "Who Shall Take Care of the Poor?" *Catholic World* 8 (1868–69): 706–7.

40. Anon., "Who Shall Take Care of the Poor?"

41. Morris Goldstein, "Causes of Poverty and the Remedial Work of Organized Charity," in *Proceedings* of the second biennial meeting of the National Conference of Jewish Charities, Detroit, May 26–28, 1902, reprinted in *Trends and Issues in Jewish Social Welfare, 1899–1958,* ed. Robert Morris and Michael Freund (Philadelphia: Jewish Publication Society of America, 1966).

42. Harold Silver, "The Russian Jew Look at Charity," in *Trends and Issues in Jewish Social Welfare, 1899–1958,* ed. Robert Morris and Michael Freund (Philadelphia: Jewish Publication Society of America, 1966), 58.

43. Abraham Cronbach, "What Makes Jewish Social Work 'Jewish'? Historical Aspect," *Jewish Social Service Quarterly* 6 (Sept. 1930): 3–5.

44. Cronbach, "What Makes Jewish Social Work 'Jewish'?" 214.

45. Edward Devine was secretary of the Charity Organization Society of New York City from 1896 to 1917 and director of the New York School of Philanthropy at Columbia University.

46. "Report of the Inspection of the Boarding-out and Placing-out Work of the New York Foundling Asylum" [dates of inspection, Nov. 21, Dec. 13, 1916], Archives of the Sisters of Charity of New York, Mount St. Vincent, 7.

47. "Report of the Inspection of the Boarding-out and Placing-out Work," 40.

48. "Babies Unaided If Not Citizens," Scrapbook, 1917, Foundling Hospital, Archives of the Sisters of Charity of New York, Mount St. Vincent.

49. See, for instance, Edward Devine to Hannah Einstein, Nov. 15, 1913, folder A3106-78, New York State Archives; William H. Matthews, president of the board, "Report of Work of the Board of Child Welfare of the City of New York, for the Twelve Months Ending August 6, 1916," New York City Municipal Archives, folder 015, record group MJP-161; Sophie Irene Loeb, *Everyman's Child* (New York: Century, 1920), 73–74.

50. Catholic and Jewish women also organized distinct groups separate from their male counterparts, including the New York City–based, all-female Association for Catholic Charities, and Jewish Sisterhoods. The National Association for Colored Women included many explicitly "religiously-based" church groups but did not use a "religious" label, making clear their primarily Protestant affiliation but their "difference" based on race.

51. Anon., "Facing Reality," *Jewish Social Service Quarterly* 7 (Sept. 1930): 15.

52. The mutability of the actual racial and ethnic or cultural background of the demonized "welfare mother" historically, from Irish Catholic in the mid-nineteenth century to

African American today, speaks to the immutability of class status in targeting particular poor women's mothering as necessitating state intervention. In other words, each of the demonized groups has in common a class status and history of long-term poverty rather than a particular cultural background. Recognizing the mutability of the actual racial and ethnic backgrounds from which demonized mothers come therefore wards against positing race as an essentialized identity used to explain why particular groups of poor mothers are targeted. Mink, *The Wages of Motherhood*; Jill Quadagno, *The Color of Welfare: How Racism Undermined the War on Poverty* (New York: Oxford University Press, 1994).

14. Feminization Revisited: Protestantism and Gender at the Turn of the Century

ANN TAVES

IN 1900 GEORGE ALBERT COE, a liberal Methodist and professor of moral and intellectual philosophy at Northwestern University, wrote concerning the "persistent excess of women in the Churches":

> If we view the problem psychologically we shall feel perfectly safe in assuming that any large and persistent excess of women in the Churches is chiefly due to a superior adaptation of Church life to the female nature. It is because the Church looks at things with feminine eyes, and calls chiefly into exercises the faculties in which women excel men. A feminine element is as necessary to religion as woman to the life of the species. *But,* in the spiritual as in the natural realm, whatever tends to isolate this element tends also to make it barren and unfruitful. Neither the man alone nor the woman alone is a perfect type, but rather the family, in which the two complementary qualities are balanced the one over against the other.[1]

At first glance there is nothing remarkable in any of this. Coe, it would appear, was reacting to what scholars have described as the widespread feminization of American Protestantism during the nineteenth century, expressing a common turn-of-the-century concern regarding the disproportionate number of women in churches, and calling for a church more suited to men.[2] Based on a careful reading of Coe and re-reading of the secondary literature on the feminization and masculinization of Protestantism, I will suggest that we have oversimplified what is, in fact, a more complex and interesting situation.

First, the words *feminine, masculine,* and their derivatives were neither univocal in meaning nor fixed in terms of referent. Failure to recognize that point has led to a conflation of bits of historical evidence, as if they were all referring to the same thing, and the tendency to impose categories (e.g., "feminization" and "masculinization") on the past uncritically, as if historians were always describing the same thing. Second, I want to raise the possibility that the "feminine church" of the nineteenth century was the invention of turn-of-the-century Protestants rather than something that had existed as such since the early national period. In other words, perhaps turn-of-the-century depictions of the feminine church were re-readings of the past in light of contemporary, turn-of-the-century concerns. In Coe's case, it is clear that his depiction of the church as feminine tells us more about Coe's modernist views than it does about the traditional form of Methodism he was trying to displace. Third, the variety of meanings and referents associated with the words *feminine* and *masculine* at the turn of the century suggest that we might better understand what historians usually depict as a masculinizing reaction to a feminized Protestantism in relation to competing (but not mutually exclusive) models of gender and society that were implicit in contending views of Protestantism.

My underlying contention is that we as historians have been guilty of what Wayne Proudfoot has termed "descriptive reduction" in our interpretations and guilty of uncritically accepting into our sources' descriptive reductions of others. In the first instance, we have too often failed to specify experiences in question "under a description that can plausibly be ascribed to the person to whom we attribute the experience" before going on to explain them as (to their way of thinking) feminized or masculinized.[3] In the second, we have not paused to reconstitute in their own terms the experience of those whom our sources want to characterize as masculine or feminine. My methodological aim in this essay is, insofar as I can, to avoid both pitfalls and, through "peeling off" successive layers of descriptive reductions, reconstruct some of the contending views of gender and Protestantism operative at the turn of the century.

I will focus on Coe and the Methodist tradition more generally for several reasons. First, Coe made his remarks about the "'Eternally Feminine' in the Church" in the context of an overall argument that we can analyze to reveal how his feminine church was constructed. Second, as a professor of religious education at Union Theological Seminary in New York as of 1909, Coe played a leading role in promoting modernist ideas in theological schools (through the publication of widely used textbooks) and churches (through Sunday school curricula).[4] Third, Methodism, the largest Protestant denomination for much of the nineteenth century, has been overshadowed by the Reformed tradition in discussions of the feminization and masculinization of Protestantism.

Feminization Revisited

The feminization of American religion thesis has had remarkable staying power, especially among historians of American religion, despite numerous significant critiques.[5] Ann Braude, for example, points out that historians of American religion have used the term *feminization* in at least three ways: to signify demographic shifts, to characterize changes in ideology, and to express normative judgments. Richard Shiels's essay "The Feminization of American Congregationalism" illustrates the use of the term to describe changes in religious demographics, specifically the changing ratio of women to men in pews. As Braude points out, everyone, including Shiels, agrees that women outnumbered men in pews throughout American history, except perhaps in the very earliest years of the Massachusetts Bay Colony. Although the ratios of men to women in pews may have had locally significant fluctuations, Braude argues that the fact that women consistently outnumbered men over the course of three centuries means that American Protestantism was not feminized in any overt demographic sense.[6]

In a longitudinal study of Center (Congregational) Church in New Haven, Connecticut, Harry S. Stout and Catherine Brekus found that women from the mid-seventeenth century to the 1980s consistently outnumbered men in pews by a ratio of about 2:1. Given this overall consistency, they argue for more subtle demographic signs of feminization, such as a shift from men to women as "carriers of the faith" and the severing of connections between conversion and male communal leadership. In a similar vein, I have argued that shifts in the nature of parenting, connected to the decline in the household economy in the northeastern United States during the early nineteenth century, led to an intensification of the mother-child relationship, as well as a tendency for adults to view their mothers as the sources of their religious feelings and conflate their feelings for sacred figures with love of their mothers.[7] These studies, both centered on the more established denominations of the northeastern United States, link feminization not to the ratio of men to women in pews but rather to changes in gender roles.

More commonly, as Braude points out, historians have used the term *feminization* to refer to ideological changes.[8] Focusing on a theological trajectory running from the orthodox Calvinist Joseph Bellamy through the liberal Congregationalist Horace Bushnell, Ann Douglas argued for a shift from a "basically paternal (or gubernatorial) and authoritarian view to a fundamentally maternal and affective one."[9] A close reading of her sources indicates that the changes involved an increasing focus on Jesus as an object of devotion along with or instead of God and changes in the metaphors used to describe both Jesus and God. Although there was increasing emphasis on the love, rather than the wrath, of God along this trajectory, maternal (as opposed to paternal) metaphors for this love do not appear in Douglas's sources until Bushnell at mid-century.[10]

When it comes to shifts in ideology, historians have counted any number of changes as evidence of feminization, including an increasing emphasis on emotion, experience, relationality, suffering, and self-sacrifice. Usually the historians in question assume that people at the time would have associated whatever change they were lifting up with the feminine, but that is usually assumed rather than argued. The use of feminization to refer to changes in ideology, when not rigorously rooted in the literal and often contested use of gendered metaphors and ascriptions, risks imposing our understandings of the feminine and masculine (and our normative associations with those terms) on our historical sources. Ann Douglas did this explicitly, using a Freudian developmental model to disparage the changes she described.[11] Others have not been so candid and have tacitly replicated the normative judgments of their sources.

In an analysis of the early-twentieth-century "Men and Religion Forward Movement," Gail Bederman rightly recognizes that turn-of-the-century church leaders' sudden preoccupation with gender imbalance in pews did not result from a change in demographics. Rather, she concludes, "Churchmen[,] . . . ignoring the fact that the churches had been two-thirds female for over two hundred years, . . . discovered—or, more accurately, *constructed*—a '*crisis*,' pointing to the 'excess of women over men in church life' as a new and dangerous threat, requiring immediate attention."[12] Traditionalists attributing gender disparity to recent causes constructed it as a new threat. Coe, a modernist, blamed the "excess" on traditional, and thus longstanding, features of Christianity. For Coe, Protestant modernism was not a cause of the crisis, as traditionalists contended, but a potential solution to a longstanding problem.

In light of the many meanings ascribed to feminization, it is important to note that Coe did not equate the "excess of women in the Churches" with the feminization of the church but rather with the "adaptation of the Church to the female nature." He personified the church as feminine ("the Church . . . with feminine eyes") and offered the adaptation of the church to the female nature (presumably an evolutionary adaptation to the excess of women in the church environment) as an explanation for why so many women were in churches in the first place. He personified the church as feminine because it had taken on attributes he associated with the "female nature." If we reject his circular evolutionary logic, then we are left simply with a church that

Coe coded as feminine based on characteristics he associated with "female nature."

There is nothing in what I have quoted so far that indicates what Coe took those attributes to be. For him, the church's chief feminine attributes were emotionality, subjectivity, and introspection. But—and this is a critical but—for Coe these attributes had less to do with gender ratios in pews than with certain ideological features of "old-time" Methodism that he coded as feminine. Coe's feminine church, that is to say, was his particular brand of feminine church and not necessarily the same as the next turn-of-the-century church leader's. Linking gender disparities in membership ("the excess of women") with disparaging characterizations of Christianity as unmanly or feminine created a sense of crisis and legitimated calls for change while masking the constructed character of the feminine church.

Constructing a Feminine Church

Coe's explanation of the "persistent excess of women in the Churches" appeared in his first book, *The Spiritual Life: Studies in the Science of Religion* (1900), a pioneering work in the psychology of religion. Like the work of his contemporaries Edwin Starbuck and William James, Coe's study focused on the conversion experience of Protestants. He contended that such experiences placed too much emphasis on the subjective, inward, and emotional. Coe coded these attributes as "feminine" and argued that they reflected the church's adaptation to the disproportionate number of women in pews. Two years later, in *The Religion of a Mature Mind,* he offered a modern, scientific alternative designed to appeal to the "modern man" of mature mind. Coe depicted this alternative approach, which downplayed the conversion experience, as objective, rational, and outer-directed. Coe's books immediately appeared on recommended reading lists for Protestant clergy and were widely read in seminary classes. They were also discussed in the press, both religious and secular, under such headlines as "Sex in Religion: Are Women Really More Religious Than Men?" and "Why Men Are Not in Church."[13]

The Spiritual Life was based on an empirical study of the conversion experiences of seventy-four college students (fifty male and twenty-four female), the large majority of whom had been "brought up under the influence of the Methodist Church."[14] More than half had a dramatic conversion experience, and more than a quarter experienced "mental and motor automatisms" (e.g., the striking dreams, visions, or involuntary bodily movements associated with the old-fashioned Methodist conversion experience). Coe found that the same sorts of phenomena were associated with the experience of "entire sanctification," a second experience that Methodists traditionally expected sometime after conversion.[15]

Coe's central concern was less with those who had had traditional conversion or sanctification experiences than with those who expected to have such experiences and yet did not. As he put it, "Why is it that of two persons who have had the same bringing up, and who seek conversion [or sanctification] with equal earnestness, one is ushered into the new life with shoutings and blowing of trumpets, as it were, while the other, however earnestly he may seek such experiences, never attains them at all[?]."[16] That, it turns out, was Coe's own question. The son of a Methodist minister, he was raised with a traditional Methodist understanding of the importance of religious experience. When he was young, he said, Methodists "laid great store by 'testimony' to a 'personal experience' of 'conversion' and 'witness of the Spirit' or 'assurance' that one had been pardoned and 'accepted' of God." Like many of his modernist peers, however, he never had a personal experience of conversion in which, in classical Wesleyan fashion, "the Spirit witnessed with his spirit that he was a child of God."[17] That lack caused him considerable anguish until he finally, as an undergraduate, decided to "cut the knot by a rational and ethical act." Doing so not only "ended the turmoil[,] . . . it led on towards endeavours to explain the experiences that some had while I did not have them."[18]

As Edwin Starbuck noted in a review, Coe's distinctive contribution and the "chief interest of the volume [*The Spiritual Life*]" was its focus on "temperament, both as a factor in the variety of religious experiences and in the determination of the peculiar types of religious expression."[19] Actually, Coe argued that there were "three sets of factors [that] favor the attainment of a striking religious transformation—the temperament factor, the factor of expectation, and the tendency to automatisms and passive suggestibility."[20] He found that those for whom emotion was the predominant faculty and those whose mental processes were melancholic or sanguine were likely to have dramatic conversion experiences, whereas those for whom intellect was the predominant faculty and those whose mental processes were choleric (i.e., oriented toward practical action) were not. Those least likely to experience a sudden conversion, in other words, were intellectuals who had an orientation toward practical action—that is, people like Coe himself.

Coe's statements about gender were derived not from an analysis of his data but from a reading of Havelock Ellis's *Man and Woman* (1895).[21] From it, Coe concluded that "[t]wo of the best established general differences between the male and the female mind are these: first, the female mind tends more than the male to feeling; and, second, it is more suggestible." Bringing

these differences to bear on his own research on conversion, Coe argued that
women were not more religious than men, as was commonly believed, but
rather temperamentally distinct. "[T]he real difference is less in the degree
of religiousness [between men and women] than in the general make-up of
mind."[22] Coe, in short, used Ellis to argue that women's emotional nature
made them more susceptible to a particular way of being religious that was
too often regarded as the *only* authentic way of being religious. Specifically,
Coe drew from Ellis the idea that women were more susceptible to hypnotic
phenomena, which Ellis defined broadly to include not only the phenomena of mesmerism and animal magnetism (hypnotism proper) but also the
"allied phenomena of ecstasy, trance, and catalepsy" (what Coe referred to
as "automatisms" and traditional Methodists as trances, visions, and the
power of the Spirit).[23]

Ellis linked hypnosis, religion, and gender and placed the whole within an
evolutionary framework. The control exercised by the "higher intellectual
centres" was "more highly co-ordinated" and demonstrated a higher degree
of "mental integration." As one ascended the evolutionary scale, "the [nerve]
centres . . . become more and more intimately bound up and associated with
each other in action." Civilized races thus were characterized by a higher
degree of mental integration and less liable to the loss of higher mental control associated with hypnosis. This higher mental control was associated with
reason, whereas hypnotic phenomena were associated physiologically with
the emotions. Thus, said Ellis, "When . . . we conclude that women are more
liable than men to present hypnotic phenomena, we have but discovered in
a more definite and fundamental manner that women are more 'emotional'
than men."[24]

The process of cultural evolution for Ellis was not simply a movement from
the feminine and primitive to the masculine and civilized. Rather, he argued
that "[s]avagery and barbarism have more usually than not been predominantly militant, that is to say masculine, in character, while modern civilisation is becoming industrial, that is to say feminine, in character, for the industries belonged primitively to women." For him, industrialization tended
to "make men like women," a process he referred to explicitly as "feminisa-
tion," where the masculine was associated with warfare and the feminine with
manufacturing. Overall, he said, the periods least favorable to women are
those that are "very militant . . . and those so-called advanced periods in
which the complicated and artificial products of the variational tendency of
men are held in chief honour." Ellis described Greece and Rome as "emphatically masculine states of culture" and indicated that "when the feminine
element at last came to the front with Christianity and the barbarians, clas-

sic civilisation went, and for a long time the masculine element in life also largely went."[25] That, I suggest, is the source of Coe's claim that the church was feminine.

For Ellis, and for Coe as well, the ideal was not a reassertion of the masculine over the feminine. Rather, as Ellis stated, "The hope of our future civilisation lies in the development of equal freedom of both the masculine and feminine elements in life. The broader and more varied character of modern civilisation seems to render this more possible than did the narrow basis of classic civilisation, and there is much evidence around us that a twin movement of this kind is in progress."[26] Coe's ideal, following Ellis, was neither the "emphatically masculine state of culture" associated with Greece and Rome nor an emphatically feminine state of culture associated with the church, but "the equal freedom of both the masculine and feminine elements of life." Or, as Coe put it, "Neither the man alone nor the woman alone is a perfect type, but rather the family, in which the two complementary qualities are balanced the one over against the other."[27]

Throughout, Coe's analysis was premised on a redescription (or descriptive reduction) of traditional Methodism such that what old-time Methodists referred to as trances, visions, or falling under the power of the Spirit were recast by Coe as automatisms and Ellis as hypnotic phenomena. Experiences of the "power of God" or the "witness of the Holy Spirit" were redescribed as subjective, inward, and emotional. Once redescribed, they could then be analyzed in terms of temperament, explained in terms of psychology, and characterized on the basis of prevailing views of gender differences. Redescription provided the foundation for Coe's depiction of the church as feminine and did not, generally speaking, reflect the language of those who had, and continued to advocate, such experiences.[28]

In referring to old-fashioned Methodism as emotional, Coe articulated a view that was to become a common-place in the psychology of religion. In everyday language, it found a place in (usually disparaging) references to "emotional religion," where what was being coded as "emotional" was, among other things, the traditional, supernaturalistic Methodist conversion experience. Coe's use of the term *emotional* was evaluative rather than descriptive. As he acknowledged, he used the word to refer to what he took to be "feeling for its own sake." Thus, "When we speak of emotional temperament, emotional novels, emotional religious meetings, and the like, what we really have in mind is not merely the abundance of emotion, but also the quality."[29] When he described traditional Methodism as emotional, he was targeting what he viewed as its one-sided emphasis on subjective experience. Coe's research thus represented a fundamental recasting of the traditional

Methodist understanding of religious experience, such that what had been understood as signs of the "power of God" or the "witness of the Holy Spirit" were now merely manifestations of temperamental differences.

As the many congratulatory reviews and letters in his scrapbooks attest, Coe's early work spoke to a definite hunger on the part of the more progressive Methodist clergy for a modern, scientifically justifiable way to move away from their experientially oriented evangelical heritage. Coe's redescription of the tradition was not uncontested, however. In a series of letters written on the stationary of the Cincinnati Camp Meeting Association, the Rev. E. S. Gaddis of Loveland, Ohio, criticized him for attacking what he took to be true Wesleyanism. Coe denied any such intent, and Gaddis ultimately reconsidered his claims in light of Coe's argument. In an abject capitulation to modernity, Gaddis conceded, "My conclusion therefrom must be, according to your book, attributed to my peculiar temperamental qualities. . . . I believe I need just such teaching to keep me from trying to push people through the same mold, I went myself. Please count me one of the pastors who have received help from your book."[30]

The Rev. D. C. John, a Methodist presiding elder from Milwaukee, was less traditional in his outlook than Gaddis and more experienced in the ways of the academy. He criticized Coe for attempting to eliminate emotion from religion but was not overawed by Coe's denials of such an intent. Despite Coe's disavowal, he insisted, "the trend of [Coe's] book was in that direction" and added, for good measure, that he thought that Coe's "treatment of feminine mind [was] . . . unjust and in violent antagonism to the facts." Pulling no punches, he forthrightly declared, "Women did not shout more and get the power more in the emotional epoch of Methodism than did men. To come to close quarters [Coe's hometown], Evanston never had a greater or more masterful mind, masculine or feminine, than Frances E. Willard. The attempt to show that women are more emotional and less intellectual than men is a self-complacent assumption untenable in the face of current history. You will surely have to revise this part of your book or fall under just condemnation."[31]

Coe did in fact avoid such claims in his later works, perhaps because he was not entirely convinced by his own arguments. Although, in keeping with common nineteenth-century usage, Coe often used the words *feminine* and *masculine* as synonyms for female and male, he did not do so consistently. Sometimes, as in the opening quotation, he seemed to presuppose the complementarity of the sexes. At other points he seemed to make a distinction between women and the feminine. Thus, although he coded the church and certain temperaments as feminine, he stated, "The temperamental interpretation of Christianity is likewise one probable reason for the aloofness from the Church of a strangely large proportion of the most high-minded, morally earnest, and intelligent men *and women.*"[32] Moreover, Coe's own marriage was untraditional. Like others married to socially progressive, modernist men, Sarah Coe was college-educated and committed to pursing her own career. The Coes had no children, and George enthusiastically supported Sarah's career as a musician, composer, and professor of music throughout their seventeen-year marriage. When she died unexpectedly in 1905, her hometown newspaper commented, "Mrs. Coe's character was a rare one, combining an intellectuality almost masculine, with a remarkable feminine intuition and a thorough womanliness in every direction. Mrs. Coe's life was a particularly happy one. Professor Coe, who . . . is a man of great intellectual power, was perfectly in sympathy with the aims of the wife, whom he adored."[33]

Within a few years, the overtly gendered language of Coe's earlier writings was replaced with generic references to selves and parents. His primary concern, as his subsequent works made clear, was to institutionalize a Bushnellian vision of Christian nurture by allying religious education with the movement for progressive education led by John Dewey. Religious education, in Coe's view, was neither ancillary to secular progressivism nor to the ministry of the church, but rather integral to a full realization of both. Coe's vision as a religious educator encompassed all institutions that engaged in the nurture of the young, from the family and the Sunday school to public schools, colleges, and universities.[34] Implicit within that vision was a new understanding of gender and society that differed in significant ways from two older understandings it sought to displace.

Competing Models of Gender and Society

Coe's modernist understanding of the relationship between gender and society was one of three competing models implicit in the thought of Protestants at the turn of the twentieth century. Both of the competing models had earlier, nineteenth-century roots. Early American Methodists and the more radical wing of the late-nineteenth-century Holiness movement generally advocated what I refer to as the "patriarchal model"; bourgeois Methodists of the mid-to-late nineteenth century advocated what I refer to as the "maternal (or domestic) model"; and modernists of Coe's generation what I refer to as the "scientific model." Each model could be adapted to more or less egalitarian ends. In their less-egalitarian forms, each agreed that women's primary place was in the home and that her primary role was as a wife and mother, albeit for different reasons. Conversely, in their more egalitarian forms, all three approaches agreed, for very different reasons, that at least some women might legitimately speak as Protestants in the public arena.

Although for heuristic purposes, the three models can be distinguished on the basis of their understanding of the relationship between gender and society, the lines between them often blurred in practice. Distinguishing among them, however, allows a view of the fluid, competitive context in which Coe articulated his understanding of gender and Protestantism. In place of the usual depiction of a twentieth-century masculinizing backlash against a feminized Victorian Protestantism, a more complex picture emerges. In it, the more egalitarian versions of all three approaches found at least limited expression during the opening decades of the twentieth century only to be displaced by less-egalitarian approaches during the 1920s.

The Patriarchal Model

The patriarchal model had its roots in the Greco-Roman world. It was revitalized in the early modern period in the form of a political theory—classical republicanism—that identified "the health of the polity as a whole with the *virtus* or virility of an ancient warrior ideal." That ideal was particularly influential in the American context around the time of the Revolutionary War.[35] Two historians, Susan Juster and Christine Heyrman, have suggested that it had particular impact on early American Methodism.[36] The Greco-Roman version of the model, however, was presupposed in the New Testament and in various ways adapted to Christian purposes in the New Testament itself. In that form, it was accessible to any close reader of the Bible.

This model divided society into the *oikos* (household) and the *polis* (city-state). Citizenship in the polis was open to free men capable of fulfilling military obligations. Non-warriors (children, women, and slaves) were all excluded from citizenship. The male property-owner was the head of the household. In this model, the health of the polity depended on the *virtus* (virtue or virility) of those (free males) designated to defend it. Free males of virtue were simultaneously heads of their households and citizens of the polis. In the household codes of the New Testament, Christ is explicitly described as "the head of the church" just as "the husband is the head of the wife" (Eph. 5:23). The most important metaphors for conversion to Christianity were based upon relationships within the household. Converts gained a place in the Christian household via marriage to Christ (as brides) or adoption as sons of God and joint heirs (with Christ) of the kingdom. In either case, God was the presumptive head of the Christian household.

The metaphor of adoption was particularly important in the Wesleyan tradition, where the experience of conversion and sanctification was linked to the indwelling of the Spirit of God such that "[t]he Spirit itself beareth witness with our spirit, that we are the children of God: And if children, then heirs; heirs of God, and joint-heirs with Christ" (Romans 8:16–17). When Coe said that Methodists in his youth "laid great store by 'testimony' to a 'personal experience' of 'conversion' and 'witness of the Spirit' or 'assurance' that one had been pardoned and 'accepted' of God," he was referring to testimony to one's adoption as "sons" or "children of God." As Coe indicated, early Methodists in England and America experienced the witness and in-dwelling of the Spirit in concrete ways.[37] Those who held to the centrality of a distinctive experience of the Spirit were drawn toward Holiness camp meetings and into the independent Holiness denominations at the turn of the century.

In this model, identity, at least on the spiritual level, was unstable. Both men and women could and did metaphorically switch genders to become brides of Christ, sons of God, and brothers in or soldiers of Christ. Like Paul, they saw visions and were confused about whether they were in their bodies or out of their bodies. They were also at times overcome by the power of God or the Holy Spirit, who sometimes caused them to fall to the ground and sometimes spoke through them while they preached. When the power of God caused them to fall or speak out, it was no longer they who acted but God or the Spirit through them. When the power of God acted through them, they were not acting as themselves, much less as men or women. Turn-of-the-century women, particularly women associated with the more radical Holiness groups, gained access to traditionally male activities such as preaching when the power of the Spirit acted through them. They did so, however, not as women but as mouthpieces for God or the Holy Spirit.

This model could also be adapted so as to rule out the manifestation of the spiritual gifts of inspiration and prophesy in this life and thus effectively to rule out female evangelism. Thus, late-nineteenth-century evangelicals in the Reformed wing of the tradition worked out the dispensationalist understanding of biblical prophesy, in part, as Margaret Bendroth has noted, to combat the "the rising popularity of female evangelists, especially in the holiness wing of evangelical Protestantism." In contrast to the more radical Holiness exegetes who interpreted spiritual gifts mentioned in Scripture as available in the present, dispensationalists emphasized the irreversible nature of original sin (with Eve taking most of the blame for the fall), the impossibility of realized (as opposed to imputed) holiness, and thus the impossibility of authentic spiritual gifts (e.g., inspiration, prophesy, and speaking in tongues) in this world/dispensation. Promises of spiritual gifts and equality in Christ were relegated to another place (heaven) or time (the final, millennial dispensation). Both dispensationalist and radical Holiness exegetes agreed on the promises but disagreed on whether they could be authentically claimed in the present as men and women were doing in the radical wing of the Holiness movement. From the dispensationalist perspective, the rising social and religious prominence of women in Holiness or progressive circles was a sign not of holiness or progress but of the impending cataclysm awaiting those who, like Eve, brazenly rebelled.[38]

The Maternal Model

The roots of the maternal or domestic model go back to the early nineteenth century. Historians have discussed this model in relation to the emergence of "separate spheres" and the "ideology of domesticity." As a social theory, it owes a debt to de Tocqueville and to the efforts of those such as Catherine Beecher who popularized and elaborated upon his ideas. It is usually understood as arising in response, on the one hand, to industrialization (with its concomitant separation of work and home) and, on the other hand, to a need to reconceptualize the social order in the wake of political democratization and ecclesiastical disestablishment.[39] This model has been widely associated with nineteenth-century Protestantism, but in my view it should be more narrowly associated with Protestantism of the respectable sort.

The maternal model divided society into a domestic and a civil sphere, but the civil was not merely equated with the state. In keeping with the theories of de Tocqueville and various eighteenth-century thinkers, the civil sphere was made up of associations, understood as loci of self-rule and the foundation for democratic society.[40] The domestic sphere was understood as loci of self-sacrifice (subordination of self to the needs of the other) and a necessary corrective to the self-rule inculcated in civil sphere. Where in the patriarchial model the household was conceptualized as "not-male," in the maternal model it was positively characterized in terms of maternal virtues. These virtues stood in opposition to the male virtues of self-rule demanded in the civic sphere. Where in the patriarchal model military virtues alone were sufficient to ensure the stability of the civil order, in the maternal model the virtues of both the domestic and the civic were necessary to ensure stability.

This basic interdependent opposition between domestic and civic gave rise to others: home/work, self-sacrifice/self-rule, maternal/paternal, and woman/man. The model was accompanied by a tendency (which gave rise to the feminization theories of Douglas and Welter) to associate religion, especially in the wake of disestablishment from the state, with the domestic sphere and to associate maternal virtues with Christian virtues. The "sentimental fiction" of the mid-to-late nineteenth century, much of it written by women, tended to heighten the association between maternal and Christian virtues, focusing theological attention on Jesus' death on the cross as an act of voluntary self-sacrifice. Harriet Beecher Stowe's *Uncle Tom's Cabin* epitomized this tendency.[41]

In the maternal model, gender identity and gender roles were understood as polarized and fixed, either biologically or normatively. There was little gender switching, even at a metaphoric level, and few trance-related behaviors (visions, ecstasy, and falling or preaching under the power of the Spirit)—at least in public. The play in this model emerged in relation to two factors: the way gender was fixed and where the boundary between the domestic and civic was located. Those with a more traditional view of women's roles tended to associate maternal virtues with a domestic sphere narrowly conceived in terms of the home and motherhood (i.e., a social location and role). In their view, the benefits of women's influence on society would only be realized if women remained within the domestic sphere so conceived. Those who had a more progressive view of women's roles tended to root maternal virtues in female nature (biology). Because, in their view, the virtues were biologically rooted, progressives believed that the benefits of women's maternal influence on society would be most fully realized by a metaphoric extension of the domestic sphere beyond the literal confines of the home or even, according to some, through direct participation in civil society.

The maternal or domestic model was the dominant understanding of society during the Victorian Era. It was embraced most fully by the "respectable" classes and the denominations they frequented. It was the enthusiastic embrace of this model by Unitarians, Congregationalists, Presbyterians, and Episcopalians that caused historians to depict nineteenth-century Protestantism as feminized. Denominations that had more populist or working-class constituencies, such as Methodists and Roman Catholics, were more complex.[42] In its more egalitarian variant, that model informed the rise of Protestant women's organizations such as the Woman's Christian Temperance Union, denominational home and foreign missionary societies, and deaconess training schools in the wake of the Civil War. Under the leadership of Frances Willard, a Methodist, the WCTU allied itself with the suffrage movement but did so to "protect the home" from alcoholism rather than to promote "women's rights." Similarly, Willard and other Methodist women pressed for access to governing and clerical authority within the church, but did so on the grounds of maternal virtues rather than equal rights.

By the end of the nineteenth century, progressive Victorian Protestants faced contradictions inherent in using the virtues of the domestic sphere to gain access to the civic. Although women's organizations were explicitly established to extend the maternal virtues attendant on the domestic sphere, they were also associations, in de Tocqueville's sense, which inevitably and in contradiction to their explicit ideology trained women in the habits of self-rule essential to democratic civil society. As the first generation of "new women" entered colleges and the newly co-educational universities during the 1880s and 1890s and in record numbers chose careers in women's colleges and settlement houses over heterosexual marriages, the contradictions among ideology, aspiration, and practice became acute.[43]

The Scientific Model

The scientific model emerged at the turn of the century. Broadly speaking, its roots were in the new social sciences, especially psychology, sociology, and anthropology, associated with the modern coeducational university. More narrowly, it is associated with the functional psychology of William James and the Chicago School, especially John Dewey and George Herbert Mead. In Protestant circles, its chief exponent was George Coe. It began as a philosophically informed (social) psychology that was simultaneously empirical, functionalist, evolutionary, and pragmatic and expanded into education, sociology, and anthropology. The model was generated by progressive intellectuals who desired a way of life consistent with what they took to be the implications of modern science. Although they were intellectuals, they were anti-elitist in orientation and convinced that the ideal of inquiry upheld by science was accessible to the "rank-and-file membership of an educated, democratic society."[44]

Two key concepts informed the scientific model: a developmental conception of a self that emerged through social relationships and the idea of society as a social organism. Social evolution and self-evolution (the development of the self) were considered correlative once the self had arisen out of the life process. The emergence of the self (a distinctively human feature based in language) made possible the emergence of human society. Society, made up of groups and communities of various sizes and degrees of complexity, arose out of family relationships that made the emergence of the self possible. Schools, churches, and government were understood as extensions of parental relationships. Democracy, in its ideal sense, depended upon the development of selves that exhibited their own individuality and at the same time took the attitude of those they were affecting (Mead) or selves that could mutually attain freedom in the world as it is (Coe).[45]

The scientific model stood apart from the others in its rejection of dualisms. Family, school, church, and society were not divided into separate spheres but rather were conceived as progressively wider, more inclusive instances of community. Balance was a virtue and led to an emphasis on the importance of a balanced approach to the masculine and the feminine. What that meant in practice depended on whether masculine and feminine attributes were identified (normatively or biologically) with men and women. Those who upheld the less-egalitarian variant of this model correlated gendered attributes (e.g., the masculine and feminine) with actual or ideal male and female natures. They viewed marriage and motherhood as the most suitable path for women and understood heterosexual marriage, the site where complementary natures were joined, as the foremost means of realizing balance. Those who did not conform to this model (e.g., effeminate men and masculine women) were labeled as moral or biological deviants. If gendered attributes (masculinity and femininity) were understood as independent of gender identity and roles, then a balance of attributes (androgyny) could be either found or cultivated. Balance could then be achieved in the individual independent of heterosexual marriage.

Changing views of sexuality, especially women's sexuality, profoundly affected the scientific model. In the maternal model, bourgeois Victorians associated mothers and children (both understood as asexual) with the domestic sphere; in the scientific model, twentieth-century modernists defined the family in terms of the husband and wife. In keeping with the findings of the "sexologists," intimate relations between women, accepted in the maternal model, were increasingly viewed with suspicion by all but the most progressive. Sexologists introduced the terms *heterosexual* and *homosexual* to define what was "normal" and what was "deviant." Where the maternal model encouraged homosocial institutions and relationships, the scientific model tended to undercut them as long as gendered attributes (masculinity and femininity) were linked with gender identity and roles.[46]

Conclusion

The scientific model was in competition with the two other models at the turn of the century, and its most progressive advocates were not in churches. Intent on overturning the old canons of masculinity and femininity and upholding an androgynous, independent, self-supporting ideal for women, they described themselves as feminists (rather than feminine), thus introducing a modern term into common English usage.[47] Although university-related academics and Protestant modernists generally embraced the scientific model, most did not adopt the radically egalitarian version associated with the second generation of new women. Coe, who appeared only moderately progressive on women's issues when compared to the most egalitarian progressives outside the church, was probably as progressive as any within the church.[48]

By the 1920s, large, coeducational universities had abandoned the nineteenth-century ideal of "educated motherhood" (the maternal model) for the new, sociologically informed, and sexualized ideal of the "wife-companion" (the scientific model).[49] The patriarchal model in its less-egalitarian form lived on among fundamentalists, however. The spread of dispensational exegesis among traditional Protestants gradually undermined the more egalitarian exegesis associated with the radical wing of the Holiness movement. The multisided battles of the 1920s between fundamentalists and modernists within the churches and conservative and progressive proponents of the new science in the broader society led to the marginalization of both fundamentalists and progressive new women. By the 1930s the less-egalitarian variant of the scientific model was dominant among the educated classes, and neo-orthodoxy was displacing modernism among bourgeois Protestants.[50]

Coe's call for masculine balance in the turn-of-the-century church carried potentially radical implications for women insofar as it separated gender attributions (masculinity and femininity) from gender identity and roles. Pushed to its most radical conclusions, this model created room for androgynous selves and independent career women, married and single. Coe, however, did not push the model that far. Although he was identified with radical causes over the course of his career, his activism centered on economic and military issues. Although he was privately supportive of many early-twentieth-century feminist goals, he did not, as far as I know, explicitly embrace feminism, nor did he take public stands on issues such as woman suffrage. Moreover, while not pushing the feminist possibilities inherent in the scientific model, Coe's promotion of the modernist approach to Protestantism undercut the bases of women's authority in the other two competing models. By explaining Methodist supernaturalism in naturalistic terms, *The Spiritual Life* undercut the authority of women called to preach by the power of the Holy Spirit in the Holiness tradition. By stressing the complementarity of the masculine and feminine and linking it to an emphasis on the complementarity of the husband and wife in marriage and the family, the scientific model undercut the dualisms that informed the idea of separate male and female spheres.

Although to speak of Protestantism as masculinized at the turn of the century is, in my view, overly simplistic, the eventual collapse of the maternal model in its progressive variant and the marginalization of the Holiness movement were significant losses for women in the absence of an aggressively and successfully feminist Protestant modernism. It is those losses that historians' depictions of the era as masculinized have rightfully attempted to capture.

Notes

1. George Albert Coe, *The Spiritual Life: Studies in the Science of Religion* (Chicago: Fleming H. Revell, 1900), 247, 242–43.

2. Gail Bederman, "'The Women Have Had Charge of the Church Work Long Enough': The Men and Religion Forward Movement of 1911–1912 and the Masculinization of Middle-Class Protestantism," *American Quarterly* 41 (Sept. 1989): 438; Betty A. DeBerg, *Ungodly Women: Gender and the First Wave of American Fundamentalism* (Minneapolis: Fortress Press, 1990); Margaret Lamberts Bendroth, *Fundamentalism and Gender, 1875 to the Present* (New Haven: Yale University Press, 1993).

3. Wayne Proudfoot, *Religious Experience* (Berkeley: University of California Press, 1985), 180–81.

4. On Coe as a modernist who attempted "a massive institutionalization of the Bushnellian theories of Christian nurture," see William R. Hutchison, *The Modernist Impulse in American Protestantism* (Durham: Duke University Press, 1992), 155–64. On Coe's role as a founding father of the Religious Education Association, see Stephen A. Schmidt, *A History of the Religious Education Association* (Birmingham: Religious Education Press, 1983), 11–15, 36–39. There is as yet no published biography of Coe. For biographical information, see George A. Coe, "My Own Little Theatre," in *Religion in Transition*, ed. Vergilius Ferm (New York: Macmillan, 1937), 90–125, and "In Memoriam: George Albert Coe, 1862–1951," *Religious Education* 47 (1952): 65–176.

5. David Schuyler, "Inventing a Feminine Past," *New England Quarterly* 51 (Sept. 1978): 291–308; David S. Reynolds, "The Feminization Controversy: Sexual Stereotypes and the Paradoxes of Piety in Nineteenth-Century America," *New England Quarterly* 53 (1980): 96–106; Terry Bilhartz, "Sex and the Second Great Awakening: The Feminization of American Religion Reconsidered," in *Beliefs and Behavior: Essays in the New Religious History*, ed. Philip Vandermeer and Robert Swierenga (New Brunswick: Rutgers University Press, 1991), 117–35.

6. Ann Braude, "Women's History *Is* American Religious History," in *Retelling U.S. Religious History*, ed. Thomas A. Tweed (Berkeley: University of California Press, 1997), 87, 94–96; Richard D. Shiels, "The Feminization of American Congregationalism, 1730–1835," *American Quarterly* 39 (1981): 45–62.

7. Harry S. Stout and Catherine Brekus, "A New England Congregation: Center Church, New Haven, 1636–1989," in *American Congregations*, 2 vols., ed. James P. Wind and James W. Lewis (Chicago: University of Chicago Press, 1994), 1:40–45; Ann Taves, "Mothers and Children and the Legacy of Mid-Nineteenth Century American Christianity," *Journal of Religion* 67 (April 1987): 210–13.

8. Braude, "Women's History," 94–95, 99.

9. Ann Douglas, *The Feminization of American Culture* (New York: Avon Books, 1978), 143–51, quotation on 146.

10. Taves, "Mothers and Children," 204–8.

11. Douglas, *The Feminization of American Culture*, 162.

12. Bederman, "The Women Have Had Charge," 438, emphasis added.

13. The following are all in manuscript group 36, George A. Coe Papers, Special Collections, Yale Divinity School Library (hereafter, Coe Papers): George Willis Cooke, "Sex in Religion: Are Women Really More Religious Than Men?" *Boston Transcript,* Nov. 10, 1900 (Scrapbook 1:46–47); "Are Women More Religious Than Men?" *Literary Digest* Nov. 24, 1900, 621 (Scrapbook 1:55); George Willis Cooke, "Men and the Church: A Further Look into the Reasons Why They Do Not Attend," *Boston Transcript,* Oct. 20, 1900; and Wilbur C. Newell, "Why Men Are Not in Church," *Zion's Herald,* Aug. 30, 1902 (Scrapbook 2:46).

14. George A. Coe, "A Study in the Dynamics of Personality," *Psychological Review* 6 (1899): 487–88.

15. Coe, *The Spiritual Life,* 105.

16. Ibid., 104.

17. William R. Hutchison, "Cultural Strain and Protestant Liberalism," *American Historical Review* 76 (1971): 410.

18. Coe, "My Own Little Theatre," 92–93.

19. Edwin Starbuck, *Psychological Review* [Nov. 1900], Scrapbook 1:52–53, Coe Papers.

20. Coe, *The Spiritual Life,* 504.

21. For late-nineteenth-century assumptions about human nature, see Helen Bradford Thompson [Wooley], *The Mental Traits of Sex* (Chicago: University of Chicago Press, 1903), 169–82, as summarized in Rosalind Rosenberg, *Beyond Separate Spheres: Intellectual Roots of Modern Feminism* (New Haven: Yale University Press, 1982), 69–70.

22. Coe, *The Spiritual Life,* 236.

23. Havelock Ellis, *Man and Woman,* 4th ed. (1904, repr. New York: Arno Press, 1974), 258–61.

24. Ellis, *Man and Woman,* 294, 296.

25. Ibid., 393, 395–96.

26. Ibid., 396.

27. Coe, *The Spiritual Life,* 242–43.

28. The desire to accommodate a diversity of experiences within the Holiness movement did lead to a certain amount of internal redescription. Late-nineteenth-century Holiness leaders who wanted to legitimate a range of experiences, from the silent meditation associated with Phoebe Palmer's Tuesday-night meetings to the crying out and shouting associated with old-fashioned camp meetings, related these differences to differences in education and temperament. A. McLean and J. W. Eaton, eds., *Penuel; or, Face to Face with God* (1869, repr. New York: Garland, 1984), 264–65. I have seen no evidence in Holiness literature to suggest that they viewed their experiences as feminine.

29. Coe, *The Spiritual Life,* 219–21.

30. E. S. Gaddis, Loveland, Ohio, to George A. Coe, Feb. 24, 1902, Scrapbook 2:41, Coe Papers.

31. D. C. John, presiding elder, Milwaukee District, Wisconsin Conference, MEC, to George A. Coe, Feb. 16, 1901, Scrapbook 1, Coe Papers.

32. Coe, *The Spiritual Life*, 249, emphasis added.

33. George Coe and Sarah Knowland married with a "mutual understanding of her ambition." When Coe was at the University of Southern California early in his career, Sarah Coe became the director of the piano department. When he was offered a fellowship in Germany, they accepted so both could advance their educations. When he was offered a position at Northwestern University after a year in Germany, "he insisted that she stay on for two additional seasons in Berlin, he returning in the summers to be with her." Charles S. Braden, "In Evanston," *Religious Education* 47 (1952): 91; George A. Coe, *Sadie Knowland Coe, a Chapter in a Life* (Privately published, 1906). Rosenberg (*Beyond Separate Spheres*, 62–68) contrasts psychologists at Columbia and Clark universities, who had more traditional marriages and were unsupportive of women graduate students and research on gender, with those at Chicago. "Music Matters of the Past Week," *Alameda* [Calif.] *Argus*, Aug. 26, 1905, Coe Papers.

34. Hutchison, *Modernist Impulse*, 158–63.

35. Linda Dowling, *Hellenism and Homosexuality in Victorian England* (Ithaca: Cornell University Press, 1994), xv; Robert E. Shalhope, "Republicanism and Early American Historiography," *William and Mary Quarterly* 39 (1982): 334–56; Linda K. Kerber, *Women of the Republic* (New York: Norton, 1980), 269–88; Ruth H. Block, "The Gendered Meanings of Virtue in Revolutionary America," *Signs* 13 (1987): 37–58.

36. Susan Juster, *Disorderly Women: Sexual Politics and Evangelicalism in Revolutionary New England* (Ithaca: Cornell University Press, 1994), 135–44; Christine Leigh Heyrman, *Southern Cross* (New York: Alfred A. Knopf, 1997), 206–8, 225–26, 228–52.

37. Coe, *The Spiritual Life*, 141–42, 216.

38. Bendroth, *Fundamentalism and Gender*, 44–46, quotation on 44.

39. Kathryn Kish Sklar, *Catherine Beecher: A Study in American Domesticity* (New Haven: Yale University Press, 1973); Nancy F. Cott, *The Bonds of Womanhood: Woman's Sphere in New England, 1780–1835* (New Haven: Yale University Press, 1977).

40. Charles Taylor, "Modes of Civil Society," *Public Culture* 3 (1990): 114–15; Craig Calhoun, "Civil Society and the Public Sphere," *Public Culture* 6 (1993): 267–80.

41. Jane P. Thompkins, "Sentimental Power: *Uncle Tom's Cabin* and the Politics of Literary History," in Uncle Tom's Cabin *by Harriet Beecher Stowe*, ed. Elizabeth Ammons (New York: Norton, 1994), 501–22; Taves, "Mothers and Children."

42. A number of scholars have identified points at which Catholics and Methodists began appropriating this model. See, for example, Colleen McDannell, *The Christian Home in Victorian America, 1840–1900* (Bloomington: Indiana University Press, 1986); Gregory Schneider, *The Way of the Cross Leads Home: The Domestication of American Methodism* (Bloomington: Indiana University Press, 1993); and Richard Bushman, *The Refinement of America: Persons, Houses, Cities* (New York: Knopf, 1992).

43. Carroll Smith-Rosenberg, "The New Woman as Androgyne," in *Disorderly Conduct: Visions of Gender in Victorian America*, ed. Carroll Smith-Rosenberg (New York: Oxford University Press, 1986), 245–96; Nancy F. Cott, *The Grounding of Modern Feminism* (New Haven: Yale University Press, 1987).

44. David A. Hollinger, "The Problem of Pragmatism in American History," *Journal of American History* 67 (1980): 99, 93.

45. George Herbert Mead, *Mind, Self, and Society from the Standpoint of a Social Behaviorist* (Chicago: University of Chicago Press, 1934), 164, 227, 238–41, 253, 326; George A. Coe, *Psychology of Religion* (Chicago: University of Chicago Press, 1916), 42, 142–43, 320.

46. A new vocabulary of deviance emerged in response to changing views of women's sexuality at the turn of the century (e.g., "sexual invert" and "lesbian") and led to new categories: "homosexuality" and "heterosexuality." Smith-Rosenberg, "The New Woman as Androgyne," 275–78; Jonathan Ned Katz, *The Invention of Heterosexuality* (New York: Penguin, 1995), 19–32.

47. Cott, *Modern Feminism*, 3–50; Smith-Rosenberg, "The New Woman as Androgyne," 288–89; Rosenberg, *Beyond Separate Spheres*, 238–46.

48. Janet Fishburn depicts social gospel theologians as quite traditional with respect to gender roles (*The Fatherhood of God and the Victorian Family* [Philadelphia: Fortress Press, 1981], 120–127). On Coe's more egalitarian views, see Margaret Forsythe, "At Teachers College," *Religious Education* 47 (1952): 96.

49. Sheila M. Rothman, *Woman's Proper Place: A History of Changing Ideals and Practices, 1870 to the Present* (New York: Basic Books), 178–79.

50. Smith-Rosenberg, "The New Woman as Androgyne," 288–89; Rosenberg, *Beyond Separate Spheres*, 238–46.

Contributors

Margaret Lamberts Bendroth is professor of history at Calvin College and the author of *Fundamentalism and Gender, 1875 to the Present.*

Virginia Lieson Brereton teaches at Tufts University and is author of *Training God's Army: The American Bible School* and *From Sin to Salvation: Stories of Women's Conversation, 1800 to the Present.*

Mark Chaves teaches sociology at the University of Arizona. He is the author of *Ordaining Women: Culture and Conflict in Religious Organizations.*

Christopher Coble is program director for religion at the Lilly Endowment and received his Th.D. from Harvard Divinity School.

Gastón Espinosa is an assistant professor of religious studies at Westmont College and a visiting scholar in the Department of Religious Studies at the University of California, Santa Barbara. He has written extensively on Latino Pentecostalism.

Maureen Fitzgerald has taught at the University of Arizona and is a visiting professor of American studies at the College of William and Mary.

R. Marie Griffith teaches in the religion department at Princeton University and is the author of *God's Daughters: Evangelical Women and the Power of Submission.*

Susan Hartmann, a professor of history and women's studies at Ohio State University, is the author of *From Margin to Mainstream: American Women and Politics since 1960* and *The Home Front and Beyond: American Women of the 1940s.*

Paul Harvey teaches history at the University of Colorado at Colorado Springs and has written *Redeeming the South: Religious Cultures and Racial Identities among Southern Baptists.*

Laurie F. Maffly-Kipp is associate professor of religious studies at the University of North Carolina at Chapel Hill and the author of *Religion and Society in Frontier California.*

Colleen McDannell teaches in the history department at the University of Utah at Salt Lake City and is author of *The Christian Home in Victorian America* and *Material Christianity: Religion and Popular Culture in America.* She has also contributed to *Riders for God: The Story of A Christian Motorcycle Gang* by Rich Remsberg.

James W. Opp is assistant professor of history at the University of Lethbridge in Alberta, Canada. He has published on the history of Canadian evangelicalism and fundamentalism.

Ann Taves is professor of church history at the School of Theology at Claremont. She is the author of *The Household of Faith: Roman Catholic Devotion in Mid-Nineteenth-Century America* and *Fits, Trances, and Visions: Experiencing Religion and Explaining Experience from Wesley to James.*

Timothy Tseng is associate professor of American religious history at the American Baptist Seminary of the West in Berkeley, California, and has written extensively on Asian Protestants in the United States.

Rumi Yasutake received her Ph.D. in women's history from the University of California at Los Angeles and teaches at California State University, Long Beach.

Susan M. Yohn is associate professor of history at Hofstra University and author of *A Contest of Faiths: Missionary Women and Pluralism in the American Southwest.*

Index

abolitionism, 6, 7, 48n71

abortion, 54, 55–56, 119, 128, 270

abstinence, 110n24

Abzug, Robert, 300n17

acculturation, 45n25, 145

activism: of African American women, 166; "Black Manifesto" and, 51; Chinese immigrants and, 134, 143–44, 145, 154; of Christian Endeavor, 87; of Coe, 320; domesticity and, 143; historians' view of, 285; of IAWM members, 268; of Japanese constitutionalists, 95; of Jews/Catholics, 293–95; of Latinas/Latinos, 41; political/economic impact of women's organizations, 215; transnational, 93–108; of WCTU, 94

activists: resistance to casework, 291–92; separate spheres and, 283–84; welfare state and, 281

Addams, Jane, 285

adolescence, 79, 120

adoption, 314–15

advocacy, 268

Advocate, The: African Americans and, 205n4; anointed cloths and, 197; content of, 189, 199–200; discontinuance of, 201; on otherness of Pentecostals, 192, 193; prayer requests in, 190

affirmative action, 55, 58

African American cultural life, 164–79

African American Pentecostals. *See* Church of God in Christ (Memphis, Tenn.)

African American Protestantism: charity work and, 297; history of, 167; literature of, 170–79; welfare state and, 281

African American Protestants: activism of, 51–52; alliances of, 7; Annie Armstrong and, 16; as arch of church, 180n9; as authors, 169–74; Carrie Judd and, 238; denominational journals of, 134; entrepreneurship of, 231; feminism and, 50; Frances Ellen Watkins Harper and, 164–65; goals in missionary societies, 215; healings and, 238, 239; interracial cooperation and, 6; JFW program and, 57; Maggie L. Walker and, 227, 228; Maria Stewart and, 49; Nannie Helen Burroughs and, 227, 228; NCCC and, 56, 58, 64; as outsiders, 280; Pentecostalism and, 205n4; role in churches, 166; as WMU speakers, 15; women as arch of church, 166

African American women, 302n52. *See also specific name*

African American Woman's Convention, 227

The University of Illinois Press
is a founding member of the
Association of American University Presses.

Composed in 10.5/13 Minion
by Jim Proefrock
at the University of Illinois Press
Manufactured by Thomson-Shore, Inc.

University of Illinois Press
1325 South Oak Street
Champaign, IL 61820-6903
www.press.uillinois.edu